North Country Cache:
Adventures on a National Scenic Trail

*To Arlene —
Take the
High Trail!

Joan Young*

OTHER BOOKS
by
Joan H. Young

Would You Dare?

North Country Cache:
Adventures on a
National Scenic Trail

by
Joan H. Young

Books Leaving Footprints
Scottville, Michigan

Copyright © 2005 by Joan H. Young
All rights reserved
For information about permission to reproduce
selections from this book, inquire in writing to
Books Leaving Footprints, 861 W. US 10,
Scottville, Michigan 49454
www.booksleavingfootprints.com

Young, Joan H.
    North Country cache : adventures on a national scenic trail / by Joan H. Young.
    p. cm.
    Includes index.
    LCCN 2005903382
    ISBN 0-9765432-1-4

    1. Young, Joan H.--Travel--North Country National Scenic Trail. 2. Hiking--North Country National Scenic Trail. 3. North Country National Scenic Trail--Description and travel.   I. Title.

GV199.42.N67Y68 2005   917.304'931
                              QBI05-600055

Printed in the United States of America
by Sheridan Books, Inc., Chelsea, MI
05 06 07 08   4 3 2 1

To Marie:

Could we have imagined
such a trail ahead,
when we watched shooting stars
from the pebbled shore of Cayuga Lake?

Naming Conventions

Throughout this book it has been necessary to distinguish words which are a part of the name of a plant or animal from descriptive words. Although scholars generally are not capitalizing the common names of species these days, it seemed appropriate to do so in this book for clarity. For example, on page 165 the following sentence appears: "The sun is bright; small marshy areas near the road are filled with Golden Alexanders, Michigan Lilies and milkweed, surrounded by busy butterflies: large, orange Great Spangled Frittilaries, and small orange skippers with an occasional black-and-white White Admiral." Upper case allows the reader to recognize that "Golden Alexanders" is the name of the flower, rather than just Alexanders (capitalized because it is named for a person) which are golden. In this same sentence, "skippers" is not capitalized. This is because there are many kinds of butterflies known as skippers, and I have made no attempt to specify which exact species was present. Similarly, Eastern Hemlock is capitalized, hemlock is not, although in the region covered by this book it is probably safe to assume that any naturally growing hemlock is Eastern Hemlock. To be consistent, Osprey and Beaver are capitalized; only one species by those names exists. On the other hand, deer is not, although, like hemlock, the only species of deer one is likely to see in the northeastern U.S. is the Whitetail Deer.

Similarly, geologic names such as Black Hand Sandstone are capitalized, generic sandstone is not.

Mileages

The miles reported at the end of each chapter are only the miles which count toward the North Country Trail total. Any given hike might have been longer. Most hikes of more than a few days were longer. Backtracking, extra miles to pick up supply boxes, repeated sections which did not count, and day hikes to visit points of interest off the NCT are not tallied in this book.

Locations

This is not intended to be a guidebook. The short description beside the locator maps may or may not include county names. I have only tried to make it possible for a reader to locate generally the hike on a road map. Not all counties or towns through which the trail passes appear in the index. The red line on the cover map indicates approximate trail sections covered in this book. For trail maps, contact the North Country Trail Association.

Graphic Credits

Map compliments of the North Country Trail Association: cover, p. 5
North Country Trail logo used with permission of the National Park
   Service: cover
Cover Design by Shark Enterprises
Text is set in Century Schoolbook
Index is set in Futura

Photographers
Addington, Angie: p. 219, 221
Altenau, Marie: cover(2), cover(4), cover(5), p. 23, 31, 74, 77, 84, 197, 221(2), 221(3), 222(3), 223(1), 224, 350
Castro, David: p. 7
Pfeiffer, Rich: p. 213
Szabo, Irene: p. 340
Unknown: p. 10, 14, 337, 375
Young, Joan: cover(1), cover(3), cover(6), cover(7), cover(8), cover(9), cover(10), p. 6, 8, 17, 19, 27, 33, 34, 41, 47, 51, 58, 60, 64, 66, 68, 71, 85, 87, 91, 93, 100, 103, 104, 106, 112, 115, 117, 123, 127, 133, 137, 142, 145, 146, 148, 151, 153, 154, 158, 162, 166, 168, 170, 174, 175, 181, 185, 194, 202, 205, 208, 211, 214, 218, 220, 222(1), 222(2), 223(2), 223(3), 223(4), 228, 230, 233, 237(1), 237(2), 241, 244, 247, 248, 251, 253, 256, 258, 263, 274, 279, 283, 284, 287, 291, 294, 295, 298, 304, 309, 313, 318, 325, 328, 333, 335, 343, 345, 349, 353, 357, 364, 368, 370, 371, 380
Young, Omer: p. 238

Cover Photos
Front
1. North Dakota sky over West Park Lake
2. Joan Young, Minnesota
3. Eben Ice Caves, Rock River Canyon Wilderness, Michigan
4. Maggie Scheid, Joan Young, Grand Portal Point, Pictured Rocks National Lakeshore, Michigan

Spine
5. Joan Young, Lookout Mountain, Superior Hiking Trail, Minnesota

Back
6. Chips, Adirondacks, New York
7. Conotton Creek Valley, Ohio
8. Showy Orchis, Ohio
9. Unknown Mushroom, Michigan
10. Marie Altenau, New York

Foreword
Undiscovered Secrets

There are people who understand the desire to carry your life in a backpack and walk for days on end, finishing each day with something resembling supper and starting each morning in rinsed-out socks sort of resembling clean. People not so inclined are puzzled by a backpacker's contentment with such spare existence on what is supposed to be a vacation.

They ask endless questions about the daily routines of life on a trail. What do you do all evening, just sit and talk? Doesn't it get a little boring staring at the stars night after night? You mean you actually don't mind going without a shower, even with the way the dust sticks to your stinky, sweaty skin? Their questions, whatever form they take, are all really variations on the same question. Why do you enjoy this?

A friend once told me he was convinced backpackers were part of some secret society, that when they got into the wilds there was some reward – something! – that made it worthwhile. And that only they knew about it. Why else would they go, other than the ability to eat 6,000 calories a day without gaining weight?

Yes, I joked, it is a secret society. And he had been chosen to join. I invited him into the woods. For five evenings in the White Mountains, at least 40 times each night, he asked: "So, this is it? Really? This is all there is? That's it!?!" He was mildly incredulous.

Oh well. I'd failed to recruit a member to the cult.

But for the remainder of the time I knew him, about two years, he would recall some moment of that brief trip – how we had shared a stew he'd made with two hikers who hit camp late, how enchanting is the morning fog, how cozy a tent can feel when you don't want to go out into the cold night to pee.

A year after the hike, while yakking in a tavern, his eyes lit up as he climbed over patrons to reach someone he recognized. He was beaming the smile of a person who had found a long-lost companion in an unexpected place. He waved me over – apparently this was someone I knew too, and while I couldn't find the name, the face was familiar. The "trail crew" t-shirt jogged my memory; it was a hiker we had encountered the previous summer.

Our two hiking parties, by happenstance, had dashed under the shelter of the same rocky overhang just below tree-line to wait out a thunderstorm. We talked for an hour. They had made coffee; we offered up our precious chocolate Ho-Ho's. When the sun reappeared, we hiked together less than a mile to the next junction, then went our own ways. Now, in a Jamaica Plain Irish pub, we were old friends.

Decades later, I remember the encounter at the bar clearly, but can scarcely recall the route of the backpacking trip. Perhaps in another ten years it will come to me again.

Hiking, like all travel, is a way of discovering one's lifetime stories. The tales are not always – or often – linear. In speed-reading, the instructors emphasize that it is not important to read all the words in the correct order. Your mind will make sense of it. A backpacking trip might last five days, but its discoveries could be revealed to you over many years, in random order.

Imagine the days and nights of a 4,000-mile walk. If you had the time, you could do it in less than a year. You would be one person when you started, and certainly someone else when you finished.

Imagine that walk over a decade. Or more. By year 10, you are someone else many times over – you are not the same person making different parts of the same journey. And the way you discover your journey today or tomorrow is altogether different from how those other "selves" experienced the early miles.

Walk 4,000 miles in a year and it is the trip of a lifetime. Walk them over many years and you see just how many lives you have lead.

North Country Cache is that kind of journey. Joan Young's wonderings along the North Country Trail are episodic. In each the landscape and the physical experience of travel are capably brought to life, but more importantly, we see that we take from travel, and life, what we bring to it. We see that travel is the ultimate way of re-discovering over and again one's self, friends, and country, and, at least from this hiker's shoes, that there is no better way to enjoy and learn from the world than on foot, step by step.

A secret society? To be sure, there are secrets to be discovered. And all are welcome.

David Lillard

Shepherdstown, West Virginia, May 2005

Table of Contents

	Cache	1
	Introduction to the Trail	2
	Wanderlust	4
1-	The Kernel	5
2-	Twilight Trail	8
3-	Shamu	10
4-	One Crystal, Sunlit Moment	13
5-	Baby Steps on the Giant Trail	15
6-	Where the Trail Begins	28
7-	Patches	42
8-	Connecting to Ohio	44
9-	Buckeye Beginning	45
10-	Losing the Way	49
11-	Incident Report	50
12-	Defiance	55
13-	Breaking the Chains	56
14-	Buckeye Buck	66
15-	Forever Wild	71
16-	The Ghosts of Rose Hollow	95
17-	West, Wes, Wet	99
18-	King Relish to Kentucky Fried	102
19-	Chips Tells the Truth	104
20-	Set Your Compass for Adventure	106
21-	Hale-Bopp and Other Fading Dirty Snowballs	109
22-	Great Scot! The Ugliest Mile in Army Boots	112
23-	Enjoying the Classics	115
24-	Testing in 3-D	119
25-	Rocky and the Rock	123
26-	On a Roll	126
27-	Tales from Paul's Woods	130
28-	Linger, Linger	144
29-	White Lace and a Million Fireflies	147
30-	A Trail of Her Own	151
31-	A Trail of My Own	154

32- Ephemerata	156
33- A Nice Walk in the Woods	164
34- Wheelin' @ 3FPR	177
35- Down a Memory of a Lane	180
36- Call the Police	187
37- Spirit of the Woods	192
38- A Golden Chip of Sunshine	194
39- Puzzled	199
40- April Ambitions	209
41- She Who Builds Fire	211
42- Rain First, Umbrellas Last	216
43- Back to the Beginning	219
44- The Song of Hiawatha's Friends	221
45- Big Mac, Michigan Style	238
46- Walking Backwards Down the Stairs	244
47- Lightning and the Snail	246
48- Look Your Dream Right in the Eye	248
49- W2K	249
50- Ice is Nice	255
51- Sneaky Valley	261
52- Emily, Mama Rita and Dick Have their Way with the Regenwűrmer	267
53- May the Road Rise to Meet You	282
54- Building Bridges	293
55- Solo, Duo, Triad	296
56- Moon Over My U P	301
57- Eye of Elk, Shade of Toad	307
58- Milk Train	315
59- Erie Canal	317
60- Philomathic Deipnosophists	321
61- Super-Duper	324
62- Fisher Settlement	336
63- Thousands of Miles	340
64- Sheyenne	344
65- The Princess and the P's	362
66- Non-Coin-Operated Amusement Devices	365
67- Quothe the Raven, "Walk, Walk"	374
68- Halfway, or Not?	384
Apologies and Acknowledgments	388
Geographical Listing of Hikes	390
Index	393

Cache

Cache- kash, n. A place where stores, supplies or provisions are hidden and preserved.

During settlement of the North American west, a cache was traditionally buried. Essential items which were inconvenient to carry were stored in a deep hole for retrieval at a later time. The location was noted but camouflaged, so that its appearance was indistinguishable from the original site, hiding it from thieves and animals. The origin of the word, from the French *cacher*, to hide, was fully realized. Requirements and language, however, evolve.

With an ATM and convenience store in every town, modern travelers would hardly consider making their way across the country by burying supplies that might be needed later. Long-distance hikers, however, seldom find towns in handy locations along the route. Most would be fairly annoyed if they did, since part of the motivation to hike is usually to get away from such plastic conventions. Instead they may locate caches along a route. Sealed containers might be buried. Many hikers mail packages to themselves at various towns before beginning their trek. Supply boxes can also be left with friends, setting pre-arranged meeting locations for delivery during the hike. These boxes, hidden or not, could all certainly be considered caches.

Campers also use the word cache to describe a bag of food, and other animal-attractive items, which is hung out of reach (hopefully) of claws and teeth. Bear resistant containers do not even need to be suspended. *Ursa* can look all he wants, but supposedly can't open the canister. "Hidden" in these cases refers only to restricted access.

What has not changed is the fact that a cache is still a collection of essential items which are assembled and stored carefully for retrieval at a future date when they are needed. And from this core of meaning comes the title for this collection of essays. Each hike, no matter how short or long, seems to take on a character of its own. There is always some defining element which makes it different from every other walk. Thus each hike must be preserved, and cherished. That essence of each trek must be distilled and stored, to be recalled and savored again at some later time. Some trips are long and meaty, while others are adventures – like spices. Some may seem less exciting, but like clean, dry underwear retrieved at the mid-point of a trip, are extremely necessary for the well-being of the whole person. So this book is a cache of those essential memories of my hikes along the North Country National Scenic Trail, extracted and refined for enjoyment, a North Country Cache.

Introduction to the Trail
August 1988

    Monotone gray streamed the road beneath the tires. Dreary straight road, dreary linear, semi-conscious stream of harried motherhood. Drive to Cadillac, Michigan. How long will it take? Guide three boys to adulthood, or even through this week. What will I fix for dinner? Route M-55. Why is another summer nearly gone?
    Plain brown sign: "North Country National Scenic Trail." Just time to register the words in my mind and note a parking area with an information board as I sped by. "National Trail?" I thought, "Here? Right in my own backyard? Where does it go?" Now alert, I determined to stop and check it out on the return trip.

    I can no longer recall the goal of the trip to Cadillac, but the message of that modest signboard forever changed my life. Later that day I did indeed check the bulletin board at the trailhead I had seen earlier. With amazement I read that this trail extends across the Eastern United States, from Crown Point, New York, to Lake Sakakawea, North Dakota. The headquarters address given was White Cloud, Michigan; again, just a few miles from my home. My head was spinning with possibilities and incredulity that I had never even heard of this trail. I copied the address, locked my car, and began what was to become a 4000-plus-mile trek.
    The bulletin board indicated that I should be looking for blazes painted on trees. But I was about to learn lesson number one about hiking a trail which has many different groups that maintain it; some sections are better marked than others. After searching the woods all around the parking area, and not finding any blazes, I set off down the fire road, thinking that this must surely be the way to go. I needed to pay attention to what I was doing since this was an unplanned jaunt and I had no compass, map, or anyone who knew what I was doing. Might as well start off completely wrong... It was late afternoon of an August day, and whether I was really on the trail or not, the appeal of sun filtering through the trees to highlight Smooth Asters' blue petals did not fail to capture me. As I marched deeper into the woods, following more fire roads but never seeing blazes, I realized that I was certainly not on the actual trail.
    Emerging about four miles later on Scocelas Road, near the northern boundary of my own Mason County, the trail crossing sign could be seen some yards down the road, confirming that I was near, but not on, the trail. I reluctantly turned around to retrace my steps, needing to hurry back to the world of family responsibilities. My head again filled with questions, but they were no longer gray.

"How much of this national trail is in my home county? Why haven't I ever heard of it? How long would it take to hike it?" Already my lifelong dream to hike that grandmother of all long-distance trails, The Appalachian Trail, was morphing in response to the call of the North Country.

Wanderlust
Autumn 1991

There has been a need this autumn to be outside that is more compelling than anything in recent memory.

It has been like the sweet and painful longing I used to feel as a child when I would kneel on my bed at night, looking out the window with my elbows propped on the windowsill. I would stare at the dark woods across the road, and smell the damp leaves, and think of all the lovely places there that I knew, and all the really exquisite places that must yet be waiting to be explored. The tears would run down my face; I wanted, so much, to be outside. I've felt that same kind of aching again this year.

>Wanderlust
> has sprinkled
>   Wonder Dust
>into my eyes and ears and brain.
>
>Wonder Dust
> has tickled.
>   Go I must,
>into the wind and sun and rain.
>
>Wind's fey sweep
> has prickled
>   urges deep;
>This restive spirit never tamed.
>
>Sun shaft bright
> has flickered.
>   Dappled lights
>excise the crushing, brindled pain.
>
>Rain soft cries
> have trickled,
>   gath'ring sighs
>to cascade, trembling: cleansing gain.
>
>Wonder Dust
> has quickened
>   Wanderlust.
>Impatient voices call my name.

The Kernel
1 - September 8, 1991

Armed with maps and information from their headquarters, I now am aware of the basic facts concerning the North Country National Scenic Trail. The trail was commissioned by Congress in 1980, and the route was originally expected to cover 3200 miles. Reroutes and the reality of building trail rather than drawing lines on maps pushes the expected total, 25 years later in 2005, to 4600 miles.

The Trail is managed by the National Park Service, and supported by the non-profit North Country Trail Association which seeks to build, protect, promote, and preserve the Trail. It's a tall order!

From the eastern terminus at Crown Point, New York, the North Country Trail (NCT) traverses the Adirondacks, joining the established Finger Lakes Trail (FLT) south of Rome, New York. It follows the FLT through the Finger Lakes and Southern Tier to the Allegany State Park near Salamanca, New York.

Dropping southwest through the Allegheny National Forest, then Cook Forest, Moraine, and McConnells Mill State Parks, Pennsylvania, the trail curves west into Ohio. At Zoar, the NCT joins the Buckeye Trail. The BT is the longest loop trail in the United States, and the North Country route mostly sticks with it around the southern tip of Ohio and up the western edge of that state. One diversion from the BT is made in southeastern Ohio, through the Wayne National Forest.

After a jaunt along the route of the famous Wabash Cannonball Railroad, NCT hikers head north into Michigan. Michigan boasts the most miles of NCT, almost 1200 of them! The route angles northwest to enter the Manistee National Forest, where I became acquainted with the trail. North of this forest the NCT heads back toward the center of the state where it must turn north again to cross Big Mac, the Mackinac Bridge. Hiawatha and Ottawa National Forests and Pictured Rocks National Lakeshore miles lead west across the Upper Peninsula of Michigan to the Porcupine Mountains.

Wisconsin boasts Chequamegon National Forest (home of the original "North Country Trail"), and Minnesota paths include the Superior Hiking Trail, Border Route and Kekekabic Trails, and also through Forests with legendary names like Chippewa and Paul Bunyan.

The trail enters its westernmost state, North Dakota, south of Fargo. Sheyenne National Grassland, Lonetree Wildlife Management Area, and Lake Sakakawea define the prairie portions of the North Country Trail. By carefully choosing his or her route a hiker could almost cross the United States twice in the number of miles this trail wanders to cross seven states. The distances are overwhelming.

Well, I can't hike it all at once anyway. Three years since finding the NCT I finally will walk a few official miles. Boys, like dreams, grow. Sam, Joshua, and Steve now need nurturing less, the dreams more. Husband Omer has agreed to take me early to Hodenpyl Dam in the Manistee National Forest, and to pick me up later at Dilling Road. Hiking is not his idea of fun, but he's willing to help me develop sore muscles and grandiose ideas. We do not share the same dreams.

This time I am prepared. I carry lunch, compass, maps, flower identification guide, sketch pad, sweatshirt and emergency gear in a day pack. The sounds of water pouring through the dam's floodgates, and of some piece of heavy equipment, fill my ears as I head across a field and into the woods searching for blazes. They are easily located, and the forest of tall pines quickly engulfs me, shutting out the "real" world. This section of the trail is well-marked and maintained.

Soon the noise from the dam is left behind. In fact, when I stand still to quiet the sound of my footfalls, there are no sounds of human origin at all! This is a rare gift of the trail. During the summer months I had made several overnight or weekend campouts elsewhere. Not one of these was free of man-made noises. Heavy equipment back-up beepers had awakened me on two mornings. The muffled pulse of distant traffic was almost impossible to escape, but was never in tune with the beating of my heart. Often, just as I thought I was free of the sound of motors, a plane would roar across the sky. So now, to stand quietly in the bracken and pines with only the soft swish of the breeze in my ears feels incredible.

TOADFLAX
9-8-91

There is no feeling quite like this sense of being the lone human in the center of the world. I am that theoretically motionless molecule at the exact center of one turntable slice of the universe. Objects captured near me move slowly, hushed. Sounds of the forest revolve dreamily around me. A late warbler calls; sparrows twitter, senseless with this imposed lull in their busy schedules. A squirrel insistently urges me to move on, to let her world turn faster again. Some small beast rattles the leaves beside the trail. Perhaps his tail is trapped at the calm hub, while his feet scrabble to keep pace with the faster concentric circle a body length away. A late-season insect hums, shifting gears to pass from one spiral to the next. Farther away the world careens out-of-focus, too fast to see, beyond my comprehension or concern. Peace is ownership of this one breath-space. Within the orbit defined by the acuity of my hearing, the world is tethered, Creation-fresh, forces counter-balanced at the escape-to-insanity velocity. This inner circle of tranquillity is the original Design, and I hold it tightly for another minute lest it whirl off into mad oblivion.

Releasing the universe with a sigh, I step along the path again. The charmed "silence" is broken but not completely dispelled; the tone of the day is set. The woods warms in the September sun to a dry and glorious mid-day. Cheese and crackers fill my stomach as the spell of the morning fills my soul. I sketch a lone flower, a Toadflax.

One short rest, and another brisk walk, I am concerned a bit about time. It has been years since I really hiked a trail and I have no good sense of what my pace is. But I reach Dilling Road two hours before Omer is expected, so I am glad that I have also packed a book. Sixteen miles of beautiful trail is a satisfying beginning.

Have you ever touched a twig to water which is just on the verge of freezing? Magically, ice crystals grow from that spot, called the kernel, and form marvelous branches and patterns. So too, my amorphous dream of becoming a hiker is poised to crystallize around this tiny kernel into a fantastic plan.

16 miles this hike
Marilla Trailhead to Dilling Rd
Manistee County, MI
16 miles total NCT

Omer, friend Marie, and Joan in 1990

Twilight Trail
2 - October 21, 1991

My friend Marie and I have both driven to Interlaken, the small town in New York where I grew up. My mother broke her hip during the summer, and it is now certain that she will never go home again. Our goal for this weekend is to empty her little house so that it can be rented. This is not the house where I spent my childhood, so there is no emotional attachment there for me, just a busy time to complete the job. Marie is willing to help even with monumental moving tasks to give us some time together. We are hoping for a few spare minutes to find a section of trail to hike.

By Saturday afternoon the bulk of the job is done. The truck is loaded with things that I will take back to Michigan. Most everything else is packed in boxes ready to go to the attic for storage. A group of people from church have come to help with the packing and lugging, and the work has moved along swiftly. Mom's cozy little home in town is bare and plain again. She had bought this house and fixed it up after my Dad died and the farm was sold. Marie and I sit on the floor and sigh at each other. "Do we want to hike? We had better go now while it is still light." We decide that a break is in order; the boxes can be hauled to the attic after dark. So off we go to Treman State Park, just south of Ithaca, to meet the trail where it crosses Route 34.

Since it is off-season, there is no one in the campground. We drive through the silent loop to reach the trailhead, change shoes, and plunge westward into the October woods. The falling leaves easily sweep the cares of the weekend away. Our greatest concern of the moment is to watch the time; we estimate that we can hike in for an hour, and then will need to turn around, to be out of the woods by dark. Somehow the magic of the moment reaches out and transforms us into two younger girls, discovering afresh the wonders of autumn. We collect brilliant leaves, colored rocks, snail shells, and bits of decorative fungi. Witches' Butter fungus gleams dull yellow in the late afternoon light. Many-colored Polypore grows profusely on stump and log. Its gray and brown lines and patterns seem richly subtle rather than dull as its colors might suggest. For the first time ever we see Crowned Clavaria, its spongy coral-like arms reaching out of a knothole in a downed tree. In the dimming light

Crowned Clavaria

its whiteness glows, otherworldly. When the trail swings close to Enfield Glen, the sound of water rushing in the depths of the gorge is our evening symphony. But the light does predictably fade, and we reluctantly have to turn back after the prescribed hour.

    We stop in Ithaca to eat and to visit my mother in the nursing home. She is so weak and unaware of her surroundings... We tell her of our walk and of our "finds." Life does come full circle; this is the shell of the sturdy lady who took me to the woods as a toddler, introducing me to wildflowers, birds' nests and rabbit holes. She is the one who helped me press my first collection of autumn leaves into scrapbooks, to label them and learn the names. Now all I can do is to leave a green and orange maple bouquet in her line of sight, and to tell her of the twilight woods. Somewhere inside that frail body does your bright mind yet reach out for new experiences? Are you still in there, Mom?

2 miles this hike
Robert Treman State Park
Tompkins County, NY
18 miles total NCT

Shamu
3 - July 17-19, 1992

My bright new teal and black backpack is screaming to be put to use. I have taken several overnight trips to brush up ancient camping skills. No empty-nest syndrome for me! The youngest son, Steve, graduated from high school this May, and I am ready to re-discover activities that appeal to me which never interested my family. One fact has emerged from the "test run" campouts. If I truly want to backpack, I must have a good pack and a light-weight sleeping bag. The rest of the equipment can be faked a bit, but these two items are required. I purchased the sleeping bag several months ago, and the pack last week. Now the plot thickens.

Marie and Joan, 1960

Marie, my close friend since the summer we met at Camp Comstock as gangly 12-year-old Girl Scouts, visits us almost every year. My strategy is to convince her to try backpacking with me. She takes the bait; although I confess that it wasn't much of a fish story. She more or less jumped into the boat as soon as I tested the water. We begin to plan for three days on the North Country Trail. I decide to go just far enough away from home that I might be able to connect with my first hike on a weekend alone. Thus we choose to follow a piece that is concurrent with the Shore-to-Shore Riding Trail. We will leave one car at Darragh, and the other near Mayfield, Michigan. There is much flurry of preparation as I read backpacking guide books, plan menus, mark maps, and practice packing my pack. Its internal frame needs to be molded to my body shape. All the zippers and pockets are grand fun. Should I put the cup and spoon here on the side? The top pouch seems great for keeping a light jacket handy. Marie finds a faded but still-useable external frame pack among her old Scout Camp gear. We carefully choose and weigh gear, food, and total pounds FSO: what the how-to books call "from the skin out." Marie carries 28 pounds, and I will have 33. Even though I'm smaller, I've always been considered the tough one.

On a warm Tuesday morning we leave Marie's car at a turnout in the shade of a woods' edge. We then plant my car at the eastern end of this hike, off-road in the sand and bracken. After about a half mile

I realize that I have forgotten to change my shoes... I doubt that I can hike the whole way in sneakers, so I leave my pack with Marie and trudge back to change to heavier footwear. Rather an ignoble beginning. Well, call it a lesson learned – double check everything, because backtracking on foot is most depressing and time-consuming.

It soon becomes apparent that I am the one having trouble carrying a pack. This isn't the way it's supposed to work. I'm the tough one, remember? This is the maiden voyage for this pack; I probably just don't have it adjusted correctly. Thus begins a day-long chain of adjustment events, tweaking, re-buckling, shifting and groaning as my shoulders and back learn the points of contact with a real pack, and as we learn how to make the weight ride properly on my hips.

Compacted sand fire roads and railroad rights-of-way are the surfaces we walk most of the day. After about ten miles and a few lessons about watching for inadequately marked turns we poke our way into a small stand of pines to camp for the night. To be in the woods, resting beside a fire with Marie, seems so right. The world is ordered as it should be for a small space of time.

The next day we encounter sections of trail that are heavily traveled by horses. This is not fun! The sandy soil is easily broken up from their weight and the churning of their hooves. The path is a channel about two feet wide and eighteen inches deep with six to twelve inches of loose sand in the bottom. It is like beach walking with a pack; every step is a calf and ankle-searing effort. The sky decides to sprinkle rain on us in the afternoon. The educational portion of this day's hike regards signs. One section of the trail passes through a camping area. According to the signpost we have managed to hike only three-fourths of a mile in an hour. We decide that we could have crawled that far, even in the sand, and add a new lesson about official misinformation to our store of trail knowledge. I am becoming firmly entrenched in a commitment to carry maps from at least two different sources on all future hikes.

Today my pack rides securely and easily. However, the internal frame provides no easy handles when I'm not wearing it. Its rotund bulk is considerable; I'm long-waisted, and have consequently purchased a large pack. "This pack is like a beached whale!" I exclaim while awkwardly hauling it yet again into some position to be donned. I can't seem to figure out any efficient way to slip into harness with this creature. However, once on my back (now properly adjusted) it becomes a part of me, fluid and connected, like the whale in its ocean environment. Thus it is christened with its name, Shamu, for the famous captive Orca. Marie's pack, although old and nameless, seems to fit fairly well. Her test is to endure encounters with the horses we meet on this bridle trail. She finds horses big, unpredictable, and frightening.

Treasures for the day include finding Racemed Milkwort with purple blooms, then Squaw Root, and Shinleaf in a rich woods. We camp here the second night. I try to sketch the Shinleaf, but am too tired to complete the drawing before the light fades. Probably just as well; the waxy translucent blooms defy capture with colored pencil. Weary but happy, Marie and I decide that backpacking should become an established part of our summers from now on, and one more piece of the amorphous idea settles into the pattern of our future.

Thursday as we are walking along, a great revelation hits me... I subtracted wrong! When we weighed our gear "from the skin out," we first weighed ourselves naked, then added all clothes, pack, and attachments and weighed ourselves again. The difference is the weight carried, FSO. Somehow I subtracted 110 from 153 and got 33 pounds. I have been carrying 43 pounds in a pack which was not initially adjusted properly. I feel very stupid at the math mistake, but lots better about my fitness! No wonder this load seems much heavier than the 25 pounds I had been carrying in a day pack; it is.

We reach Marie's car in good time. A man in a pickup truck, with his two young daughters, sees us emerge from the woods at the road edge and asks where we have been. We tell him we just hiked from Darragh. His eyes pop; he is incredulous, even when we explain that it took us three days. He wishes us well and drives on. Our car is parked near a cold stream. We soak our overheated feet and also wish ourselves well at a small but most definite beginning.

33 miles this hike
Darragh to Mayfield
Kalkaska and
      Grand Traverse Counties, MI
51 miles total NCT

One Crystal, Sunlit Moment
4 - May 28, 1994

The great plans Marie and I made for backpacking had been put on hold. In the spring of 1993 Marie broke a small bone in her foot. Although it was healed by summer, she could not yet carry the weight of a backpack. So our plans were reformulated for that year to a week of camping with short hikes. We had a wonderful, wacky week at Apple River Canyon, Illinois. Marie's teenage son, David, joined us. He apparently didn't find camping with two mothers oppressive. We tried out equipment and campfire recipes. My new puppy, Chips, began to learn tent etiquette. It was good to sharpen all these skills. But it was not on "The Trail."

My mother's condition has deteriorated. She only occasionally recognizes me on my twice-yearly visits to New York. Her wish was to remain in New York State, nearer to most of her friends. So here I am, spending Memorial Day Weekend frenetically trying to make many short visits to her bedside at an Ithaca nursing home. This way there are more chances that she might be alert at one of these times. There is a renter in the house to check on. There are legal and banking issues to be attended to. Marie has met me at her parents' house in Waverly, which is a reasonable distance from Ithaca to use for our home base. They are a generous, caring couple. But I am overwhelmed with people and responsibilities. The weekend has been a mad rush from one town and appointment to another.

As we drive Route 34 from Ithaca toward Waverly yet one more time, checking our watches, we surrender to the call of the woods. We decide to park just opposite Treman Park and hike in the other direction (from the autumn hike) for a short distance. Construction of a new intersection has made the area a dusty, rock-strewn mess. But this is a holiday, and the bulldozers sit idle. The equipment tracks form a good place where I can maneuver my little 4-wheel drive Colt safely off the road. So far so good. We find blazes leading along the edge of a hot field and then up a rocky creekbed lined with softwood trees: Cottonwood and Pussy Willow. The sun beats with august fervor on our heads and backs. Our footsteps are loud, echoes created by the distinctive "chunk" of slabs of shifting shale sitting half-submerged in water.

Just a few yards farther and, as if we had passed out of the footlights' glare, behind the velvet curtain and onto the dark and waiting stage, we enter a forest both still and cool. Peat deadens our footfalls. Deep green Eastern Hemlocks rise around us to block the sun and absorb extraneous noises. The trail climbs immediately along the edge of Lick Brook, and the sound of the gurgling water recedes below us in proportion to the rising of the cliff. As we near the top, we also reach the head of the gorge and are rewarded with a crystal cascade tumbling in the sunlight, breaking into beads like shattered safety glass, laughing coyly as it polishes the shale wall to faux-obsidian and disappears into the depths below. If we had not looked at the right instant we would have missed it... turned the bend and walked right by... lost the moment. This is no Type A personality stream, falling sheer and aggressive, bent on keeping rocky appointments, leaping to heart attacks. This rill wants to play, wants to display its beauty. But oh, only one secret at a time! I can almost hear it, "Careful now... you must peek around that branch to see this gem... See that little splashy spot on my southern wall? Watch closely. If the sun will play, I'll make a rainbow for you... Come with me, I'll never run away."

Catherine Leary, Mom, 1947

We are dazzled, blinking from the dim woods at this sparkling playmate. Tinkerbell lives! Only a mile, only a few minutes stolen from a hectic weekend. Yet like memories of the smiling, energetic woman my mother used to be, these minutes are the ones remembered. All the people and paperwork are forgotten; all the checks on the checklist are faded and filed. But the beckoning laughter of the brook still calls me to follow, follow The Trail.

1 mile this hike
NY 34 to Sand Bank Rd
Tompkins County, NY
52 miles total NCT

Baby Steps on the Giant Trail
5 - July 20-31, 1994

"I'll see you in about six hours!" I hang up the phone, ending this conversation with Marie. Then putting the dog dishes and the dog into the car, we roll eastward. The rest of the gear is packed... in boxes or in Shamu. We are really and truly going to take a long enough trip to test our independence. We will start at the New York/ Pennsylvania border and walk south along the NCT through the Allegheny National Forest for about 100 miles. David, having completed his freshman year in college, has decided to join his mom and me.

The hours in the car give me plenty of time to think and there is plenty to think about. The past few years have been ones of swift changes in my life. It feels as if I am moving into a new lifetime. My husband has taken a new job working with test tubes and chemicals after 24 years of working with people. The boys are grown and finding their own ways through life. The youngest, Steve, has completed his sophomore year in college. I had invited him to join us, like Dave, but was not surprised at the negative response. No hiker, he. "You're weird, Mom," he always says.

"Thank you, it's one of my better qualities!" I always retort.

I am finishing my second year in the Environmental Engineering program at the University of Michigan, headed for a Master's Degree. I get home only for holidays or an occasional long weekend. Omer is accepting of this arrangement, but eager for me to finish. We have built a new house on our property, and we have said a sad farewell to our 100-year-old home, which turned into a pile of rubble while being moved (but that's a different story). It feels like everything I own is packed in a box somewhere; things from our old house, things from my mother's house, things I have brought to Ann Arbor. Sometimes I don't know where home is, except maybe in my car. And that is where I am now, with more things in boxes, and with a wonderful friend who will also have the chance to test his endurance.

That friend is Chips, whom I am determined to train to be a good camping dog. Chips is 35 pounds of mixed-heritage assets and liabilities, but he looks like a mini Golden Retriever. My mind wanders again to last spring when I had to say good-bye to a key player of that "previous life." My old dog, Hezekiah, at fourteen could see or hear little. He was incontinent, and could hardly walk. We joked that he looked like a drunken semi-truck driver who could manage the cab but didn't have a clue as to what his trailer was doing. Omer had patiently cared for him while I was away at school. But I had to make that most difficult of decisions, to put Hezekiah to sleep. Heze (HEH-zee) had been born on a hand-braided rag rug in our kitchen, with our two youngest boys watching in wonder. He earned the reputation over the years for being the dumbest, but funniest dog we ever owned. He was 65 pounds of hilarious, rock-stupid mutt. He looked something like a white short-haired German Shepherd with black spots and ears that flopped at the tips... except when he looked like a fuzzy pig, or a sheep, or a bat... Well, you get the idea. When I started renewing my camping skills I tried to teach Heze to go with me. One incident explains the result of this experiment pretty well.

Hezekiah and I had carried the camping equipment just over the hill onto the back section of our five-acre lot. This was just to be an overnight, with no trips to the house allowed, to make sure that I was including all essential gear. If we passed this test, I would next plan for a weekend outing. All went well. I cooked dinner, boiled water, set up my pup tent, and enjoyed the evening. At dark I crawled in the tent and zipped Heze and myself in, away from the mosquitoes. This may have been a pup tent, but my "pup" certainly wasn't used to such sleeping quarters. He insisted on sleeping on the bottom half of my sleeping bag. He woofed at every night noise, and tried to poke his nose through the mosquito netting. I tried closing the flaps so that he couldn't see out, I tried tying the flaps back so that he could see out. We finally settled on leaving the bottom of the zipper open so that he could sleep with his head poked outside. After several restless hours of attempting to appease both the dog and the god of ideal camping, I fell into a deep sleep.

Some time later I became semi-conscious and discovered that I was unable to move. It was dark, very dark, too dark somehow. Why couldn't I move? I concluded with a fuzzy brain that the dog must be on top of me. "Move, Heze," I muttered, giving the bulk above me a shove. Nothing. "Get off!" Nothing, maybe a wiggle. I pushed, and tried to roll him off. Why couldn't I seem to move properly? This is nuts; I still couldn't see anything either. Usually this white dog is readily visible except on the blackest of nights. I shoved harder, and with a dog-voiced "oof" the weight slid off my body. But I still couldn't freely move my arms and legs, although there seemed to be nothing wrong with them. Slowly I regained full consciousness and began to realize that Hezekiah, now treading heavily on me, trying to re-settle himself on this wonderful warm spot in the chilly night, was separated from me by layers of maroon nylon. "This dumb dog is outside the tent," I said to no one in particular. More shoving and struggling and I finally extricated myself from the sleeping bag and tangled tent. Heze smiled happily at me. He had collapsed the poles, and found everything he wanted, an unimpeded view of the world and a warm spot to stretch out and rest.

The old dog and I camped a few more times together, but he never did get it quite right. Hezekiah is now gone, and gone with him what felt like one of the last connections to my former self. Heze may have been dumb and funny, but he was also the most empathetic dog I ever owned. He had jumped and celebrated at all the victories and joys of three sons. He had cried with me as I agonized over the boys' poor decisions, growing pains, and other sorrows of life. His tongue was the softest and smoothest of any dog's I've ever known and he would lick the tears carefully from my face and gaze into my eyes with near-human sympathy. Then he would sigh and stretch his long frame against mine, patiently comforting. "I'm here for you," he always seemed to say.

Chips is off to a much better start at camping skills. He is one-year-old wild, but at least he is intelligent.

"Ie-ee-ee-ee!" I am jerked from my reverie. What is that in the road ahead? It is nearing midnight and I have turned off Route 17 to enter the town of Allegany, New York. Some long-spindly human form is jumping and flapping around in the street ahead of me. A drunk? He's running at the side of my car! Can I avoid him? He's trying to grab the door! Oh! It's only David (you can stop hammering now, heart), making sure that I don't miss the turn to St. Bonaventure's where we are to meet. Marie's aunt lives here, a retirement home for nuns. Early next morning we attend mass in the red-marble, ornately painted and gilded chapel. This is all strange enough to Protestant me to seem mystical and old-world; a sense of praise with hushed awe pervades. Breakfast is the counterpoint — sharing hearty bowls of steaming oatmeal with the nuns, who wear simple and practical brown dresses, laughing and chatting casually, a contrast to the formal worship setting.

Next stop, Sheffield, Pennsylvania. Don and Brita Dorn live near the center of the Allegheny National Forest in a crossroads town. They have agreed to help us place a cache box of supplies with a family near the mid-point of the trail. Their home is a lovely colonial building on a corner lot with a white picket fence. Don, a retired forest ranger, gives us ecological previews of the forest trail. Brita gives us slices of homemade pie. Both gifts are welcome. We leave our cache box with a family only a half mile off the actual trail, and then return to Dorns'. We know that we have everything that we need with us, but it is not distributed in the three packs. This job takes most of the afternoon and all of their porch. We sort and weigh, and adjust and give all the extras to Dave. Having a teenage fellow along who hardly notices 50 pounds on his back is a

Dave & Marie sign a trail register

great idea! Before dark a car is stashed at each end of the Forest, and we spend the night at Willow Bay campsite. In the morning we walk north to the New York State border and backtrack to the trailhead to ensure that we hike all the Forest miles. Now for the reality check – we must shoulder the packs, sever the vehicular umbilical cord which ties the day hiker to the placental resources of city and store, and be born as backpackers.

Our first few days together are a shakedown for all of us. Marie's pack with new hipbelt and straps is pressing painfully on a nerve. She is annoyed that I seem unconcerned, while I blithely assume that she will get it adjusted. I have always packed Shamu just so... everything in its perfect compartment. Marie points out that we need to pack differently to make camp set-up faster. I am offended. Dave and I had each assumed that we would be the one navigating us with the map and guide. He doesn't like the way I check it less than continuously, and I think that he is TOO presumptuous to want the map. This is MY hike. Marie is a morning person, frustrated by my slow wake-ups. I am a night person, irked by her terse fumbling in the evening. Ah, yes, backpacking is not for the inflexible. Friendship of long-standing wins out and conflicts are eventually resolved. Marie is right, packing differently makes much more sense. Perhaps the fact that Marie and I function better at different times of the day can be an asset to the group efficiency. Dave and I agree to be navigator on alternate days (after a tense exchange covering what we do not like about each other's map-reading style). No modest victory, this; two only children apparently can learn to share! These moments are not chemically preserved in our bright photos of Great Spangled Fritillaries (orange) on purple Heal-All, or sparkly sun on Johnnycake Run, or Tracy Ridge rising steeply from the level of Allegheny Reservoir. But such moments of contention and compromise must also be remembered and their lessons internalized.

The other member of our gang, Chips, is unaffected by all the tensions around him. He is ecstatic, racing from one exotic smell to the next, sampling them all. His dog-mind is a tangle of experiential riches. Bound after that chipmunk ("where do those shifty fellows disappear to?"). Check out this log ("don't know what's marked this spot; file it for reference"). Time for a pat on the head ("yup, the humans approve my reconnaissance plan"). Poke nose under these leaves ("snff-fff, musty leaves mean salamanders"). Lap at a rocky trickle ("sure am thirsty, but this oak-leaf tea is pretty great"). Run ahead to find David ("got to keep these people herded properly, they might get lost without me"). The commentary at a level three feet above Chips' brain runs more like, "That crazy pup must be running five miles for every one we walk."

On the third day out we take a half-day off, and for once our timing is impeccable. It rains all afternoon, and we laze in the tents, cozy and dry with books and maps and each other for company. Chips is nearly comatose. He had "crashed" under a fern when we reached this site, and moved slowly to the tent to join us when the rain began. For the rest of this hike, and ever after, he has paced himself to the rigors of trail life. He still has to occasionally rip through the leaves after some real or imagined

Chips rests in the ferns

exciting smell; he still tries to keep his humans herded up tighter than they usually are, but he generally trots sensibly along the trail. Now he probably walks only a bit more than we do. "Since Chips has four legs, does that mean he's walked twice the distance you have?" a friend would later ask me. I hope he was making a joke.

Bears. I have yet to meet one on the trail, and that's just fine with me; I have friends who have met them and this is one adventure that I am content to experience vicariously. Supposedly there are bears in this Forest so we must cache our food each night to keep it safe. Well, that's the theory. If any bears really wanted our dinners, I suspect they would have had them. According to the backpacking guides what we really needed each night was a cliff. Two cliffs, at least 20 feet apart, with sheer walls, with one of our party placed strategically on each side. Then we simply had to string a cable from one wall to the other, and hang the cache bag in the middle. Right. Given the cliffs, in between the time needed to do and undo our cache we could hike a mile or so each day (staying near the cliffs), maybe even find time to eat some of our carefully hoarded food.

Option two. Act I. Climb at least 20 feet up two trees with no lower branches which are at least 20 feet apart. Tie a stout rope between them, and suspend the cache bag in the middle. "Oh, Dave," we implore sweetly. Our site the first night has politely provided such trees. Dave shinnies up a rough bole with the rope clenched in his teeth, as we watch. "Is this high enough?" We agree, and he ties off the first end and descends to earth. Not bad, this has taken only ten minutes. On to the second tree. Marie and I are beginning to be bored with watching Dave grunt and heave himself up trees, and even our energetic teen is losing his enthusiasm. After another twenty minutes or so the second end of the rope is tied. "I'm not sure I can do this every night," he casually comments while collapsing at our feet and spitting bark fragments from between his teeth. Now we only have to suspend all food and toiletries in the middle, at least 8 feet from any side branches, and at least 12-15 feet from the ground. This means ransacking the packs for every article of such description. So much for each person carrying his/her own things. If we must do this every night the cache-requiring items will need to be kept together. Another quarter-hour and we have a nylon stuff sack, lined with a plastic bag, filled with all bear delicacies. It's less than clear how much the plastic liner will prevent our bear from smelling this wonderful offering since she can easily open even tin cans whenever she so desires. We tie another rope to the cache bag and hoist it to the middle of our horizontal line. One hour has now passed. The bag swings a happy two feet above the forest floor. Maybe we've saved our food from an uninterested chipmunk. We give up for tonight. At least the delicious items are out of the tents. Except for us.

Act II. Tonight we look for just one tree, and divide our food into two bags. We find a maple whose top bends to one side, and tie the heavier bag securely to our rope. After a dozen tries we manage to throw the other, weighted end over the curved trunk, at what we judge to be the best location. Tonight's lesson is: do not tie a rock in the end of the rope for a weight, no matter how many books confidently suggest such a plan. Gravity works, and the rocks occasionally fall out of their rope cages, bent on redesigning our heads. We'd rather not, thank you. Few rocks come with grooves to hold the rope in place. We are not enchanted with the idea of taking a day off for a participatory stone-age history lesson on rock shaping, to learn how our ancestors accomplished such tasks. Besides, we would then feel obliged to carry our carefully prepared rock whose status would be elevated to implement. This runs counter to the backpacker's credo to reduce the load. A stout, short piece of stick turns out to be the best weight, the rope tied to the middle with a clove hitch. This creates a T-handle to grab and pull the rope once it's over the branch. We hoist the first bag as high as we can, tie the second bag to the free end, and push it upwards to counterbalance the first bag. Wow! We did it, and in only thirty minutes. Tonight our bags are safe from chipmunks and clumsy squirrels! Well, hey, it's an improvement. "Are you enjoying the show, all you bears who hold tickets to this event?" Hopefully we are so hilarious to watch that you will spare the cache just to see what Act III will be.

Maybe in bear country hikers should eat all their food the first night, and skip this cache comedy. However, we do become better and faster at finding and choosing trees, appropriate heights and diameters of horizontal branches. "Is there a cache tree?" becomes a key question in choosing a campsite. We actually succeed, some nights, in getting the bags high over our heads and several feet from the tree trunk. We are either lucky, there are no bears nearby, or the show continues to be too amusing to eat; the bears never sampled our Baco-spuds or Crest. It seems to me that what is really required to be bear-proof is a skyhook or a guardian angel. I'll take the angel. Ours seems to be on duty.

Crossing creeks we often stub our toes on chunks of Pennsylvanian sea. That is "Pennsylvanian" as in 300 million years ago. Now the seas are the Pennsylvanian hills. This makes the wading more treacherous. Red and yellow sandstone do not belong only in the Painted Desert, so it seems. My guidebook informs me that the floor of the inland sandy sea settled and then rose without wrinkling to form a plateau. Rivers with rocky teeth sawed the plateau into tiles in high relief which were then rounded into the pointed knobs we now call the foothills of the Appalachians. The sea floor was above the present tops of the peaks. We are stepping carefully along the edge of the Allegheny Reservoir, through pre-history, at the bottom of the bottom of the sea-floor, seeing things already hidden from the Brachiopod's gaze. The bottom of his kingdom ended 800 feet above us. We live after him, and walk through a sandy world formed before he hatched. The guidebook does not warn us to watch out for the Pennsylvanian Dragonflies with the 30-inch wingspans. Would it be so incredible to see one, here on our journey through the ancient past?

Interspersed with the sandstone is a rock with the descriptive but unromantic name, conglomerate. This is shale with pebbles of gray or pink or white quartz embedded like tapioca pearls in a chocolate pudding. When I was small and found my first such rock I showed it to an adult, and asked what kind it was. I was told, " it's conglomerate." Serious child that I was, I stamped my foot and replied, "I can see that, but what is its name?"

Most of the sandstone and conglomerate which we must deal with on this humid July day is still cemented neatly into a conical hill in front of us. Not that we can actually get a perspective on the hill from where we stand. At this point it's just trees and trail heading upwards from Chappel Bay, at 1328 feet, to reach the high point of the Kinzua Watershed at 2110 feet. This climb is carefully routed up the hill, and without much difficulty we ascend to the high point for lunch. Our topo map tells us that is where we are but the forest is closed around us; no vista is awarded for a job well done. Lunchtime pleasures include freeing our feet from boot-prison, sock-drying in any available sun puddle, munching on various portable, mold-resistant breads with spreads, and resting. Declaring these to be pleasures is no careless boast. Such humble activities bring genuine delight, strategically placed in the middle of the day's toilsome miles. After lunch we descend into the Tionesta Watershed, 672 feet down again to the Bay! Intersecting Route 321 we turn right to follow the road to Red Bridge, in order to cross South Branch River. We pass Red Bridge Campground, a memorial monument, and the road winds ahead of us into more woods. Marie and Dave are far ahead; I have stopped to read the monument. Finally I catch up. Where is this bridge? A careful re-survey of the maps indicates that we should have turned left at the highway. Groan. It is already past 6 p.m. and we must yet walk far enough to get away from the road to camp. Returning past the campground, Marie and Dave walk in to see if any sites are available, despite our desire to camp alone. I guard the packs. They determine that established camp-grounds are designed for people in cars! Not wishing to hike three more miles just to learn that the site is full (it seems well-peopled), they return and we shuffle on. At least we are now headed in the right direction.

The sun, low in the sky, is beautifully reflected as we cross Red Bridge, but we are too preoccupied with finding a tent site and eating supper to grasp the possible ruby origins of the bridge's name. The trail turns off the road and becomes a dragon with three hikers and a dog wearily trudging up its backbone. It need not turn its head to breathe fire, cook and eat us; it has cleverly sat up and is waiting for us to fall exhausted, dead at its feet. On our left is a wall of dragon spine-spikes, and to our right its side drops away around the ribcage. We follow the six-foot-wide path along our dragon's vertebrae. He (she?) sits angled at an average of 14 degrees, a 26% grade. "Couldn't you lie down, Mr. Dragon?" Regulations state that camping is permitted away from the path, but fifty feet straight up or twenty feet straight down are the only "away" options. It is quickly becoming dark in the woods.

"How many hikers have we actually seen in three days?" Marie queries.

"Only one group," comes the answer in all our minds.

"How does this flat spot look?"

"Wide enough for a tent."

Well, it is, barely. We eat a supper of cold odds and ends, and carefully ease around the edge of the drop-off into the tent door. "Be careful not to roll to your left," are Marie's last words to me that night. The day's 14 miles of hills at least guarantee there will be no trouble falling asleep. (Guidebook note: "there are no good campsites between Red Bridge and Route 6")

Z-z-z-z-zip. Opening the tent door next morning, Sunday morning, I am greeted, blessed breathless with a favorite and familiar hymn come to life.

> Morning has broken, like the first morning.
> Blackbird has spoken, like the first bird.
> Praise for the singing, praise for the morning,
> Praise for them, springing fresh from the Word.

Sweet the rain's new fall, sunlit from heaven,
Like the first dewfall on the first grass.
Praise for the sweetness of the wet garden,
Sprung in completeness where His feet pass.

Mine is the sunlight, mine is the morning,
Born of the One Light, Eden saw play.
Praise with elation, praise every morning,
God's re-creation of the new day.[1]

Celebrating in the green morning light

What had seemed so dragonish and bone-wearying the night before is transformed into one of those perfections for which I will keep venturing into the woods for as long as I can walk. Cool white shafts of sunlight burst in a gleaming aura from behind dark tree trunks. Yellow-green and grass-green leaves glow on each black twig and stalk. Beads of dew cling to every leaf-tip, poised at the decision-point to fall or evaporate. Miles of spider webs hang in wet-white nets just below me, over the cliff-edge. The whole world is green and shining white. An early crow caws a greeting, and a spring in the lower hollow answers in bubbly, yet subdued, glee. I lie quietly, stunned into worship. No other response is possible. Marie and Dave are soon sharing the riches; there is plenty, freely given to all of us. This is indeed the Lord's Day.

Let me explain the theory of laundry. Hiking guru Colin Fletcher clearly advises taking two pairs of socks. One you wear, and the other you have washed the night before and hung on your pack to dry during the day. Mr. Fletcher did most of his hiking in the arid West. Well, I knew this. So I theorized that it might take two days for a pair of damp socks to dry in an Eastern Forest. Thus we take three pairs each, one to wear and two to have clipped outside in varying stages of dryness. We dutifully wash our first pair of socks at lunch on

---

[1.] Farjeon, Eleanor; from *The Children's Bells*; Oxford University Press; 1931; used with permission.

day two and find various ingenious ways to fasten them to buckles or through straps. Of course these are not dry by the next morning; this was not expected. So we wash our second pairs of socks and wear the third. Being in a courageous mood, Marie and I also wash underwear. By now the collection on the pack clothesline is becoming impressive, but not to worry, the first pair of socks is almost dry. Then it begins to rain. The semi-dry laundry is quite wet before we get the packs covered in their plastic rain jackets. O.K., tomorrow we will again wear the socks we have on now, and the others will all dry. It rains again. The daily soakings continue for the duration of the hike. It doesn't usually rain for long, just regularly, and long enough to thoroughly dampen the laundry and sometimes us as well. This also inspires a game: should we stop and put on the ponchos and pack jackets, or will it stop in two minutes? We almost always guess wrong. Photos reveal us wearing plastic bags in sun, or with wet hair and clothes plastered wrinkly about us with not a poncho in sight.

Thanks to the deer we lost our last pairs of dry socks. Deer had overbrowsed areas of the forest and the only plants that succeed in growing back in the openings are ferns. This creates huge fern-fields which have to be crossed. The walking is easy but we might as well be fording a stream. The closely spaced, compound, curved leaves hold buckets of rainwater. After 30 seconds in one of these fields we are soaked to the knees. Despite careful pre-trip waterproofing, our boots do not hold up to this continual assault. They soak through, and with this insult we give in to having constantly wet feet. By mid-hike pretty much everything we can wear is wet. Dave gives up and bags the mess in his pack, till his mom gets a whiff of it one night. Truthfully, we are all feeling quite nostalgic about being dry, so we begin cooking our clothes along with dinner. Open fires are allowed (with certain restrictions) so we have been building a fire each night anyway. We now begin stringing a clothesline above the fire and playing musical socks and t-shirts to keep each item above the fire for a carefully prescribed amount of time. The strategy is to let the item directly over the fire begin to steam, without letting it get hot enough to scorch. It is then moved to the farthest spot to cool and let the water evaporate while sliding the next item to the middle. We become adroit at sock and stew manipulation and don't come home with too many blackened briefs, or eat too many dinners flavored with ripe foot. It feels so grand to have dry socks for a few miles of each day, until we encounter a stretch of ferns, that we decide to go for broke. We also begin to dry our boots around the fire. We are probably shortening their life-spans a bit by doing this, but we don't really care. Dry feet make happy hikers.

When we had begun the hike, at the northern border of Pennsylvania, we had entered a rich, northern hardwood forest community. Indian Pipe poked through deep, scrunchy leaf litter below;

oak and hickory leafed in a canopy high overhead. Glimpses of turkeys flashed in the shadows and Ruffed Grouse feathers were so numerous on the trail that we stopped collecting them. Once we passed a bathtub size patch of Northern Maidenhair Fern. It was so unusual with its crayon-green leaves carefully outlined in black, it made me think that someone used the cut and paste function to copy it there from some careful child's coloring book. After climbing away from Sugar Bay on day two we topped the ridge at the source of Hemlock Run and, without noticeable transition zone passed into an ecosystem dominated by acid-loving plants. Sphagnum Moss, Bog Cranberry, and Goldthread covered the ground. Goldthread hoards its gold in the fine roots underground. For public viewing it displays a carpet of deep green waxy leaves with delicate white star blossoms sprinkled liberally above. The understory consisted of Moosewood with carousel striped bark, and blueberry.

Time out from the ecology lesson for Dave to go nuts, er, berries... They were ripe. He ate so many that he could hardly manage dinner, and that is saying something! We made blueberry pancakes for breakfast, a genuine north country treat. Even Chips got into the act. He carefully pulled berries off the bushes with his lips and sampled them. (No, I'm not pulling your leg. He does this with raspberries and strawberries too.) The trees were almost all mature Black Cherry with its distinctive "potato chip" bark. Sadly, they all had no leaves! An inch-long marauder, called the Cherry Scallop Worm, has pursued his passion with vengeance. These worms ingeniously choose two cherry leaves, stack them carefully and chew around the perimeter, cementing them together. The edge-pattern of this no-seater-kayak-shaped breeding house is scalloped, hence their name. Don Dorn assured us that the permanent damage is slight unless they attack in several successive years. The destruction occurs late enough in the season that the trees don't expend much energy trying to refoliate. But it is strange to walk beneath bare trees in July.

Our gradual descent along Hemlock Run is one of those seldom-encountered ideals of hiking. The trail wanders gracefully along the bank above the rock-strewn, splashing Run. The sun sprinkles flakes of light around the forest, spicing the day and enhancing the flavors of hemlock and tannin which hang in the air. This is apparently a popular, but well-tended section. We pass several neat campsites with fireplaces and seats built of the ubiquitous sandstone.

On day five we enter the Tionesta Scenic Area. This is the largest stand of virgin forest in the eastern U.S.; six square miles, a diminutive but mature forest. Three-hundred-year-old Eastern Hemlocks watch us pass. How many different travelers have they watched: Algonquin, Iroquois, Redcoats, Tories, Bluecoats, Senecas, oil-drillers, narrow-gage rail engineers, and now backpackers? But not loggers, they missed this tiny patch. Are all the details of this history stored in tree-ring memory if we could but learn to read the code? Could we tap the trees, install a jack, and listen to fife and drum of a passing column of Loyalists? Would the memory-sap be spilled and gone after one listening? Someone would commercialize it. "Jars of home-canned Indian war-whoops." "Get your gen-u-ine Pennsylvania oil-boom, mood music here! Sounds of the forest with a track of rhythmic oil-well squeakings. Guaranteed to cure insomnia."

Trees here are so tall we can not see their tops from any vantage point beneath them. For several days we had been finding ROCKS, calves of the mountain tumbled like giant-baby toy blocks around a playroom, but here we encounter ROCKS! Perhaps the giant-baby had abandoned them, but we can not. Despite the late afternoon hour and the fact that regulations require us to leave Tionesta before camping, we stop to play. These rocks are scattered willy-nilly down a gentle slope. They are nearly covered with moss and ferns which glow, fiery emerald trailer-size cut gems in the slanting sunlight. Dave climbs the scalable faces, I take inadequate photos, and Marie and Chips circle the blocks searching for treasures. We need to focus on miniatures to counter our feelings of insignificance in this quiet giant-world. A wavy band of waxy, apple-green Chrysoprase gleams opalescent from one granular yellow and umber wall. Tiny terrariums, more carefully planted by nature than any I ever succeeded in making, are tucked into angles of the rocks, flung carelessly over stony lips, strewn in wondrous abandon down slanting ledges. Scaly rashes of orange, red, brown, white or blue-green lichen erupt where moss can not yet wiggle its toes in deep enough to hold. Mysterious rows of small elliptical holes honeycomb some bands of the blocks forming geometrical, abstract art borders. A Red Eft is silhouetted as he pauses mid-scramble against the violent green moss, but paler orange somehow when he crawls across my hand. And the greatest mystery of all: in a tent-size pool at the base of one forward-tilting cube, from the entire bottom of this shallow, shadowed hollow something emanates a metallic-yellow phosphorescent light. A luminescent bacteria? Some strange algae? Witchcraft? In this eerie, silent realm of disproportions and oddly angled lights the golden phenomenon fits appropriately; we do not even shiver at its inexplicable, alien presence.

At length the light changes and the magic dissipates. We hoist our packs and move on to a comparatively drab and "normal" campsite. Another two days and we enter the final ecosystem. Instead of ankle-turning rock-litter the trail now smoothly works its way over humps and down hollows of a maple-beech forest. Its openness, comparative youth and light is a cheerful change from the dark and closed hemlock-rock experience of the days before. We had not realized the effect of the deeper forest until we felt the contrast of this lighter world.

Triumphantly we hug the sign at the southern boundary. In the car we zip northward, covering superficially in two hours what we have studied with feet, fingers, ears, noses, eyes and muscles so carefully over the past ten days. A restaurant meal treat for the people and ice cream for all (don't forget Chips) completes the adventure... well, except for the fact that I spend the next three days curb-camping in Bradford with car trouble. Such inconveniences are easily discounted in the overwhelming fulfillment of a quest.

I have somehow neglected to mention the puffy, creamy peach fungus as big as a platter, the twenty-eight hummingbirds, names as descriptive as Cornplanter Bridge, Sheriff Run (which parallels Fool's Creek) or as plain as The Branch, the private jokes, the night camped in the deer conference grounds with the herd stamping and snorting around our tents, the giant slugs, a hundred other details, and the sign to "Heart's Content – 28 miles." I knew that was a lie; I have found mine right here.

In ten days we walked through five counties, four ecosystems, two watersheds, and 300 million years – several times. We were tired. But sometimes it is the little things that stick with you. Pun intended. For more than a year afterwards we would occasionally find unique, green Pennsylvanian stick-tight seed pods in our socks.

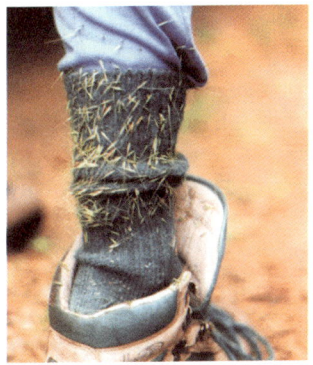

Memories that stick with us

98 miles this hike
Allegheny National Forest, PA
150 miles total NCT

Where the Trail Begins
6 - July 3-15, 1995

"All right, I'll come right out and admit it. I want to hike this entire trail in my lifetime. Let's see, if we hike about 100 miles each summer, that means 30 more years. But Ed (Talone, end-to-ender) says the trail is actually at least 4000 miles, rather than the projected 3000-something."

"Wait just a minute!" Marie exclaims. "If you think I will walk 100 miles when I'm 77 you can think again. We will have to take a couple of summers and do longer pieces."

"Great! Do you think we can do 130 miles in our two weeks this year? And let's do something really different... for us, anyway. Let's try out the plains and hike to the western terminus of the trail."

I was off and running with plans and priorities to make the next hike happen, and it was only November of 1994. I started telling friends that I would hike next in North Dakota. "North Dakota!" they would shriek. "Why? There's nothing there!" The better-informed would respond, "Oh, the Badlands?"

"No, east of the Missouri River," I answered, becoming more wary with every encounter. Stubbornly I would explain about The Trail, and my goal.

Responses deteriorated from the hopeful, "Tell me what it was like when you get back," to the disdainful. "Phooey. You should go out west and do some real hiking."

I completed my Masters Degree in December. My mother died in February. The metamorphosis to whatever the new self was to be seemed nearly complete except that I could not see who that new self was. I began course work toward a doctorate, but felt alone, surprisingly lost for someone who had always cared little about the connectivity of human experiences. On my father's side I am an only child of an only child who was adopted. My mother was the only one of three children who lived to adulthood. My three sons are adopted. I felt isolated in a puddle of indefinite emotions. Adoptive families had never seemed less real to me than biological ones. But for the first time ever it really bothered me that I had no blood relatives closer than cousins of my mother. We have papers to trace my bloodline back through my mother to the Mayflower and Peregrine White, the first Caucasian child born in the New World to survive. I became acutely aware that I was now the end of that line.

Perhaps these emotions contributed to my focused obsession with the North Country goal. I pored over maps and mileage legends. I wrote to administrative agencies, trail authorities and individuals.

Setting the emotional issues aside, it's a good thing that I spent time planning this hike. There are few certified miles of trail in North Dakota and the hiker must assemble maps, routes, varying regulations, and miscellaneous information and tips without assistance from published guidebooks. We integrated lessons learned the previous year. Boiling water for a group takes too long; we bought a filter. The dog pack needed to be more sturdily remade. Chips had destroyed the old one snagging it in Pennsylvanian undergrowth, thus cleverly manipulating the humans into carrying his load for the last two days of that hike. Firewood would be scarce; we bought a stove. Maybe we could leave the two-pound hatchet home. Marie bought a new pack. We didn't need so many flavored drinks; water was refreshment enough on hot days. Individual mess kits were a nuisance, we bought stainless steel bowls which stacked neatly, and smaller ones for the dog. He had flattened and split the foil pans, and then the plastic dip can we had used for his food dishes last year. Lighter is not better if it does not survive the trip!

Time is counting down. There are only three weeks, 21 days, until we will leave for North Dakota. Marie and I plan to hike alone. On a whim (but anchored in the reality of her fitness for the enterprise) I decide to invite a housemate, Mathilda, to join us. She decides to think seriously about it. At T-minus-15 days Marie calls and says that David can't find a summer job that pays enough. He is thinking about coming along. In a frantic e-mail message I insist that he decide by the next day because I must have the final two weeks to prepare food. He readily commits his fate with ours. Mathilda decides on day minus-14 that she will also come. We are suddenly a group again. The final two weeks of preparation are described by a third housemate as "crazy." Or maybe that was us he was referring to. Mathilda has never backpacked. We must shop for a pack, and bring her up to speed on essential personal gear. Food must be bought, dried, measured, packaged. Mathilda and I work intently at this task. Marie, in New York, and David, at school in St. Paul, Minnesota, jack up phone company stock as they try to determine what equipment is in which state (geographically and conditionally!), and who needs to buy new this, or repair old that.

The logistics of even getting started are a bit impressive. Marie will drive the 14 hours to Ann Arbor. We have gone back and forth on the issue of taking two cars several times. Public transportation is not available to return us to wherever we might spot one car, but Marie is meeting her sister-in-law in Bismarck after our trip. Virginia (who incidentally thinks we are interesting but nuts to hike hundreds of miles), will rent a car and meet us at the termination of the hike. We are all set. We think. On the night Marie arrives in Michigan it is decided that this option is outrageously overpriced. We will take two cars. Remember, I said that hiking is not for the inflexible. It works well for those who can say "organized" and "haphazard" in the same breath without feeling like a split personality. From Ann Arbor it is 18 hours to St. Paul. Mathilda rides some with each of us, getting acquainted with Marie. We have planned to spend this night with David at his college-town apartment. Quick, blink and change plans. Dave informs us that his housemates, who have majority and seniority, are planning a late-night party "which quite likely involves various illegal substances." We are getting good at running through the options. We find a motel that will accept dogs. They are full. I call all the people I know in Minneapolis. No one is home. Marie calls the motel's reservation hotline. They tell us there is indeed a room in St. Paul, the motel just doesn't know it. We call the motel back. "Oh, yes, we do have one room left, if it's a small dog."

"Hold that room!"

"Kneel, Chips!" Marie orders hopefully.

Somehow we also manage to eat supper and breakfast, walk the dog twice, jockey Dave's gear into a vehicle, sleep some, and attend church before returning to I-94 and the final leg to North Dakota. Where did that all that activity fit?

Sunday, July 2, we sail past the Exit to Fargo, across the flat surface of Lake Agassiz to Valley City. No matter that we are 10,000 years late for sailing. Its floor is as flat as the water would have been, and we have brought a car instead of a HobieCat. At Valley City we abruptly leave the valley and climb 250 feet, straight up the Pembina Escarpment to the first of several wide north-south plateaus striping across the Dakotas, called coteaus. This one is still considered a lowland coteau. And here North Dakota giggles and tosses the first of many surprises our way. Each laugh is expressed in a bubbly green hill, roiling away to the western horizon and the Missouri Escarpment. No flat prairie, this. Our visions of level, wind-swept, xeric brown-and-yellow northern deserts impressed into agricultural service explode in a green reality of prairie potholes, wetland plants, and water birds. Alas, I have brought the wrong plant and bird identification book!

We turn left off Route 3 onto a road which would be called a "two-track" in Michigan. Here it is one grade better than the dim breaks in the grass which cross it and are marked "Minimum maintenance road." Our destination is Faul Campground, in the Lonetree Wildlife Management Area. The WMA requests hikers to use the established camp sites, and we will try to do so. Tonight it serves us well. A pump, latrine, and fire ring are available for use. There are also three cement slabs, one rectangular, and two round ones. An ominous sign on the outhouse warns, "Do not dispose of garbage or bird remains in the latrine!" Someone has shot this argument full of holes.

Literally. We will pitch the tents, leave our gear here, spend tomorrow spotting the cache box and cars, and then hike eight miles from the eastern edge of Lonetree to our already-set-up camp. The highlight of this plan is that these miles can be hiked with only odds and ends in a waist pouch, rather than with full packs!

It seems unlikely that anyone except the hunters uses this lonely campsite, but to our surprise a pickup truck and car roll in. Two couples, one younger, one older, emerge and wander around the site, pointing at various spots, shaking their heads. Finally they approach us. "We used to live here and wanted to show our new son-in-law around," the elder woman explains. I am thinking that their old home must be nearby, then realize with a shock that she does mean here, right here. How could I not have recognized that the rectangular concrete slab is a driveway, and the round ones are grain bin pads? Suddenly I see their farm in my mind. The access road was their driveway, the windbreak the fencerow behind the house. The mother is doing most of the talking. When the government bought the land for the lake/ canal/ irrigation project they were forced to sell. She is still sad. Her husband is bitter. He turns away from us, too emotional to face the strangers whose tents now rest where perhaps his own bed stood. I want to apologize for even being a nameless part of some master plan for recreational usage that I represent to him. But I don't. Instead we commiserate with them on their loss, and they share the feelings of coercion they experienced. "It's a good well; enjoy the water," they finally offer us, the only resource from their farm which has retained its value. Our education in North Dakota politics has begun.

Next morning we drive, still in caravan, to Harvey. The tourist bulletins have urged us with quarter-page insistence to "Visit Harvey, home of the famous Og!" The small monochrome photo shows a gorilla growing out of a field. We have to see this. A big breakfast at a small café provides us with a final kitchen-cooked meal, and supplies the locals with something to talk about. North Dakota may advertise for tourism, but they are not yet used to the fact that tourists may indeed come. It isn't always clear whether we provoke suspicion or just provide a diversion. While checking out I ask the doughy, aproned man, "What's the story about Og?"

Visit Harvey, home of the famous Og!

Looking as if I had queried him in Chinese, he says, "What?"
I repeat the question, and he ruminates on the words.
His sudden response: "Town didn't want it. Guy built it anyway. It's ugly."

And that's all we know about Og. It is indeed a statue of a gorilla-ish torso sprouting from the middle of a field, both arms raised with clenched fists. We park on the edge of the highway and take photos, with us making silly poses in the foreground, Og forever baring its teeth in mock ferocity over our shoulders. Cars whiz past and we supply the town with more gossip fodder. We are having great fun imagining dinner conversations, "Didya see them dang tourists fussin' over that fool THING today?..."

---- ✳ ----

To make a long-distance hike work smoothly requires the help of some outside people. The purist might prefer to walk extra distances to buy groceries en route, or to reach public (or thumb-derived) transportation at the conclusion of the hike. We have chosen, however, to plan ahead for these details so that we can concentrate our energy here in North Dakota on the trail. The Commissioner of McLean County, Tom Beierle, has agreed by phone to hold and deliver our cache box. So the next stop is his home village of Mercer, just off Route 200. Mercer has a gray, weathered grain elevator by the railroad tracks, a garage, a store or two and 104 people as of whenever someone last counted. We find Tom and Alma's house without difficulty, but no one is home, so we settle on their lawn to wait. Soon Alma drives in, flustered, excited. She is so sorry. She decided to drive out to the highway and watch for us. Somehow she missed seeing us. Then she saw us. She can see the house from the road. She came back. The fragmented explanation goes on in small explosions. It hits me that we are a phenomenon in her world. I don't recall very many people who were ever excited enough about my appearance to watch the highway for me, and I am suddenly humbled and honored. She is saying that Tom is out at the garden, and she will take us there. We all pile into her full-size, dusty auto and drive about a half mile. A solidly-built man in jeans, brown work shirt, red suspenders, and an engineer's cap grins impishly from under its brim. With a slight European accent he welcomes us.

While my check-list mind pressures me to hurry these "pre-hike details," the experiential half of my brain argues back that these encounters are also worth savoring. The garden tour is first. "Radishes came along better last year. Tomatoes are lookin' good though." He draws David into his confidence, showing him stealthily the mechanism to control his underground irrigation system. "Now I'll show you my winter hobby. You ladies go in the car. The young fellow can ride in my truck." It's hard to be offended, to accuse him of being sexist. He seems to treat it all as a joke, but one that we can be in on if we want. In a world where he is confronted with the reality of three women and a just-past-boy who are planning to camp alone for two weeks, perhaps he must find a bit of security in the old ways.

Tom's winter hobby is an entire building full of antique engines in various stages of refurbishing. It is spotless, and smells pleasantly of fresh oil and metal shavings. We learn that he is of German-Russian descent, a proud U.S. veteran of World War II who speaks four languages. He has been re-elected to county commissioner for so many terms that he has now held the office for thirty years! There seems to be no one in the county whom he does not know. Explaining the local politics is his favorite subject, with the federal-local sovereignty struggle the keynote. After a couple of hours of visiting we agree on a meeting place for later that week, and our box of food, clean clothes, and extra film is left in their keeping.

The Beierles are our second surprise. They appear to be a typical, weathered farm couple. The problem with the word "typical" is that there is no such thing. Here we meet an entertaining, knowledgeable and highly sophisticated elected official. I do not mean city-slick, pseudo-sophistication. I mean the genuine sophistication of a person who knows his world, his worth, the extent of his abilities to improve that world, and who both stands out and fits in, with no hypocrisy. As we leave, Tom hands us his business card. The bald man in the suit staring placidly from the corner of the card seems to have no connection with this vibrant public servant we have just visited. Well, some conventions must be served.

Alma and Tom Beierle

Next we drive to Lake Sakakawea State Park, the western terminus of the North Country Trail. My car is left in the safekeeping of the maintenance man, and we all pile into Marie's sleek and silver New Yorker. I always feel a little silly riding around the woods and fields in this car, but Marie's husband, Ed, insists. "It's the trip car," he says. Back to the eastern end of Lonetree we cruise. A few hundred yards down a minimum maintenance road the low-riding auto begins to scrape a bit too often for Marie's comfort. We back out, drive around a country block and approach our starting point from another side. At

6 pm we leave the sleek silver machine at an almost invisible crossroads in the middle of four square miles of green fields. Lonetree officials have been notified that it will be there, but it doesn't look like anyone will care very much.

One of the few certified sections of trail in North Dakota is through Lonetree. That official status had been attained just months before we arrived to hike it. Markers are yellow Carsonite® (the flat composite ones) stakes spaced at irregular intervals. We stand at the 8x10 inch metal sign marking the Lonetree boundary and scan the tall grass for such a marker. I get out the binoculars and look harder. "There it is!" Off we march, straining to keep the yellow speck in view. This sequence of activity describes the next three days quite well, except that sometimes the response is "I can't see one anywhere, can you?" In that case the next activity is to check the map and compass, head in the right direction till we hit a road and then determine where the next marker should be. (Ed Talone, who traversed this section in November, says, "You should try to find them when the grass is yellow too!")

Lonetree is indeed lonely and wild in a prairie way. The wind pulls our hair into cartoon streamlines. Squirrel-tail Grass, in tones of chartreuse and maroon, is ever out-of-focus flowing like water buckled to the earth. Incongruously, gulls wheel and scream overhead; the wet year has coaxed them inland to smaller ponds. Water in Coal Mine Lake is raised into whitecaps and we feel sure we will be blown off the

Prairie hiking above the Sheyenne River

narrow causeway which separates it from Sheyenne Lake. The old and lazy Sheyenne River has thus far eluded capture by the irrigation/canal projects. (Only because they ran out of money.) It wanders in slow loops through the plain, forming a wide marsh dense with reeds. If it weren't so marked on the map, we wouldn't know that we were seeing a river. At the western edge of Lonetree we climb the Missouri Escarpment and camp on its slopes, facing a vista of river, prairie potholes, the bubbly hills, and not a mote of human activity.

Climbing the Missouri Escarpment takes us to the next level in more ways than one. Geologically we are now on the Missouri Coteau. Each coteau, moving westward, is hillier than its eastern neighbor. We reach the end of the McClusky Canal on Friday morning. We almost wonder what alien race had left such a monstrosity in the green wilderness. The sluiceway rises from a small pond, ominous and white, dozens of feet high and studded with monoliths of unknown purpose.[1] Behind it, the watergate is sealed. No water or secrets escape its lips. In back of the watergate a trench stretches to the horizon. For the next 74 miles we will follow this wound in the Dakotan hills. For a wound it is, largely unused and unhealed. This section is not even filled, and the sour ooze in its depths matches the souls of residents who feel they were deceived and defrauded. A bench halfway up the engineered slope of the trench carries the access road. It is this line of crushed rock which we will tread. The hills we might have seen and walked are abased into a tame two percent slope. The sides of the waterway are lined with rock trucked from Minnesota. The water beside us used to flow to Nebraska. Now it sits idle here in North Dakota. The banks above us exclude even the wind. This is a monument to government projects.

The story according to Tom goes like this. The federal government masterminded a plan to control flooding in Nebraska and provide irrigation water for Dakota. The Garrison Dam would be built on the Missouri River, creating Lake Sakakawea. No small idea, this! The dam was the largest packed earth dam in the world when it was completed in 1954, and the lake is the third largest man-made lake in the United States. The cheap water from the irrigation canals was to be the reward for all the land the Dakotans would have to forfeit for this venture. The land was possessed. The dam was built. Nebraska got its flood control. Most of the canal system was built but not fitted with pumping stations. The money ran out. Several groups protested mixing Canadian and U.S. fish. Dakota got a useless ditch full of unavailable water. At least if you need water to grow crops it is considered useless.

On the other hand, the string of the canal is beaded with deep blue lakes. Dusty farmers are discovering water recreation. I never quite got used to seeing cabin cruisers on trailers being towed by the ubiquitous pickup truck, in the midst of the prairie. Sounds of fishing, cruising, water skiing, or jet-skiing replace the rumble of tractors and balers on weekends.

---

[1] We have since learned that they are to slow the velocity of the water to prevent erosion, when it flows out of the canal.

Two items of note from Lonetree:

One: A friendly, wrinkled man who could have been 50 or 70, stopped his pickup in concern for us. It's common for people to know nothing of the trail, but he even found it hard to believe that folks would come from the east to see North Dakota, and planned to walk to do it, no less. He shook his head in disbelief that we did not require a lift, but finally admitted that all the rain had made the state "real pretty" this year.

Two: Chips earned a blue ribbon, grand prize, "Good Dog" award. He is intelligent; the Lab half of his mama gave him that. Mama's other half, however, is Beagle. The hound shows up only occasionally, in his deep, liquid brown eyes, a seldom-used but wonderful little warbly howl, and the often-used attitude, "I'll come when you call as long as there is nothing more interesting to smell or do." This condemns him to being leashed more often than either of us would like. But this evening there were no cars or other immediate dangers, so he ran free and exuberant. We were chatting, probably about the lack of trail markers, and I looked up to see Chips approaching a furry form silhouetted on the road, about 200 feet ahead. The approaching sunset made details difficult to see. The form shifted, sporting a broad pale stripe down its back. "Chips, come!" He paused and looked casually back at me, then moved toward the skunk a step or two. Now we all took up the cry. "COME, CHIPS!" He stopped, confused at this unanimous interest in his activities. For at least a year (oh, all right, maybe a minute) he debated the merits of obedience vs. checking out this interesting critter, looking alternately at us and the polecat who was now squared off, facing him, with tail twitching. We ordered, reasoned with him, implored, "Come, baby dog, ple-e-e-ease." Suddenly Chips sighed and trotted to us, where he was duly fussed over and praised. We contemplated the alternative ending a bit... two weeks in a tent with a skunk-scented dog. We praised him for his wise decision even more adamantly.

As we march along the canal road the heat increases daily. The temperatures climb to over 100°. The coarse gravel road surface is torturous to feet. The sloping canal walls offer no shade, and serve only to block the breeze. At least the water is nearby; Chips can dip his belly often for relief. The wide maintenance road does make it possible for us to hike side by side, rather than single-file as is usually required on woods trails. We overcome being obsessed by the pain and heat by singing. *Dakota Hymn* becomes our theme:

> Many and great, O God, are Thy things,
> Maker of earth and sky.
> Thy hands have set the heavens with stars,
> Thy fingers spread the mountains and plains.
> Lo, at Thy word the waters were formed,
> Deep seas obey Thy voice.
>
> Grant unto us communion with Thee,
> Thou star-abiding one.
> Come unto us and dwell with us,
> With Thee are found the gifts of life.
> Bless us with life that has no end,
> Eternal life with Thee.[2]

Ballads with many verses also help to pass the time. "The fox went out on a stormy night..." well, it was early one morning, but we did see a fox. Dave wakes us each morning by flapping around our tents bellowing "Good morning sun, good morning sky!" Hopefully we chorus, "We're bound away, 'cross the wide Missouri." And I never fail to choke up while singing, "I love to go a-wandering until the day I die, and may I always laugh and sing beneath God's clear blue sky."

We stop at the Operations and Maintenance Building for one lunch. There Bob Olmstead, the maintenance supervisor, gives us a different perspective on the canal. He assures us that it is being used for irrigation in one section, and that progress is being made toward full utilization. This is a good reminder that there are always two sides to any issue. He also tells us of some tough miles to come near Turtle Lake where the canal walls have collapsed.

Contrast. Joy. Plunging into the canal clad in a two-ounce swim suit after hours of trudging, hot and dusty, laden with 45 pounds of pack and boots. Joke. "How far do you think we could swim with the packs?" Sky. Blue wrapping around the green circle of our horizon, providing light shows of titanic proportions. Distant thunderheads building, sunsets with color reverberating from west clear to the east, and stars seemingly close enough to gather like wildflowers. Mathilda chooses to brave the mosquitoes and sleep in the open several times to soak in the "big sky" without being fried in the unrelenting sun. Night is the only time she dares leave her pale, sensitive skin exposed to feel the air. Birds. Rounding a bend with expectations of only more treeless canal walls and the boring ditch, to find instead an unmapped lake with

---

[2.] Renville, Joseph; 1842; public domain.

trees and accessible shore where we can soak our feet and filter water. The dramatic White Pelicans with black tips on their nine-foot wing spans play keep-away when I put the zoom lens on the camera. Photos show only elusive dots above the water, but our brains have recorded their awesome flights from just a few feet away. Bonaparte's Gulls laugh at us with eerie, human voices in the night. Yellow-Headed Blackbirds, Little Gulls, Cormorants, ducks, grebes and many others offer us tours of their prairie pothole homes.

    Everyone's feet are blistered and raw. Mine are the worst. If you add up all the blisters I have had anywhere on my body over my entire life the total is fewer than I now have on my feet. It is a humbling change for me to be the one slowing down our progress. We add an extra day to our itinerary and ask Tom to bring us more moleskin. Marie is becoming a specialist in padding, taping and protecting sore heels and toes. We cover our feet with baggies before putting them in the water to cool so that the moleskin patches will stay dry.

    The mercury climbs to 105° in the shade at our rest stop. I am too busy just trying to move my feet to check the thermometer while we are walking. We scan the trail ahead hoping for a tree. A huge Cottonwood shelters us for lunch. Did it also shelter lunches served from covered wagons? We know the kinship of shared experience with the pioneers who braved this grassy inferno. Unbeknownst to us until later, Tom is concerned about our health in the heat, and is following our progress from a distance with his binoculars. This is genuine hospitality.

    At 7:30 pm the temperature has dropped to a delightful (by contrast) 90°. We pitch our tents on the bluff above the canal to catch the breeze and the view. And it is quite a view. We are the highest point for miles around. The sky is cloudless and the daylight fades to a spectacular starry night. At about midnight we awake to the sound of thunder. Will the storm go around us? The answer is an unequivocal "No." In just a few minutes we are at ground zero of a bank of storms. The wind is so strong that the tents are pushed flat against our bodies. I realize with a sudden clot of fear that I have metal tent poles, and our wonderful, high vantage point is now the least favorable place to be. "Dave! We have to take the tents down, now!" I yell. He and I emerge into the wild night and wrestle poles from their casings and clips, flinging them away from the tents. Mathilda and Marie lie under the loose fabric, clutching it to keep the tents from leaving the county. We huddle, flat under our nylon shrouds, trying to be inconspicuous to a lightning bolt. I learn new facts about plains storms. They come in banks, not as a single storm. The old trick of counting the seconds between lightning and thunder is useless; the light and crashing are continuous. It is impossible to tell which flash and boom are a match. I give up trying and concentrate on holding the nylon down tight to keep it from shredding. A perverse pleasure develops in seeing the next flash of light; I figure that if I can see it then I am still alive.

After an hour the storms have passed and the wind eases. We decide to set the tents up again. Dave and I crawl out to find the poles. While Act I for the night was pure drama, Act II is a comedy. Every mosquito in the world has chosen to come to our plateau for a post-storm feed, and Dave and I are the entré. Marie and Mathilda laugh themselves silly watching Dave and me perform with poles and flashlights, slapping and dancing.

We later bought a newspaper saying that the winds exceeded 70 mph that night. Fiberglass poles have a tensile strength of about 55,000 pounds per square inch. One of Dave's fiberglass poles broke. My tent has E9 aluminum poles rated at 96,000 psi. One of these was bent. All in all, this was the scariest night I have spent outside. It was also a warning. As an experienced camper I should have realized that the late, hot evening would set up thermal currents and create storms. We were protected from our own stupidity, or you may conclude just lucky, but the experience was a serious reminder of the consequences of a wrong decision in the outdoors. Nature is a beauty with teeth.

Let me tell you about the ticks. This paragraph is not for the queasy. The ticks were without comparison or compassion. Pamphlets outlining how to deal with ticks contain such sensible phrases as "check yourself each day if you work or play outside." Or, "the best time to check for attached ticks is while you are in the shower." Shower? Shower! We wish! Checking ourselves and the dog became a continuous exercise. Long pants tucked into socks or repellent were no deterrent to the hordes of arachnid invaders. At each rest stop we brushed several, sometimes dozens, from the warm and humid hollow between pack and back. We became adept at pulling them, kicking and screaming (we presume) from our skin, wherever they had attached for a lovely, warm meal of our blood. Chips patiently endured having them torn from his ears, neck and belly. We found dog ticks, wood ticks, a smaller tick (but not the deer tick), and the horrors we named "the big gray ones."[3] Thankfully these preferred the dog. They swelled to a blood-filled gray balloon about a half inch in diameter. Their tiny legs

---

[3.] As it turned out, these were just the dog ticks, swelled with blood to proportions which seem unbelievable, given how tough and inflexible ticks seem to be when you try to squash them.

then became useless and looked like a row of threads protruding from the edge of the balloon. No matter to the tick. It was then ready to settle in to a few weeks of digestion after which its body would shrink and become studded with bright orange eggs. Joking about it all was the counter-measure for the primal distaste of crawly things with many legs. We stacked ticks – the art of holding more than one tick at a time. We passed ticks – the person away from the tent door had to relay ticks in the night to the person who could reach the zipper. We squashed ticks with increasingly deft techniques. We stooped to photographing ticks. Even those of us who aren't much bothered by thoughts of creepy-crawlies had had enough. I knew that accurate explanation of the scope of the situation was beyond the grasp of those who have not lived outdoors when a doctor asked me sincerely, "Did you save the tick that bit you?"

At last we reach the watergate at the beginning of the canal, the eastern end of Lake Audubon, which is the eastern bulge of Lake Sakakawea. We are not sad to say farewell to the watery gash. Our feet are healing; are the wounds in the Dakotans' pride healing as well? We have seen repairs being made to a canal section where irrigation water was being drawn. We have hiked through a section so damaged that the canal was reduced to a trickle, drains were bent like pipe cleaners and we had to step from block to block of cracked and fallen wall. The islands dotting the lake are refuges and nesting sites for water birds, but the prairie soil is unstable at shorelines. One ranger predicts that the islands will be gone in ten years. We saw 40 local farmers attending a seminar on Integrated Management: how to manage the land to benefit both agriculture and wildlife. The next day we hear angry words concerning the decision to hold the Lake at high water in order to protect plover nesting sites downstream from the dam. Healing is often a slow affair.

Our final days of this hike are on county roads, and then state Route 200, as we near Riverdale and the Garrison Dam. The dam is a triple-point, the meeting of three phases. The Missouri Upland is separated from the Badlands by the Missouri River, and Lake Sakakawea sits high above them, across Route 200 and the dam. It is three more hot miles across the huge Garrison Dam, but our goal is in sight and we are motivated. Lake Sakakawea State Park projects into the lake on a peninsula just west of the dam. We are met at the entrance by the rangers. They are as excited as we are. One of them takes the requisite group picture – four tired hikers and a dog – grinning beside the entrance sign. Ranger John Tungee directs us to the spot which is marked as the western terminus of the North Country Trail. His enthusiasm for encouraging hikers to visit North Dakota is contagious. "This is where the trail begins!" he insists, countering the usual description of the trail as running from New York to North Dakota.

Winding down emotionally from a major hike always takes some time. After we have stowed the packs in the car, showered, shampooed, and changed to clean clothes, we are indistinguishable from all the other campers at this park. Now only we know how unique we are. We gradually work our way back to the ordinary world. As we travel eastward the alchemy fades and the golden elements of a backpacking venture devolve to more common matters. A restaurant meal is set before us with no effort on our part, ice cream tempers the blazing afternoon heat, we drive to see sites of particular interest rather than taking whatever comes into our line of sight. We stop in Mercer to retrieve the tag ends of non-priority baggage which Tom has held for us. Reaching Marie's car in the evening, we drive to Faul Campground where we began this hike. The stated purpose is to sort gear, and we do accomplish this. But here the transformation from hikers to ordinary travelers is completed. We visit late into the night, singing, rubbing each other's backs and feet, and each sharing what the trip has meant to us. In the morning, Marie leaves to meet her sister-in-law. By evening Dave has been delivered to St. Paul. The next night Mathilda, Chips and I are back in Ann Arbor. So quickly the trip is ended and the group dispersed. Yet not all the gold is lost. Nuggets of lessons and adventures and friendships gleam brightly in the magic of our memories.

Wood Lily

Three photos typify the North Dakota we expected: a weathered church, farmland dotted with haymows, and a windmill standing lonely in a field. We did find these on the plains. But we also met the unexpected: green hills, wetlands, birds and flowers everywhere. We tested and stretched ourselves in ways not possible in woods or larger hills. Like the ever-changing clouds in the big sky, the variety of attitudes, experiences, history and landscape to be found along the North Country Trail calls me to sample them all.

131 miles this hike
South of Harvey to
   Lake Sakakawea State Park, ND
281 miles total NCT

Patches
7 - October 27-28, 1995

Common perception often labels people who collect embroidered patches as "nerds." So be it; I am one of those people. Colorful symbols of many of the milestones of my life adorn a flannel shirt which I actually wear to an occasional, appropriate function. Various Scouting roles and events are memorialized on my shoulder blades. Some of my patches simply advertise favorite locales: Sleeping Bear Dunes, or Maine. The Allegheny National Forest hike earned us end-to-end patches for its 95 miles. Most recently I added a patch from the North Country Trail Association's annual conference where I examined the prospects of becoming more than just a hiker of this trail. One sleeve is reserved for major accomplishments. The Allegheny patch is here, as is one earned for a Pacific-to-Atlantic-Ocean bicycle ride. Delegates to the 1965 Girl Scout Senior Roundup would recognize another of these special patches. At the NCT conference in August, four end-to-end patches were awarded. I covet one of these.

The NCTA also offers patches for sale: one showing the trail's route, and individual ones for the states it traverses. Mileage patches must be earned. If someone else verifies that you have hiked 5, 10, 15, 20, 25, 30 or 35 miles of the trail in one day, you may then sport a patch with that number. I already have the three lowest, but my next goal is to earn the aqua and gold rectangle for 20 miles.

I persuade friends Phil and Nan to drive with me on a cool Friday evening to Osseo, Michigan. They are flabbergasted as I nonchalantly leave my car in the parking lot of a garage and fasten a note to the door of the building explaining that I will retrieve it the following evening. Next we steer their car along back roads until we find the spot I have selected to camp, near the tiny village of Medina. I quickly set up my tent in the glare of their car's headlights. Then they are gone, leaving Chips and me to our own brand of insanity.

At 8 am the dog and I are on our way. This section of the trail, like so many at this stage, is only proposed. I will hike on roads lined with small farms. Even in this rural setting the day becomes crowded with passing pickup trucks, herds of curious cows, angry geese, snorting and cantering horses, and unchained, performance-enhancing dogs. I am glad that there is a reason for this hike other than to have fun. A cold rain begins to fall and I am also glad that one of the requirements of this day is to walk briskly. By noon my hands are numb. With blazing stupidity I have forgotten to bring gloves. Too bad the heat of that embarrassment won't warm my fingers. I realize that I do not dare stop unless I can find a sheltered place where I can truly warm up, or I will not be able to work the buckles of the pack. Just past 12 o'clock

I am rescued from the consequences of my mistake by the misfortune of some other family. Where a house once stood on a corner lot, now remain only charred steps and a basement full of refuse. Chips and I quickly scramble down into this shelter expecting to only find a leeward wall. To my delight there is a cinderblock cave to be claimed. Where the water pipe once entered the house there is a crawlspace two feet wide, four feet high, and about six feet deep. I struggle with the buckles, unable to grasp anything tightly with my deadened fingers, but I finally manage to remove our packs, and deploy my sleeping bag. Huddled in the nylon cocoon, in our dry hole, munching cheese and crackers, we warm to the remaining miles. In less than an hour I can use my hands sufficiently to work the buckles and clips. Chips is whining; he knows that we need to move on. An extra pair of socks goes on my hands for the afternoon; at least I have that much sense.

We march on purposefully through the drizzle, but by mid-afternoon the rain has ended. We are comfortably warm but we are definitely tiring. At least on days when I know I must reach the car there is motivation to keep hiking. By 4 pm Chips has had enough. He trots steadily along but looks over his shoulder at me plaintively every few yards. I assure him that we are almost there. It is doubtful that he understands the message, but it helps to reassure me that we are close to reaching an end of this day. At 5:05 we arrive at the car. Chips collapses with a happy sigh in the back seat; I, however, must drive home.

The many irritating encounters with farm animals, vehicles, and people throughout the day, and the cold rain prevents this from being described as an enjoyable hike. But like episodes of life, hikes are not all wonderfully pleasant experiences. This does not negate their value. This day has met its stated goal. I will have my patch.

23 miles this hike
Lake Hudson State Park to Osseo
Lenawee and Hillsdale Counties, MI
304 miles total NCT

Connecting to Ohio
8 - November 2-3, 1995

Most of my close friends are well-trained to accept my eccentricities. Since I met Phil and Nan only a year ago, they are still learning this skill. But I have convinced Nan once again to dump me off alone in the middle of nowhere. We find a farm near the road I will be hiking, one mile into Ohio. A quick chat with the owner, and my car is safely parked for the day. Back we go to the spot where I camped just one week earlier and I again set up the tent in the car's headlights. Nan is not really comfortable with my independent whims, but she bites her tongue and drives away.

The air has turned much cooler in the last week. Winter is nipping at the heels of autumn. My camping equipment is really not adequate for truly cold weather, but I can make do for nights near freezing. Sometime during the dark hours Chips lets me know that his equipment is not adequate either, so I teach him to come in the sleeping bag with me. Once he catches on to the trick, we are both toasty warm. When he gets too hot he squirms out again and curls his nose into his tail until he cools off.

The morning is clear and crisp and at 7:45 am we are headed south from this campsite, instead of north, as we did the previous week. The blacktopped country lanes are straight as arrows, flat, and lined with stubbled fields. However, they are less populated with people and domestic animals than last week's roads. For this I am thankful. The temperature is hovering around 32°, but the wind is shrieking angrily across the open fields. I have remembered my gloves, and am wearing several layers of warm clothes. Still, I am glad that this will be a short hike, with no chilling stops required. There is no glamour or gold in this day's miles, with the wind chill creating an apparent temperature of $-2°$. I will not try to romanticize it. The dog squints into the wind and pulls me as fast as I will walk. It is basically a miserable morning. We reach the car at 11:10, shut the wind outside, and head for home with the heater on full.

But one more small piece of the quest is fulfilled. I have crossed into Ohio on the North Country Trail.

10 miles this hike
Lake Hudson SP to US 20
Lenawee County, MI,
   and Fulton County, OH
314 miles total NCT

Buckeye Beginning
9 - December 16-18, 1995

As independent as some of us like to think we are, when pressed we must admit how much we rely on the help and achievements of others. The modern sport of backpacking would not have been viewed as recreational by pioneers of past centuries. To pack their belongings into a mobile contrivance, usually a wagon, with some salt, flour and bacon and head into the unknown was an adventure to be sure, but one which could not so blithely be assumed to end as cheerfully as most modern hikes. Disease, injury, enemy attacks, ferocious animals, hunger and exposure were ever menacing. For many of these travelers there was not even a warm house to shelter them at the end of their trail until they could build one for themselves. The risk was high and the dangers many. Recreational activity which increased personal risk would have been regarded as lunacy.

But it is my opinion that humans require some measure of adventure and danger to feel truly alive. So, encapsulated in our much safer century, we must create thrills, adventure and danger. My husband rides roller coasters, some folks bungee-jump or climb mountains, I backpack. Comparatively speaking, it's still quite safe. Technology increases the warmth of fabrics while reducing their weight. Moisture can be wicked away from the body to guard against hypothermia. Packs are suspended on our bones and muscles by computer-designed frames, enabling us to walk more miles with less pain. Boots contain supportive ply of various materials to cushion and protect feet and ankles. A well-planned hike involves a network of support people who contribute help with transportation, cache boxes, or emergency aid. I hope I will never become ungrateful for all the assistance I receive as I hike across the north country.

When I hike alone, I am especially dependent on others for transportation aid. I am feeling a little guilty at the number of hours of driving I have asked of Phil and Nan in recent weeks. As I complete the miles nearest to Ann Arbor, each trek to spot my car requires a longer drive. So this time, I have asked another friend, Theresa, to go with me to Defiance, Ohio, where I will leave my car. She will then drop me (and Chips, of course) at the farm where I ended the short hike in November. Actually, Theresa is wishing that she had time to come with me. However, she adds danger to her life by playing ice hockey in a city league, and she has a game later this day which precludes hiking with me this weekend.

Again, most of this hike will be on roads, but before I reach Defiance I will connect with the route of the Buckeye Trail, which is concurrent with the North Country Trail through much of Ohio. December is bleak and brown with no snow yet to cover the patchwork of fields which stretches to the horizons, polka-dotted with houses and barns. But I am determined to knock off sections of this trail on weekend hikes. The road miles are more endurable in short segments, rather than for days on end. The main point of this trip is simply to cover some miles, but it will also offer me the challenge of winter camping. The weather reports predict temperatures near or just below freezing. I have prepared for this, but if it gets really cold, I will need to bail out. Again, the safety nets of modern communication, law enforcement agencies, and transportation make such options possible.

My expectation is for many miles of boring blacktop. In this I am not disappointed. But the weather cooperates at least. Days are above freezing, and nights are not much below that. I have a new toy to quantify this information. Its packing box calls it an "electronic wrist instrument." My friends call it "quite a fancy watch." Temperature and elevation are two of the data points available to me with this toy. Since the elevation in northwestern Ohio doesn't vary enough to affect anything except maybe ants, the temperature changes are much more interesting to track. Like all technology, it has practical limitations.

First I learn that the wrist instrument is not accurate if worn on the wrist. If it is inside my jacket it reads a toasty 75°. That is good. Now I know that I am dressed warmly enough just in case I had lost communications with my personal internal body thermostat. Next I verify that if the instrument is outside the jacket but still on the wrist it is also affected by my body heat. I doubt very much that it is 54° outside, even though it is a mild December day. I remove the "watch" and clip it to my belt pack. In about 10 minutes it more accurately reads 49°. This is still very warm for winter, giving me the reason why I am rapidly overheating inside my layers of clothes. Inside the jacket, I am now surrounded by a steamy 84° layer, but some quick zipper work solves that problem. The nights turn out to be more consistent with the anticipated temperatures. I am also able to check out the reality of how much warmer it can be inside a tent than outside. At dawn it is 35° inside where the dog and I have snuggled, while outside the reading is 29°. The second morning the spread is 33°/25°, and the condensation of our breath has caused it to snow in large flat flakes inside the tent. On the final morning the temperature remains near freezing, and a dreary mixture of snow and sleet is falling to soak my shoulders and boots.

The final ten miles of this hike are by far the most interesting. At Florida, Ohio, we connect with the Buckeye Trail. There is a three-mile section here which follows the towpath of the old Miami-Erie canal. With the canal on our right, and the Maumee River to our left, we are insulated from the road, and Chips can run, unleashed and exuberant. This towpath leads to Independence Dam State Park, then connects with the road again, and reaches the city park in Defiance.

Photos of this section are dull gray and brown, flat, without dimension or interpretation. Word pictures come a bit closer to conveying the mood which begins to develop. I am tired of tracking sterile data points, and solitary hiking encourages reverie. Huge Sycamore trees tower a hundred feet above the river. Bark on their smaller limbs peels in puzzled gray-green contemplation of the century of history which has flowed beneath. But the lower trunk, the oldest tissue, has ceased to puzzle and has settled into a lumpy acceptance of all that it has experienced. Does this make it older and wiser, or is it bitter and resentful of the changes effected since it was a sapling?

After making camp, I sit in the late afternoon winter light which angles through the branches, and watch the gulls wheel and dip above reedy, golden islands on the river. With each turn to the east the sun catches their wings and flashes of silver-white punctuate the dusk. Are the birds aware of the grace and light they reflect toward a solitary camper on the bank, or are their only thoughts of fish? Do I reflect any beauty to some observer unknown to me, while I concentrate on my personal, narrow concerns?

Approaching Defiance the next day, I pass monuments to historical figures. John Chapman, better known as Johnny Appleseed, lived in Shawnee Glen. Blue Jacket, Shawnee War Chief who may have been a white man, sat in power here along the Maumee. Chief Pontiac was reputedly born in the village of bark houses which the Indians built here at the confluence of the Maumee and Auglaize Rivers. Here, too, is the preserved stump of the largest known apple tree, 9 feet in diameter with a 60-foot spread. It sprouted in 1670, and as

An ancient Sycamore

late as 1872 bore 200 bushels of apples, finally dying in 1887. Perhaps all of these notable people sampled its fruit, and rested in its shade.

And the name, Defiance, is a living memorial to the power struggle for this important watery junction. U.S. General Anthony Wayne marched through swamp and forest, in 1794, to reach the hill above the meeting of the two broad and navigable rivers. He declared, "I defy the English, the Indians, and all the devils in Hell to take it." A fort was built, and named Fort Defiance. The quiet midwestern town, on this chill December day, seems insensible of the angry, hot blood and tears of the sons and daughters of four nations which flowed in the quest to possess these lands. Maumee, "the river, our mother", from the Shawnee. Auglaize, French explorers simply described this river, "like clay." Defiance, the bold attitude of an emerging united community of states severed from the British monarchy. Now these names roll without intrinsic meaning from our tongues. Only two defunct cannons, aimed across the river from what is now the placid lawn of the city library, prod us to recall the suffering. Is this peaceful inclusion of cultures sincere, or do we yet nurse 300-year-old racial and national grudges?

This weekend seemed filled with meditation as well as miles. Soliloquy and sleet vied for attention. Gold and silver shafts of light pierced the air where bullets and arrows once pierced walls and bodies. Were my thoughts worthy of gold and silver, or were they more like weapons, wounding and maiming my future attitudes?

37 miles this hike
US 20 to Defiance
Fulton, Henry,
    and Defiance Counties, OH
351 total miles NCT

Losing the Way
10 - January 26, 1996

"Follow the blue blazes." The admonition of the Buckeye Trail literature sounds so clear, so simple. "Pursuing a doctorate in Environmental Engineering." My stated goal at Michigan sounds so straightforward and purposeful. Both statements are fraught with pitfalls this bright but chilly day. But my thoughts are not bright, and there is a chill pervading my hopes as well as my bones.

Just four days ago I stood nervously facing a board of four professors. Years of my future were to be determined by the strength of this two-hour pivot. This dreaded "Qualifier" exam was the next challenge on the trail to the Ph.D. program. I failed.

Today I am on my way to spend a weekend with close friends in Indiana. I seek comfort and some salve for my wounded pride. En route I decide to seek comfort in walking a few miles of trail. I do not have the maps of sections south of Defiance, Ohio, but surely I can find and follow the blue blazes from the city park. I fail. I find no blazes in the park. I find no blazes along the street I believe the trail takes out of town. South of town I drive both east and west along a cross road looking for some sign of a trail crossing. I do not find one. I know that the trail passes through Delphos, south of Defiance. One point of my knowledge pins the trail down at the city park on the north edge of town. I leave the car there, and I am able to find a dim blue streak on a telephone pole. I head north along this road. In less than a mile I reach a junction. But there are no blazes, no guidance or direction is offered. Retreating to the car, I walk to the south, through Delphos. For now, to continue where I know the trail must go is all I can do. At the south edge of town I turn and retreat to the car again.

My committee wants me to try the qualifying exam a second time. Retrace my steps. Search for direction. To follow the blue blazes they must first be found. Wait months in order to face the same inquisition a second time. Without a support vehicle each mile of trail must be walked twice. Why don't the Buckeye volunteers keep their trail marked? Where are the blazes I followed so clearly on the trail to my Master's degree, God?

2 miles this hike
Delphos, OH
353 total miles NCT

Incident Report
11 - March 1-2, 1996

A letter and a few phone calls have brought into my possession the Buckeye Trail map set, and the aid of a cheerful young man who will help me spot my car on Friday for another day of hiking Ohio roads. I hope to connect Delphos to Defiance on this hike. Mathilda and another friend, Brook, will join me for Saturday and Sunday. The observant reader will have noted that this three-day plan does not match the two recorded dates for this hike. Plans often go awry.

Friday's miles slip by calmly enough. I do note that the rule-of-thumb for northern Ohio seems to be that if a house is set far back from the road the owners tie or pen their dog(s). If the house is close to the pavement, the dogs roam free. But each encounter between Chips and a resident canine is resolved reasonably, much to my relief.

There are not many places to camp along the Buckeye Trail. I have left my car at a lovely roadside park outside of Cloverdale, but no overnight parking is allowed. I had checked, and Defiance has no motels which allow dogs. So we drive to Grand Marys Lake State Park for the night. The effort seems wasted. The cold wind howls off the lake and across the flat and open campground, gusting to around 50 mph. There is no shelter even in the lee of the small rest room building. I can have my choice of 170 deserted campsites. However, I figure I no longer have to prove that I can camp under adverse conditions. Chips and I rest snugly in the car, but we could have done this any number of places closer to the trail.

Saturday morning we meet Brook and Mathilda right on schedule at the tiny village of Junction. This name is descriptive of Ohio's canal history. Once the Wabash and Erie Feeder Canal here met the longer Miami-Erie Canal, forming this junction. Now the few remaining dilapidated houses and their sprawling piles of junk sullenly continue to mark the junction of only a minor state route and a county road. We spend about 15 minutes in the parking area of a defunct café and gas station to plan where we will leave our vehicles for the day. Brook is more concerned about his car, and chooses to place it in the park at Cloverdale. Mine will go on a country corner. In even this short time the owner ponderously emerges from the house behind the block building to inform us that we are on private property and he wants us to leave, now. It is easy to comply since we are ready to go anyway. But I am sad that he is so bitter as to order us off with no interest in hearing what we are about.

The day is bright and crisp, just right for hiking. It is very pleasant to have company on these miles. We walk and talk of issues with small import, but it is enough to share and enjoy being with each other. I am especially looking forward to the evening hours with friends. One drawback to solo winter camping, with short daylight hours, is that the dark evenings are hard to fill. It is hard to sleep for 10-12 hours. Reading can be done by candle lantern, but you must stay partly outside your sleeping bag to turn the pages. If it is cold this becomes uncomfortable. I had concluded on my earlier hikes that what is really needed is a friend to visit with. This night I will have two friends. During the afternoon the temperature begins to drop and flocks of snowflakes gather in the swirling breeze, like birds, to perch on our scarves and eyelashes.

Chips asks for a snack from Brook and Mathilda

    The final two miles we will cover are on un-maintained two-track roads. Chips is happy; he can roam the fencelines. Nor I am sorry to be released from his tugging on the leash. The last mile, until we reach my car, passes along the edge of a field directly beside a remnant of the canal. All that remains is a straight-sided, wide ditch, but trees have grown up since its abandonment, and the result is not unattractive. Major chunks of the concrete walls of what might have been a lock still stand in one place, and the local population has clearly turned this into a summer fishing spot. There is room for one car to pull off the road to an area where old chairs and numerous beer cans litter the banks. The wind speed has increased as the temperature dropped, and now we begin to discuss plans for the night. Driving many miles for the privilege of camping in the unprotected expanse of state park sites does not sound appealing at all. The "road" we are hiking on is quite deserted. In fact, except for big-wheel trucks, it is impassable. The deep ruts have frozen into ridges which make it look more like a plowed field. We decide that after we retrieve the cars we will drive to the nearest intersection and creep as close as possible to the old lock. Its sheltering walls, within the trees, will provide the protection from wind which we seek. This decision will cost us dearly.

    My car, with 4-wheel drive, easily makes it to the turn-off spot tucked into the trees. It is just past here that the road becomes unrecognizable as a thoroughfare. Brook does not make it quite so far, but he parks at the edge of the rutted section and walks to our chosen tent site. And it is a nice site. None of us owns adequate winter camping gear, but knowing we would have the cars near at hand we compensated by bringing lots of layers. Brook has brought a tent large enough for all of us, and we have each contributed mats, quilts, and blankets. He and Mathilda set about to arrange the tent into a cozy nest, while I build a fire and stew a pot of Burgoo. Warm cups of hot chocolate, and bowls of the steaming stew keep our spirits up as the temperature goes down to 6°. The wind is still howling over the remains of the lock. Who knows what the wind chill factor works out to be; cold, no matter how you figure it! But after clean-up we snuggle into the middle of our nest. The puffy piles of layers seem almost two feet deep, a regular ocean of comforters. We spend a lot of time congratulating ourselves on managing to be toasty warm on such a bitter night.

As I drift off to sleep I am thinking about how sensible some aspects of the 1990's are. Here we are – two girls and a guy – sharing a tent with no sexual implications at all. I remember in the late 1960's my mother was horrified that I went off for a weekend of hiking with a guy.[1] No matter to her that his father was with us except for a few hours of day-hiking, and that we slept in separate rooms in their cabin. It is so much more practical, and fun, to share the experience (and the body heat) of any one who is willing to participate.

The rest of the night is remembered as a bizarre collection of freeze-frames. If you consider your five senses to be five dimensions, these images can be considered as flat – not fully dimensional, separated from the way reality is usually experienced. Separated from each other too, by the dark and cold of the night, and unknown periods of time.

Frame one: In what must have been a dream, I hear a male voice yelling at us that we are on his property and we have to get off, now. I try to wake up to tell Brook and Mathilda, but can not fight my way to consciousness.

Frame two: Brook wakes Mathilda and me to tell us that he hears a vehicle on the road. It is gone before I am awake, and either from being groggy or indifferent, I ignore him. It is hard to believe there would really be a vehicle; the road is as close to impassable as you can get and still be called a road.

Frame three: Brook wakes us again. He hears voices. These are real; they sound like teenage boys from the direction of my car. One of them yells, "You check the glove compartment." Chips starts to bark, and in a burst of speed that surprises even me, I jam on my boots and run through the dark trees in only my long johns and flopping, untied footwear. By the time I reach the car there is no sign of anyone; the roar of a retreating motor is heard. I check the car, making sure the doors are locked this time. But it seems that we have frightened the boys away and nothing is missing. We all heard this, proving its veracity, but its occurrence in only the sound dimension heightens the

---

[1] see Pastor Paul in Chapter 15: "Forever Wild"

feeling of unreality. (Before returning to the tent my temperature sensors do kick in and inform me that long johns and boots are inadequate for extended outdoor activities this night.)

Frame four: This must also have been a dream. I see the silhouette of a man through the tent wall. There is some bright light behind him so that his shadow is flat and distinct. I would think that this really happened, except that he sported a "Sherlock Holmes" type hat and pipe. It seems unlikely that this could be real, given the weather conditions. He walks all the way around the tent, his shadow looming large and menacing against each green wall in turn. But there is no sound.

Frame five: Brook wakes us again. He is agitated and claims, "Someone just ran into my car!" By now I am so disoriented by the previous events, that I really doubt him. I have not heard anything at all. But in just minutes (seconds?) more, we hear spinning tires, a screech of grinding gears and brakes, and a sickening THUNK, followed by more spinning, grinding and roaring, as a vehicle bounces away. Brook can not seem to decide if he should go look, or hide. The flat audio image imposed on the blackness of the night seems eerie but manageable. To add a visual dimension is almost too frightening to face. I am groggy and feeling that since it is his car, he should go. Finally, Mathilda dresses and goes to check it out. With stunning diplomatic finesse she reports that it looks kind of bad, but that she doesn't understand much about cars, and she thinks Brook should come look. This bridges the gap to conscious reality, and Brook finally scrambles out of the tent. It is bad. His little Toyota looks like an accordion, and has been pushed about 20 feet. So at 1:30 in the morning, this frigid morning, we break camp and set out to find a law officer. By now, there is no way I am going to leave anything of value unattended, so we stuff all our gear, and our bodies into my car.

We do find a sheriff's deputy, and report what has happened. There is no open doubt of our story, but they find our claim to be camping curious on this cold night. However, seeing the car jammed full of equipment, and a return to the site quickly convinces them that we are "for real." The officer, with Brook, drives the quarter-mile from the access corner to his car, telling the rest of us, in my car, to stay at the dark intersection of the two county roads.

Frame six: The patrol car's spotlight is suddenly turned on the remains of the cream-colored Toyota. We are too far away to hear any of their conversation or vehicular noises, but the flat, bright image of the crumpled car floats in the dead black of the February night.

The car is towed, addresses are exchanged, and we begin to allow ourselves to react to the shock. This abruptly ends our weekend plans, so after a restaurant breakfast at 4 am we return to Ann Arbor.

The car was totaled, and rests in peace at an Ohio junkyard. No lead to whoever did this has ever turned up. One blotch of blue paint (not the kind of Buckeye blaze we wanted to find) on the front of Brook's car was the only clue.

Brook says he would go with me again. I'm glad he is a good sport. Infamously, this becomes the first National Park Service Incident Report on the North Country Trail.

31 miles this hike
Delphos to Twp Road 156
VanWert and Paulding Counties, OH
384 total miles NCT

Defiance
12 - March 23, 1996

Word quickly spreads of the "incident." I am asked over and over if this will scare me off the trail. I suspect that the questioners do not know me very well. Perhaps it is appropriate that the section I need to cover, to connect the two previous hikes, terminates in Defiance. I defy anyone to keep me from hiking this trail. I finish what I start, no matter what the cost. I just wish my feelings about graduate school were equally determined, but today I will not let myself think about this.

Omer is trying to be supportive of my crazy compulsive hiking. So after a weekend together in Ann Arbor, we drive to Ohio. He drops me off at the corner where the ill-fated hike ended, on which Brook's car was totaled, and heads for the Defiance Library to wait for me. It is a warm spring Buckeye day, there are only a few miles to walk, and all's right with the world. Sunlight glitters on streams, freshly released from winter's ice. One small off-road segment of about a half mile is still deep in snow, providing this day's biggest challenge. I stumble along, and Chips bounds over the drifts, but we soon return to the road and accelerate to full speed.

Rejoining Omer in good time, I sit on the warm parking lot surface letting my bare feet cool in the fresh breeze. How can I explain the joy of such a tactile focal point as cool air flowing over hot toes? It is moments like this when I feel really alive – interactive with my surroundings.

12 miles this hike
Twp Road 156 to Defiance
Paulding County, OH
396 total miles NCT

Breaking the Chains
13 - April 22-25, 1996

Chips and I leave for Ohio at about 1 pm. Anxious for some warmer weather and some attractive off-road trail, I have planned a few days on the southernmost section of the NCT. Pat, a friend of a friend, has agreed to take me to Pike Lake State Park, keep my car, and pick me up when I finish hiking. I arrive at his home around 6 pm. It takes a while to meet everyone in his family and get organized, but before dark he leaves me under drizzly skies at Pike Lake. I confess to an ulterior motive for choosing to hike here. Bill Menke, National Park Service Manager for the North Country Trail, may be hiking this same trail section this week. Bill and I have been discussing our vision for the Trail via e-mail this spring. He has planned a long hike through Ohio, and has shared his itinerary with me. If he is on schedule, we may run into each other. Much to my delight Bill is there at the park, and we agree to hike together for a day or two.

It is raining quite hard in the morning and my preference for dispersed camping is reinforced. The park tent sites are all bare packed mud, so our tents are a spattered mess, but must be packed up anyway. We get an early start, and the rain eases, but the trail immediately climbs straight up to the top of a ridge, goes down the other side, and up the next one. Bill starts to explain basic principles of trail construction. There are a lot of specific things that should and could have been done differently to take this trail over the same area. Hiker that I think I am, I have never before really looked at THE TRAIL; I have just followed it! I begin to learn what constitutes good trail layout. I see firsthand how benched construction, just below the ridge top, could have made the muddy treadway drier. Bill teaches me to pay attention to how often the track goes up and down the same slope instead of sensibly following a contour. A ten-percent grade standard for trail slopes not only saves hikers' knees and muscles, but helps protect the trail itself from washouts. Instead, this trail is steep, painful to walk, and a rutted, yellow-clay morass. A new world of information and observations is opened to me this day.

The sky continues to spit little showers on us until mid-morning when a cold, hard rain begins and soaks me to the skin. I did not come prepared for cold in southern Ohio in late April. This is embarrassing since I would like Bill to consider me an experienced hiker. Despite assurances from Bill to the contrary, I feel pretty stupid! We stop for lunch in an old barn which has wonderful piles of straw to curl up in. We each pick a pile and sit and eat and shake from the cold until we are miserable enough to start walking in order to warm up again. The afternoon miles are mostly off-road, but the trail sections again are poorly laid out – too steep and lots of horse damage. With the rain, this makes them just uneven tracks of clay muck which become creeks instead of trails. Because of our earlier e-mail correspondence, Bill is aware of the singing my "hiking crew" and I enjoy, and asks me if I have a song for Ohio. At first I apologetically say no, then I realize that we are in southern Ohio, near the river of the same name. And it is raining. "Yes, I do!" I almost shout.

> O, the boatman dance and the boatman sing,
> Boatman do most anything.
> When the boatman come on shore
> He spends all his money and he works for more.
> Hi, ho, the boatman row, up and down the river on the O-hi-o.
>
> Did you ever see where the boatman live,
> In a house in a hollow with a roof like a sieve?
> Boatman say that he have one wish,
> If you get much wetter that you'd rather be a fish.
> Hi, ho, the boatman row, up and down the river on the O-hi-o.[1]

Cheered somewhat at boisterously sharing the sloppy plight of the boatman, we take our afternoon break on the porch of an old store which is more ugly than quaint. Mercifully it is not raining so hard, but the temperature is falling. Bill's weather radio informs us that it is supposed to get down to 32° overnight, and we hike on through the chilly afternoon. The yellow clay sucks at our boots and makes walking very difficult indeed. It is clear that Bill's pace is faster than mine. This is not surprising since he is both taller and has been out on the trail, becoming conditioned, for ten days already. But it does nothing to change my feelings of inadequacy.

We poke our way into a woodlot at about 6:30 pm, after walking 17 miles, finding a nice upland site with a stream not far away. A Barred Owl welcomes us, asking his priority question, "Who cooks for you?" Tonight, I do. We pitch the still-wet tents, then Bill goes to filter water and I get a fire going. There is a lot of Sassafras around, and that seems to remain crisp and burnable even when damp. We eat spaghetti, discuss the merits of stoves vs. open fires, and dry our wet clothes over the flames before heading for our tents.

Much to my surprise, I am not cold during the night. It does get down to 32° outside, but only down to 43° in my tent. Bill is already up and has the fire going before I awake next morning. He makes oatmeal for us, and filters some more water. I don't know just what I am doing

---

[1.] Public domain

except not being very efficient. I make several packing goofs which make me rather late to be ready to leave. I suppose that the mistakes are just a matter of getting back into the swing of backpacking, but the reinforcement of my feelings of stupidity continues. First I pack my sleeping bag with clothes I need still stuffed in the bottom of it . Next I fold my tent with my watch still tucked in the inside pocket. Then, twice, I close up the dog's pack before it is ready. Since one side is currently fastened with a safety pin instead of the clip, this takes precious seconds to unfasten. The mud-covered metal zippers are a problem too. Anyway, we do not get on the trail until 9:10 am, a full hour later than the previous day, and mostly my fault.

The climbing sun begins to warm our bones, and the sky is a patchwork of blue and puffy white offering no liquid contributions today. I realize that it is my birthday. What a glorious day to celebrate! There is a little local grocery store where the trail crosses US 23 and we take our morning break there, and buy ice cream. Chips, aka the "dairy dog", is very happy about that, of course. While we rest, we discuss our satisfaction at finding a small store that is not part of some franchised chain. We agree that we are sick and tired of every place in the country looking just like all the rest.

Redbud trees along the trail

After some fence climbing, trail hunting and a few more miles, we stop for lunch at a brook with a mini-cascade. While soaking our feet in the cold water we eat crackers and bean dip, soaking the rest of our beings with dappled sunlight. I am thinking that this is just about the perfect birthday, but can't quite bring myself to tell Bill about my holiday. I was glad later that I didn't. My right knee has begun to hurt going down hills. This is of some concern to me; it is the ligament on the outside. I don't want to do any kind of serious damage that might prevent me from enjoying the "real" hikes later in the summer. This is supposed to be just a fun trip – not a marathon. Again it takes me longer to ready myself for the trail after lunch than it does Bill. I do not manage to anticipate that he is ready to leave. I take a couple of pictures, change films, and pack up the dog stuff again, but Bill is already buckling his hip belt, and picking up his walking sticks. Am I doomed to being everlastingly slow, or is this just the normal result of hiking with two people instead of solo?

Bill is going much faster than I after lunch. We climb a long, steep uphill, followed by a long, steep downhill. (Is this beginning to sound familiar?) My knee is hurting a lot. I can tell that Bill is becoming increasingly frustrated with waiting for me. He asks me how I would feel about him moving on, and I assure him that this is fine. We hold this discussion multiple times, at the top and bottom of the next few inclines. He is feeling guilty at leaving me behind, despite the fact that he should feel no obligation to me at all. Finally he conquers these feelings, we wish each other "happy trails," and he hikes on ahead. The biggest problem now is that Chips has readily accepted Bill as part of our "pack" and I have to keep him fastened to me so he won't go chasing off to try to check on the missing human.

We rest for a while to give Bill a good lead, and then I hike for another hour before stopping by a quiet-flowing brook for the night. The evening is calm. It is one of those warm, dry, quiet days of early spring when the world seems to perch on your shoulder in anticipation of what may happen next. I putter and relax by my fire, deciding that Marie's oft-stated philosophy of hiking trips is pretty good. If all you care about is making a lot of miles, without taking time to relax and enjoy the beauty, and have spaces to rest, then you've missed the point. Although I was a little bit down at first after Bill left (I just felt like a not-very-good hiker), yet I am glad to not push so hard. Slower is fine. The enforced stillness and acceptance of my slower pace reminds me of the ongoing internal turmoil concerning school, and I finally am able to unlock some of my fears and anger, letting them trickle down through chemical pathways, nerves and graphite to spill out onto paper. The comfort of the trail does not always erase thoughts of other difficulties, but gradually the peace washes over the angry words and thoughts. Perhaps the sharp gravel of hurt and wounded pride is beginning to erode, to become yet more shingle on the long beach of experience.

The next morning is cloudy, but warm and dry. I take my time getting ready – savoring a cup of coffee, cleaning the tent, and making sure the site looks like no one has camped there. My knee is still really hurting on the downhills. The trail continues to go steeply up and down ridges, but at least it is drier now since there have been two days since it has rained, and not as much horse traffic is evident on these sections. Spring is about four weeks late by local reckoning, so the trees are not yet leafed out, but the wildflowers are rampant. The Redbud trees are just blooming, and provide florescent pink-purple sparkle whenever the sun shines. Over the course of the three days I have seen one late Bloodroot, and multitudes of the following: Spring Beauty, Rue Anemone, Bluebells, Quaker Ladies (Bluets), yellow and purple Violets, Trout Lily, yellow Large-flowered Bellwort, Coltsfoot, Lesser Celandine, Jack-in-the-Pulpit, Cut-leaf Toothwort and Trillium. There have been gorgeous little rills with water falling over sandstone shelves. Unfortunately many of these little hollows are also filled with a century of trash, where people have used them for dumps. How sad.

Chips and I eat lunch at the top of a ridge overlooking the Scioto River Valley. After this there are to be only a couple of miles left for the day, and those will be on roads. This is sort of the emotional end of this hike for me, knowing that I will be out of the woods in just a few yards. I take off my boots to let my feet feel this fresh spring air too. Chips lays his head in my lap, and shares with me the peace of a creature who accepts the pleasures of the present.

Chips and I take a rest break

Just about two miles on a county road brings me to US 35. There is a home-owned store there which offers slightly naughty lawn ornaments for sale. I can't say that I would want a wooden "pee-boy" in my yard. I raised three real live ones, thank you! But, since it is a business, I go in and ask the proprietress if I may have some water. In confusing contrast to the "pee-boys" she seems to be very proper. She replies hesitantly that I can if I have my own container. Then I ask about using the phone. Well.... she says that the only phone is in their bedroom and her husband doesn't want anyone in there. Then she asks with a tone of incredulity, "Are you hiking all alone?! I have seven daughters" (sweeping her hand back to show me their pictures displayed in a row on the wall behind her) "and I would never let them do that!" I go out to get my map and re-enter the store to ask about where the closest phone might be. "Gracious, that pack is almost as big as you are," she comments. She says there is a truck stop about two miles west on the highway. That probably translates to five miles – people who drive don't pay much attention to short distances. Then she points out that there is a town just two miles east. This is also the direction the trail jogs along the highway for part of a mile, so I decide to go that way. Just about then a man (I assume her husband) comes from somewhere and up to the door. Chips decides to growl and jump on him, making a poor ending to a marginal conversation.

The town is off the highway a bit – one of those little burgs that used to be on the road until a bypass was constructed and labeled as an improvement. Small-town business owners seldom see it in that light. Coming into town I find a cracker-box restaurant with a pop machine and a pay phone outside. Chips and I flop down to rest, and I buy a cold drink. After a bit I decide to go inside and see if they have ice cream. I'm not sure how a room can look tired, but this one does. It has been worked hard, and needs a nap. Four tiny booths line one wall and a counter with stools follows the other side. One young, rather dirty couple sit eating sleepily at one of the booths. Chips, fastened outside, begins his whining and howling routine to convince them that he is dying. I assure them all that he is not being killed, it only sounds that way, but no one even smiles at this joke which usually yields at least one grin. A grim-faced, sixty-ish lady with a neat figure, polyester slacks and blue hair stares suspiciously at me from the back room. I ask if they have ice cream while trying to scan the menu board posted behind the counter, but I can't find any desserts listed. The taut-lipped lady asks me tightly what I want. She does not look sleepy; ever-vigilant is more like it! I say again that I was wondering if they have any ice cream... bars or sandwiches maybe.

Her response bangs down on the end of my sentence with the finality of a judicial gavel, "All we have is vanilla."

"Well, vanilla is fine." Meanwhile she walks to a freezer by the door, an old one with four metal lift panels on top. "Oh, there is the freezer," I say, and try to lift one of its doors, thinking to look for an ice cream sandwich.

She puts her hand querulously on the door I am reaching for and again asks tersely, "What did you want?" I try to ask once more about bars or sandwiches, but she interrupts and pronounces the sentence, "I could put some in a cup."

I tell her that this would be fine. She opens the freezer and there I see four ice cream drums, all open, with vanilla, chocolate, strawberry, and some fourth flavor! I decide not to comment, since I really do like vanilla best anyway. I ask her to put one scoop in one cup, and two scoops in another, but that I only need one spoon. She looks at me without moving her head, rather like a reptile. A lizard-lady judge of strangers. We complete the transaction, and I pay her. I comment that even though I am rather grubby, and my money is still wet from the rainy day, that it is probably still good. She remains silent and stiff, but Chips and I sit on the curb and enjoy our treat whether it makes her happy or not. She probably needs some of our dappled trail sunlight to warm her blood.

Later I take my trash, and some extra litter from the edge of their sidewalk in and ask if there is a trash can since I had not seen one outside. Although it is my habit to clean up extraneous trash, I am also motivated by a perverse desire to see just how annoyed this lady will get before I move along. Silently she takes the messy pile from me. I decide to live dangerously and ask if there is a rest room. She replies (I swear her lips are so tight that they hardly move), "There's one at the public library, and there is a gas station down the street." Giggling inwardly, I respond with overt politeness that I am probably a bit grubby for the library, but that I will try the gas station. It's too bad I can't stay to watch this lady's blood freeze, but I really do need that rest room.

I call Jane, Pat's wife, and she says they can pick me up in about two hours. So Chips and I load up again and walk the block to the venerable gas station/ general store. The two gas pumps are directly on the sidewalk. Car owners park in the street to fill their tanks. The atmosphere here is certainly different, as I discover when I go in to ask about the rest room. The building is old and dark, but clean, and filled with wooden cases of groceries, convenience items, and general merchandise. The dim room smells of old varnish, linoleum, soap, and that undefined but unmistakable essence of small grocery store. Two older men in overalls sit on the front windowsill, chatting. They want to know where I am hiking, and why... all the usual. The gal at the register is cheerful and smiling. She had seen me walking on her way to work and wondered how to find out more about me, and now... here I am!

The rest room turns out to be a certainly illegal outhouse which is squeezed between a garage and a fence. There is just enough room to get in the door, and only the space around the hole is not filled with garden tools. But, hey, there is toilet paper!

Outside again, the breeze blows a turkey feather against my pack. I grab it and tuck it safely into my map. This hike began on the opening day of turkey season; how appropriate that a memento of that should come to me at its end!

The time waiting for Jane is spent observing life in this small town. Pat had told me that the local attitudes were very much those of poor Appalachia. I begin to see some of this as I watch the steady stream of customers coming to the market. School lets out and I hear about the girls' softball game that is scheduled for that day. A lot of the kids stop to talk to me or pet the dog. One young man tells me that he has just gotten his driving permit, having turned sixteen. A number of the teens seem to have nice cars to drive.

On the other hand, it appears that folks who stay in the area to raise families are of a different ilk. Most of the young couples who come to buy something are a sorry sight. Most come in beat-up cars, with two or three dirty children, complete with runny noses. It is hard to explain the impression of poverty and apathy that I receive. When my kids were small they also were often dirty... I don't want to pass judgment on that score. But many of the parents are not much cleaner. Hair is uncombed. These folks do not look as if they have just worked hard today but are on their way home to shower; they look as if they have not been clean for weeks. One mom in her twenties has no front teeth, but a cigarette is clamped in her gums. The kids usually point and wave at the dog, and then at me. Only a few of the parents seem to pay the least bit of attention to what their kids are interested in.

At the house across the street one lone red tulip blooms on the left of the sidewalk, and one lone yellow one guards the right side, directly opposite. The notion grows in my mind that these two tulips are symbolic of the few bright spots of caring and beauty that might still be found in a tired, poor town which has been bypassed by the highway and most of the advantages of the late 20th century.

---- ※ ----

At 6 pm Jane and crew arrive and the mood changes abruptly. John (age 12) eagerly takes the dog. John is a spring wound tight, and ready to run! We load my gear in the van and drive to their home with Brendan (age 3) talking constantly. He is quite a verbal little guy, and explains that he is going to be an ark-ee-ol-o-gist, because he is a good digger, and he wants to dig up dinosaurs. He begins to name the kinds he will dig. We pick up Amanda (age 13) from a school dinner and she has lots to tell about the food, and pictures which will be taken the next day. I try to listen to all of the voices at once, inwardly feeling thankful that my years with full-time children are over. Keenan (age 1) at least doesn't have too much to say. He has a smile that nearly cracks his face though. It is so broad that it almost goes from ear to ear. He doesn't have much hair yet, and when he smiles he becomes a live Humpty-Dumpty. They want me to stay overnight, and I agree that a shower would feel really great. So that evening is spent getting better acquainted with Pat and Jane. Pat built their house, expanding a smaller house that was there when they bought the land. He has done a beautiful job, milling the boards himself, and is justifiably eager to show me around. Wide board floors, wood paneling, and siding are evidence of the amount of work and care he has put into the construction. Jane suggests that if she can get her mom to watch the two little boys that we go to one of the local state parks to look at the rock formations in the morning.

So Friday we drop off the little ones and drive to Rock House State Park. Jane and I eat a picnic lunch sitting on a blanket in the parking lot. She wants to share her concerns with me about her kids, and the fears and hopes they have as parents. Strange, but Pat had just shared a lot of the same feelings with me the night before. I just walked into these people's lives three days ago and yet they want to open up to me. So we talk about kids and about "hanging in there." We all are so lonely for someone who will listen, aren't we? This trip has been a strange meld of trail and family life for me.

Leaving the blacktop, and entering the park, the Redbuds glow brightly in contrast to the dark green of Eastern Hemlock. Clear yellow-green Larch add their cheer to the sunny patches. The rock faces are of red and yellow sandstone, weathered by wind and water into sensuous and fantastic shapes. Little trickly waterfalls splash and putter their way down the walls to drip into cool, dark pools at the base of the rocks, in the shadows of the hemlocks. The walkways are wild

Jane at one entrance to Rock House

and inviting. No frenzied concerns with maintenance and safety here. So much the better in my mind; the worn rock steps with last year's leaves puddled in the corners whisper to me to come explore. The Rock House itself is a grotto, emoting many centuries of human experience.

Geologically it is a sandstone cave: a vertical opening about 30 feet high through the edge of one of the bluffs. Several contorted doors or windows, formed by wind and water, access the front of the cave from the face of the cliff. Indians supposedly lived here in the 1700's, but there is little physical evidence remaining of their presence. Square basins with drain channels, carved into the rock may have been from this era. The cool, damp whispers of the breeze carry suggestions to the mind of moccasined feet, or corn rattling in baskets. I imagine glimpses of small copper hands holding tight to rocky ledges, securely holding their child owners in favorite sandstone hiding places. Dark eyes flashing and sounds of stifled giggles are only a small step further into the imagination.

Of course, when the spot became popular for visiting by "palefaces" they left plenty of evidence of their presence. Thousands of names and dates are carved into the soft rock. Jane enjoys looking at these immensely. There is some appeal for me to seeing dates such as 1858, or 1872. Names like Sadie and Mollie conjure up thoughts of picnics in Gibson Girl decor with admiring and proper suitors. By and large, however, I just feel disgusted at the fact that we can't seem to leave any bare surface alone, and free of words. In this technological era we can't seem to leave any blank space unoccupied. Walls and rocks are covered with graffiti. Roads are littered with advertising. The skies too are tracked with jet streams, or satellites and lights at night. Look down, see a heron track beside a french fry box; look up, see a 747 trail distorting the cloud patterns. The very air is filled with music or news... walkmen, boom boxes, or radios blast away at the "dead space" in our thoughts. I long for more and more of the "dead space." What a negative phrase to describe an opportunity for mental exercise. If my mind is constantly filled and distracted with other peoples names, thoughts or opinions, how can I discover what is really on my mind?

Individuality, to refuse to be pressed into what some franchise with a lighted plastic sign thinks I should want, seems of paramount importance to me at the end of this trip. Talking with Bill about protecting diversity, seeing Pat's careful and loving handiwork on his house, hearing Jane's concerns for helping her teens to survive peer pressures, and feeling the presence of visitors at the Rock House over three centuries has left me with a heightened devotion to treasure my right to non-conformity.

It becomes important to me to find a place to eat on the way home that is not imprisoned in a chain. I must exit from the expressway at several different towns, and really search, to find such an establishment. I finally succeed in locating a family restaurant with a wagon-wheel theme, and comfortable booths upholstered in warm brown tones. The food is wonderful; I do not know the menu and decor before walking in the door. For the moment, independence is safeguarded.

33 miles this hike
Pike Lake State Park to US 35
Pike and Ross Counties, OH
429 total miles NCT

Buckeye Buck
14 - June 10-14, 1996

Sister-in-law Loretta has been eager to join me on a short backpacking jaunt. Her teaching school year in Tennessee is finished, and I have taken the summer off to ponder my future plans: re-take the qualifier exam or move on in some other direction. So far all I can decide is that the future will include continuing to hike this trail.

Loretta drives eight hours north, and I eight hours south. We arrive at the agreed-upon campground, near Spring Valley, Ohio, within 15 minutes of each other! The evening is spent spotting one car and checking gear. I am beginning to learn that novice backpackers simply don't yet comprehend with their backs and feet my request, "think lightweight." Loretta has all the right equipment, exactly what I put on her list. So how can it weigh so much? I have not yet learned how to make people understand ahead of time that a three-pound poncho is not significantly more useful on a four-day trip than a five-ounce thin one. To someone who has not previously carted their world on their back that cozy, bulky sweat suit still seems more appealing than a couple of thin layers. I cringe. It is too hard for me to be ruthless and demand the removal of some of these items. After all, the fault is mine for not explaining better, and now these are the items she has brought. Neither am I willing to make a beginner carry too many extra pounds. Thus we begin next morning with Loretta carrying 42 pounds. Chips carries his normal eight-pound panniers, and I have 51 solid pounds to haul.

But hey, I'm in good shape, there is really no problem for a short hike. The problem is more likely to be the miles planned. In order to find legal campsites we will need to hike about 14 miles a day. My goal is to create a positive backpacking experience for Loretta, and she says she's game for the challenge, but I'm secretly a little worried. Masking my concern, we confidently swing down the road in the morning to meet the Buckeye/ North Country Trail at the north end of Caesar's Creek Reservoir. The maps indicate this route as an alternate. What they do not make clear is that this is the horseback rider's main route. Hooves have sculpted the trail into a continuous array of clamshell gouges.

Loretta encounters muddy trail

The clay mud in this section of Ohio is unique. A sign at one interpretive kiosk claims it to be the stickiest clay in the world. I don't have an independent source to verify this information, but its truth seems likely to me! In some sections the clay even slimes over the tops of our boots. So, you ask, why not hike along the edge of the trail?

Well, how about because of the lush, armpit-high Poison Ivy? Nevertheless our spirits run high and we steadily progress along the lake. The goal set for the day is Hopewell Lodge. Only groups can reserve it, but we have been assured that there are tent sites available on the grounds. By 5 pm Loretta is getting anxious for that Lodge. It has been a sunny, warm early summer day until now. But gray skies are sneaking up on us and thunder growls a warning. Thinking that the Lodge is just a few minutes ahead I urge us on. Suddenly the storm lunges at us and within two minutes we are drenched, with the ponchos – of whatever weight – safely stowed in our packs. Chips chooses this moment to tear through the brush and rip his pack straps completely from their moorings. He damages it so completely that there is no way to tie or pin it temporarily. I add his 8 pounds to my 51 (not to mention the weight of the water in my clothes). I am getting anxious for the Lodge myself now. In about 45 more minutes we arrive at a trim and empty building on the edge of a ravine: our goal. Let me assure you that we have no qualms about setting up the tent on the covered back porch of that Lodge rather than in the slimy mud. I'll even confess to checking to see if the doors are really locked.

The rain stops in a few more minutes, and we actually manage to dry out a bit as we dine on hot rice curry before crawling into our sleeping bags. I mend the pup's pack and return him to the category of backpacker for the morrow.

In the morning, Loretta is definitely sore. Not a complaint do I hear, but we are moving slower and slower. My concerns are rising higher and higher. By noon we have slowed to one mile an hour, and I know that we must go to plan B. I'm also feeling great chagrin at failing to plan a hike at which she can succeed. We decide that it is reasonable to try for the small burg of Oregonia, and to try to find a ride back to the campground from there. As the alternate trail we are on joins paved rail-trail just north of our new goal, the hiking becomes easier at any rate. People are generally so kind! There are only a few houses in Oregonia, but at one of them we find a young woman willing to drive us, our packs, and the dog back to Spring Valley.

We spent the rest of the week with an altered itinerary. Our week changed from a hike to a history and culture tour. The Blue Jacket Festival moved me to tears as a segment of Shawnee history was played out under evening skies. We explored antique shops in Lebanon, rode the Indiana and Ohio Scenic Railway, saw *A Chorus Line* in dinner theatre, visited the Hopewell Indian Fort Ancient site, and drove over the I-71 bridge. We had walked under this amazing structure which minces from bluff to bluff in neat white triangular trusses, 239 feet above the Little Miami River. I was impressed. Loretta also played spotter and allowed me to hike six more muddy miles one afternoon.

But the trip was defined forever by an event having nothing to do with hiking or exploring the area. The afternoon that we bailed out of the serious hiking we returned to the private campground. Loretta headed for the showerhouse, and I began preparing dinner. Chips was clipped to the picnic table on his tie-out, and I was sitting on the table tinkering with the Zip Stove. We were the only campers in the tent area, far from the campground office.

Walking under the I-71 bridge

I sensed a presence and looked up to discover a huge Rotweiller standing between the road and the table, staring at me. Chips approached him... there was little I could do at this point except see how the meeting would go. Not well. They touched noses, made a few tentative sniffs, and then the big dog had Chips in his teeth by the neck, shaking him. I smacked the Rotweiller across the nose. At this point began one of the strangest encounters I have ever had with a dog. The hundred-pound animal let go of Chips. He still had hardly moved his hindquarters. He continued to stand still, but raised his eyes to mine and gave me a look that clearly communicated, "All right, if you don't want me to bite him, I'll bite you." Turning his head to the side he took my calf in his mouth and chomped. This was not acceptable to my brave and loyal, but much smaller dog.

Chips took on the attacker. Now the calm of the Rotweiller was disturbed. The two dogs bounded the length of the table. Chips' cable wrapped my legs and I was now flat on the ground. Disentangling myself to rise on one elbow I saw Chips, with one rear leg in the black dog's mouth, being pulled backwards at an awkward angle. I ran to re-join the fray. I'm no screamer, but by now I was yelling for help. Everyone was too far away to hear me. I smacked the big dog in the face again and was bitten on the hand for my efforts. But he did let go of Chips. Somehow all in a few seconds, I realized I was on my own for solutions, managed to unclip Chips from his tie-out and throw him into Loretta's car. The dogs growled and snapped obscenities at each other through the glass. But that was fine; it gave me time to find a big piece of wood with which to chase the assailant away.

I was wearing nylon wind pants over shorts. I could feel the wet, sticky pull of the fabric where the blood was gluing it to my leg. Too mad to care, I stomped to the showerhouse, and informed Loretta, "I think we have a problem." Together we went to the office to show Nancy and Paul, the horrified owners. Seems that Buck the Rotweiller was not unknown to them. The neighboring trailer park had been unable to make Buck's owner restrain him properly, and he had been terrorizing the campers by virtue of his size. But it was my honor to be the first to be bitten.

Examining the wound revealed that medically it was not serious. The nylon pants had made Buck's teeth slip. There were only two punctures, neither of them dangerously deep. Multiple scratches traced the impression of the rest of his dentation, and my hand was turning ugly purple, but was not bleeding. Chips was shaken (literally), but fine. His dense fur had protected him from perforation.

Obviously a report would have to be filed, and here is where the comic relief kicks in. Buck's mistress began to claim that it could not have been Buck who bit me. First she asserted that Buck was not loose, and no one was home who could have let him out. The neighborhood teens quashed that motion by offering the information that her son had indeed been home. Then she began to claim that it was another Rotweiller who lived in the park, named Jet. You may have noticed by now that I'm a dog lover. I didn't want to get the wrong dog in trouble. I had written out a lengthy report and description for the county Animal Control Office. But I said that I would look at this other dog to see if I could tell the difference. I had some doubts; don't all Rotweillers look pretty much alike? The extent of this lady's efforts to get her dog off the hook (and hooked up was all the sentence was to be... he only would have to be restrained, not destroyed) began to become laughable. I went to visit the other dog and its nervous owner.

I'm guessing that the lady had not counted on my ability to observe details. Jet was female, not male. She was much older than Buck, with a gray muzzle. Her head was much more triangular. She was fat. And her tail was about two inches shorter than Buck's. She wagged what was left of it and snuffled a gentle geriatric hello.

Do you think that this would deter the determined owner of Buck? Wrong again. In my report I had written that the attacking dog wore a red nylon collar. She now claimed Buck had never owned such a collar, and of course he was now wearing a brown leather one. I know, because unbelievably, he came back to the campsite, loose again, the next day! This time I knew what to do. I immediately threw Chips in the car. Oops! One window was open and out he sailed, heading straight for Buck's yard. So after him I ran with leash in hand, now being in the guilty position of having my dog unrestrained in her yard.

The tale is nearly told. Not surprisingly, after the observation period I received a letter saying that Buck showed no signs of rabies. We learned that he and his family moved away later that summer. I have two small scars on my left calf. They provide a nice balance for the two on my right calf which were a gift in my childhood from a dog named Pal who used to bite the tires on the school bus as well as the neighbors.

The sad part of the story is that Chips has become a much more aggressive dog. We had also been attacked while walking near home earlier in the spring by a dog that broke its chain. The cumulative effect is that Chips is no longer a carefree pup of ready friendships with others of his species. I am not able to predict his criteria for friend or foe, so we now must avoid contacts with other dogs as much as possible. We will remember Buck.

31 miles this hike
Spring Valley to Oregonia, OH
460 miles total NCT

Forever Wild
15 - July 12-23, 1996

      The Adirondack Forest Preserve cannot "be leased, sold or exchanged... nor shall the timber thereon be sold, removed or destroyed... The forest preserve... shall be forever kept as wild forest lands." This amazing provision of Article XIV of the New York State Constitution was ratified in 1894, and has become known as the "Forever Wild Provision." Its regulations apply to the nearly three million acres owned by the state in the middle of a larger area designated as the Adirondack Park. The astonishing foresight of those who drafted this proposal over 100 years ago can be appreciated by understanding that until 1980 when Denali National Park in Alaska was expanded, it was the largest park in the United States, containing six million acres. It is greater than the 5.5 million acres obtained when you total the areas of Olympic, Glacier, Grand Canyon, Yosemite, and Yellowstone National Parks. Areal measurements are often compared to the state of Rhode Island, and indeed the Adirondack Park is larger than our smallest state. But it is also larger than Hawaii, Connecticut, New Jersey or New Hampshire. The Park finally meets its match in the size of Vermont, its neighboring state to the east.

      The Adirondack Mountains rise in a rough circle between Lakes Champlain and Ontario, south of the St. Lawrence River and north of the Mohawk in northern New York. Geologically separate from other

The Adirondack Mountains, viewed from the north

eastern mountains, a pool of molten rock bubbled them into existence a billion years ago. The peaks are some of the oldest mountains in the world, and yet they still rise high enough (over 2000 feet above sea level defines a mountain) to be called mountains. Consider their heights in their youth! Granite, garnet, iron, taconite and talc were carved from their slopes one-hundred thirty years ago by my ancestors without much changing the mountains' visible shapes. However, relentless time has surgically imposed a transvestite destiny on their primordial, lean and rawboned slopes, now muted into sensual mounds of high appeal.

The High Peaks call us to the eastern end of the North Country Trail. Although the terminus of the trail is anchored at the Crown Point Bridge, the route of the trail through the Adirondacks is still in dispute. By hiking now, before decisions are made, we can choose our own combination of trails to cross the park. The higher and wilder the better, I say. This will be the major hike of the summer, with as many of our core group as possible. Marie and Mathilda are counting on it, and in February I begin studying topographic maps with glee. David resigns himself to a summer of work, sad at having to pass up rock-strewn capers, his favorites. Chips presumably can not grasp the details of planning, but his dancing enthusiasm for the project is apparent whenever I so much as move any item of hiking equipment.

The maps fascinate me. I make copies of all the sections we will hike and color the elevations within the contour lines. Everything above 4000 feet I shade with purple and am delighted whenever our projected path crosses a purple blob. The abruptness of the High Peaks is shown graphically by the colors. From Lake Champlain at a mere 100 feet above sea level, in only 35 crow-flight miles from white through yellow, orange and green, Mount Marcy rises from the center of a purple amoeba on my map to a blue spot: over 5000 feet. 5344 feet, to be exact. The highest point in New York. We will climb its slopes in just a few weeks.

The guidebook excites me. I contemplate such promises as "the climbing increases to the top of the Wolf's 'Chin'... The trail then descends steeply to a col and soon begins an exceedingly steep climb to the summit of Lower Wolf Jaw." I learn a new word: "col," an elevated pass between two mountain summits. The anticipation increases. "Stupendous gorge," "impossible tangle of boulders," "the grade... winds among large boulders and ledges," "ladder necessary;" all such phrases pump adrenalin through my system. My tiny Ann Arbor room for the first time seems too small. On graph paper I sketch a vertical elevation map of our route. The line wiggles satisfactorily up and down across the long strip of taped-together pages.

The place names alone send me scurrying for more information to match the mental images. "Noonmark Mountain," so named because from the village of Keene Valley the sun hovers directly above its acute pointed summit at noon. "Wolf Jaws," the twin peaks seen at a distance from a certain vantage point appear as the lifted muzzle of a howling wolf. "Tahawas," Cloud-splitter, the native name for Mount Marcy. "Hogback," a name which appears in many locales besides the Adirondacks. In fact, Ann Arbor has a road of that name. I learn that the word applies to a narrow, steep-sided ridge of rock resistant to glacial forces. This serves as a reminder that the glaciers have passed over these mountains several times, leaving only stumps of their former selves, and yet they still stand in blue majesty. "Opalescent River," an iridescent blue feldspar called labradorite in its bed creates the play of colors in its waters. "Lake Tear of the Clouds," source of the Hudson River.

Over-stimulated as a hyperactive child, I welcome these provocations. Their contrast with the disappointments of graduate school are as alluring as any siren song. I am more than ready to do battle with mountains I know I can conquer.

At the end of May I move home to west Michigan, giving up my tiny Ann Arbor room. I have enjoyed the independence of living there, but it feels good to be back in a larger space at home. The housemate who felt the pre-hike preparations to be encroaching on his freedoms the previous year will not miss the chaos. Husband Omer has at least come to tolerate my ability to fill every available space with piles of items in various stages of coming and going from a multitude of projects. I know I am supposed to be thinking about school and plans for the fall, but how can I, with trail to be hiked and gardens to be cultivated? The warm earth is a salve for my wounds, and I have missed having time to absorb the joy of watching the grass grow. Seedlings speak their mind slowly; time and patience are requisite to be able to hear even one phrase of what they have to say. It has been much too long since I have listened to their whisperings and I am hungry to catch up on the news.

Between conversations with the plants and soil, food for the hike is dried and packaged. Like kids in a toy store, we each make purchases to upgrade our equipment. I order a lightweight but larger tent so that we can all stay together and visit at bedtime. Mathilda decides that backpacking will remain on her list of regular activities and buys her own pack. She had rented one for the North Dakota hike, and had at least learned what features she did not like! Marie decides to get a better sleeping bag. Chips gets another new and strengthened pack. His ability to destroy one each year is consistent.

Before we can quite believe it, it is time once again to pile in the autos and head for the High Peaks. The plan is to meet at the home of an old friend of mine. Paul actually introduced me to the Adirondacks when we were 20-year-old college kids. I have not been back since, but Paul lives there, surrounded by the peaks, pastoring a church in the hamlet of Indian Lake. He and his wife, Shirley, have generously agreed to help us with cache boxes and car spotting. In the golden light of sunset, Mathilda and I arrive at the foot of Blue Mountain. It rises, cool and lonely at one western gateway to the High Peaks. The anticipation has not been overstated; I am compelled to stop, to attempt to capture the moment on film. Experience tells me that the pictures will be disappointing, but I can't keep from trying. From here we plunge into the peaks, so close they are no longer discernable as separate entities from our low vantage point of the road. We drive through the valleys, over passes and around the curves, delighted at whatever is next revealed to us.

I take offense at those folks who scoff at the mountains of the East. To be sure, these old peaks are different from the raw and aggressive youngsters of the West. Different is not inferior. Eons have given them time to develop a sense of modesty, but they are no less appealing. Demurely covered in green lacy negligee they hide behind one another, perfumed with balsam; a harem willing to pleasure any who come to visit. Several coy peaks raise their heads above the green garment, sending come-hither looks to human suitors. "To reach me, you must first journey the paths of my sisters' slopes," they sing. "Each of us has surprises to offer you." I am beguiled without recourse. Lost in self-satisfaction, I drag Marie and Mathilda in the wake of my enthusiasm. I hope they too feel the allure of the cloud splitters.

Necessary tasks pull our heads out of the clouds for two more days. Since we are pooling our equipment and supplies here at the starting location we must sort and re-pack. We spend some time reviewing wilderness first aid, laughing, aghast at the treatment for a "sucking chest wound:" to place a plastic bag over the hole. Secretly we pray that we will never need to use this knowledge. We have decided to carry a length of climbing rope. A bad fall or other difficulty seems quite possible in the rocks and chasms we will traverse. Plus we indulge ourselves with a trip to the Adirondack Museum giving us some insight into the logging, mining, and tourism history of the area.

Early Friday morning we load ourselves in Paul's car and he drives us to the Crown Point Bridge. He is familiar with each slope we pass, naming the peaks by seeing only their bases. It is too much information for me to absorb at 40 mph. Sadly I resign myself to the realization that I will not recall much of what he is telling us, even if we pass this way again. I am a visitor but this is his home. At the humped, white Crown Point Bridge over Lake Champlain, the eastern terminus of the North Country Trail, we haul our gear onto the parking lot. This is an historic site, important to Colonial and Revolutionary times, that we'd like to visit, but that indulgence will have to wait: it's so early in the day that they are not yet open. Paul says with sudden haste, "I've got an appointment. Hope you have all your stuff!" He quickly prays with us, hops in his car and drives away. We too hope we have all our stuff!

Joan and Paul at Crown Point

Even Chips stares after the car as it shrinks in the distance and breaks our connection with easy solutions to difficulties we may encounter.

Well, we do have all our stuff. And we even have managed to leave extra sweatshirts and sneakers correctly in Paul's car. We are off to a promising start.

Put a clear level path beneath Mathilda's feet and it's all we can do to keep up with her. But we do stop for a moment at Bulwagga Bay to see the long list of names of the people who claim to have seen Nessie's cousin, the sea monster of Lake Champlain, who is sensibly named "Champ." We hope for a glimpse of Champ ourselves, but it is not to be.

Instead of Champ of Lake Champlain we are about to meet Rex of Crowfoot Pond. Late in the afternoon we reach the head of a road marked "Private." The locally purchased map of the area only shows it as an unimproved road connecting to a hiking trail on state land, which is our goal. "Now what?" we ask each other. A jeep approaches, and the lady driver rolls down her window. "You can't go down there; that's a private road."

"We just discovered that," Marie explains. "How could we get permission?"

"Oh, you'll need to talk to Rex," she answers summarily.

"Is he likely to allow us through?" Marie asks politely.

"You'll have to ask him! Last house on the right." She doesn't exactly roll her eyes but the tone of her voice is less than encouraging.

She practically burns gravel in her hurry to leave us to our dilemma, and we turn down the road. The lane wanders for a mile past summer homes, along one bank of the small private lake. People wave and smile at us as we pass, raising our confidence. We are expecting that "last house" at any time, where we might receive permission to continue our hike. Finally we near the end of the houses. Small scraps of information are forming into meaningful patterns, and we begin to suspect that we may soon need to duck or run, or both. Straight ahead is the boundary sign for the state land. Parked in the driveway of the last house on the right is the lady's jeep, and a man with no good intentions for our future is stalking across the lawn towards us.

Inwardly gulping, I begin cheerfully, "Hi, are you Rex? We spoke to someone who told us that you were the one who could give us permission to walk through here."

All the crow's feet nearby must be in Crowfoot Pond. Any lines on Rex's face do not seem to indicate that he has laughed recently, if ever. "You can't walk through here. You'll have to go back and walk around on the road."

We may be polite, but we are not fools. The "walk around" is 17 miles, and the boundary sign for the state land is 150 feet away. Mental telepathy sometimes works, because in the next two seconds Marie and I agree with a glance that we can probably run, even with full packs, and reach the safety of public land before Rex can get to his house and return with a shotgun. We hope Mathilda is tuned to the same frequency. Chips is clipped securely to me, ready to follow, or at least be dragged, in whatever direction I may jump. Nevertheless, we agree to try diplomacy first.

I pull out my maps and carefully show him where this is indicated to be a public road. I explain that we cannot possibly walk 17 miles before dark. I point out that we've already nearly walked the length of the private road, and to retrace our steps will cause us to bother people twice. Changing tactics, I mention that I am an NCTA board member and that we do not encourage people to cross private land without permission. That is why we are here, to ask permission. I may be able to help assure that other hikers will not come this way. I promise to write to the map company and ask them to change the map. I implore him to see how sensible it would be to let us walk those final 150 feet. Marie and Mathilda are edging slowly eastward; their potential sprint now reduced to 146 feet. Rex is unmoved by any plea, and our hopes for negotiating a mutually satisfactory solution are sinking with the evening sun.

Finally I ask him what he will do if we choose to simply walk to the end of his road. Not cheerfully, he admits that he can't stop us if we do just that. Figuring that we'll never do better, I make a final promise to write to the map publisher, and although we don't exactly sprint for the boundary, we don't wait for any rocks or lead shot to catch up with us. From the safety of the state land, and around a good bend that puts us out of view, we collapse for the night in exhaustion, relief, and laughter.

Two days later this scene is repeated with Santa Claus' evil doppelganger. Well, without the red suit. Careful study of the maps and guides ahead of time had revealed that although we knew we could not take the dog through the AuSable Club Mountain Reserve, the bridge we need to cross to climb away from AuSable is outside the Reserve. Santa disagrees, and he is the bridgekeeper. A right jolly old elf, his belly shakes when he laughs like a bowlful of jelly. His eyes how they sparkle, his dimples how merry, but we will not cross his bridge with a dog, walked or carried. It's only a 20-foot long footbridge, but there aren't to be any desperate sprints here. Santa's gift to us is a three-mile roadwalk detour to Hedgehog Mountain in the rain.

Throughout these first few days, we also have to deal with Bertha's tail end. That's Bertha the hurricane, if you don't happen to remember the big storms of 1996. Mid-afternoon of the day after Rex, we are still stomping at Mathilda's amazing pace up Route 73, drenched by a cold downpour. A snack of Wild Strawberries keeps the chill off our spirits, but we doubt that we need the cold spring water flowing from a pipe in the rocks. The rain lets up by the time we reach Round Pond, climbing a steep 800 feet to the campsite. We are ready for a good

Soggy, but ready to climb to Round Pond

night's rest, but Chips finds the frogs in the pond more alarming than our moaning and imprecations, and barks all night long. With nothing like enough sleep, we head out next morning to cross the pass between Round and Noonmark Mountains. We drop again to AuSable, where we collect our first supplies and are gifted by Santa with those three miles and then by Bertha with the rain. After a dry night on Hedgehog we begin, Monday morning, the climb I've been anticipating, which ends in that "exceedingly steep" ascent of Lower Wolf Jaw. For the first few miles we easily meander farther up Hedgehog with views of the AuSable Valley alternating with tunnels of forest beauty.

The wind and rain begin gently, dribbling just enough moisture to slick every rock, and just enough breeze to chill exposed skin. The trail takes a turn ahead, not left or right, but up, straight up for about 50 feet. I'm almost too busy climbing hand over hand on wet rocks and clay with a full pack to worry about everyone else. Almost. I turn Chips loose to find his own way up. The biggest risk while attached to him is for one of us to drag the other down as the result of a slip. I'm sure that Marie will gamely climb to the top, but I'm not counting on much joy from her about this one.

Mathilda won't be happy that I'm bringing up this topic, but there's no way to continue the saga of this hike without giving you more information. Mathilda is visually impaired. This has made no difference in any other situation we've been in together to this point in time. In fact, I lived with her for six months before I even realized that she could see very little. But now I wonder if she will be able to scale this wet wall when she can't see more than one hand and foothold at a time.

Despite my worries, we all arrive at the top in good spirits, wet and muddy but not harmed. Bertha's final farewell greets us at the top. As we work our way around a ledge the wind takes aim at us and fires horizontal needles of rain. My relief at successfully reaching the top moves me quickly around the ledge, in the lead. Behind me, Marie gasps as a gust of wind bends an eight-inch diameter tree, which is rooted in the near vertical cliff wall below us, in toward the trail and then out again, buckling the treadway. I turn to find her shaking. "Slow down and be more careful, please," she implores sensibly with a slight quaver in her voice. The drama has occurred completely behind me; she has to explain the cause of her emotional condition.

Actually, speeding up seems more logical to me, to get out of the wind zone, but we continue to tread, at least more observantly, along the narrow ledge. The wind and rain never abate, but the trail does eventually work its way off the ledge and back into more protected woods. Now our concern is in becoming seriously chilled, although we all seem to be fine as long as we keep moving. After a while I realize that I am feeling light-headed and a bit weak. A glance at my watch reveals the reason for my sensations. It is 3 o'clock in the afternoon; we've been so focused on the challenges that we haven't paused for any snack or lunch! Yet stopping in an exposed location is out of the question as the wind continues to knife through even our nylon rain suits. Finally, after another thirty minutes of searching for shelter I crawl down off the trail under some hemlocks where a pair of giant boulders drop off six feet and create a calm in their lee. "Come down here, there's no wind!" I call to my soggy companions. Crackers and peanut butter never tasted so good! We realize that for the first time in hours we can hear each other over the whining of that incessant wind.

While we eat, the weather does ease up a bit, and after resting until we begin to feel cold we continue eastward through gray drizzle – just enough to keep us wet to the skin. Coming down off the chin of our drooling wolf the day and our energy are waning. Although not as steep as the ascent, we must scramble or slide over bare rock surfaces at angles too sharp to risk walking upright. By 6 pm I am very cold and chafing at our slow progress – we've made three-tenths of a mile in the past hour. I have concerns about finding a tent site before the early dusk of a gray day in thick forest settles around us. I keep finding myself far ahead of Marie and Mathilda, but seem unable in my impatience to pace myself to go slower. I decide to do something I have not done before or since, split up our group. I tell my companions to watch for me, and that I will under no circumstances go farther than a trail junction which we know to be less than two miles ahead. I hope to find a tent site, get set up and get dinner started. I'm not sure how they feel about this plan since I'm not hearing any answers except, "Fine, we'll look for you or your pack."

A flat spot to put our tent would be the joke of the day, except for the rain and the wind and the mud. The trail drops 1400 feet in two miles, and I know that I'll be lucky to find even a semi-flat space large enough for the tent. My frustration mounts with each foray into the woods where it looks as if there might be a more level area in the sloping mountainside. I feel that I'm using way too much time taking off and putting on my pack, leaving it on the trail as a signal to Marie and Mathilda of my whereabouts. Several quick-paced side trips through the thick birch and hemlock saplings warm *my* bones, but my concern at being able to provide a warm dry refuge for my friends continues to mount. Then, just to the south of the trail, my architectural dream comes true! One flat rock sprouts horizontally from the hillside out of an area of gently sloping sphagnum moss. "It will be too wet," I surmise. But it seems slightly feasible, so I decide to take a look. Oddly enough, the moss is not massed on a soggy lump of peat, but seems to be cushioning the edge of the rock and the area just above it. Water runs down the slope, into the mossy area, and is emerging in a small stream between rock layers at the lower end of the great flat stone! I carefully pace out the area, and the tent will fit, just barely. I have found a Frank Lloyd Wright Waterfall Tent Site! By the time Marie and Mathilda arrive, the tent is perched on the rock and the moss. Plus, a small trench (which can easily be filled in the morning to leave no trace) has been scooped on the high side of the tent so that extra rivulets which come down the hill will flow into the sub-petranian stream, and I'm setting up the kitchen area on a flat rock just below the tent where the "waterfall" flows past in artistic rhythm with the rest of the site.

Marie and Mathilda appear, but they are not quite ready to appreciate my Walter Mitty-ish adventures in architecture land. They are downright unhappy. "I didn't know I could be any wetter than completely soaked, but I am!" Marie growls. "One of those huge slopey rocks that we had to slide down on our rumps had a stream of cold water running down it that flowed right into the back of our pants while we were sitting there."

"I just want to go to bed," sighs Mathilda.

"Oh, no, we are going to eat some hot dinner first," I explain. After some coaxing they agree, and besides, what else can they do when handed hot bowls? The warm soup revives all our spirits, not to mention that the rain has tapered off. But we've only hiked 3.7 miles in this whole miserable day.

Tuesday, mid-day, the skies are clear, but our mood has blackened. We are hunkered down on the porch of Johns Brook Loj facing the fact that we are, even now, four miles short of our planned goal for the previous day. At least Marie is trying to make us face that fact. Mathilda crouches with her knees hugged to her chin in the corner of the porch railings, crying. I straddle a post, ten feet away with my forehead slumped against the rail, crying.

"We can't possibly complete the miles you have planned, and meet Paul on the agreed day." Marie points out.

"But yesterday was different," I whine. "We can make up the time."

Mathilda sighs, sobbing quietly, knowing that she is the cause of all the unrest.

This triplet is repeated a dozen or more times, with varying phrases and nuances. The bottom line is that we have to change our route, and we have to do it now. This is the only place where we have a chance to contact Paul in time to change the planned pickup. From Johns Brook Loj they can radio in a request to call him, but we have to decide what we are going to do. There are only two feasible choices. We can eliminate going over Mount Marcy (the very mention of that idea brings a new wave of tears from me) and take a shorter route to our original end point. Or, we can instead choose to shorten the hike considerably, hike fewer miles in a day, and take in Marcy as a day hike.

I don't like either choice. Every selfish cell in my body is poisonously turgid and oozing. "It's MY hike," I hear myself saying. "I want to go over Mount Marcy and see Lake Tear of the Clouds, and if I can't then what was the point of coming?" Worse yet, I'm not even horrified at hearing these words come out of my mouth!

Marie, furious with me, stalks off to the sanctified privacy of the latrine, a quarter-mile away. In all of my self-righteous shepherding of the group yesterday I have failed to notice what Marie has learned by hiking behind me, with Mathilda. Although younger than we are, and fully fit, and as intrepid as Jack the Giant Killer, Mathilda simply can not hike this rough terrain at the rate I have planned for our group. She can not really see her feet, and walks almost entirely by feel. These trails are so rocky and uneven that each step is different. The toll is extracted from her speed and her knees. Mathilda and I huddle in our respective corners, weeping.

A little-known fact is that tears are sometimes a good antidote for poison, although their rate of effectiveness can vary. After a while the two surviving logic cells in my system randomly wash into each other and lock arms in desperation. Eventually they bump into one stunned molecule of maturity and an injured corpuscle of kindness, which they succor and bandage. With a hiccup I momentarily flirt with the idea that Marie's suggestion to do Marcy as a day hike might be workable. Those four cells needed only that brief flash of acknowledgment to begin their counter-offensive growth, suffusing me with resignation to the new plan.

You'll have to ask Mathilda if I eventually apologized for my behavior. I hope I did, even though no simple apology could make up for such an uncharitable display. With coughs and sniffs and much wiping of eyes with grubby hands we accept the reality that the hike will now be 40 miles shorter than planned, and that we have lots of time to fool around. The challenge of a new puzzle helps pull me further out of any remains of my selfish morass. We have to notify Paul. We have to reassess our food supplies. The whole plan will work if we can come up with one more day's worth of food, and the caretaker at the Loj has just the solution for us. An occasional hiker leaves some unwanted item there and she lets us choose from a scant collection of odds and ends.

We scoop it all into our possession! With a can of spinach, two packs of ramen noodles, a few slightly-crumbled, cellophane-wrapped saltine pairs, some instant oatmeal, and left-overs of our own we are now provisioned for some strange, but passable meals to tide us over till our supply pick-up.

With our new plan, we will hike only a mile along the trail toward Slant Rock, and camp for the night. This gives each of us a chance to rest from the rigors of the trip so far: emotional or physical.

The tent site we have chosen is resplendent with pink striped Wood Sorrel, rich umber Red-belted Polypore, and miniature hemlocks sprouting from every rotting log. Nestled in this delightful setting, and tired from our earlier wrangling, we perform the evening chores – Mathilda cleans up after dinner; Marie mends a split sleeping-bag seam. My job is to find a cache tree and hang the food bags. There aren't any really good trees for this job near the site. Everything seems to be either large old hemlocks or too-small maple saplings. But finally the bags are slung over a slanting maple branch, "kinda low," I admit to myself, "but probably o.k." Now the three of us are cozy in the tent, reading and ribbing each other over the day's events. An occasional gust of wind rustles the treetops, harmony to soothe away any remaining lamentations. The food cache is hanging in sight of the tent screen, its bright orange and blue bags easy to spot against the deepening shadows. The trees sway once again, then come to rest, but the cache bags are violently swinging in an extremely localized gust. Suddenly the blue bag zips earthward, while the orange-bag counterweight heads straight up! Hardly believing my eyes, I holler, "Something's got our cache!" Not a profound observation, but certainly an important one. I burst from the tent with empty cooking pots, banging them and yelling, "Hey, get out of here!" Where is a good guard dog when you need one? Oh, remember the camp at Round Pond where Chips spent the entire night barking at the FROGS? So now he's tired, and could care less about a BEAR! He's sprawled in peaceful comfort, oblivious to the current excitement. Marie finds his apathy most provoking. "Arf, Rrrarf!" she exclaims for him.

Our banging, yelling and barking may be approaching circus velocity but they are effective. A small bear glances at us, surprised but without malice, and shuffles past and out of sight! Well, it's another sewing project for the nimble-fingered Marie! Three slashes on each side of the blue bag show how close we are to having our plans changed yet again. Now we have another challenge: to make a much better job of hanging the cache than before, but now we get to do it in the dark, by flashlight. By snagging a tall young maple and bending it down we are able to spring load our bags and send them skyward. A guy rope lashed to another nearby sapling guarantees that we can pull the cache back down in the morning. Any small animal could gain access, but we know the bear can't climb these skinny trees. Pan lids tied to the rope will sound the alarm if the bags should be molested in the night.

Despite wondering if our bruin might want to return and sample our eggplant with marinara sauce we sleep well. After a leisurely half-day rest the next morning we mosey up to the Slant Rock campsite. Slant Rock is a natural lean-to shelter used by generations of Indians and early explorers. The rock itself stands about 20 feet tall above another bare flat rock creating a perfect place to rest. The heat from a fire built in front will reflect from the slanting rock to warm a camper. However, to preserve the historical integrity, hikers are no longer allowed to camp under the rock. Designated campsites have been established here, complete with fire rings, and high bars for hanging food caches. Signs indicate that you are supposed to camp only in these improved sites. The area is at an elevation of 3360 feet, and camping is not allowed above 4000 feet due to the sensitive nature of the ecosystem. Luckily, we capture the very last tent site.

Next we explore the trail in the direction of Marcy. Just a few paces beyond the end of the campsites the angle of the trail takes a distinct upturn, and we read this sign: "Warning. Weather subject to severe change. Do not proceed beyond this point without proper gear." For those of you who still scoff at eastern mountains, this is no idle threat. The weather in the Presidential Range of mountains in New Hampshire, and in the Adirondacks, is considered to be some of the most severe weather on the planet. Until the very week that I find myself at my computer writing this chapter, the highest wind speed ever recorded on Earth was on Mount Washington, NH, in 1934. Winds at the peak reached an astonishing 231 mph on April 12 of that year. (But yesterday, September 15, 2003, a plane flying into the eye of the treacherous Hurricane Isabel took a windspeed reading of 236 mph, setting a new record.) Actual temperatures in the region have been recorded to be as high as 107° F and as low as –50° F. The record high 107° F is hotter than the all-time high temperature taken in Miami, Florida, and the –50° F low is colder than the record low temperature in Anchorage, Alaska or International Falls, Minnesota (which is commonly considered to be the coldest location in the continental United States).

There are four major reasons for the often violent weather of the New England region (considered to include upper New York). First, the area is about half-way between the pole and the equator, where warm moist air moving north meets cold dry air moving south. But hey, you can travel all the way around the globe at this latitude and not meet severe weather everywhere. This is not enough in itself to generate really interesting weather. But next add a cold ocean current moving along the Atlantic coast, and a warm current flowing along the south shore of Connecticut and Rhode Island, in Long Island Sound. These different-temperature currents spawn sea breezes on a nice day, yet

New England is not truly a maritime climate due to condition number three, which is "westerlies." The entire area is downwind of the rest of the continent, and these continental air flows meet and mix with the breezes from the ocean currents, within that 45 degree latitude mixing zone. Last, and definitely not least, throw in the mountainous topography, and it's like tossing rocks in a blender. Don't try this at home! But you can imagine that any liquid swirling smoothly around in your Hamilton Beach would begin to act strangely if you were to drop in a mini-mountain or two. To quote a meteorological report: "The region's weather is notorious. It is known for its diversity over short distances and changeability in a matter of minutes."

After being reminded of the need to pack our wits along with our lunch, and assured of our direction for the following morning, we head back to Slant Rock itself to check out its awesome contours. We are hoping for a nice calm-weather morrow.

As we come down the path we meet a misplaced family on their way up. Mom is dressed for the seashore: shorts and t-shirt with sandals on her feet. She's only missed the beach by six-tenths of a mile vertically, but her horizontal calculation is off by something more like 200 miles. A pair of sneakers, laces tied together, is slung around the woman's neck. She has no pack, nor even a jacket. I think they are lost, but I am wrong.

"We're looking for a place to camp," the woman begins.

"Oh, um, we just took the last of these campsites. You're supposed to stay only in designated sites here," I reply cautiously.

"We want to go higher up and camp on a rock with a view."

It's pretty obvious that they will be able to enjoy their view all night, wherever they camp. We can see that they have no tent. In fact, they appear to have only one sleeping bag. Dad has a pack, sort of... a very small pack and a roll-mat tied on the frame. One unrestrained nylon sleeping bag slithers over an arm, more loose items are grasped in that hand, and he carries a gym bag in his other hand. Clambering restlessly over nearby rocks are their two teenaged boys wearing pack frames with only roll-mats tied on.

"Well, no one is supposed to camp above 4000 feet, and you are already very close to that here."

"Why can't you camp higher?"

"Because you are approaching the timber line, and the ecosystem is very fragile there."

"Oh, how would we know that?"

The closest access by car to this place is over six miles away. They now appear to have come here on purpose, but it's difficult to be a true believer. Then again, perhaps these people are super-hikers in disguise. Maybe they are some of the first people to go ultra-light. Are they feckless tourists, or perhaps their foam mats are military prototypes with secret tabs which, when pulled, self-inflate to become fully furnished shelters... with beds... with food... with brains?.

"Do you have a map?" I ask.

"No. Maybe you can tell us where we are."

Gawking behind carefully applied masks of 1990's "whatever-works-for-you" philosophy, we smile and show them where they are on the map. Still not quite able to accept that they are seriously planning to spend the night outside, I ask if they have enough food.

"We have some candy bars and granola," they cheerfully explain.

I'm beginning to be concerned for their safety, but can't quite muster the moxie to just plain tell them to go back to their car. "Well, you need to be sure to hang it out of reach of animals. A bear got our cache last night."

"Really?" Mom snaps to attention. "I didn't know bears were interested in cash."

"Oh yes," I continue gravely, "one pulled ours down last night. We managed to scare the bear off before it got away with anything." I ramble on, seriously worried that these people should not be let loose in the woods.

Mathilda and Marie, unable to swallow their reaction to the homophonic breakdown in communication, are definitely giggling.

For some reason, I have reverted to the completely dead-pan serious self I was as a child, and can't for the life of me figure out what is so funny about these people who don't have enough sense to know that bears like candy bars, or that they need a map, jackets, or sleeping bags.

My friends pull me away, as I continue to sputter warnings about camping. Marie and Mathilda wish them well.

The top of New York State is now only 1984 feet above us; spread out over 2.3 miles of trail, that's about an average 16% grade! Mount Marcy's highest point is 5344 feet. The Indians called it Tahawas, the "Cloud Splitter." As you climb higher, you are also moving through ecosystem changes which are the equivalent of traveling poleward. Thus, with Marcy rising just over a mile into the sky, you could roughly

Marcy: the final ascent above timber line

compare the habitat to one 600 miles or so farther north, but at sea level. The Adirondacks are at about the latitude of Toronto, Ontario. At sea level, 600 miles north is Hudson Bay, a habitat which most everyone would agree is inhospitable. And the High Peaks of the Adirondacks do indeed have harsh alpine climates. In fact there are 85 acres of genuine alpine ecosystem on the Adirondack summits.

We begin our climb to the alpine clime early and are thinking that we might be the first to stand on Marcy's dome today. Even though the trail clambers up and over boulders the size of small cars we make good time without the heavy packs. Alas, during the final ten minutes, two young men pass us, striding confidently to the top. They are there taking in the awesome view when we arrive. Wearing only shorts and their boots they have a lot of skin exposed to the cool mountain air... and to the morning blackflies.

"Hey, how do you keep these flies from biting?" they call to us.
"You might start by putting on a shirt!" Marie quips.

It doesn't matter that we aren't first. We are indeed at the top of the local world. The weather is fantastic. A slight breeze blows up and knocks down the flies. Puffy clouds soar high above, sending shadows sailing up and down the blue slopes which undulate away from

Mathilda atop Mt. Marcy, 5344 feet, view eastward

our feet in every direction. Haystack, Algonquin, Colden, Skylight, Whiteface, Rooster Comb, the Gothics, Avalanche, Gooseberry, and Tabletop – the names alone make me want to run to each one, or ride the magic carpet clouds. Layers of blue magic which seem so close, yet even the closest is over a mile away in a straight line, not to mention how far it would be to walk to each peak.

The experience on the mountain is so pure and personal that each of us is drawn to a separate hump of rock to savor the slice of time we have to spend there. Mathilda chooses the highest point to sit and watch the clouds, just north of where I've selected a special panorama of Colden and Avalanche to the west. Marie likes Haystack, the closest and second-highest peak, for the changing colors of cloud shadows playing over its slopes. Chips is as close to heaven as he can get. He can always be counted on to leap to the top of any rock, log, or piece of furniture (unless forbidden with stern warnings). To be "Top Dog" is always his heart's desire. Today he revels in his position at the apex of the state. Somehow he is aware that there is not a higher rock to be found. And truly, each of us surveys a private kingdom under the mellowing sunlight.

Jan, the caretaker who helped us at Johns Brook Loj, marches purposefully to the top of the hill. We recognize her and ask her if she's just out for a little exercise. No, she's on her way to pick up her mail and get a shower. This is her weekly treat on her day off. Of course it's three peaks away. Now there is a gal who is in shape!

A few more hikers appear on the ample curve of the mountain's bosom, but we never feel crowded with over 300 open square miles in view around us. One particular person of interest appears at about 10 am. This is the Summit Steward. This volunteer program exists to educate people about the fragile alpine ecosystem, and to help protect it. The alpine world found above 4000 feet is a series of mountaintop islands marooned in a glacial landscape sculpted 13,000 years ago. As the area warmed, conifers and then maples slowly climbed the Adirondack slopes. The maples are mostly unable to survive higher than 2500 feet, and the spruce-fir forests dominate at the next level. Above 4000 feet, even the hardy conifers have trouble breathing and they become gnarled and dwarfed, old, yet with trunks and branches so twisted they stand barely five feet tall. This is the "krummholz" (crooked tree) zone, bonsai created by wind-blown ice. This gradually gives way to the alpine zone which resembles arctic tundra. All plant life here is confined to a layer two feet thick. Under the shallow roots of these plants lies impenetrable bedrock, and whistling overhead are killing winds. The plants are literally trapped between a rock and a hard place! The Stewards come to teach people about the delicate yet hardy plants, and to ask people to tread carefully to avoid disturbing the remaining plants which have survived after decades of little protection from thousands of climbers' boots.

With the Steward's help, we learn to look closely at the tiny plants and discover a world of diverse beauty and rare botanical specimens. First lichens and mosses grasp tenuous toe-holds in the bare rock. Acids which leach out of the lichens with every rain storm help dissolve the rock. We see Haircap Moss and Mountain Sandwort, a bright white, five-pointed star of a flower. These are pioneer species which can move in when the lichen has dissolved just enough rock, and has created enough organic debris, to form a shallow layer of peat. Caught in a fierce windstorm you would want to hold on tight to others standing near you, and this is indeed one of the survival strategies of these plants. They grow tightly packed together, and hunkered down, low to the ground.

Bearberry Willow trees

Also blooming just for our visit is Small Cranberry, with tiny, pink orchid-like blooms having recurved petals and protruding stamens. Alpine Goldenrod glows, in full bloom, barely four inches tall, surrounded by Deer's Hair Sedge, so named because its leaves are so fine that they resemble hair. Patches of cotton-grass wave puffy white heads. Perhaps most astonishing to us are the catkins of a small woody plant, opening and blowing in the wind like small cottonwood seeds. The Steward explains that those six-inch tall plants are mature trees, the Bearberry Willow! Despite the harsh conditions, over a hundred different species of plants may be found by a curious and determined explorer who could revisit the 85 acres over the seasons of the year.

There are 46 Adirondack peaks which still retain heights of more than 4000 feet. Alpine plants are incredibly sensitive to footfalls. They must use every bit of energy they have to carry out their life cycle, and damage by trampling usually kills a plant. When the plants die and their roots are lost, soil that took more than ten thousand years to accumulate is easily blown or washed away. It can take centuries for a damaged alpine meadow to recover. There are over 20,000 hikers who trek up Mount Marcy alone each year. Imagine the impact on these fragile plants if any significant number of those hikers take careless steps.

From May to October each year, Summit Stewards provide an educational presence on the peaks that are most threatened by hiker trampling. Stewards spend up to five days at a time in the backcountry interacting with hikers and encouraging them to stay on trails and bare rock, not to pick the plants, and to share the message with others.

While we are exploring Marcy, our food bags have been hanging twelve feet off the ground from the center of a horizontal pole, eight feet from each side post. No bear is going to get our cache or our cash while we are mountain-tripping. We return to find it hanging securely as described with a large hole in the side, scraps of tinfoil packs and plastic containers scattered on the ground, and one precocious Red Squirrel sitting on a log holding a crumb of breakfast bar in his adorable little paws. But we are not feeling fondly toward this camp-wise marauder. We chase him away and assess our losses (and mend the poor tattered bag yet again!), while he audaciously runs up and down the campfire ring logs chattering and scolding us. When Mathilda discovers that *Sciurus hudsonicus* has concentrated his thievery on the chocolate she is so mad that she grabs the one remaining half bar of chocolate and eats it right in front of him, while returning his scolding with some of her own. We can adjust to the lost food; this squirrel is so sophisticated and well-provisioned that he is a most selective burglar.

Nevertheless, we aren't as stupid as he thinks... he'll have to work a lot harder to steal a snack from us tonight. We take the smooth plastic-coated dog cable and use it in place of the rope to hang the bag. Sure enough, our little friend tries to climb down it in the morning. We are actually watching as he discovers, much to his surprise, that there is no purchase to be had on the plastic. Those darling little paws slip and slide, he makes a wild grab for the bag, misses, gets points for hang time, and lands on the ground, twelve feet below. I'll confess that we even cheer a bit. He shakes himself, and staggers off to the woods. Don't worry; he isn't injured. Before long he's back, scolding us loudly from the edges of the campsite. But we are ready to hike, so we'll leave the campsite to the squirrel-burglar's next victims.

The Adirondack Mountains are keeping their promise of unpredictability. Morning is born wet and foggy and ripens into rain and wind by the afternoon. We are still so thankful for our perfect day on the mountain that we just don our rain gear and hardly give the weather a second thought. The revised schedule is turning out to be a wise choice. Our progress is steady, but very slow. The trails are rugged, and uneven. Mathilda and I joke constantly about the steps built for the Jolly Green Giant. Trail crews have gone to the effort to install steps made of squarish rocks in many places, but each step is so high that Sprouts Mathilda and I, at 5'4" and 5'2", can't step up on them. So we have to climb up along the edges which nullifies any benefit of erosion prevention that the steps were supposed to provide. The Adirondack mud is also a force to be reckoned with. It is mostly peat, and black as coal. In many places the mud holes in the trail are wide and deep. In the rain, it's deep enough to ooze over our boot tops. Supposedly, good hikers just walk through the mud rather than try to find a higher edge, because that just widens the trail. But filling our boots completely with muck really isn't something we want to do.

Here is Marie's version of the next adventure. "Joan often walks a few paces ahead of Mathilda and me. We are climbing along Klondike Brook, or at least slopping along in the rain. Joan is already around the next bend and we hear her give out a loud yell. Mathilda and I turn to each other in consternation. 'Joan never yells,' Mathilda notes. 'It must be BAD.' We hurry around the curve, and find her, thigh deep in the mud in the middle of the trail!"

They extricate me from the peat pit, thankfully without losing a boot, although the mud sucks hard and tries to keep one of them. We soon meet a couple walking down the trail. We try to warn them about the mud hole, but they speak only German, and we don't. We point to my black legs and keep saying "mud, mud!" "Ja, ja" they exclaim cheerfully. We hope they will still feel so jolly after a few more yards!

Every stream is swollen and tricky to cross on rocks of various sizes and stabilities. The mucky trail continues to try to steal our boots. Slippery steps and slippery slopes are the norm. Progress continues to be excruciatingly slow. Mathilda has always refused to use a walking stick. In her mind it would be an admission of being handicapped. No matter that Marie and I constantly show her how we use one all the time to provide a "third leg" while making stream crossings, or to boost ourselves up the big steps. Mathilda does not like us pointing out successful routes around mud holes, downed trees, or across creeks. To her it sounds like we are patronizing her and treating her as if she can't do it on her own. No matter that we tell each other about secure steps, or bad footing, or good handholds all the time. She insists that she is better off just finding her own way across obstacles. Although she always succeeds, the method is very slow, and involves backtracking at times when her original choice of a route comes to a dead end. Of course, we can see that she is going to come to these dead ends long before she can. The frustration of this entire situation comes to a head in the middle of this slow afternoon.

While crossing another of the many, many rocky streams, my patience with Mathilda's independence comes to an end when she refuses yet again to follow a suggested route or let us offer a hand to help her up the final step. I decide that I just have to say something or we will never finish even our reduced mileage route. In what I hope is a tone of true friendship I appeal to her to accept the fact that we do not think of her as handicapped, and never have. I point out again that Marie and I exchange information about these little issues of good and bad footing all the time, and that we use a stick for stability, not as a substitute for eyes. Then of course comes the hard part where I tell her that she has to stop thinking that we are patronizing her. In fact, we are treating her exactly like we treat each other, and her stubbornness is forcing us to treat her differently, and slowing us all down a lot. "You have to stop thinking that we think you are handicapped, and get that chip off your shoulder."

Mathilda has said nothing during my entire speech, but her face is getting redder and redder. She crosses the creek with us and then turns on the speed that we certainly know she possesses. Neither Marie nor I can catch her. We hike nearly a mile with no sign of our friend! Worst of all, we soon come to a triple fork in the path. We aren't sure until we consult the map which direction we need to follow, and of course we have no idea which trail Mathilda has taken. Marie continues straight ahead while I look down the two side trails trying to possibly identify boot prints in places where the treadway is less rocky. Hollering at the tops of our voices gets no response from anyone but the echoing rocks. I am just returning from exploring a creek crossing to the south when Marie arrives at the junction and announces with a sigh, "I've found her. She's fine, just angry." Well, a few more tears can't make us much wetter than we already are, and a hug or two goes well with an afternoon snack. Mathilda agrees to let us help her a little, and I apologize for losing my temper.

Gray layers of shadows and fog soften the hard edges of the day as we spend a cozy night at the Klondike Shelter. We all seem more comfortable in our roles tonight, and the outburst, though unpleasant, does seem to have cleared the air.

Our scaled-down schedule gives us time for some great side trips in the next few days. We spend a day on top of Mount Jo, a small mountain set apart from the other peaks. This lonely location places it perfectly to be the spot from which you can really view the High Peaks, without being a part of them. We explore the old skid road to Scott's Pond, and visit the small museum near the Adirondack Loj. Chips is glad of the extra time too. Now there are plenty of chances to fetch sticks thrown for his pleasure in Heart Lake.

Even without any side trips we continue to find trail adventures. Crossing South Meadow, which is actually the northernmost section of our hike, we reach a very shaky and long beaver dam. Several other hikers turn back when they reach this point. But we have no choice, so across we go, fortunately without incident. Our boots are now wet through from days in the damp, so there's no point in worrying about that. We've actually discovered that having really wet feet all the time doesn't seem to be a problem: none of us has any blisters! After leaving the meadow we reach the West Branch of the AuSable River. The cribbed, triangular abutments for the bridge can be seen, but the bridge itself abandoned the site long ago with some flood. The water is cold, and thigh-deep on Marie, our tall one. And here at last, Mathilda finds a walking stick a good idea to provide stability against the strong current!

On the far side we see a small stream flowing toward us. Turns out that stream is the trail! Well, onward we slog, often calf-deep, for half a mile or more. Marie natters on about a warning, but I can't figure out what she's referring to, so I ignore her. When we reach the junction to Adirondack Loj, Marie triumphantly points to a small sign, "That's what I am talking about! There was one of these at the other end too." The sign is not bold, but its message is meant to be: "NOTICE, Trail impassable during high water conditions." Ah well, accomplishments are often achieved in great oblivion.

At the Loj we discover that we are quite an attraction as we pick up and sort a box of supplies. Most hikers who pass through here are day-hikers, taking the easiest ascent up Marcy. They are very curious about how and why we are hiking for many days on end. We also learn that the very next day after our perfect Marcy experience the weather on the mountain was so bad that people were turned back out of concern that they would be literally blown off the rocks. Unpredictable!

Our motto on this hike has become, "It's a beautiful trail except for the trail!" The next morning while wandering around a wetland looking for a trail marker we meet up with a group of teenage Boy Scouts, who are also hunting the missing trail markers. They too have been in the woods multiple days and one of them exclaims with gleeful sarcasm, "Yeah, we found a piece of real trail for a while back there and thought we must be lost!"

Ahead of us looms Wallface, the vertical wall of rock beside Indian Pass. We've been watching it for several days, and now, on the final day of this hike, we are ready to ascend the pass. This wall is the second-highest sheer rock face east of the Rocky Mountains. It is surpassed only by Cannon Cliff in Franconia Notch, New Hampshire. The cliff is reputed to be 900 to 1300 feet high (depending on what the measurer considers "sheer"), and rises precipitously from the floor of a cleft in the mountains littered with boulders the size of houses, ships and castles. The guidebook, which has been a never-ending source of understatement, reports casually, "The trail passes above this rock jumble on the SE side of the pass, but nevertheless the going is often difficult." Charles Fenno Hoffman, a 19th-century journalist, wrote more honestly that Indian Pass "was...savage and stupendous...cloven through the summit of a mountain."

Wallface, still two days' walk ahead

It's not long before we can no longer see the hunched profile of the cliff because now we are beginning the ascent. Truck-sized rocks are strewn with abandon down a deep declivity, and occasional ancient disks on trees indicate that this is indeed the way we are to go. Walking is no longer an option, we are simply scrabbling and clambering upward over the rocks. The Scouts have now also found the trail and their young legs carry them past us. Still full of joy, but panting a bit, one of them comments, "I don't know how you can do this; it's killing us!" Their speed forces them to sit and rest before long. Now we pass them, grinning with the satisfaction of having learned how to pace ourselves. In our vast maturity we refrain from teasing them in return. But the last laugh is yet to come, and it will be ours.

We reach the top of the pass around noon. As the guide notes, the trail is not at the bottom of the valley, but benched part way up the opposite, less perpendicular side. The awesome cliff is beside, below and above us. Tiny sprouts of plants below to our right are the tops of tall Balsam Firs! With nothing for scale our photos are meaningless. Three rocks tumbled together have landed so as to leave a space beneath them. The snapshot looks just as I've described, but one of us should have gone to stand in the open space to show that the "room" beneath the rocks is a large as a cottage, and the rocks themselves are 20 by 50 feet!

Wanting to find a place to stop for lunch, and perhaps motivated by some inner "little-girl" urges to play house in the rock cottages, we begin hunting for a place where we might be able to get off the narrow trail. Soon we spot a break in some rocks and then feel cool air as we pass this space. We scramble down about 20 feet and find ourselves in a small rocky alcove that is indeed at least ten degrees cooler than it was up on the trail! Some exploration reveals the cause: the sun never reaches this hidden spot and crevasses in the rock are filled with solid ice, in mid-July! Before exiting our private ice-box, we hear the Scouts pass us again, on the trail above. But they can't see us, down here in our grotto; so, as far as they know, we are still ahead of them!

———— ✷ ————

A young boy at the Loj, who heard that we were hiking the mountains, saw the rocky trails from a perspective closer to the ground, and recognized a potential difficulty. He asked me, "Will you have to carry the dog?" Chips is a dog bristling with energy, stamina, and wits, who is usually offended at the idea of being carried, although he did accept rides in North Dakota to cross the cattle grates made of piping. Nevertheless, he faces his own challenges on Indian Pass. Forty pounds of muscle and willfulness are enough to keep him ahead of us even when he has to find longer routes over the rocks. He has four legs, to be sure, but they are shorter than ours. I'm wishing my own were longer as I try, for the dozenth time, to locate a foothold that isn't somewhere above waist level. Sort of beside and above me I hear a thump-slosh, the sound of Chips' pack (filled with water bottles) hitting bare rock. A glance left freezes one cartoon frame of a small, blond dog with a red and blue pack, spread-eagled against vertical, gray granite. Claws extended like a cat, he tries to grip the surface, but slides as surely as gravity is functional to an inglorious heap at the base of the rock. Not to worry, even with recovery time for his pride, he still beats us to the top of the pass.

For the trip down, we have a dog contingency plan. The guidebook has forewarned us that there are two ladders affixed to the rocks in places where there are vertical drops in the trail. Chips is willing to climb ladders which have flat steps, and a bit of incline, but we don't know exactly what configuration of rungs and angles we will find here. So as part of the preparation for this trip I have taught Chips to ride in my backpack. In a pinch I could climb down, empty my pack, return to the top of the rock and ferry the dog down. The training for this shenanigan had a much higher entertainment value than the final result. Two days of the recommended maximum training time, fifteen minutes, were wasted trying to get the pup to back into the empty pack. This activity was beneath his dignity, but when I asked him to crawl in head first, he readily agreed. The obvious thing to do next was turn around and stick his head out, and being a sensible pooch, he promptly did just that. After that I simply had to pick up the pack, put it on, and carry the dog.

The only real difference between 40 pounds of gear and 40 pounds of dog is that the dog packs less firmly. Over the next few weeks Chips and I worked out the kinks in this operation. He determined where to brace his hind feet, and I only suffered a couple dozen kidney punches during this learning process. Initially he had had enough of this activity after about two minutes, but I give him a stern warning that he would not be able to go on this hike if he didn't agree to stay in the pack longer. To Chips, such a possibility was about the same as threatening to murder him, and he quickly acquiesced. After much wiggling he found the optimal position for riding, his hind feet pressed against my back, and his front paws balanced on my shoulders. Whispering sweet nothings in my ears (and occasionally licking them), he rode, and I marched around the house and yard for five or ten minutes each day. Any concerns I harbored about how he would perceive the addition of a vertical dimension were unnecessary. We added stair-climbing, step-ladder mounting, and finally going up and down our narrow spiral staircase. Chips, the wonder dog, was ready for the hike!

After lunch, we reach our first view of Henderson Lake and the first ladder at the same location. We can hardly comprehend that when we reach that lake the hike will be over. Not only does it seem impossible that it is the last day, but it looks mighty far away! The ladder drops, almost vertically, 15 feet

Marie coaxes Chips to finish

off a block of stone with no other feasible route of descent. It looks like the pooch-packing plan is going to be needed. For a few seconds getting Marie to go down the ladder seems like it might be more difficult than Chips, but after some customary whimpering about why she lets me get her into these things, down she goes.

Chips takes one look over the edge, and with no whimpering or hesitation, walks headfirst down the ladder! He gets about eight feet down, now closer to the bottom than the top, before realizing what he has just done. The magnitude of his accomplishment stalls him on the spot! He tries turning around, but that's not going to be an option, even for my agile dog. He contemplates jumping, and Marie is now below him, trying to second-guess his next decision. With some world-class coaxing from her, Chips decides to walk the rest of the way down the ladder. What a pup! And what a friend, my ladder-dreading, dog-enduring pal.

The next ladder is even longer, but there is an alternate route of descent which our four-footed hiker quickly finds. We all climb down this last steep ladder easily, and add a burst of speed to cover the final three miles, passing more gigantic rocks, caves, and one more shelter. Our transition to civilization is swift. Broken bottles, tin cans and trash appear; it's clear that we are not far from the trailhead. The car has been correctly delivered by Paul. We leave the woods just at dusk, rushing to find a phone to let him know that we are safely off the trail, as we have promised. His confidence in us appears to be greater than we expected. He's gone to bed, and answers the phone in foggy confusion. We just hope that he is processing the message so that he won't call out the rescue squad in the morning!

Hamlets, as they are called in the Adirondacks, tuck in their sidewalks early, and we pass through several before finding a place to buy something to eat. And so we end the hike at a carnival food booth, surrounded by teenagers in leather and studs, celebrating some summer passion. A large toad jumps on my foot, and doesn't complain when I pick him up. Eyeball to eyeball, I give him a kiss on his broad lips and he croaks in satisfaction. My toad is no prince, but continued kisses elicit more contented croaks, until we both tire of the affair. A false lover, my non-prince toad, but there's no surprise in this. My kingdom has been the Castles of the Mountains, and we three Princesses, with one Princely Pup have surveyed our realm and found it fine, and our wealth immeasurable.

59 miles this hike
Crown Point to Henderson Lake, NY
519 miles total NCT

The Ghosts of Rose Hollow
16 - August 19-21, 1996

"Tick, tick, tuck, chick, chuck, thunk." Something trots briskly through the dry evergreen needles and twigs, down the slope of Rose Hollow, and stops just short of our tent.

Rose Hollow, a natural bowl, seemed the ideal place to pitch our tent on this warm and dry evening. If there were any chance of storms it might have turned our tent into a bathtub, but Marie and I had no such concerns today and had skittered down the steep sides to the flat floor of the bowl and set up camp in the golden sunset light slanting down the western wall of our hollow.

"I wonder what that is?" *It sounds too big for a chipmunk or squirrel.*
"Well, it's waiting right outside the tent." *Maybe a large raccoon; they can be tricky. Why isn't Chips bristling and barking?*

Relaxed and satisfied after two days of hiking, and with the prospect of only a short morning walk to reach the car, we serenely settle in for a comfortable summer night.

I open the tent flap and peer about. No creature catches my eye. "It's gone now." *But how did it leave so quietly after such a noisy entrance?*

As good friends will, we mull over the events of the past few days. Several beautiful, hemlock-hidden waterfalls were definitely the high points of the trip. Children of the eastern forests, we both love the dark and damp dripping ledges of rock overhung by sweeping green boughs.

"Tick, tick, tick, chick, tuck, chuck, chunck, thunk." Once again the footsteps stop just short of our tent. We are being watched. "OK, now you've got my attention, little critter, let's see what you are." I poke my head outside. There's nobody there. "Must be behind the tent." I crawl back inside.
"It didn't sound like it was behind the tent," Marie points out, with a mind toward the practical application of physics. I leave the rain fly open so we can see out the screen door.

The sun is sinking below the rim and one possible source of Rose Hollow's name becomes apparent as the entire valley fills with rosy glowing light.

"It really sounds quite large."
"I know."

"I loved the view of Labrador Hollow, when we walked across that open space above the valley," Marie sighs.
"That was great, " I agree.

"**Tick, chick, tick.**" "There, it's moved away," I point out.
"Not very far," Marie protests, her voice keening ever so slightly. It's getting dark.

Rose Hollow is odd, even by the standards of little hidden bowls in the woods. It is so small in diameter it doesn't even appear on topographic maps of the region, heightening the sense of unreality. It is an almost perfect circle with no saddles or dips in its rim. The sides fall steeply and symmetrically, thirty or more feet down to the smooth bottom where we are certainly not sleeping. Ranks of spruce, with natural but regular spacing, march down the walls, reaching ever taller to catch the sun. Brown branches at the lower levels tell the tale of needles shaded out of life. The side path to reach it from the main trail is darkly overgrown, noted only by a broken brown sign.

"**Tick, tick, tuck, chick, chuck, thunk.**" *Rocketing as if from a coiled spring, I burst from the tent and look 360 degrees around the lower edges of the slopes. Our visitor cannot be seen, but once again it is not heard to leave. How many invisible guests are we now entertaining? Three? Four? It's really too dark to see anything except perhaps the flash of glowing eyes. Chips still naps, unconcerned. Some guard dog he is.*

Prickles begin on the back of my neck, but there is no way I'll confess this to Marie. Leaders instill confidence, not jitters. We lie tensely in the tent; I grip the flashlight tightly, awaiting the next round of insistent footfalls. We do not have long to wait.

"**Tick, tick, thick, chick, tuck, thuck, chunck, thunk.**" *I spring for the door.* "**Tuck, tuck, chuck, chink, thwack, tack!**" *With flashlight I search for gleaming eyes. There are none.*

Uneasily, we lie back and explain to each other that there is just nothing out there. The dog is uninterested. There are no creatures moving around the hollow. Whatever is making that noise is quite regular in rhythm although each series is unevenly spaced from the next. The noise or its maker does not seem to be harmful. It is too dark to do anything more about it. The logical portions of our brains convince us to suspend the search for meaning in the sounds, and we doze off.

"Tick, tick, tuck, chick, chuck, thunk."

Yet the less sophisticated, atavistic centers of the subconscious rule the hours of sleep. Marie dreams of huge raindrops falling on the tent. I restlessly conjure up phantom images of unknown assailants and persuing adversaries. Chips alone sleeps deeply, unmolested by our ghostly guests.

"Tuck, chuck, thuck, thump."

Sometime in the night the sprites leave the hollow to our keeping and we awake with golden rays of sun streaming from the other side of the high rim. With the pleasurable confidence of survival we search for clues in the forest floor. I can find no trails of roughed up needles where small, or larger, feet might have run down the sides of the bowl. "Come look at this funny little pile," Marie beckons. At the base of one of the spruce trees is a cone of rounded wood chips.
"So?" I bluntly dismiss her finding. "What we heard had substance, not some little pattering of falling wood chips." Not to mention that we would need to mentally invent some curious mechanism that might have caused a pile of wood chips to fall from a tree.

The ghosts are silent this morning, offering not one clue as to their identity.

"Look, here's another... and another," Marie points out stubbornly.
"Well, those chips could be a chewed up spruce cone," I admit tentatively. We pose an unlikely theory: "Maybe a squirrel started to eat a cone here and then carried it up the tree and it banged on branches as he climbed." A few minutes, and several more chip pile discoveries later, we remember that the sounds always moved down toward the tent, never up the sides of the hollow.
"It can't be a squirrel carrying a cone up the tree." "Besides, here's an old core of a cone right here next to the pile. And another.... and another."

With a flash of brilliance born of the exhaustion of other logical pathways we realize that the squirrels were sitting in the trees eating the cones. We could not hear the small pieces of the cone petals dropping one by one. However, when the cone was stripped to the bare core the squirrel would discard the "cob" and it would fall, noisily bouncing off the dead branches on its way to the ground. "Tick, tick, tuck, chick, chuck, thunk." In our bowl of a campsite the sound was gathered and amplified, resonating across the enclosed space, loud and ominous.

Ever since, the sight of a pile of chips at the base of a spruce tree is enough to send us into a fit of giggles. Are we relieved to have lived out the night with the Ghosts of Rose Hollow, or have the Ghosts possessed us, compelling us to laugh in admiration of their conquest of our subconscious minds?

19 miles this hike
south of Fabius, NY
    to Randall Hill Rd.
Onondaga and
    Cortland Counties, NY
538 miles total NCT

West, Wes, Wet
17 - December 12-13, 1996

Here I sit in my pajamas, at the Jonesville laundromat, experiencing genuine American culture along the North Country Trail. Today I have changed my mind about what constitutes a Hike. I've always been one of those diehard minimalists (secretly cursed by their friends), a pioneer wannabe, who scoffed at those who want to carry less weight, sleep in a warm dry place, or take a shorter route. If there was a hard way to do something I would find it and exult in the discovery.

Today I have realized that despite eating my dinner in the car with the heater running full blast, despite the fact that I have "wimped out" and chosen to dry my wardrobe with the aid of coin-activated technology, that this hike counts.

"West" will be the theme of my winter months. Two roads diverged through a sallow fog as autumn approached. The yellow-brick road to the Maize and Blue City was lined with high expectations but led to disappointing realities. Should I continue along the bumpy educational pavement? To follow the winding road back home is the alternate pathway. The yellow smog hanging over a marriage which has benefitted from the years of separation is beginning to lift, but neither pathway is appealing. Whichever of these roads I follow will indeed make all the difference.

With great agony I resign my graduate fellowship and choose not to return to school. The years apart have given Omer and me a chance to remember some of the things we like about each other. And there will be no abrupt removal from the Ann Arbor culture. The wetland project at Matthaei Botanical Garden in Ann Arbor has a monthly monitoring commitment, so one week per month I'll be working on the east side of the state. It seems to be a no-brainer to incorporate the many miles of roadwalk required to cross southeast Michigan into these trips. With every monthly jaunt I push the red line on my wall map farther west. This path at least is clear.

Wes Boyd is my trail angel for this section. Wes is editor for the *North Star*, magazine of the NCTA. He's also a board member, organizer of spontaneous campfire storytelling sessions, and all-round good guy. "Trail magic," one of his favorite themes, is real because he practices it. His home is nearby, and a few phone calls have settled the logistics of spotting my car for this two day roadside adventure. He's also planning to call on a friend to help with the next section west of here in another month. Wes writes for his local paper and does some radio interviews as well. Even with fewer than 600 miles to my credit, he thinks my quest is newsworthy, and we record a brief question and answer session before Chips and I tumble out of his warm car to stand on the wet and shimmering pavement.

But I digress from the fly-spotted yellow laundromat. As you may have guessed, a hike, the highlight of which is watching my pants twirl around the thumping drum of a dryer, can't have too much to recommend it. Ten miles of certified asphalt from Hillsdale to Jonesville keeps us off the road, but just barely. This bike path meanders from exactly curbside to a few feet away and back to the edge of traffic. It is hardly bike-worthy, being littered with gravel, broken glass and metal scraps. Chips winces as the trucks zoom by, their hub caps just inches from his shoulders. "Flam, blam, blam!" Chips and I both jump at the unexpected battery of noise. A grain truck, with loose tarp flapping in the wind, blasts past. The rain falls relentlessly and we walk hunched, with heads bowed, wet and miserable. I am comforted by the knowledge that I can draw a red line on a paper map. What satisfaction a dog, even a highly intelligent one, can find in such a day, I'm sure I can't say. But with the loyalty of the species Chips trots along, droopy and forlorn, yet ever trusting that his silly human must have a reason for such a dreary activity plan.

Wes Boyd practices trail magic

Unless you count the parking area, I also miss seeing Lost Nation State Game Area. Trail had been built across its length in the past, but for lack of maintenance it is lost to briers and saplings. The parking area is my campsite, and the car my tent. The damp weather fogs the windows so completely that I'm secure from prying eyes. Gray is the color of the world.

"Wet" is what I remember about this hike. Yet my photos prove that in reality a few bright spots exist. The short but picturesque Baw Beese section is a palate of textures – golden vertical cattails and mottled rusty leaves against a pale blue sky dusted in fine snowflakes. Hillsdale fairly bristles with historic homes, decorated beautifully for the holidays. In Litchfield a storefront display of century-old tools attracts the eye. Also in Litchfield stands a bell, mounted on a fieldstone plinth bearing a plaque commemorating Rose Hartwick Thorpe who graduated from high school in the town. Rose was the author of a sentimental poem "Curfew Must Not Ring Tonight." To our modern ears the verse is maudlin and foolish. A young maiden risks death to muffle the ringing of the evening bell since her lover is to be executed when it tolls. Yet, in its Victorian day, the fable was highly popular, and Thorpe an honored daughter of the town.

What constitutes a "real" Hike? I pounded each foot on the pavement about 32,000 times. That's real! Hikes with slow-roasted evenings beside a glowing campfire linger in memory, but my laundromat memory is no less valid, only less pleasurable. Fragrant stew followed by s'mores may be perfection, but eating a cold lunch in the car at 2 pm, followed by a cold dinner at 4 pm, just because I am hungry, also satisfies. Even my pictures are beginning to exhibit my changing perception of The Great Hike to The Great Adventure. Previously I have carefully framed each shot to capture photos of idealistic scenes. Such "editing" is not dishonest, but my hiking mentality is expanding to include the laundromat, the Burger King, the nights in the car, and the smiley face painted on an oil storage tank beside the road. "Smile...," it said to me. "There's a smile in every situation!" I plodded westward, and I'm sure I saw it wink.

30 miles this hike
Osseo to Homer, MI
568 miles total NCT

King Relish to Kentucky Fried
18 - January 20-21, 1997

I begin both days of this hike with relish – pickle relish, that is!

Consider the odor of pickle relish so strong it hurts your nostrils. Consider how many plain hot dogs you could wolf down just with the condimentary power of that scent. Imagine five-gallon pails of green vinegar-and-brine soaked chunks stacked to the ceiling. How much more American can you get!? I suspect that the pungent power of this cultural icon is propelling me for the first five miles of each of these long days.

Wes' friend Jim has dropped me off at the King Pickle Relish Factory where I will walk east to my car. The next day I'll drive to the relish factory, leave the car and hike west to Fort Custer Recreation Area where I will be picked up by friends, Janet and Peter Payne, from Ann Arbor.

"You-all just walking!?"

"Yup," I reply to this king-size owner of the auto-body shop who is kind enough to let me use his restroom. His astonishment surprises me less than usual since the weather has been pretty astonishing itself. Days of heavy snow have slowed parts of southern Michigan to a muffled crawl. Cities and counties here are not used to dealing with feet-deep drifts. Sidewalks and shoulders are not plowed. Don't even think about urban pathways and bike paths! Chips and I stagger through drifts, we walk on semi-frozen curb edges with the cars at nipping at our heels. By mid-afternoon of the second day even the super-pup has had enough. An open UPS step van stops in front of us for the red light at an intersection and Chips tries to climb in the cab!

The most pleasant space has been the Linear Pathway through Battle Creek, where in one section the snow is shallow enough that we can walk through it. The ducks float in lazy sunshine on shimmering blue water. Mostly we walk as fast as we can. Finally we reach the western edge of Battle Creek and the map says another five miles to go. It is already after 4 o'clock in the afternoon. How could there be so many miles yet ahead? We pace, we force each sore ankle to lift each sore foot, we nearly jog in our effort to reach the meeting place with the Paynes on time. At about 4:30 I can see a brown road sign ahead, too far away to distinguish the words. But that spacing, color and size all indicate "recreational information." Could it be? "O frabjous joy!" cry Lewis Carroll and I. The last map in my set is printed at a different scale and the final five miles are really only two and a half!

Ducks on the Kalamazoo River, Battle Creek

    Just as we turn the corner into the Recreation Area, Peter and Janet appear with their warm car. Chips is ecstatic and jumps and dances in circles. I leave out the jumping and dancing, but I, too, feel pretty good about seeing them. They arrive bearing Kentucky Fried Chicken box dinners, a cultural cure for the common cold, damp, hungry hiker.

38 miles this hike
Homer to Fort Custer
    Recreation Area, MI
606 miles total NCT

Chips Tells the Truth
19 - February 3, 1997

Chips is always ready to hike, with a smile!

I knew something exciting was going to happen when they told me to get into Omer's car before it was even light. I don't get to ride in his car very often. We traveled a long time on the wide roads where they drive fast, but finally I heard the turn signal click, and we slowed down. That's how I can always tell when to get excited. Joan told me to calm down because we had a ways to go yet, and I tried, but it's hard to be calm when there are going to be new places to smell. I tried to get in the front seat several times to let them know how important this is to me, but they pushed me back. They just don't understand.

Finally the car stopped, and Joan got out. This is the really scary part. What if she walks away and leaves me in the car? I always make sure she won't forget me by whining and wiggling. But she remembered me after all (she usually does), and clipped on my leash. Omer drove away. I knew this would not be a long walk because Joan didn't have that big pack she carries on her back, and she didn't even fasten my pack on me. The weather was perfect. It wasn't too hot, and not raining or windy. There was snow piled alongside the road for quick nibbles to quench my thirst. Every once in a while there were slick patches of black ice on the road, but they don't bother me much, what with having four feet. Joan always slows down walking across those. It must be so un-handy to have only two feet. Maybe that's why she doesn't notice all the great things that I detect, if she has to spend all the time concentrating on just walking on those two feet.

This was such a great walk! There were lots of houses on the roads we traveled. Most of them had those big black cans on wheels by the road that smell like everything that came from the house. You can tell what people had to eat, if they have a cat, and some of the things they do, just by sniffing those cans!

Actually it is serious business when we pass lots of houses. Most of them have already been claimed by some other dog, and that has to be fixed. These are mine now. Joan gets annoyed when I stop very often though, so I had to figure out a way to keep her from bothering me. I'm just trying to fulfill my traditional canine responsibility, you understand. I've learned that if I trot ahead to the very end of the leash I can pull for about two steps without being yelled at. This gives me time to take a little sniff of a mailbox post, or snowbank, or one of those black cans, and lift my leg before she is pulling on me to come along. I know the leash means that I get to go for a walk, but I really wish she would let me take it off more often. Especially on a day like today when there are so many posts and things to take care of.

Also today I had several chances to meet other dogs. Joan still seems nervous when some other dog comes to meet us. Maybe she doesn't realize that I would give my life to defend her. Actually I only got to meet two of the dogs. Joan always yells at them to "go home" or "stay." But one big guy named Coco came out and said hello. He and I started discussing who owned that piece of road. We showed each other our weapons and exchanged a salvo of nasty comments. It was just getting interesting, but Joan kicked Coco in the chops, and his man called him and made him go home to his pen. I knew that piece of road was mine!

I like to walk fast to get to the next exciting spot. There is so much to do. Joan complains when I pull on the leash all the time, but I pretend not to understand what she wants. I've nearly got her trained to leave me alone. The way she walks is so boring... just at a steady pace. Why can't she hurry when there is nothing interesting to smell? Then there would be time to check out the important places properly and salute them.

In the middle of the day we stopped under a big tree and sat down. I thought this was silly; Joan didn't even get out snacks for us. But pretty soon Omer came along and picked us up. This is a nice way to end walks: a soft car seat to sleep on with my food and water dishes right there. What a great day! I'm tired, but not exhausted. (I wouldn't be so tired if Joan would stop yanking on me all the time, but I love her anyway.)

Note from Joan: I have to confess that this hike was not the most exciting part of the day for me. Omer and I viewed the re-release of *Star Wars* with digital surround-sound that evening. Oh, since Chips can't read the map I guess I should explain that we walked from Fort Custer Recreation Area around the east side of Gull Lake.

11 miles this hike
Fort Custer Recreation Area
    to Hickory Rd
Kalamazoo and Barry Counties, MI
617 miles total NCT

Set Your Compass for Adventure
20 - February 17-19, 1997

Mathilda wants a winter vacation from her job supervising sheltered workshop teams. I, of course, want to continue walking across southern Michigan. We take a lesson from Chips. The pup is ever ready to seize any adventure — ready to walk, ready to explore any location which comes within the scope of his senses, or ready to rest in the car. He attacks each moment with complete acceptance and joy in the present.

The adventure is set in the compass housing of the soul. If the points of the compass all lead the seeker to exciting discoveries and happy endings, then long road walks always have golden moments and gray clouds always have silver linings.

Four-year-old Danny's eyes grow large, and his mouth twists into an incredulous grin. "Naaaaw," he growls in response to my claim that his mother is going to throw Mathilda, Chips and me out of the van on a corner, and watch us walk away in the snow toward our unseen car. But we do it anyway. Danny is relieved to learn that his mom is going to stop the car before we get out! Four-year-olds can be very literal.

Mathilda and I walk 38 chilly miles. Our path is mostly on roads. Some is on trail with missing blazes where we occasionally get "misplaced" and need our real compass to get "re-placed." But those facts are not the things we will remember. Instead, we will box our memory compass with these eight points:

Two pure white swans float gracefully on a wedge of deep blue in Crooked Lake. The rippled blue water is framed with snow-topped ice, sparkling in the winter sun.

As we walk and talk, we explore the idea that most people have one sense which they use much less

Swans on Crooked Lake

than the others. Mathilda is trying to train herself to use her vision, to bother to look at things she can see, rather than to just feel or listen for the input she needs. My weakest sense is auditory. Interestingly enough, I have recently been trying to make myself listen better, to close my eyes and use my ears. Mathilda works at learning some trees by their winter shape, and I am amazed at how early she can detect vehicles approaching us from behind, and can accurately judge their distance from us.

Mathilda names her borrowed down sleeping bag "Genie." Releasing it from the compression of its stuff sack, to puffy normalcy, is like letting one of the djiin out of its bottle!

The moon is bright, casting tree-shadows on the snow around the tent. Cold, bare branches rattle in the wind like a room full of children beating with toy drumsticks on the furniture. We sleep warmly, despite a cold night, and wake slowly, drifting in and out of the new day. Even Chips is content to stay warmly curled in semi-slumber.

Approaching a rise in the slick, icy mud of the two-track we are following, the sound of spinning tires is unmistakable. It's difficult to believe, but we come upon a young man in a full-size station wagon, stuck in ruts of his own spinning. He sheepishly admits that this was a poor choice of roads to follow. We take off our packs and with much pushing and grunting and sliding manage to get him turned around and headed back to a "real" road. Then we are overdue for a good grin and chuckle, joined by Chips with great enthusiastic yips.

Rows of Red Pines glow in the slanting afternoon light. The shallow snow has persisted only in occasional checkered squares beneath the trees' ordered ranks. Green needles contrast with the white patches, giving cover and floor to the red-trunked boxes, the air of each box shimmering with rosy warmth.

Walking on single-track trail, gravel roads, paved roads, dirt roads, hills and flat places provides variety. One road drops, in one mile, through a steep dip to a valley and immediately rises to the same level at the other end. Although dirt-surfaced, the road is so icy that we have to walk in the dead leaves and loose snow at the edge, holding on to branches to keep from sledding to the bottom. Any driver foolish enough to try this road today will be sitting at the low point of the dip waiting for a thaw!

Chips knows as well as any human that it's warmer to rest off the damp ground. Or is it just that he must be top dog? We park our rear ends on one trunk of a double-trunk fallen tree. This configuration is perfect for a four-legged friend. Chips jumps up and nestles between us. His rear half settles comfortably on the back log, while he curves his front paws over the slightly higher front log. Smiling at us contentedly he echoes our mood: "Great hike, great friends, great fun!"

38 miles this hike
Hickory Rd to 72nd Ave,
Yankee Springs Recreation Area, MI
654 miles total NCT

Hale-Bopp and Other Fading Dirty Snowballs
21 - March 16-17, 1997

Too early for wildflowers and buds, too late for snow. The landscape lies gray and brown, my least favorite time of year. Only dirty remnants of snow lie in ditches or shaded areas. There is no bright blue water to serve as a backdrop for the swans this time. The pair I see swimming today lift their bodies and walk bent-kneed across the gray pond, a cartoon of squished bird shapes reflected in the muddy surface. I shake my head, not believing my eyes, and then I realize that there is a layer of water lying above the ice and the swans are walking on the submerged ice!

Spring is but a hope carried in the hearts of two young brothers. Mom and Dad are headed to the orchard to assess the swelling of the buds on their apple trees. The younger boy, about four years old, rides in the car, his bicycle stowed in the trunk. The older brother, maybe eight, can't wait to feel the cool air on his face and smell the fresh earth being opened by his tires. He's determined to ride across the muddy field from their house. He leaps to his bike seat just as the car begins to move, pedals with all the strength his young limbs can muster, and manages to reach the orchard just as the car also turns in at the gate. The other bike is quickly lifted from the car and the two boys pedal furiously down the orchard lane, their parents smiling after them.

By far the largest and best of the dirty snowballs to be seen on this hike is the comet, Hale-Bopp. It sounds and looks something like a cartoon itself! I had arisen early several times previously, at home, to view what is being touted by the news media as "one of the most impressive astronomical events of the 20th century." Despite such foreknowledge, when I leave the tent this night to deal with the entire bottle of water I drank just before turning in, prickles rise on my neck and my heart thumps in atavistic alarm when I glance up and see this strange night object.

The first thing noticeable about this snowball is its size. There just shouldn't be anything else that big, besides the moon, up there. With a diameter of 40 kilometers, that would be 75 miles to hike around, if it were solid, and had an atmosphere, and I could get there... but it's not part of the North Country Trail, so I don't need to plan that adventure! Hale-Bopp has two tails, one bluish, the other yellow, spread about 30 degrees from each other. The blue one is composed of ion gases, and streams directly away from the sun. The dust tail, the yellow one, is curved. The head, like any other comet, is a loose amalgamation of gases, ice and dust. Just one humungous dirty snowball hurtling erratically through the universe. Or is it?

Comets, to be sure, are not homeless wanderers. They are the backpackers of the universe, and when they return home, they live in the Oort Cloud. Their trails are not bound by the workaday chains of the sun's gravity which hold the planets to their Day-Timer schedules. Comets hang out in Oort, at the very edge of the Sun's influence. Oort is a big town. It surrounds our galaxy, and some locations are a meager 1000 astronomical units (AU) away. What's an AU, you ask? Just merely 93 million miles, the average distance from the earth to the sun. Most of Oort is a bit farther though, as much as 100,000 AU's from my back porch, or even yours...

Comets are very independent creatures, preferring to be left alone, but every so often a Star passes through the neighborhood. Celebrity lifestyles have huge effects on some comets, luring them to try their luck in Hollywood. Or sometimes a cold hydrogen wind will blow and raise the blood pressure of one little iceball, making wanderlust irresistible. And Earth is not the only place where heavenly bodies call waves and werewolves to their spring highs. Tidal forces from the Milky Way jostle and crowd comets most unkindly. Such potent disturbances send comets scurrying from time to time. One may forget to pack her compass and find herself lost in interstellar space. But Hale-Bopp (or whatever name he goes by to his friends) was ready one fine noon when the temperature soared to a balmy four degrees above absolute zero. Little H.B. leapt into the sunshine. I forgot to ask him if he was seeking to be a Star, or if he just shivered in anticipation and raised his arms when that wind blew through his soul. But no matter why, he just had to travel that winding trail that led him to explore the world outside of Oort. And he's been here before.

H.B. last appeared to humans in 2213 BC. That's before glass was discovered. That's before the patriarch Abraham lived. In Great Britain, humans were beginning to figure out how to turn rocks into metal implements. The Egyptians had discovered pen and ink by then, but no one recorded the passing of the strange horned monster in the sky. The Egyptian nobleman Harkuf, who lived around 2300 BC, is thought to be the first documented explorer. He led expeditions up the Nile to the land of Yam. So perhaps there was some early backpacker outside on a clear night gazing up at this heavenly hiker, and surely giving it a more poetically emotional name than Hale-Bopp. (We named it for its "discoverers." That's scientific notation for the first people to write down something they notice.)

Now, I know it's just a big ball of gas and ice. I know that it won't hit the Earth. I can picture its elliptical orbit through the solar system in my mind thanks to 6th grade science class. And even so, the emotions of a primitive civilization rise in my body. What must Harkuf and his friends have thought? Perhaps they called it the Streaking-Horns-of-Night. H.B. didn't know he was so frightening.

The next earthlings to view Hale-Bopp will be those who are alive in 4300 AD. So that's only 2300 years away. But the comet was last seen 4300 years ago. Although most comets have regular elongated orbits and return on a regular schedule, H.B. is a true wanderer, and doesn't want to follow the beaten path. He checked in with Jupiter on this loop to see what was happenin', and old Jup' gave him such a slap on the back that little H.B. just had to hurry up a bit to keep from tripping.

And then there is the theory which says that a spaceship can be seen lurking in the shadows of the tail. Just a few days after I returned home from this hike, 39 people committed mass suicide in Sante Fe, California. As Hale-Bopp reached its closest distance to Earth, Marshall Applewhite and 38 of his followers drank a lethal mixture of phenobarbital and vodka and then lay down to die. They were hoping to leave their bodily containers, enter the alien spacecraft, and pass through Heaven's Gate into a higher existence. H.B. is supposedly towing the spaceship. But of course, no sensible backpacker would carry such a heavy piece of unnecessary equipment.

Well, these people who died for a dream are some of the ones who can't quite accept that Hale-Bopp is just a dirty snowball. They are some of the many who wish the mystery had not been taken out of the universe by the analysts and organizers who turned the world into particles and forces... and who can blame them for that wish?

30 miles this hike
76th St. to Ramsdell Rd.
Kent County, MI
684 miles total NCT

Great Scot! The Ugliest Mile in Army Boots
22 - March 31- April 1, 1997

I want to name this chapter "The Ugliest Mile," but I can't do it. Not that the mile being mentioned is not ugly. I have judged it, in my own kangaroo court, the Ugliest to Date. More about that delight anon. But to focus singly on that theme would be to leave out the great Scot, my good friend Robert, who has accompanied me on just this one hike so far. And Robert can not be dismissed so lightly.

Robert is about six feet four inches of highly intelligent determination who is ready for any adventure. He's taking stab number two at a Ph.D., this time at Michigan State, after a "character-building" experience at the University of Michigan. We met through a group of people who love to experience the outdoors, and have many things in common. He wants to hike some of the North Country Trail. This route will include some road miles, but also a certified section through the Rogue River State Game Area (SGA). With high hopes for a satisfying escapade we, at 6'4", 5'2" and Chips at 1'8", set off on a bright Monday morning.

Robert and Chips are ready to hike

It certainly does not matter that we are walking roads this morning. I never notice the scenery at all. We chat seriously about the vagaries of graduate school, including his current study of dendrochronology and the dating of forest fires throughout Michigan's history. We commiserate over family crises of larger and smaller consequence. Robert's long-term dream is to be a missionary in the Near East. He's been prepared to go twice but the instability of regional politics kept him out. Now he hopes to cooperate with an existing forestry research facility there after he finishes his degree, and to be able to pursue the mission goal on the side, preferably with a red-headed Scottish lassie at his side. He's still taking applications for that role.

Irene Szabo, President of the Finger Lakes Trail Conference, says, "A trail should be a trail, not a trial." We agree. Rogue River SGA turns out to be a bigger trial than we had planned on. The northern trailhead is not to be found. Robert has decided that since the Army marches people all over the map that they must know a thing or two about footwear. He has purchased a pair of Army boots for this trek and the phrase "breaking-in period" can be applied to his feet rather than to the stiff leather. We march up and down 22-Mile Road, an extra mile-and-a-half all together, looking for the elusive trail. The solution is to follow a two-track which isn't the trail, but eventually leads us to some faded blue blazes, and then to another old road where we meet a rusty van coming our way. Now we have found blazes where they definitely are not supposed to be, on roads open to vehicles. Next we follow some off-road treadway. The hunters here want us to be sure to know that it's their playground, not ours: the blazes are more often than not blasted full of shotgun pellet holes. Some are even blown off the trees. At road access points where mounds have been bulldozed to prevent ATV entrance there are multiple tire tracks snaking around the mounds. Or just for fun, the tracks buzz straight over their tops.

By the end of the day the blazes give out entirely. A random guess at which way to turn at the corner of a farm lane fortunately turns out to be correct. We finish ignominiously, following a bike tire imprint to find the path out of the SGA. Luckily, a cheerful campfire and fresh, hot corn fritters to share with a good friend make up for any deficiencies in the trail.

Robert and I also share an interest in all aspects of nature. No academic these days is allowed to be a mere generalist. A century ago someone like one of us could be a "Naturalist" with a passion for studying, drawing, cataloging, and finding all kinds of bugs, birds, beasties, or plants. No longer: a specialty is required for higher education. Both of us long somehow for those broad educational fields, and on this hike we have a chance to pool our knowledge of the species we see. Musclewood trees often line the trail, their striated gray bark the obvious source of their name. Black Willow are easy to tell from their cousins because of their wider leaves, always acknowledging that any willow may be a promiscuous hybrid. We identify the voices of Spring Peepers chirping, and the Green Frogs' "gunk." Another amphibious sounding "chuga, chuga" we are never able to identify, unless it is a tee-totaling Bullfrog who can't quite bring himself to say "jug-o-rum." It is too early for wildflowers, but a slim brown and green Garter Snake is content to be picked up and examined before we return him to his warm spot in the sun. Many a footsore mile may pass when the surroundings offer a variety of familiar and challenging natural wonders.

But oh, let us go back to that ugly mile, so that you can experience it with us! It wins the hands-down, hog-calling, most stupendifying, un-scenic award of all the miles of the trail I've seen. To begin with, it is survey-line straight and laser-line level. No relief is offered wherever the eye can see. The fields on each side have no more topography than the road. These plots are plowed black dirt, cut open and oozing a horrid smell which turns out to be rotting onions. Stalking along the west edge of the road are high-tension power-line towers with concrete pads for boots. The east edge of the road drops off to a steep-sided ditch. The ditch has collected every bit of trash straggling across that indefensible landscape from the force of every temperamental wind. For the entire distance we observe a linear accretion of plastic bags, cardboard cartons, styrofoam cups, fast-food containers, bottles, and an occasional chair or tire protruding from the green-coated slime which floats on the oily water huddling in the bottom of the gash.

No mercy from the sun, the smell, or the sights is given to the hiker of this mile. We gladly will say farewell to this one when a suitable off-road route can be found!

30 miles this hike
Ramsdell Rd. to 96th St.
Kent County, MI
714 miles total NCT

Enjoying the Classics
23 - April 25-28, 1997

Marie, Chips and I are huddled in the deteriorating cab of a classic 1950's era pickup truck. There is no windshield. The doors are missing. The seat cover has moldered away leaving bare springs. The dashboard and steering wheel's plastic has disintegrated into a black, crumbly grunge that clings to whatever comes in contact with it, like for example... us. But we are happy. Happy campers! The rain falls in vertical sheets through the open woods, darkening the sodden leaves, disheartening the sodden hikers. Yet, with a plastic poncho laid across the windshield opening we are temporarily dry, although blackening with rotting bakelite (probably its younger cousin). With care, we can eat a snack without ingesting too much crumbled hydrocarbon residue. We are so happy!

Alas, all too soon, we are also cold and so we head out under the dripping trees for a classic afternoon on the trail.

Our four-day hike through the spring forests of central New York, east of Cortland, provides all the classic joys and trials of backpacking. The discouraging rain is bracketed with warm sun on our shoulders. Chilly nights which refuse to release the frosty edge of winter give way to sparkling days with crisp, clean air.

The brown carpet of leaves is broken in many places by new shoots of green, or purple. Broad, bright Clintonia reach for the spring sunshine. Later each plant will send up a single stalk bearing three or four lily-like yellow blooms. But Clintonia is better known for its deep blue berries, and thus it is often called Bluebead. When DeWitt Clinton scouted a prospective route for the Erie Canal in the wilds of western New York (and they were wild then!) he was so impressed with the distinctive plant that it now bears his name: *Clintonia borealis*.

Clintonia, Cohosh, and Spring Beauty

Complementing the wide, yellow-green leaves, Blue Cohosh offers naked purple stalks. In April, each stem has a tangle of purple "hair" streaming from one side of the stem. This tangle will open into fern-like leaves, then a cluster of inconspicuous yellow-brown flowers will appear. Finally, the Blue Cohosh will also produce three or four blue-black berries. But the two plants certainly look nothing alike at this time of year. And twining over all in ivy-like profusion are several kinds of Lycopodium, the Ground Pine. These plants are fruiting, their primitive structures punctuating the interwoven strands like musical notes painted on a helical staff.

Such beauty is offset by the piles of trash. We are plodding up an old woods road which climbs Mt. Roderick steadily for a mile through the forest. We are puffing and panting and vowing to keep going until we reach the top. Marie and Chips win this race. I stop in disgust to photograph the most recent addition to the many deposits of discarded household items. Old dumps do not disappear even after many years, and the new dump sites are not more attractive, even with the bright colors of plastic bags and rot-resistant fabrics. I can forgive the generations of our ancestors who chose a gully in the woods and used it for the household dump site. This was accepted behavior, and considered much more tidy than letting the trash pile up around the house. Old washing machines, bathtubs, bottles, car parts and bedsprings are part of the normal topography of second-growth forest. Perhaps a clean-up campaign will some day get to these piles, or perhaps the state archeological committee will have a thing or two to say about these sites. But contemporary dumpers are just plain abusive or cheap. I can't really believe there is a person in America who hasn't heard by now that solid waste should be disposed of properly. I guess I can't call such litterers lazy though. It must be a lot of work to load the car and sneak off with adequate stealth to unload the trash illegally in the woods. It's all part of the trail experience, not my favorite part, but there's American culture for you!

Soon after cresting this long hill we stop in a sunny patch where the trees seem to be not so old or dense. There are slabs of dark shale lying about and we choose two of these for seats; they are warm and dry. Many more of these rectangular stones are scattered around – easily identifiable as the foundation for a building with no basement. Spreading our checked tablecloth over more nearby stones we set out our lunch. As we are munching there on the hilltop we realize that we might be sitting in some homesteaders kitchen, sharing lunch with the memory of some young woman who swept her floor and gazed over the softly falling sides of this hill. The dark and gnarled trees we had walked through just before reaching this hilltop are the remains of the apple orchard. All the trees within fifty paces of our dining area are certainly no more than thirty years old. At the edge of the thicker and older woods I see some spiky green clumps. A quick examination proves them to be budding daffodils, planted, no doubt, by our hostess. An eerie wistfulness pulls at our thoughts as we ponder the stories the young woman might have to tell of life at her hilltop home, her pride in the apple trees and flowers poised to bloom in a few days. But she cannot chat with us: more than a few years have passed since these stones were placed for the foundation of her new home and life.

That evening we camp early, having reached the boundary of a State Forest. We need to camp here rather than proceed on to private land. We pitch our tent on the brow of a hill overlooking the valley, 300 feet below. The brook, farm buildings and country road lie muted in pastel shades, the softness of springtime not quite ready to burst into substance. The sounds, too, are indistinct, a fuzzy reminder of the privilege we have to be camping here, so close to more ordered needs of humanity.

Our early bedtime leads to an early rising. Blue mist hangs translucent behind the black boles of the forest. The world is small and so perfectly ours for these few moments in time.

The dry stone fences have climbed the hills before us. Often our trail follows some former property line, marked neatly by low-lying walls, or sometimes by linear humps of fallen stones. We like to think that we can tell something of the character of these farmers. Those who were careful and hard workers built the walls which still stand neatly squared. Sometimes the fences are backed with a row of tall and wide maples, providing shade to the fence row, or the lane which followed the line. When we are following a line of fallen fence we speculate that the builders were hasty, planning to work the land only until some better opportunity came their way.

Marie resting on a carefully built stone wall

The stones we pass on Freetown Road are definitely not scattered about, but are beautifully crafted into a structure. The fieldstone walls of this home stand clean and glowing in the sunlight, beneath the high bridge carrying Interstate 81 far above our heads. The green, arching span of steel soars 100 feet above the road we tread, as it bears cars on its strong wings from one hilltop to the next. Such examples of the melding of engineering skill with a pleasing design which does not detract from the beauty of its surroundings is American culture at its best.

Classic moments of this hilly hike include more high points than just our luncheon with the wraith of Mt. Roderick. Near the end of our hike the trail tops Virgil Mountain, the highest peak for 70 miles around. But along the way the alternating names tell the story well: Randall Hill and Wiltsey Glen, Cuyler Hill and Taylor Valley, on to Mt. Roderick and Pritchard Brook, Mt. Tego to Trout Creek, Solon Hill to Hoxie Gorge and the Tioughnioga River, Snyder Hill and Woodchuck Hollow, then Tuller Hill to Gridley Creek which was also high. Not high in elevation, but high in springtime flood.

And so our hike is nearly at an end with another classic trail story... the road-walk detour. Thigh-deep, roiling, muddy water cancels any thought of wading this usually placid stream. Chips barks his frustration too as we grumble and march the extra mile-and-a-half to reach the blazes we could see from just across that rushing flood, thumping and crunching stones for dinner in its passing. Up one more hill past Greek Peak ski area, a quick trip to retrieve the other vehicle, a hurried dinner together, and one more good-bye to be said.

"I don't like the good-bye part," says Marie.

44 miles this hike
Midlum Rd. to Van Donsel Rd
Cortland County, NY
757 miles total NCT

Testing in 3-D
24 - May 10, 11, 1997

A good friendship is one that can stand up to testing.

Kevin is explaining a computer program he wrote which can graph equations on a 3-D wire grid, as we sit around the campfire. His mom, Jessie, is off at the campground lodge swimming and enjoying the jaccuzi. He's cheerful and animated. This is the longest speech he's made on our entire weekend together. He tells me how he needed to test the graphing program in many different scenarios in order to be sure that it worked properly so that he can sell the game he has designed over the internet. And we've certainly got three dimensions in operation among the three of us. I'm happy with the campfire, Jessie's in the pool, and Kevin's probably busily programming in his head while he carries on a minimal conversation with some small morsel of cerebral matter.

And 3-D is how the weekend began: Delayed, Decisive and Doubtful. I am Delayed. In fact, I am just plain late. I hadn't started packing for this hike until 5:00 on Saturday morning. I made it out of the house and on the road by 7:30, but this is about thirty minutes behind schedule. Jessie and Kevin however, arrive on time at Croton Dam. Jessie, never one to hold still if there is a detail to be roped and hog-tied, has Decisively rushed around to scout out all the places we could possibly park one car and leave it. And Kevin Doubtfully watches as I sort gear into our three packs and carefully weigh it, being sure to give the large teenage male the heaviest of the set!

We quickly shift to Dramatic, Dismayed and Diffident. "My friends who live right near here," offers Jessie with a Dramatic wave of her hand in the general direction of their home, "say they can't understand why we are hiking this section of trail. It's nothing but muck. They say the bike riders have been through here so much that you can't even find the right trail. Do you know that there's a motel right near the corner where you've planned for us to camp? Do you realize how close we'll be to the road if we camp where you have planned? Do you see that there's a campground on this map just three miles farther? I don't like to hike so close to roads; we always hike [in California] in more remote areas. Why don't we stay at the campground and just do two day hikes?"

"Sure, we can do that," I falter. I am Dismayed, and trying not to show it. When we had discussed the planning for this hike we had talked about a backpacking trip of not more than ten miles in one day. (I'm planning to do the final six miles on my own). Jessie was specific about the length she was willing to walk in any one day, so I had not even looked into the campground. And I really thought she wanted to camp primitively. Now she seems completely unhappy with the plans I've made. And we'll have to completely re-pack the packs for dayhiking.

"Well, this is the civilized East," I finally offer. "You aren't going to find anywhere that is far away from the influence of people in the same way as you would in the West. Staying at the campground will make today a thirteen-mile day, and I thought you didn't want to walk that far." Jessie decides to go with our original plan, but she does not seem happy about it. I want my friends to have a good time, and will try to adapt to anything which will add completed miles to my tally sheet, but it seems that it will be difficult to please everyone. We load the full packs into one car and head for the northern end of our hike. As we pass the turnoff to the campground we decide at least to take a look at it. It is a huge, 200-site, franchised campground with lodge, indoor pool, jacuzzi, tennis court, mini-golf and a partridge in a pear tree (disguised as a Robin in a maple tree).

Jessie is thrilled! "I checked," she bubbles, returning from the office. "I can swim in shorts and t-shirt, the dog is welcome, two cars are allowed. Let's camp here tonight."

I'm wondering what Kevin expects from the weekend. I ask him what he wants to do. Even though we are out of Jessie's hearing, his response is hushed. "Do whatever my mom wants; I came for the credit for PE class," he clarifies Diffidently. So we drive back to the dam to get Jessie's car, bring it to the campsite, and re-pack all the gear again. It's just fortunate that I threw in a daypack at the last minute. That "last minute" now seems to be months ago, rather than just three-and-a-half hours.

But finally, at 11:00 am, we are at the northern end of our planned hike and walking away from the vehicle with me wearing the daypack containing the few things we will need. Throughout the morning Jessie seems to be in great Distress at our situation. She worries that we will get to the campground too late for her to swim. She's afraid we will have to cook dinner in the dark. At the first rest stop I dole out shares of trail snack. Included in the mix are commercially dried bananas.

"Oh, no! I can't eat sulfured foods!" Jessie cries. I apologize, wishing however, that she had told me of this when we decided that I would prepare the food for the hike. At the end of the break we rise, and I hand the daypack to her.

Without a thought of any adverse consequences I proclaim, "Your turn."

I am frankly Dumfounded when she replies, "Oh no! I can't

Testing in 3-D

carry that kind of pack. It would hurt my shoulders too much." Kevin Dispassionately shoulders the small pack for this walk, and he and I take turns carrying it for the rest of the hike.

At 1:00 pm we stop for lunch in an open space to enjoy the warm spring sunshine. Jessie is Determined that we will not waste a minute of time. As soon as we have eaten and checked our toes for hot-spots she announces that it is time to hike again. She doesn't want to stay here any longer because there is nothing left to do except sleep! Now, some people think that I am a bit too intense and always in a rush. Episodes like this at least help me to understand how they feel. I guess that sitting still for a few minutes in a warm sun-puddle to listen to the woods doesn't qualify as "nothing" in my book. However, it seems silly to make an issue of it so I choose not to Dicker, and we hike on. Kevin Dodges all the verbal parries going on around him; actually, he appears to be oblivious to the tension.

Jessie's worries notwithstanding, we arrive at the camp site at 5:00, leaving plenty of time for her swimming program, and for Kevin and me to visit around the campfire.

Sunday's conflicts are diminished, but we continue to differ in planning style. We make a rest stop in the rain in the middle of a clearcut. There is nothing to sit on but the muddy ground, and the gray sky drizzles sadly on our heads and shoulders. After that I stop being so Demure. It's possible that Jessie is not truly trying to Dominate, but that she just sprouts ideas with the speed of a Chia Pet, not expecting that they will all be taken. When she asks for another rest stop where there is no place to sit, I suggest that we walk just far enough to find some logs to perch on, and she agrees. Another time I explain that it would be good if we make it just a little farther before we stop because we can get water at the same place as our rest. These reasons apparently sound sensible. Kevin continues to Disregard all disharmony. He smiles quietly and hikes cheerfully, but his method of coping is to speak little and stay under the radar.

The strategy for Sunday has been to drive one car to the southern end, where we had originally planned to start, and hike back to the campground. We easily complete these miles before 1:00 pm. I put down my pack and uncovered camera in the parking lot and go inside to use the facilities. When I come out again it has begun to rain. I am frankly Disgruntled when I notice that Jessie has continued to putter around getting her things arranged in her van, but has left my things out in the rain. I put my gear in the van and then we all huddle inside to eat lunch. Our timing in arriving there is good at any rate; it's now pouring rain! We enjoy some bagel chips and dip. There is more dip than we need and I offer to take the cup in to the rest room and wash it out. "Never mind!" Dictates Jessie. "Kevin, just go dump it somewhere outside."

"This isn't a really good place to do that," I protest. The site is all maintained lawns, with pine trees along the edge, clipped high with only bare needles underneath.

I can't believe what I am hearing as Jessie follows with, "Oh, it will be OK. Kevin, just go do it and put some leaves over it." Well, Kevin is in front and I am in back. Before I can take any action he Deftly hops out and proceeds to dump the runny white dip on the pine needles. To my absolute horror, the owner of the campground marches out and wants to know what we are doing. Kevin shows her, and she does not yell at us, but she is not very happy. Neither am I.

I'm feeling quite Disillusioned about the weekend, but at least I get to complete it solo. Before long we have sorted our gear and parked my car at the end of my final six miles. They take me to the corner of "the ugliest mile,"[1] where I will begin my final walk. We wave "so long" as I head down the road on foot, and they drive in the opposite direction in their van. As they leave Jessie is Diligently rearranging their schedule for the rest of the day. I wonder if Kevin is rolling his eyes. InDubitably.

Jessie and I are still friends, although we've not backpacked together again. And, yes, the names have been changed to protect the guilty, at least from undue embarrassment.

26 miles this hike
Thornapple at 96th St.
to Croton Dam
Newaygo County, MI
783 miles total NCT

---

[1] See Chapter 22: "Great Scot! The Ugliest Mile in Army Boots"

Rocky and the Rock
25 - June 6, 7, 1997

"I found it! I found the rock!" crows Rocky from the edge of the woods. "I'm really good at finding things," she grins shyly, belying her thirty-some years by echoing the prideful glee of a first-grader. But who can blame her? She has indeed found the guilty rock, a smooth two-inch oval with a fine powdering of glass dust concentrated toward one impact point. The County Deputy shakes his head incredulously. How could someone pick out one rock from an area of woods and road shoulder, possibly fifty feet square? Nevertheless, upon examination, he agrees that this is the missile which has caused so much speculation and delay at the end of an otherwise cheerful walk.

Rocky and Kelly

Rocky is the nickname of my friend, Roxanne. She's been asking me to take her backpacking, and her two girls, Kelly (11) and Kaitlyn (9), want to come too. So we plan an easy hike, just five miles a day with one overnight. Rocky home-schools the girls, and this is a great opportunity to point out how academic skills are important to all of life. We spend a couple of entertaining afternoons drying and packing food, calculating how much each of them should carry based on one-quarter of their body weight, selecting, stuffing and weighing packs, and choosing clothing and shoes. Our route is near home, and I've scouted out a good place for a campsite, because I want to be sure that the girls have a positive experience for their first overnight in the woods.

From almost the beginning of the walk it is obvious that the activity, the weight, and the distance are perfect for Kaity but not for Kelly. This is a function of their personalities rather than anything objectively amiss with the planning. We walk in good time through the warm woods of early summer. We sing all the Bible choruses and then silly songs that we can

Kaity loves to pet Chips

remember. The girls tell me jokes, and I try to remember what it was like to be a camp counselor, oh so many years ago. But in between each episode of distracting fun Kelly whines, "How much farther?" or "I'm not sure I like this." Kaity just flashes me a bright smile. The two girls are nearly the same size, despite the difference in their ages. But they are so very different in temperament. I'm guessing that Kelly does not have a future in Outdoor Recreation.

We stop for the night just north of Mena Creek. Kelly, Kaity and I collect water to filter, and wood to build a cooking fire. It's great fun for me to slip into the teacher role. We pace off the distance from the trail where we may legally camp. I teach them how to clear a safe space for a fire, and explain how we will cover it in the morning to leave no trace. We talk about the microbes that make it necessary to filter the water. We fix "upside down sloppy-joes" in a pot with dried ground beef and the "buns" on the top. Chips especially enjoys all the extra attention from the girls, who love to pet him.

As we settle in the tent the girls are a little nervous at their first night camping out in the woods. I decide to sing some quiet tunes softly... memories of late evenings at Scout camps... in hopes of setting a mood of peace and tranquility. After a few songs Kelly loudly enquires, "Why are you singing?" My explanation sounds a little lame even to me, so I leave the peace to the sounds of the evening woods.

But peace is not to be the musical theme of this sunset. Two Barred Owls begin calling loudly to each other directly across the space where our tent is pitched. Soon their conversation progresses to a level far above the familiar "Who-cooks-for-you" queries. I have never heard such a barking, cawing, vibrating "you-all" celebration of Barred-Owl-ness as we are hearing tonight, and right outside the tent! The girls are somewhat reassured by the fact that I know what it is that is making such a racket, but the volume and proximity are enough to un-nerve anyone. After several minutes the owls move away, and we fall into the arms of the night wind, rocking us to sleep.

Breakfast is traditional kids' campfire food. I call them "doughboys," but they are also known as "bread on a stick." Just mix some stiff biscuit dough and mold it around the end of a thick peeled stick. Bake by holding it over the coals till golden brown, carefully ease it off the stick, fill with good things like peanut butter and jelly and eat! At least this is the way it works on an ideal day. We have a few successes, and eat more than a few pieces of broken dough with un-cooked middles, and dipped in ash. Kaity is philosophical, but Kelly is frustrated at the patience required.

Soon we are back on the trail for the last five miles of the hike. It's pretty much a repeat of the day before, but I ignore all whining and press on to the car which I know is not far ahead.

We have left the car parked on the shoulder of a dirt road. Not exactly the best choice, but it was to be there only overnight. It is a dirt road; cars are unlikely to be driving by at high speeds. And now we have arrived, to find both front windows smashed. The driver side window is just gone, and the passenger side glass is pierced with a two-inch hole. The glass is scattered inside on the driver's seat, and outside the right front door, indicating the direction of the projectile. I quickly assume that someone has shot out the windows, and that this needs to be reported to the authorities.

What an inglorious ending! We "stash" the girls just off the road at a farm lane, and Rocky and I walk to a house to call the Sheriff's Department. None too soon a deputy arrives, and the investigation becomes quite a bore for everyone. Now the girls are the ones who are displaying patience, while Rocky and I chafe at the laborious examinations of the deputy. At first he agrees with me that it appears that someone has shot out the windows. But the more he studies the hole and the angles, the more he begins to believe that the damage was done by a rock thrown by a truck. This seems unbelievable to me. Yet, he explains that gravel trucks travel this road at high speed, despite the fact that they are not supposed to do so. He points out that, clearly, the trajectory is upwards... nicking the bottom of the window frame on the driver's side and creasing the metal. The hole on the right side is about half-way up the window.

I feel a chill crawl up my spine as I realize that had I been sitting in the driver's seat when this rock was thrown, I might well be dead now. The force required for a rock to take such a path and break out both windows had to be tremendous.

And then, "I found it! I found the rock!" as Roxanne brings the stone for our inspection. She has indeed found the weapon, and she has it in her collection of souvenirs to this day. Kelly and Kaity add memories of the hike to their collections, and I trace 10 more miles on my map. Hopefully we have each learned a little bit about ourselves as well. We don't all have to love backpacking or sleeping in the woods, but we do owe it to ourselves to try new experiences, and give them a chance. For this I applaud Kelly whose forté has turned out to be music. (The adult Kelly doesn't whine any more than the rest of us.) Now I'm waiting for Rocky to join me in another adventure, as she says she will do when the girls are older.

10 miles this hike
3-Mile Rd to Pierce Rd.
Newaygo County, MI
794 miles total NCT

On a Roll
26 - June 21, 22, 1997

Drum roll please; I'm on a roll! Nibbling away at the trail over the winter and spring I've digested a respectable number of miles. In fact, I've added almost 300 miles to my total since the Adirondack hike of last summer. That's a 60% increase. Of course, as soon as I announce my total mileage, people always ask how many more miles I have yet to go, and discouragement rolls in like a thundercloud. And now I have to travel farther each time I try to arrange to hike a section I've not yet covered, and at some point this will become a limiting factor for short hikes. But not quite yet.

This time Omer has agreed to go with me to do a section of the Little Miami Rail-Trail in southwest Ohio. He can roller-blade and I can hike. I admit to conniving a bit to make this happen. The paved trail is the primary requirement, but there is a wonderful trail-side restaurant that I've offered to take him to, and the campground of "Buckeye Buck" fame has small log cabins at very reasonable rates. So, armed with all these weapons of crass manipulation I suggest a weekend hike. Omer's defenses are penetrated, and we are off to Ohio.

The economic advantages of trails have yet to be discovered by many communities. But some towns near trails, often rail-trails, have begun to learn that people actually are willing to come to them. And when people come they spend money. Admittedly, rail-trails lend themselves to this format with little trouble because railroads went through towns.

It is interesting to observe the evolution of urban centers as their primary mode of transportation changed. Where the canals came first you now often see a row of very old storefronts that face on some dismal ditch, or perhaps just an odd linear depression which no longer connects with anything. Sometimes the railroad lines followed the same rights-of-way as the canals, and then there might be a newer set of buildings, just a block away, but facing the same corridor. Perhaps the newer buildings will be on the opposite side of the combined built-up grade for the tracks running parallel to the old canal. But all too often, rail corridors are empty these days too. As trucks, buses and cars appeared on the scene the center of commerce usually shifted completely to some new commercial district. And so many small towns in America are nearly interchangeable, with their two or three-story brick buildings lining the main street, built in the early 1900's. The wooden stores, taverns and inns facing the canals and tracks sag and frown sadly, their moldering backsides turned on the modern world.

But once in a while the old transportation corridors have been brought back to life by muscle-powered transport. Rail-trails attract bicyclists, walkers, roller-bladers, skateboarders, wheel-chair users, and occasionally where allowed, horse-back riders. The grades are easy (those steam engines had to have gentle inclines to pull their loads). They lend themselves to family activities, because they are wide. Often they are paved. I admit that mile after mile of paved trail is not my favorite, but it is much preferred to road-walking with the cars and trucks. And for this trip it means that Omer will come with me.

We settle into our tiny cabin at the Spring Valley Campground. With just a double bed, one chair and a lamp on the bedside table the cabin is as full of furniture as possible. Chips lies down and occupies most of the remaining floor space. It's just perfect! This is Omer's kind of camping. The owners are happy to see me again, and are eager to tell me that Buck and his family have moved away.

Not wanting to waste any time before getting to the good part, we set out for Oregonia and the Little River Café. Oregonia has become a non-entity on a bend in the road since the demise of the railroad. It has one convenience store, and a few houses still straggle down the hill. But one enterprising businessman has taken a chance and made a mark. The Café is in a transformed Victorian house. Separate rooms on the ground floor are special dining rooms with just a few tables each. Ohio-themed decor of Cardinals (the state bird), covered bridges, and flowers add bright spots of color to the walls, and the tall old-fashioned windows let in lots of light. The food is excellent and reasonably priced.

Om takes Chips for a whirl

The strategy for the two days of hiking is this. Omer drops me off at the place where I want to begin hiking. Then he drives to the place where I plan to stop for the day. He puts on his roller blades and zooms back along the trail till he meets me. Roll on, Om! Then we sort of spend a little bit of time together. He takes Chips for a short whirl at a faster pace, which the dog likes. These more highly populated trails do, however, mean that he must be leashed. Omer skates in circles around me for a bit. We stop and have a snack and a drink. When Omer is bored enough with this he zips back to the car and waits for me, taking pictures or reading a book.

Although the North Country Trail is a National Scenic Trail, not an Historical Trail, one of the things I like best about it is the history to be found along the way. Omer also has a great love of history, and since seeing the Blue Jacket Festival with Loretta I have known that I had to come back with him. So we take in the outdoor theater production which portrays the life of this famous War Chief of the Shawnee tribe. Ohio history is also Shawnee history, and I've read a lot about that tribe since my last trip to this area. After Blue Jacket came the great Chief Tecumseh with his strange brother, Tenskwatawa, The Prophet, who molded the history of the region, and also the United States, through their encounters with William Henry Harrison. Harrison was a young Army officer, very full of himself, who became our ninth President, but only briefly. He caught pneumonia while delivering a pompous, too-long inaugural address in the snow and died four weeks later. He was elected largely due to his fame from defeating Tecumseh in battle at Tippecanoe Creek. From this he was nicknamed "Old Tippecanoe," and his campaign slogan "Tippecanoe and Tyler too" is still a catchphrase, implying having everything you could possibly desire. But did you remember that it refers to Harrison and his running mate, John Tyler?

Go back a bit further in Ohio history, to 1763, and you find Pontiac, the Chief of the Ottawas who actually succeeded in uniting most of the eastern tribes. He boldly declared, "I mean to destroy the English and leave not one upon our lands." He nearly succeeded. Ten of the thirteen forts east of the Mississippi and north of the Forks of the Ohio (Pittsburgh, Pennsylvania) fell to his confederacy, and two more were under siege. Only Pontiac's failure to capture Detroit allowed the westward expansion to continue with the steady pace we now take for granted. His allies began to desert the siege after many months, and he finally had to accept defeat. Today, few people even recognize his name except as a make of car.

In addition to the broad strokes of regional history, almost every mile along the way has some interesting story that needs to be told. Perhaps some day I'll write about more of these. One such interesting spot is at Kings Mills, where we end our second day of hiking/ blading.

Right beside the trail, because it was located for access to the railroad, stands a large, deserted factory. Many of the windows are gone, but someone is clearly doing clean-up work, perhaps even some restoration. One tall, thin smokestack rises from the building. On the opposite side an equally tall square tower is topped with a pointed roof. The office-front is still beautiful, with architectural detail of colored bricks laid in diamonds against a background of creamy ones. On the apex of the office, and at the top of the tower and stack are medallions with keystoned bezels. Each medallion has a bright red "P" in its center. But there is not one clue as to what this intriguing building might have been!

Omer strikes up a conversation with a man there who seems to know what he is doing. He tells us that this was originally a munitions factory. Due to the beauty of the building, despite being empty for so long, it's currently being renovated into artist studios and apartments.

Some research later at home reveals that this complex was constructed in the 1860's and was the home of the Peters Cartridge Company. This company manufactured bullets and cannonballs for the Union Army during the Civil War. Morgan's raiders made an 1863 foray into Ohio to target the plant, but it survived. Legend says the Raiders got lost and missed Kings Mills entirely!

G. Moore Peters, owner of the company, then invented a round-table loading machine for his cartridges and was granted patents in 1885. The machines were installed in his factory and the Peters Company kept rolling out that ammunition and expanding the factory all through World War I until 1934, when the entire plant was purchased by another familiar name in firearms, Remington. In its next life, the building was used by Columbia Records for pressing and storing vinyl disks. Seagrams Distillers, a cabinet-maker, and Lens-Crafters have since used the buildings. We wish success to the studio plan; this is a building worthy of yet another life.

Time, history, Omer, Chips and I roll on. Plans are already well underway for the summer's big hike with Marie and David. But Omer is not interested in backpacking. When people ask me what my husband says when I take off for the woods, I answer with a wave of the hand and a quote from him, "Bye, have a good time!" But for this weekend at least we have enjoyed each other's company and found ways to have fun in the same space. As I said, we're on a roll.

19 miles this hike
Loveland to Beech Rd.
Warren County, OH
813 miles total NCT

Tales From Paul's Woods
27 - August 6-17, 1997

Paul's Woods

    Although tales from Paul Bunyan have usually been confirmed by a word from Truthful Tim, the straight-forward truth of the matter is that Tim was unable to make this trip. It has been said that Tim and Paul are gettin' along in years, and that Babe is a bit long in the tooth. I'm not sure of that fact because we didn't see either Babe or Paul, so we can't swear to one position or another. However, there is a good chance that we heard Babe bellowing one night. We lay in the tent, Marie, Dave, Chips and I, listening to some very loud trumpeting coming from the woods. The locals insisted, and they should know, that no moose live in those woods. These good citizens suggested instead that we heard wolves. Now, it's not a mannerly attitude to take to be crossing the residents concerning knowledge of their own woods, so we kind of shuffled off quiet-like, but if what we heard was a wolf, then Paul has taught those wild pups to speak in a way most uncommon for their breed. Which leaves us with the likelihood that Babe was communicatin' some serious topic. Perhaps he was tellin' Paul that it's time to come home from wherever he was, since we didn't see or hear the famous Lumberjack. Or perhaps he just had a headache.

    We knew for sure that we were in Paul's Woods, at least in the woods where he does his resting, not his chopping. Maybe that's where Paul was, off doin' some work in someone else's woods. But he likes to come home here, to Paul Bunyan State Forest, to take a snooze. They named that woods for him, right where he likes to settle his haunches in between a hill or two. You can see where he's wiggled himself to snuggle in to a comfortable spot here and there, that's where those bald patches show up with no trees on them. And he's sort of pushed the extra branches off to the sides into piles, out of his way. We came upon a good many of those brush piles, so we can vouch for the truth of this activity.

    Paul likes to sleep here with his head to the west. This is obvious to anyone who knows the lay of the land. The high point is sure enough off to the west, and it's located where that little trickle of water begins its long journey south to Louisiana. Any fellow with some common sense is going to nap with his head higher than his feet, or his nose gets awful stuffed up. As far as I know, Paul never was credited with digging the Mississippi (although, as you know, his friend Pecos Bill dug the Rio Grande with nothing but a stick). However, I'm pretty sure that he did a little re-routing of that stream to push it north and eastward for a bit so as to keep the water out of his bed. Good old Henry Rowe Schoolcraft must have got a glimpse of Paul napping here when he named that little puddle he saw Lake Itasca. That Itas-ca business is a bit of a puzzle, but Henry knew one of those languages from ancient times, and he took two of those fancy words, and made up a new word! Yup, he just grabbed the word for "truth," *veritas*, and another word for "head," *caput*. His hatchet was handy to the job and he just chopped 'em both in two and slapped the pieces together. 'Course he has to keep explainin' to folks like you and me that "Itasca" means "true head." I can't quite fathom what he did with the other halves; "verput" seems like a good word too, if you're makin' 'em up. So whose head do you think he saw? Well, Paul's, of course. He was just fortunate enough to be one of those individuals who caught Paul takin' a snooze!

Just in case you've heard that the Indians used to call that water Elk Lake before Mr. Schoolcraft arrived, we would just like to adjust your thinking a bit. That seems unlikely to be a true statement, despite the fact that the lake is shaped like a set of antlers or horns. But now that it's been clearly shown that this is where Paul lies down, the only logical conclusion is that Babe was lyin' there with Paul, head to head, so as they could enjoy each other's company. And Babe must have scrabbled around with his horns a bit, digging that True Head Lake. You just can't argue with a guy who names something "Truth."

Off to the east, we also have more evidence of Paul's favorite resting spot. Where his feet repose, those who know best have named this the Chippewa Forest. Most folks think that this was named for the Chippewa Indian tribe. And I won't dispute the fact that those good people have roamed this area. But once again, we are forced to see the real reason for the name in the logic of Paul's habits. When Paul rests, naturally he likes to take off his boots and give his toes some freedom. That word, "chippewa," explains it all: the word means "puckered," because those Indians who lived there made their moccasins in a special way. The toes were sewed into a puckery seam. Of course, when Paul first lay down there, those Indian maidens were so delighted that they spent a whole summer making a pair of chippewa moccasins big enough for Paul's feet. I wish I could tell you where he keeps those special slippers when he's off running his logging camp, but we never did come across them.

Well, back to the business of the veracity of these reports. Truthful Tim was more than willing to pass along his responsibilities to Sincere Sal, who joined our faithful band at Sea Shell City. Yup, that's the one in Michigan, about a thousand miles from any sea. Sal's full name is S. Al Amander. His parents, Pete and Marsha Amander, never could agree on what the S. stood for, and they finally began calling him Sal. So Sal it is. Sal's bright black eyes never missed a trick on our hike, so you can count on him to give you the straight scoop from here on out.

A Healthy Company

Sal was good for our group right from the very beginning. The minute that he left the counter and made our acquaintance he pointed out that we had only two sleeping bags for the three of us humans. He allowed as how he, being stuffed with cotton, and Chips, who had his own fur, didn't need much extra warmth at night. But he did wonder how we would get along. This state of affairs was quite a surprise to us since we had begun with a sleeping bag apiece. The problem was easily remedied by a drive back to the place where we had stayed the night before. These folks, Jack and Betty Young, are no relation of mine, but Jack is an old acquaintance of Paul's, which is why I bring them into the story. Jack has spent his life hanging around with foresters, and Betty knows how to cook for folks like that. The fact is, she doesn't know any other way to cook! She served us a breakfast that would have filled up eight lumberjacks, but she also taught us an important trick.

Hungry Dave, as he came to be known in his early teen years, was going through a time this summer that sorely tested his patience. As it turned out later, he had to have the valve going into his stomach re-plumbed. But as we began the hike all we knew was that Hungry Dave was as hungry as ever, but eating caused him to double over with quite a belly-ache. There were only a few things he could eat without hurting himself, and he could only eat a little bit at one time. This was a test of our ingenuity as well, since all the food for the trip had to be dried and packed ahead of time. We took a lot of instant oatmeal, and instant soup packets, after checking to make sure that they were actually edible when mixed with cold water. We weren't plannin' on lightin' the stove every hour! So, that morning Betty placed a steaming cup of brown liquid in front of Jack, which he sipped with pleasure. Dave was definitely suffering from the obviously disappointin' condition of seeing all that wonderful food and not being able to stuff himself with the joyful abandon he had once enjoyed. So he asked what Jack was drinking. Turned out to be a cup of bouillon. Dave gave it a try, and there you are! We had one more menu item that Hungry Dave could keep down. You might be wondering if a tall, already cadaverous youngster can hike one hundred miles on a diet consisting mostly of oatmeal and soup. Sal kept his careful eye on the situation, and reports that while Dave's appearance was leaning toward skeletal by the end of the trip, he never lost his cheerful disposition. Pass the oatmeal please!

One of our first priorities when we reached Minnesota was to leave our food re-supply boxes with trustworthy folks along the way. The first box was left with Bill and Kathy Turgeon, who met us with a hearty northwoods welcome: "Ya, well it's good to meet you then!" The second box we planned to leave at the Douglas Lodge at that Itasca place. They were friendly enough about it all until we asked if they could keep our cheese in the refrigerator until we came through to pick it up. Seems those government rascals have folks tied up in regulations even out here in the woods. They are only allowed to keep medicines in the cooler. Right smart like, the beefy-looking manager spoke up and pointed out that things in closed bags marked "for medicinal purposes" were sealed, and they never made a practice of opening them. Sal winked his appreciation, and we soon turned in a tightly taped bag labeled "health related items" for their safekeeping.

I wasn't going to tell you about the next part, but Sal is here staring at me, and he thinks that I shouldn't cover up the facts. The very next day, our first day on the trail, I was walking along on a nice level treadway, and my left ankle turned over on its side. This is rather a handy feature of my ankles, and I use it fairly often. It allows me to take some stress off the bottoms of my feet by walking on the ankle bones for a step or two. The entertainment provided to my companions is also noteworthy, since sometimes the following activity is the dancing of a short jig, accompanied by a ditty whose words go something like "Ah, ah, ah, oooh!" Which lyrics Sal observed to be lacking in profundity, but they were certainly heartfelt. Anyway, after I hopped about a bit, Marie and Sal declared that they had heard a distinct "pop," coming from the vicinity of that agile ankle. I never heard such a sound, and it's probably as well that I didn't because it might have given me cause to believe that something was amiss. But, never mind, limping is still forward motion. It's just a bit more jerky.

Marie celebrates amid balloons and mosquitoes

The senior member of our crew hit the big 5-0 in the middle of the walk. She's always eight months ahead of me on these explorations, and we do like to keep her mindful of her responsibility to let us know what the weather is like on the other side of that hill. We reminded her, gentle-like, about six times that day. First we had 50 raisins prepared, and then 50 M&M's,

followed after a spell by 50 peanuts. Sort of like sequential gorp. There were 50 confetti dots, saved just for her from a letter she sent to me which generously included about 500 of those colorful little items – handy too, if you ever need to spot a salamander, notes Sal. She received 50 words of condolence, and 50 hearty "Happy Birthdays," since they don't tend to weigh down a pack. Well, a few balloons, and a bouquet of flowers from Dave so overwhelmed the lass that she lay down in the middle of the trail and held those flowers close to her heart so as like to scare us into thinkin' she was going on to hike some higher trail.

But never-you-mind. When we reached Douglas Lodge and retrieved that medicinal cheese it fixed us up, right dandy-o.

The Minnesota State Bird

It only stands to reason that any area which is even a vacation home to a man of the stature of Paul Bunyan would host some other extr'ordinary critters as well. Sal chose for one of his souvenirs a postcard of the state bird. He was mightily impressed with the size of that whining lady, *Anopheles Barberi*. Sal's innards, having not even one drop of blood, were not of any interest to Miss Mosquito. But the picture-card clearly showed her to be of a size comparable to Sal, and that long pointy thing on her nose was particularly frightening to the small sincere member of our company.

Unfortunately, we did not yet fully appreciate this winged resident of the Woods when we left the car on a sunny afternoon. Marie thought she'd try hiking in shorts, and the rest of us were comfy in short sleeves and open collars. In a half mile we had laid out a wide enough trail of carbon dioxide for Ano, Ana, Annie, Anna, Maryann, Pollyanna, Barberi, Barbara, Barbarous, and all their cousins and girlfriends within shouting distance to come streaking after us four luscious mammals. Marie was mighty nimble as she pulled on long pants, and we all added long sleeves, head nets, and gloves. Then we deployed the chemical defenses. Actually, not one of us is fond of store-bought repellants. They are smelly, and they are slimier than a slug's ear to have on day after day when the mobile bunkhouse doesn't have a washstand. Some are sticky or oily. One of them actually melted the plastic liner in a fanny pack we used to own, not to mention that there is something about smearing all that stuff with "Active Ingredients" on the skin that seems as downright risky as the other alternatives. A mosquito bite now and then should be less dangerous than N,N-dimethyl-meta-toluamide, a word that Paul never had to roll his tongue around in the logging days. But that afternoon we decided that chemicals were niftier than a hand-forged, double-barreled, slide-action, self-adjusting hazelnut cracker.

In the late evening of that first night in the Woods, we lay quietly in our tent. The sunny afternoon had faded into the soft shades of twilight, when a hiker's thoughts tend to stray down nostalgic paths. Yet Marie's thoughts were not so pacific. She grimly mused, "I don't care how much Joan wants me to be here; I'll go home rather than hike in mosquitoes this thick."

Next sleeping bag over, I lay there thinking, "I'm supposed to be the tough one of this group, but I'm not sure that I can take two weeks of this."

As we contemplated thus in a gloomy gray silence, the sound of a freight train arose in our ears, just outside the tent. "How can there be a train so close to where we're camped?" posed Dave, the only one of our party to be taking the mosquito situation in stride. The rest of us shook our heads in wonder at the noise. Well, we never did figure out how we missed seeing those railroad tracks so close to the tent, but we mean to tell you that it was not a freight train at all. No sir-ee... that was a passenger train bringing in the rest of Ano's relatives to the family picnic! "Last stop, Green Tent City! Multiple mammals! Don't forget your luggage!"

The thing that we really came to be perplexed about in the days to come was why those shady ladies needed to come on the train, since they were provided with more than adequate wing power. Perhaps they just needed to save their strength for the final assault, or refueling was a bit of a problem. Make no mistake about it, they did have a full assault in their battle plan. The mosquito air force spent the following days targeting us as we continued through the Woods.

One day as we were sitting in the shade of the mosquitoes, munching goldfish (raised in the fields of Pepperidge Farm), Dave lifted his head and said with a sudden burst of observation, "Ma, my elbows hurt." It might be noted that the shirt was a tad tight for Dave's long extremities, but Marie helped peel the sweat-stiffened wool off his hungry frame. The cause of the pain did pose something of a medical mystery since we were pretty sure that Dave had not been walking on his elbows. But others had been. Where the shirt fit tight over the angle of his elbow the mosquito bites were so thick and red that they looked more like a rash than individual holes bored by sharp proboscises.

We took to calling those gals the Anopheles Luftwaffe, so swift and deadly were they at their profession. If we touched our feet, even in socks, to the netting in the tent, ten or twelve of them would hone in and begin drilling through the fabric. Whenever we looked at each other a whole cloud of cousins could be seen swarming around just waiting for the netting to be lifted, or for it to settle casually too close to an ear lobe. Poor Chips' nose swelled up so from all the bites that he began to look like a different dog, and we started putting some repellant on his ears and eyebrows where he couldn't lick it off. He seemed to understand.

The effects of these constant attacks began to show in our mental condition a mite. It seems that they stimulated the creative regions of our brains, and we commenced to invent gimcrack machines to counter the enemy's advances. We designed a beanie with a big fan on top to make a breeze too strong for the biters to fly. This seemed impractical, due to the difficulty of keeping the beanie on, if the fan were to be big enough to knock down those critters. Therefore we decided that an attic fan over our heads, with supports on our shoulders to hold it, might do the job. Only problem was that the 100-mile extension cord would snag on the bushes. Dave suggested punching bags on springs attached to our shoulders to knock them off our ears. But Marie remarked that the pain threshold needed to use this device was higher than she was willing to deal with. Sal always says that the best solutions are the most simple and natural. Without a doubt all we really needed were Purple Martins tethered to our shoulders. Too bad we never figured out how to catch the martins.

We'd been reading a Psalm or two each night, and you can hardly blame him if Dave began to sense a familiarity in the plight of that famous David. The similarity was so striking that one night he began to wax poetic: "How are we cast out of your sight, O Lord? We are crushed beneath the weight of a mighty horde; we cower at the roaring of their wings; we fear for our safety! Relent, O Lord, how long will it be?"

As it turned out a friendship with these ladies had never been in the cards. It seems that we hadn't been properly introduced. Her name wasn't Ano' Barberi after all. She was probably *Aedes* Somebody, or possibly *Anopheles Quadrimaculatus*. So I suppose we shouldn't have been surprised that she took umbrage and kept trying to POINT out our mistake. Oh, and we just won't mention that we did keep trying to murder her relatives on a regular basis. The mistaken identity was our error and I am not ashamed to admit it. We just never did get friendly enough to notice how many projections she had coming out of her head, or the number of spots on her wings, or whether she preferred to suck our blood with her tail up in the air, hoity-toity-like, or just level with our skin. I guess she was probably wearing can-can ruffles and a feather boa. But the honest truth is that we just assumed that she was wearing a tiny aviator's helmet and dashing neck scarf to go with her winged assaults. You can easily see that this relationship simply had no future with so many misunderstandings.

Well, either we got used to life under netting, smeared with smelly stuff, or the air war eased off a bit. None of us quit the hike. We occasionally were able to take off the nets or the long sleeves when a breeze came up a bit, which grounded the insect air force.

So we left Minnesota with a new respect for these ladies of the evening, or the air force, whichever they were. And Sal came home with us too, without striking up an acquaintance. His honor would never have allowed him to get into a fight with a lady, no matter what her reputation. Sal reckons that the entire adventure was on a par with what should be expected on a national trail. Those mosquitoes were sure as shootin' getting a premier hiker experience.

Home Sweet Tent

Sometimes we are fast learners, and as you can well imagine, we came to be quite fond of the serenity to be found inside our dark green nylon refuge. We became immediate champions as to the speed with which we could set up the tent. One of us would find a good tree and get the rope ready for the cache, while the other two pitched the tent, laid out the bags for sleeping, and organized the gear. Then we all dove inside and closed those zippers.

Once inside we would spread the tablecloth across our laps to collect any crumbs, and eat our cold meal of the day. When we finished, we'd pack the

Dave reads to us in the tent

food in the cache bag (inside the tent, of course). Then two people would sprint that bag to the rope, hoist the cache, take a turn at the *toilette*, and return. The third person would work the zippers to be sure that the length of time they were opened was shorter than two shakes of Babe's blue tail. Then it was that person's turn for a trip to the woods. When he or she returned we would flatten any of those offensive, whining ladies that might have snuck in. Usually a chapter or two from a book put us in the mood for sleeping.

We had just dozed off, or so it seemed, the second night in the woods. Ba-WHAP! Our green nylon roof slapped down heavily on our bodies and sprang back to its dome. This rather surprised us, having never, ever known a tent to do this before. In fact, it was downright alarming! Marie, our "doc," was instantly awake and asking, "Are you all right?" I confirmed that I was fine, although a bit confused.

Chips yipped, but seemed in good health.

Marie insistently questioned Dave about his health. "My legs hurt," he replied, fighting his way out from under the pile of logs he had been sawing.

"Why? Where? Is the skin broken? Let me look?" Marie's voice began to rise in pitch.

Dave fought harder against the grogginess. "No, no, they are sore from walking," he muttered. "What's going on?"

From about ten feet outside the tent we heard a rustling, and then a snort. This was followed by the frantic bounding away of what must have been one very surprised deer at finding a trampoline in the woods. We are sorry to have to tell you that due to the darkness of the night, we don't know if that four-legged gymnast did a double-back flip or just a simple front drop. This has taken more time to explain than it did to occur that night, and I'm sure you have not forgotten what we were not thinking of at that moment... carbon dioxide. We are pretty sure that we had not given up breathing while sleeping and to the huddled masses outside, the tent must have glowed brighter than the neon sign on the cafeteria in Bemidji. That river of mammal breath streamed from a ragged hole left by the pointed toes of our dainty gymnast. Not to worry, folks, those versatile mosquitoes just swam up-current and joined our company in double ranks. We'd also like to assure you that you have never seen three people deploy a flashlight and a sewing kit so fast in your life!

To be sure, we checked in the morning, and we had not camped in the deer's pathway. Our night-time visitor had just been wandering around looking for some excitement and we were there to meet the need. Somehow our enthusiasm for repeating the adventure waned. The next night we surrounded the tent with "fences" of long, dead saplings. We called it our "Homestead" campsite.

Oh, and we added one more detail to our evening ritual. After shaking the crumbs out of our bright yellow-checked tablecloth we draped it over the tent for the night. Maybe we smelled more delectable, but at least we were visible. The tent poles never did quite recover, but Sal is happy: they now both match his initial.

Camp of the 34 Alders

Why these thirty-four alders were singled out Sal doesn't know; it was more like thirty-four thousand. Maybe even thirty-four million. To be perfectly honest, this time it was maples rather than alders, and we weren't camped there either. Well, not overnight anyway. We were camped; that's telling the truth. Marie was as mad as Sniffy McGurk and his sleepy buddies the night that Paul installed the Northern Lights so that they could work longer hours. Hungry Dave was philosophical and suggested that we should eat. We had found a spot where the saplings were slightly thinner than the hairs on a dog's back, so we sat down to rest and take stock of the situation. Eating did seem sensible, and while I rummaged with the cookstove, Dave opened his notebook and worked on a letter to his sweetie who was far away at the Falls of St. Anthony (Minneapolis). Marie's fuming stemmed from the indisputable fact that we were again wandering among the alders rather than following a trail. This condition seemed to bother her more than Dave or me.

We'd been fine that morning, swaggering down the trail of that great Chief, Ozawindib. We'd taken a right turn on the Eagle Scout Trail and passed the cabin of Hernando DeSoto, and also the lake named for that great explorer. Hernando hadn't been there for awhile and the cabin had fallen into serious disrepair. We watched a Bald Eagle spotting his lunch from the safety of a tall tree. We passed a pleasant camping site and followed the trail to the point where it led straight into a lake! Despite the many unlikely places the trail had taken us, we doubted that this was the intended pathway. We suspected that Babe had been having some fun hauling quarter-sections around the northwoods for practice, and had carelessly left Morrison Lake in the wrong place. But this knowledge was of no help to us on that day. So for the third time this trip, out came the compass.

The first time that we had lost the way we had some help. A local volunteer, whom we will call Peaceful Pete, early one morning had shown us the way from the end of the Chippewa into Paul Bunyan's Forest. Through the berry bushes we waded, westward toward the tall trees. Dave and I hung back, whispering in wonder about the apparent fact that the capricious sun had decided to swing around and spend the morning shining on our right shoulders. But good help is hard to find, so we gratefully followed Pete into the woods. After a while Pete asked us to wait for him a minute while he went to check something out. We had a nice rest that must have been good for that overworked sun as well since it calmly returned to shine on our backs. Shortly, we arrived where we were aimin' for, at the corner of Steamboat Forest Road, which also seems misplaced with not a body of water large enough to float a canoe, let alone a steamboat, in sight. Perhaps it's just the nature of this legendary woods to propose riddles. Well, Peaceful Pete never flapped an eyelash, and generously shared his lunch with us before heading back to his home.

Next time, we got misplaced all by ourselves. We were supposed to be able to find a trail to follow, used by those noisy snow machines, after the road ended in Paul's Woods. But the trail we found went very much the wrong way, or perhaps that sun was just being playful again. In any case, the logger's road ended, the snowmobile trail went south, and we struck out on our own. Dave demonstrated that he had not lost his ability to shinny up trees by climbing to the top of the highest fir he could find on a hillside. He saw a lot of trees and a few more hillsides, but we all were in agreement that this information was not particularly useful. But, no problem, there was a road on the west side of the Paul Bunyan, so all we had to do was keep a steady course, correcting a bit to the north so as to come out on the north side of the intersection we were hoping to find. Well, we pushed and shoved our way through stands of alders so thick that even Hungry Dave could not slip through without effort. This also meant that we couldn't see more than about ten feet ahead. At the end of every stand of alders was a slight downhill, which we quickly learned was to be followed immediately by a small annoying body of water which had to be circled, and our bearing re-established. Minnesota is not named the land of 10,000 lakes for nothing. In the middle of the day the landscape opened up to sky-blue water, a Minne-sota. We ate lunch beside the marsh which was decorated for us with mauve Marsh Cinquefoil, blue Harebell, and white water lilies.

Our Minne-sota marsh lunch spot

Then it was back into the alders, oh yes, and the aspen... except for that space where Paul had been sleeping. As I remarked earlier, he had heaped up those extra branches to get them out of his way. Those dratted aspen just sprout up quicker than Big Ole the blacksmith can punch a hole in a sinker. And who would care, except us on that warm afternoon? Pushing blindly through the aspen we kept stumbling into those brush piles. That was the easy part. The stumbling out was a little more tricky. Marie all but called Paul a dirty-old-bent-elbow for shoving those branches around and leaving them. Then she demonstrated a new technique for getting out of the pile called the turtle turn. The only problem was that lying on her back on top of a bumpy backpack made it real difficult to walk at all. We gave her a hand getting upright, but she seemed strangely ungrateful.

We emerged after a few hours at the exact corner we wanted to find on Spider Lake Road. I guess the mischievous woods was not able to fool us just yet. Sure as you can count on spit to dance on a hot flapjack griddle, though, we scared a local driver out of his wits. We just wanted to ask him if that was indeed the corner we were at, but I guess he thought we were pretty frightening, running after his van that way.

But this time, there was no road or stream to the west to "catch" us; even if there had been one that rascally Babe might have moved it too. So Dave counted paces while I kept us on a proper heading. Well, I tried to. Between Babe's antics and Paul's stomping around in his heavy boots to make new potholes, those little lakes we kept finding bore no resemblance to my map.

After an hour of this, Marie was, as I think I have already pointed out, piqued. So there we were, camped in the alders, er... maples. Sal, Dave and I are of a similar opinion on this, and we think that the word "lost" is just a frame of mind. We knew where we were, more or less, and had no doubt that we'd eventually get back to the trail. Marie felt a whole lot less confidant about the whole situation. So there you are. Chips, by the way, did not care. But no matter what the afternoon was to bring we had a good full stomach on which to do it. Sourdough Sam would approve. After lunch, soon after we resumed hiking, Chips decided to do some exploring on his own and raced off wildly into the thick brush. He simply has to do this once in a while to vent his natural exuberance. But he did not return, and we could hear the eagle screaming not too far away. Now it was my turn to be alarmed! But in a few minutes, which seemed like an hour, Chips returned dragging his torn pack by one shredded strap: his usual clever means to get the humans to carry his load for the last two days of the hike.

Meanwhile Dave was counting, and I was heading. Pretty soon we came into a long abandoned roadway. In just a few feet we found those cheerful blue blazes. Of course there is always a chance that we had just wandered into a space where Babe had scratched his back against a tree. But the blue markings led us right out to the place the map indicated that we should be. Shucks, I'll bet that Babe is the one who has been blazing this whole trail!

Now you might think that this was the end of the adventures for that afternoon, and we would have been happy enough if that had been so. But the playful beavers had other plans for us. There was no doubt that we had found the right path. There was a North Country Trail triangle displayed on a pole just as we came to a beaver channel connecting two lakes. This waterway might originally have been made by an ordinary beaver, but it must have been recently taken over by one of Paul's personal pets. The channel was about ten feet across. We wondered how deep it was. Dave is a helpful sort of a fellow, and he cheerfully stepped in to check this out. Within two steps he had learned that the water level came to his chest. This was not very good news for some of the rest of us, since the level of my head is also about at Dave's chest. Well, some thoughtful person had left a handy 10-inch log nearby for folks to bridge that channel. The only problem was that they had forgotten to leave the log-stretcher with it. The log was only six feet long. If you recall, that's about four feet too short.

Since Dave was already mighty wet he suggested that he might make a good bridge foundation. So we tossed in the bridge and Marie and I drew straws to see who would get to try it first. By unanimous consent I lost, and we are so efficient that we didn't even need any straws. First I tried it without my pack. Even with Dave holding the bridge it was a lot like being entered in the annual log-rolling contest at Marquette, except that they don't have a division for rank beginners. Well, I made it across to the far bank, but I'm sure you will be quick to point out that my pack was not there with me. It is not yet quite filthy enough to get up and walk by itself, so this was clearly a problem. One more trip on the log returned me to the company of Marie and the packs.

We managed to sling Dave's pack out to him without soaking it, and he hoisted it high and waded to the far side without quite going in over his head. One down, two to go. Dave began exploring along the channel from his bank, and so did we on our side. After a spell he came upon a narrower place in the channel, only one good leap away from our side. We succeeded in getting there through the marshy area without getting wet above our thighs. This depth now seemed very reasonable. Chips remarked that all our fussing was taking much too long. If only we didn't mind swimming and getting the packs wet (of course he was no longer carrying his!) the whole problem was rather simple.

One way and another we all did get to the far side of that creek. About that time the sun decided that it had had enough of watching our antics and began to doze off, slipping farther and farther down the edge of the sky. Wet and chilly, we hustled past the next road and came to a clearcut. Those logging boys just had one more trick up their sleeves. We confess that we were feeling too sour to face another joke that day. We retreated to the road and the recently graded trailhead and camped right there in the mud. After we had eaten again – funny how the grub from that mobile cook-shack would raise our spirits – Sal gave us all a piece of his mind. He pointed out that we had no cause for grousing. We were all safely together in a warm tent, now in dry clothes, with full stomachs, and back on the trail. We'd walked through fields of pink Fireweed, and tall yellow Mullein and Woodland Sunflowers. We'd floated lazy in Hazel Lake among the lily pads. We'd seen the tall pines and the shallow beginnings of the Mississippi. We'd watched a tiny snail search for his dinner, and seen the eagle soar. We'd heard the song of the loons, and felt the soft touch of a welcome breeze. We had to agree; we had no cause for complaint.

Sal and the Tiger

We had just one half day of walking to do, and this one turned out to be special to Sal. There beside the road he met an ancient cousin, the Tiger Salamander, both relatives of Axolotl. Tiger was a little bigger than Sal, but Sal was just so tickled that he didn't mind being the smaller. We never knew, but Sal had been lonely during our exciting trip. He didn't realize that there were other beautiful individuals like himself in the world. But Sal is also an easygoing fellow. That one amphibian encounter has satisfied his social needs. Ever since we returned home he has been happy enough to sit on my computer and keep me company. He's smiling at me right now.

Tiger and Sal

111 miles this hike
Chippewa National Forest
   to Gardner Lake
Cass, Hubbard and Clearwater
             Counties, MN
923 miles total NCT

Linger, Linger
28 - November 6-7, 1997

"L–in–ger–rr, l–in–ger–rr," slowly chants Mathilda to the sunlight as she, Chips and I drive towards Ohio from Ann Arbor. We have gotten a slightly late start and are wishing desperately for the twilight to hold out just a bit longer than it might on an average November day. This mini-hike is being squeezed into a week of bittersweet and swirling feelings for me.

Mathilda's lilting "linger" reminds me of a sentimental song from Scout Camp days:

> Mm-mm, I want to linger,
> Mm-mm, a little longer,
> Mm-mm, a little longer here with you.
>
> Mm-mm, it's such a perfect night,
> Mm-mm, it doesn't seem quite right,
> Mm-mm, that it will be my last with you.
>
> Mm-mm, and as the years go by,
> Mm-mm, I'll think of you and sigh,
> Mm-mm, this is goodnight and not goodbye.[1]

This song always brought tears to the eyes of all but the most callous of campers at the final campfire. And this week is the "goodnight" for one more phase of my life. I've spent the summer in Ann Arbor working on the grounds crew at the Botanical Garden, and also doing my wetlands research work. I'll need to return to Ann Arbor once a month to continue that, but I will no longer be there full time. And I'll still visit Phil and Nan, where I've stayed all summer, but I won't be as much a part of their family as I have been. Mathilda is moving on too; she's met someone special and is spending a lot of time with him. All of this, combined with the falling leaves of autumn whirling around the car in red and golden question marks, stirs my emotions. This time I'm really going home; I think I'm ready... to have my own spaces again, and my own projects, and to spend more time with Omer. But the Quest for the Trail is one project that will not change.

We arrive at "Bloody Bridge" with the maples dripping blood-red leaves around its rusty span. On a fall night in 1854 Jack Billings and Minnie Warren were returning home from a party. Bill Jones had also

---

[1] Words attributed to Livett, Elaine and Mellowshi, Pauline; *The Kids' Campfire Book;* Kids Can Press; Toronto, ON; 1996; public domain.

courted Minnie, but Jack won her favor. Bill met the couple on the bridge with an axe, and severed Jack's head from his body. Minnie was so distraught that she jumped from the bridge to her death. Years later Bill's skeleton was found at the bottom of a nearby well. Folks are reported to have asked, "Was it suicide, or was it justice?"

Our next point of interest is the spillway which was built to regulate water depth in the canal. Canals are odd transportation routes. They must be flat, except for locks to raise and lower the boats. So aqueducts were built to carry the canals across rivers and valleys. Hills were cut down. Huge lakes were dug to provide feeder water for the canals. And when the locks were used water was moved from one level to another along with the boats. Thus there needed to be some way to keep the water level constant in any one portion of the canal. Here is a wonderfully preserved example of the canal being carried over a waterway, Six-Mile Creek. Above the canal aqueduct can be seen a half-moon cutout where the extra water spills over into the creek, 20 feet below. But the mules needed to have an unbroken pathway, so yet one level higher, the towpath continues on a low-walled bridge.

Miami-Erie Canal overflow at Six-Mile Creek

The twilight does obediently linger for us and we follow the towpath of the old Miami-Erie Canal to a spot within some woods. The maples are golden and warm in the evening light, and there is something about camping in a pretty spot which sets the heart at rest for a good night's sleep. This makes no logical sense: I'm not seeing anything when I'm asleep, but reality is more than what I see with my eyes. And we are too close to civilization to escape the noises: airplanes, a barking dog, traffic, and machinery in a nearby barn. Nevertheless we are screened from prying eyes and content to be outdoors. We set up the tent and crawl in just at dark – 6:30 pm! It's a good thing that we have lots to visit about. Mathilda tells me about her work supervising housekeeping crews for a sheltered workshop, and I tell her all of the Tales from Paul's Woods, since she was not able to go on that hike.

Apparently all the difficult experiences I've had in Ohio make it impossible for my brain to relax as much as I had hoped. I awake repeatedly from strange dreams involving caves beside the towpath. A mother and child sit on a porch above one cave and invite me to come sleep on their doorstep. A young man approaches me and asks why I didn't know that the Botanical Garden has a room just for hikers; all I have to do is call the program secretary to reserve it. An eerie technician in an underground laboratory has sliced Chips into medical specimens, and then invites me to come spend the night in the lab. I'm less horrified than you might expect; the slices of Chips have three eyes, so I decide it is a dream just before waking up.

Despite the strange encounters with my subconscious we awake feeling fine, and laze in the cool autumn air for a bit before packing the tent and continuing down the towpath, with bagels in hand. The morning's adventure is our walk through "Deep Cut." A blue-clay hill which barred passage of the canal separates the St. Marys watershed from the Auglaize. Both rivers eventually flow to the Maumee and Lake Erie, but the St. Marys first takes a far westward detour through Fort Wayne, Indiana. Men labored for thirty cents a day to dig and blast their way through this hill, for 6600 linear feet, and at times up to 52 feet in depth.

Mathilda in Deep Cut

After lunch we have five miles to go, straight and flat. The Delphos water tower and grain elevator loom ahead across the ancient glacial lake bed. Mathilda tells a tale on herself as we walk toward the towers, which don't seem to get any closer. When she was a child she tried to swim to a raft that she could see. She reasoned that if she could see it, she could swim to it. But she had to be rescued, and learned one of those unforgettable lessons about personal limits. At least I suppose she learned it. Neither one of us is big on personal limits!

Delphos by 3:30 in the afternoon, a ride back to my car from some steeple-roofers while Mathilda baby-sits the worried Chips, and soon we are zooming back to "real life." In just a couple of days Mathilda is again supervising her work crew, and I am headed for Scottville with all of my belongings packed in the car.

The oaks and maples gleam gold, copper and russet. Many golden ones have red-tipped leaves. The day is gray, but the woods are infused with light, on fire with the glory of a last hurrah. Hurrah for the summer past, hurrah for the hope of good things to come. Omer welcomes me home and we order pizza. That's always a good beginning.

16 miles this hike
Bloody Bridge to Delphos
AuGlaize, Allen and VanWert
                    Counties, OH
940 total miles NCT

White Lace and a Million Fireflies
29 - March 12-13, 1998

In high school I wrote a poem which my English teacher pooh-poohed as being too difficult to understand. Of course, that hardly stopped me from liking what I had written anyway!

> Winter
>
> White lace and a million fireflies,
> Black lace against a bleached sky.

What I had in mind with the "fireflies" was snowflakes flitting through the car headlights, and just as surely, those chilly fireflies fill the air around Pam, Chips, and me on this March Friday. I've been itching to do a real winter camping overnight and Pam, a friend from church, is game to try it with me. Pam is not only a long-time friend, but she feels like family. Pam is the owner of Chips' mother, Cleo; I chose him from a litter of six tiny balls of fur huddled in a box in her kitchen, when he was just ten days old. Of course, Pam kept him a few more weeks for me until he was old enough to leave his mother.

We are only traveling about 30 miles from home, so the logistics are fairly simple. The season has cooperated by providing a nice level of snow cover, with about eight inches on the ground. Trail crossings can be difficult to find in winter. The one we want is elusive in white, but after some delays we head south from 16-Mile Road. It's mid-afternoon but we only have three and a half miles to go before reaching the place I've chosen for our campsite. Perhaps my map is out of date, or perhaps we haven't found the main trail, but the map disagrees with what we are seeing almost immediately. But soon we find the trail markers and proceed with fresh confidence. In just one mile the trail comes to an old woods road and the blazes disappear. The old guidebook we have says to continue straight across, but there is no remnant of any trail, nor any blazes. The two-track heads in approximately the right direction, south, so we settle on that pathway. After about fifteen minutes this turns out to be a well used snowmobile trail that turns back on itself and heads north toward Highbanks Lake.

I am extremely disgusted. Here we are, trying to hike just a few miles, and I can't even seem to get this right. I want to show this trail to my friends, and once again I can't even find the stupid path. It's not that I'm worried about being lost... we could bushwack straight south for a couple of miles and easily find a road, but that's not the kind of hike I wanted to lead. Taking a break to assess an unexpected situation is always a good plan, so I find a log for us to sit on, and decide it's time for a snack. Pam is amused at my annoyance; I munch on some trail mix in quiet fury and study the map.

The situation is not nearly dire enough for my anger. We need only to continue south on a two-track which the snowmobiles have not used, and the trail should cross it again. I simply need to pay more attention to the topographic map, and stop counting on finding blazes. So that is exactly what we do, passing Condon Lake, and soon Pam spots a trail marker!

The afternoon is not all frustration. The snow is perfect for displaying animal tracks and we laugh at the antics of squirrels who have passed this way. They have jumped from tree trunk to snow and on to the next tree, sometimes with slow and curious steps, sometimes with hasty leaps which leave only one deep set of tracks between trees. We find tracks of a jumping mouse, little footprints separated by the long curling drag marks of its tail. Its tracks are supposedly not found in snow because it hibernates. Yet perhaps the warm weather of a week ago awakened the shy creature. Pam gives a little mouse-like squeak of her own. A vole is running across the tops of the toes of her boots! "I think I accidentally kicked it," she chuckles. "I'll bet he was as startled as I was!"

Pam and Chips squint at the "fireflies"

We make it almost to Leaf Lake, where I had hoped to camp, before the light is truly fading. Inside the tent, under layers of sleeping bags and extra thermal blankets, we light the candle lantern and settle in for a cozy evening. Dinner is energy bars, dried fruit, and trail shakes. Pam says that she likes really cold water and drinking from our bottles which are part ice slush is wonderful. I have made Chips a sleeping suit of quilted fabric that zips around him like an extra-warm sweater. He seems to like it, and sometimes even snuggles between us under the blankets. It's only 24 degrees in the tent, even this early in the evening, so we are sure it will be much colder before morning.

The moon is near-full and we peek outside occasionally throughout the evening to see the bright globe in a matte-blue sky with the black lace of the bare branches silhouetted against its deep silence. It's nice to have a companion on a winter evening in a tent, much easier to converse with than the dog, no matter how special he is! And we do visit for a while but the quiet and the inertia and the dark overcome consciousness. We fall asleep quite early.

It is another lazy morning, waking up slowly, adding one layer of clothing while removing one layer of bedding. Nevertheless, we are hiking by 9:30. I carefully watch the topo map to avoid any problems similar to yesterday, and passing many small lakes makes it easy to be sure of our location. The largest lake we pass is Nichols Lake, a pretty triangle of water, with a small group of cottages on one side.

It begins to snow, quite seriously. We stop for lunch and find it difficult to eat if we leave the lunch items exposed because they are getting covered with snow so quickly. The going has been pretty tough, breaking new trail in 8-10 inches of snow. I have been wearing a brand-new pair of winter boots. They are broken in but I've not worn them for a whole day at a time prior to this trip. They have been wonderful: warm, waterproof, and they do not slip around on my feet like every other pair of winter boots I've ever owned. Chips seems to have foot pads of cast iron. He's never had any foot problems on any hike – gravel, heat, pavement, stone, snow or ice. I have brought a couple of booties just in case the ice does cause him some problems, but he stops only occasionally to gnaw an ice-ball from between his toes. Pam, however, has worn the best boots she owns for the adventure, but they haven't really stood up to the test. Her feet are wet and cold. As we reach a road crossing we discuss ending the trail miles here and following roads around to the car. Pam would like to do this to keep her feet from getting any wetter. I think it's a good plan because the snow is really coming down now, and the temperature is dropping. The road walk is actually longer, but it should be much easier and quicker. We decide to make this change.

The wind picks up and blows the wet snow in our faces. Chips whines and keeps trying to turn his head away from the blasts. We can't blame him! Several groups of snowmobilers pass us and look at us as if we are nuts. Perhaps we are! One rider stares at Chips so hard that he almost falls off his machine. We pass a man outside of his house cutting wood. He says that we must be kind of crazy. I mention that he is outside too. His reply? "Yeah, but I only stay outside for a while and then I go back in the house!" In any case, the fat, swirling snowflakes are so beautiful that it is difficult to be anything but joyful.

We are safely at the car by mid-afternoon. How quickly a vehicle can return us to warm houses, hot showers, and soft beds! We also learn that we have just been out in the worst storm of the entire winter. We were having too much fun to realize that people might be concerned about us.

My favorite memory of this trip is the "million fireflies," the thick snow flakes dancing around us for hours. But like my insistence on the literary value of my poem, just because I am happy with it, sometimes I am so focused on my own eagerness for new experiences that I don't realize what other people are thinking or feeling. I asked Pam a long time later what she remembered most about the hike. Her answer: "Sleeping with a wet, smelly dog!"

7 miles this hike
16-Mile Road to 11-Mile Road
Newaygo County, MI
946 total miles NCT

A Trail of Her Own
30 - March 16, 1998

Ginny Wunsch began teaching the year I began walking, literally, as opposed to crawling and drooling on my bib. But to both of us, walking is more than just a skill we learned as toddlers that then faded into an automatic action about which we seldom think. She grew up on a farm in Michigan; I grew up on a farm in New York. She loves to hike and fix things; I love to hike and fix things. She has been involved with Girl Scouts for many years; Girl Scouts provided many of my opportunities to learn outdoor skills. She always owned a horse; I always wanted to own a horse. Dogs are an important part of her life; I've always owned a dog except for my college years. Any concentrated population, even White Cloud, Michigan, is too crowded for Ginny, and I too need open space where I live.

Ginny Wunsch

As you can probably tell, I feel that Ginny and I have much in common.

Back in 1989, when I first wrote to the North Country Trail Association for information, I received a two-page, hand-written reply from Ginny. She signed the letter as Headquarters Manager. 1989 was admittedly a while ago, but not many people were still writing letters by hand, even then. I was impressed. It was also obvious that the North Country Trail didn't have many people writing for information and maps. That seemed sad.

I don't quite remember just when I first had the chance to meet Ginny in person, but today I am on my way to her house to interview her. Lots more people now want information. In 1989 Ginny had included with her letter a black and white newsletter about the trail. Now, by 1998 the *North Star* has become a 24-page magazine with a color cover, under editor Wes Boyd. And I have even been asked to write regularly for it. Ginny is to be honored for her long service to the trail with an article about her accomplishments.

Ginny meets me at the door with Rahjah the collie and Fudge Mix the German Shorthair snuffling around our knees and sniffing our hands. My "wild child" Chips is banished to the car since he does not play well with other dogs. We settle in to her cozy kitchen nook, the walls of which are covered with mementoes of the important people and things in her life. You might be tempted to assume that she's an average retired grandmother. You would be wrong. Of course she displays photos of the grandkids. There's a picture of a horse that belonged to her grandmother. The rest of the space is covered with plaques which honor her for service to the Girl Scouts and to the North Country Trail. She was Field Director for Girl Scouting in Newaygo and Lake Counties for ten years. She taught Physical Education and/or Science from 1949 until her retirement, and occasionally coached basketball. She currently is Township Supervisor and a substitute mail carrier. As I said, not your average grandmother.

And then there is the trail, the North Country Trail. "I always wanted a trail," Ginny smiles conspiratorially. She also seems to sense that we are twins, separated by 20 years. "Not just to hike a trail, but a trail of my own." I know exactly what she means. And if the NCT might be said to belong to anyone, that person just might be Ginny. When she first learned in 1980 that a National Scenic Trail was to be routed only two miles from her home, it was an easy connection for her to make that trail her own.

In the early days Lance Feild, the first president of the NCTA, had reckoned that Newaygo County was the mid-point of the Trail, so he began looking nearby for a building. Soon the Birch Grove School had been donated, and the NCTA had a headquarters, more or less. "Oh my, it was a mess," Ginny recalls. The roof was bad. The foundation leaked. Walls and windows were broken. Ginny took on the task of coordinating the renovation project. "We did the roof first," she continues. They had volunteer help, but some of these people would show up and then disappear, leaving Ginny to do the work. When they moved on to repairing the foundation they used donated, used concrete blocks, smeared with old cement that had to be chipped off. "We spent a lot of time on that project!"

Another famous North Country Trail persona is Peter Wolfe, one of the few to hike the entire trail. Peter lived at the schoolhouse for several summers, and did a lot of work on the interior of the building. Until Peter re-dug the well (by hand), Ginny hauled water from her home to the schoolhouse for every need. Ginny worked side by side with Wolfe to dig and replace the entire septic system and drain field. Once the building was useable it became the hub of Western Michigan Chapter meetings, board meetings, the Trail Shop, and storage for all the Association's literature and belongings. Ginny was Vice-President, both of the Chapter and the Association. And don't forget, she was personally answering every request for information that came in. But she is one to look forward rather than back. She is encouraged that the Association has grown enough to require full-time staff, and a larger building too. "The more qualified people there are who join the trail effort, the more other people will be attracted," she asserts. Currently the Chapter manages the schoolhouse for rentals and events.

Back to the trail itself. Don't think that the schoolhouse took all of our heroine's time. She was in on lots of the original clearing for the trail through Newaygo and Lake Counties. Naturally this is high on her list of favorite activities. Her favorite locations are near her home. She particularly loves the crossing of Second Cole Creek, which I will see later today.

The phone starts ringing, and Ginny has an appointment to keep. The dogs wag their tails in farewell, and Ginny grabs her barn coat as we head out the door. She still has time to help me spot my car for the hike before her meeting, and this says it all for me: responsible and busy country woman who always has time to squeeze in one more favor for someone else who loves her trail.

I'm walking only three miles, but they are a challenge. The new boots are great, but snowshoes would have been a good addition. We sink deeply in the snow and Chips keeps generating growing snowballs on the long hairs of his haunches. They gain in weight and annoyance, so we stop often to clear his rump. The snow is deep enough that he mostly has to spring from one spot to another leaving big belly holes and drag marks. But Chips always has energy to spare, and nothing can spoil the mood of the day. The sun is bright, the sky is as near to royal blue as I can remember seeing, and the snow is pure white, draping the forest-green pines and hemlocks. We play tag with a Barred Owl for a distance. Second Cole Creek is everything Ginny has promised it to be.

Today it is my trail too.

Second Cole Creek

3 miles this hike
M-20 to 3-Mile Road
Newaygo County, MI
943 total miles NCT

A Trail of My Own
31 - April 20, 1998

When I first discovered that the North Country Trail actually nicks the corner of my home county I was tickled pink. Even though it is a thirty-mile drive from home, somehow that six-mile piece has felt like mine ever since I discovered it. Since last week it is even more "mine." I have called the Forest Service Ranger Station and officially adopted this section (plus an adjoining three miles) for maintenance. Today I'm heading out to become acquainted with and to clean my trail.

Autumn leaves, still bright in spring

It's a perfect spring day and I simply can not stay inside. Chips has learned, in the few months that we have been home, that the hiking equipment is stored in the porch. Whenever I grab any item from the shelves he's there in a flash, whining for his pack and wiggling with anticipation. The hike itself turns out to be an easy, gently rolling section, passing by a small swamp and a bog which will be fun to explore another day. Chips and I stop for a snack at the edge of a vernal pool at the bottom of a bowl-shaped depression. The surface is shiny and bright with last fall's oak leaves in rich tones of caramel and umber, and fresh green Sphagnum Moss. Chips enjoys the water too, but he's less interested in the aesthetics. He drinks his fill and then lies down in the shallows until he's cool. I, on the other hand, have very little to drink. I thought the water bottle in my pack was full, but instead I have about eight ounces of stale drinking water. Oh well, we are soon home.

In just a few days I will turn 50. Omer has invited a few friends to a cookout dinner for my birthday. I find that I am very happy to re-discover the joy of warm garden dirt between my fingers, and the cool, crinkley texture of new Rhubarb leaves as I weed their patch. Over and over again, I find myself watching Chips playing with his ball, or sniffing in the leaves along the edge of a trail. I'm grateful for each moment with a happy, healthy dog-friend. I've learned that I am a person who cares more about the process of doing something rather than having the finished product. I love to garden, with less concern about "the garden." I have trouble finishing projects because what I like is to knit, or crochet, or build, or draw, or write; I'm not particularly interested in having the sweater, or afghan, or project, or picture, or book.

  Yet, there is one growing obsession: to finish the North Country Trail.

6 miles this hike
Tyndall Road to 9-Mile Bridge
Mason County, MI
955 total miles NCT

Ephemerata
32 - May 2-7, 1998

Change. Most of us don't like change very much. It can be threatening, leave us feeling insecure and off-balance. We'd really rather have a solid idea of what is coming next. All of us, hikers especially, often try to find refuge from the vacillations of life by escaping to Nature. The "everlasting hills," and all that. Of course, in reality the natural world is just one big simmering cauldron of change. Occasionally the pot breaks into a boil: volcanoes, earthquakes, tornadoes and hurricanes catch our attention, but we are more likely to interact with smaller bubbles of change which are less spectacular.

Any system is continually changing, trying to reach a state of equilibrium. Wind is what we experience as the planet's atmosphere tries to become homogenous. It doesn't reach that state of calm because the sun keeps stirring the pot. And we really don't want the sun to stop doing that!

Our minds boggle at the geologic evidence that Ohio was once under the ocean. Volcanoes around Lake Superior are hard to visualize. We read that the Adirondacks were once higher than the Rockies, and we are tempted to sneer and say, "No way." More recently, much more recently, we read that the Missouri River has changed course so much that those who follow it today are not really traveling the same route as Lewis and Clark. In fact, those adventurers found that the river had changed by the time they returned to it on the way home from the Pacific! A steamboat that sank on the Mississippi was excavated by two archeologists from the middle of a field a half-mile from the river. How did it get there? That's where the river was when the boat sank.

The North Country Trail is no more exempt from change than anyplace else. We've seen blue blazed trees lying in Lake Superior at the bottom of a sandy cliff. Who hasn't followed the trail only to have it end in a recently created beaver pond? Those steep gullies of the volcanic Superior North Shore fill with rushing water with such regularity that the trail folks have taken to tying the bridges to trees with cables, so that they can retrieve them after the spring rains. A tornado changed the pristine Tionesta Scenic Area of Pennsylvania in 1985. The Adirondacks are managed according to the "forever wild" provision, which means only that humans will not make any major changes; it certainly does not mean that changes won't occur.

On this hike in Ohio, Rich Pfeiffer and I will sip from that cauldron of change. Rich is Section Supervisor for the New Straitsville section, and hikes his segment each spring to check out the maintenance needs. He has invited me to hike with him this year.

Sunset overtakes me as I drive toward our meeting location in the southern part of Ohio. All sense of direction is lost once I leave the interstate highway. The roads wander up, down and around the rolling hills. In the dark, I am disoriented, following the white line and hoping that the maps I have are good enough to direct me to Boat Dock Two, which I need to find. Ahead of me the blinking glow of red police lights ripples through the rain, thrusting long pink reflections along the wet pavement. Slowing as I approach the officer who is standing by his car, I see the water creeping across the road, halfway already. Is it moving so quickly that I can actually see it rise, or is that an illusion created by the wind riffling its surface? I roll down my window, and the deputy tells me that this road is being closed, now. I am the last car that will pass this way tonight.

At the next intersection I am not so fortunate. The blinking light is yellow, from a battery-powered flasher mounted on the striped barricade. This road is closed already. Now my unfamiliar route in the dark and the rain will include a detour of unknown length.

Finally, a little after 9 pm, I am searching roads around Burr Oak Reservoir looking for Boat Dock Two. Approaching the end of a road I can see the reservoir ahead, and the moon sends a shining pathway skidding across the slick asphalt parking lot. Two men are standing in the water, fishing. Strange little docks are anchored randomly near the edge of the lake. I realize with a start that they are picnic tables, and my foot finds the brake pedal just in time to keep from driving into the water. What I had taken to be only wet pavement is really water with depth. The men glance up. The water is tickling the running boards of their truck; they are fishing in the parking lot in their waders. Fortunately they know where Boat Dock Two is located, and their comments about my interest in finding it at night seem odd, given what they are up to themselves.

So just before 10 pm I coast to a stop part way down the hill marked with an arrow as leading to my destination. Ahead of me the road runs straight into the water, and 30 feet beyond that, by the light of the now bright moon, I can see the top of a Carsonite® post with a trail emblem poking out of the water. Well, this is where I am supposed to meet Rich in the morning. I back the car up so that I am at least five feet higher than the water level, roll out my sleeping bag in the back, and Chips and I curl up to wait for dawn. Hopefully those hours will include some sleep.

Some time later I awake to a tapping on the car window. The moon is gone, and Rich is standing beside the car trying to get my attention. "It's about 2 am," he tells me in his careful voice which isn't quite a drawl. "Sorry to wake you, but I think we need to move." Unbeknownst to me, he had come earlier and was camped nearby along the trail. For some uncertain reason he awoke just in time to find the water nearly at the door of his tent. And the ripples, which were five feet below me when I parked, are now touching my front tires. "I think if we go to Tom Jenkins Dam we should be fine," he adds. Struggling to wake up enough to drive, in just a few minutes I am behind the wheel. Rich stows his gear in back and folds his long frame into the passenger seat. There is no turning around here; I back up the hill until the road widens enough to maneuver. The parking lot at the dam is indeed high and dry. Rich takes his sleeping bag and stretches out in the picnic shelter, while the dog and I resume our sleeping places in the car.

When the dawn arrives we discover that we are not alone in the parking area. An apparently homeless man seems to be living there in his truck. Life for him is probably defined by the changes that brought him to that condition.

We are dry and safe, but surrounded by a fog that has settled thickly into the low areas. The top of the dam appears to be just a green causeway, only slightly higher than a white level plain beside it. There is still no way for me to orient myself to my surroundings. Joining Rich at the picnic shelter, I can no longer see where the car is parked. I'm glad that he's familiar with the trail here. We decide to begin from this point and skip the four miles between Boat Dock Two and the dam. Rich says that they are surely under water.

This is a new experience for me in several ways. I am hiking with someone whom I barely know. This bothers me much less than the fact that I am not in control of the maps. In fact, I've hardly seen the maps! I am trying to trust Rich, and am doing fairly well, but without maps for me to follow the feeling of disorientation continues even after the fog lifts.

Rich has chosen a camping spot for us in the Trimble Wildlife Area beside a little used road. We reach there and set up our tents by 1 pm; Rich likes early starts and early stops. I am enchanted by wildflowers uncommon, or even unfamiliar, farther north. Bright red Fire Pinks explode from their stems like little showers of fireworks. Blue-Eyed Marys fill entire meadows with small

Rich checks the map

pansy-like faces of royal blue and white. Allegheny Foamflower fills low areas with white froth, and Blue Phlox beautifully complements the deep purple Larkspur. Rocky hillsides are covered with a white-blooming stonecrop.

We spend the afternoon getting acquainted and swapping camping tales. Each of us has some good ones to offer. I have brought a humorous book to share and Rich has brought his harmonica. We have a good time, never getting to that phase of awkward pauses that can finish off a budding friendship like a late frost.

The nearby road is indeed little used, but not abandoned. And Chips is not to be trusted around moving vehicles. A jeep roars by, lifting clouds of dust into the air. Too fast for me to snag his harness, Chips is gone, racing up the steep hill, incredibly, catching up to the vehicle. I stumble after him with my heart in my throat, but experience has taught me that I'll never catch him until he is ready to return. Instead of speeding up to get ahead of the dog, the driver has slowed down, so now Chips is even with the wheels as they turn the bend, out of my sight.

I hear a series of yips just before I reach the curve. I am running so hard that I hardly have time to consider the possibilities, but after one of those split seconds that last a year I see Chips still chasing madly after the jeep. Thankfully the driver now realizes that the solution is to get out of range. Experience with naughty dogs has taught me that the thing to do is to turn around and head back. To continue to follow Chips will only convince him that I want to come along on this adventure of his choosing. I start downhill, calling for Chips to come. He arrives at the campsite shortly after I do. Bands of dirt and small gravel across his body suggest that he was rolled by the car, and one front foot is covered in blood. Careful examination shows that the foot itself is uninjured, but his dewclaw is halfway separated from his leg. First aid kits work fine for dogs as well as humans, and we soon have him cleaned up and bandaged. Now I only hope I can keep him from tearing off the gauze, and that he will be able to walk tomorrow. At least he decides he's had enough car-chasing for one day, and spends the evening curled up on my sleeping bag.

Those who wonder why I am continually amazed at the resilience and strength of this dog were not there for this chapter in Chips' life story. Except for being annoyed by the bandage, in the morning he seems unaffected by his romp in the gravel. Not even stiff—what a dog! Of course our first challenge of the day is to wade a creek, followed by a steep climb up a muddy horse path. So much for keeping his cut clean. For the rest of the day we climb up steep muddy hills and then slide down steep muddy hills. We are exhausted; Chips is fine.

That night we camp at Tecumseh Lake in a grove of mature trees whose trunks are black from the days of rain. Light from the lake glows between the dark columns. Rich tells me a tale of the ephemeral nature of human influences on the land. While that section of trail was being improved, they dug up a number of pieces of broken glass and several complete bottles. Thinking nothing of it, they took some of the interesting ones home. Word got around, and the Forest Service Archeologist had serious things to say to the trail crew. Even though the artifacts were less than 100 years old they needed to be preserved. No surface trace now remains of the miners' camp which was located on this site, and only the informed know that Tecumseh Lake itself is an abandoned coal mine pit.

In the morning we meet three turkey hunters dressed in full camouflage, guns cradled in their elbows. We nod as we pass, acknowledging each other's outdoorsy-ness. Yet, in the slight air current stirred by our passing wafts the strong scent of Irish Spring soap. Rich and I are glad they can't see our faces as we grin at the incongruous odor in the woods. We also expect that we smell a bit more *au naturel*.

We don't know if the soap will keep the turkeys away from the hunters, but we manage to attract one. A fine tom struts his stuff for us, spreading his tail and parading around before finally losing interest and flying away. I guess we don't smell right to be his girlfriend at any rate. We also come upon a turkey egg. It is as large as a duck egg with maroon speckles. Here it is, alone in the middle of the trail, with a small blood smear across one end. Perhaps a Raccoon has raided a nest and dropped one egg as it fled. The blood probably tells the fate of the egg's siblings, and this one is almost certainly doomed as well, but is undamaged for our inspection.

Life itself can be ephemeral for woodland creatures. The tom was looking for a hen. Perhaps he found a shotgun blast instead. A hen found her nest raided, her instinctive priorities thwarted. But the Raccoon found a meal. It will live to see another day.

We continue through a beautiful old White Pine forest. If blue-green can have an odor it is the odor of pine, not the indoor pine of cleaning fluids but that of the outdoors: damp sap, deep in a warm, rich woods. Brown stalks of Squaw Root poke through the leaf litter, and an unidentified fern spreads grass-green fingers from a chocolate stalk. We come across a small dead Copperhead snake.

In two places we experience the afore-mentioned trail re-routes compliments of the Beavers. One of these involves a hands-and-knees scramble up a steep hill with Multiflora Rose snagging our clothes and skin. In fact, one of those bushes still owns one of my sandals. Once again, I've inadvertently littered the woods. I would rather have had the sandal.

We come upon the perfect campsite at three o'clock in the afternoon. The Beavers have created a two-level pond among the small hills. We are drawn to the edge of the upper pool by the glint of sunlight on water, broken by the twin wakes of two Canada Geese who hardly notice our arrival. With some careful hunting we find flat spaces large enough for our tents, so Rich and I break out the nylon homes. Rich heads for the water to wash up, and calls me to come see the first of many wonders of this marvelous site. Crawling on the leaf-covered lake floor, in about a foot of water, is a male Red Eft in his adult phase. Most U.S. easterners have seen these bright red-orange teenage salamanders. Like many teens, they are not shy about modeling bright colors, particularly showy against green moss. However, fewer people are likely to encounter this eft in the adult phase, or to know what they are seeing if they do. Thrilled that my habit of occasionally thumbing through the field guides has provided me with the knowledge to recognize the dull yellow-brown salamander, we watch him in awe. He's about three inches long, and his tail has a large translucent fin on both the dorsal and ventral sides. The fin ripples lightly when he moves. The females are similar, but without this fin. All adults do retain their spots, which line the back. For quite a while he crawls slowly around on the leafy bottom, poking his nose under edges and occasionally opening his mouth to grab things which we cannot see. Then he folds his legs tightly against his body, gives one flick of that tail-sail, and shoots like a long bullet through the water.

Looking around further we notice that the Beaver lodge is located in the upper pool, and appears to be occupied. On a log near the far shore a large Spiny Softshell Turtle raises its prehistoric head to glance slowly around its world. A pair of Hooded Mergansers cruise by on the pond, followed by a pair of Black Ducks who choose not to stay. Zebra Swallowtails and Painted Lady butterflies flutter by.

Along the shore Soft Rush has formed spiky tufts. American Rush is also present, a three-sided exception to the alliterative mnemonic "rushes are round." Most of the nearby area is coated with soft Ground Pine. We play "fetch the stick," Chips' favorite water game. He dries soft and silky, a clean and happy dog.

Later, Rich explains that all these small hills are old slag piles left from coal mining. Given time, nature softens slag piles as surely as the Adirondacks were worn down to stumps of their former selves. Despite their ecologically unpopular genesis the pools are clear and unpolluted as evidenced by the presence of the salamanders. We are hoping the Beavers will also entertain us. And indeed, one does appear. We watch it head for shore, strip the juicy twigs and leaves from a sapling, and carry them back to the lodge. He (or she) shows us that the lodge has a back door in a small bay on the far side of the conical home. As the twilight deepens an odd rattling call comes from a tree-top. "What bird is that?" Rich asks. I have no idea. The call is answered by one similar, but farther away. More and more of the odd calls chime in till the sound is deafening. "Tree frogs!" we exclaim.

With the addition of a chorus of Peepers as night falls, we wonder if we will be able to sleep at all. As it turns out, I can sleep with a thousand frogs in the trees and the water. As I drift off, somehow I hear a Barred Owl who-who-ing beneath the high-pitched din. But I cannot sleep with one frog singing between the tent and the rain fly. His leggy silhouette shows through the nylon, throat pulsating with every breath. In vain I try to drift off despite the screaming just above my eardrum, but eventually I slink outside. I can't catch my soloist, but I manage to chase him back to the trees. Sleep comes to me again.

Morning completes the magic. The fog has returned and the sun, in trying to burn through, has dipped the world in molten gold. The Beaver, also edged in gold, treats us to another appearance before we leave this delightful campsite.

A magical, golden morning

But leave we must. This is a hike after all. Today we walk by small, dirty shacks, also reminders of the coal-mining history. To all appearances, the occupants can barely feed themselves, but most places have two or more dogs chained outside. This culture is also ephemeral; the developers have bought out whole hillsides and the starter castles are sometimes back lot to back door with the shacks.

A man in a truck stops to chat with us. He is a Buckeye Trail supporter who owns the farm on the next corner. When we reach that turn we meet him again in his yard. He invites Rich to return and paint blue blazes on his fence posts. The barn is blazoned with the family name and four generations of given names from "Silas- 1880" on down to "Paul- 1990," the man we are visiting with. He sadly shares that he has one non-farming daughter, and she has no children. No more generations will be painted on the barn. The names will fade and peel; perhaps the barn will never again be used to store sweet summer hay. It will sag and return to the earth. More ephemerata.

We have one more night before the hike is completed. We camp, with permission, in a private woods on a hill. Tonight's music has an out-of-tune rhythm section. Just over the ridge an oil well motor is humming and sputtering "put-put-PUTTTT----put-PUT. At dusk a Whip-poor-will adds the melody line... maybe. The sound is so insistent and repetitive that we aren't sure if it's a bird or just a new voice from the pump. It lasts till we fall asleep. In the morning Rich says that he awoke later in the night. The pump had turned off, but the

Whip-poor-will was still playing the same tune.

A few more miles and we reach the end point for this trip. After retrieving Rich's truck we decide to try to pick up the four miles we had skipped at the beginning. The water has fallen significantly. We have to bushwack around only two places where the trail is still under water. But Rich points out seven places where we would have had to make long detours if we had tried to hike it the first day. Change. Conditions always change.

I am especially happy that we have walked these four miles. Adding them puts my North Country Trail miles over 1000. This total is a number that I definitely want to change regularly.

We've had a good time and agree that we would be happy to hike together again. We part ways in stages, stopping once at a convenience store, and then finally we go our separate ways where we take different routes around one of the detours which is still in place.

Another hike completed, this one forever defined by the magical campsite of the Gray Tree Frogs and the golden morning. "And where is this wonderful place?" you ask, desiring to visit it too.

You won't find it, for like Peter Pan's Never-Never Land "it might be miles beyond the moon, or right there where you stand." Remember, Rich did the mapping for this trip; I never was sure exactly where we were most of the time. I doubt I'll ever find it again.

"Then was it only a place in your imagination?" you ask. "Did you take too much literary license and invent this mystical pond of the eft and the turtle?"

No, it was real. It was real, but it lasted only one wet spring season. Rich returned to that same place later in the year. The Beavers and ducks were gone; the wetland plants withered and brown, the water all evaporated away. Only the green fire of the Ground Pine burned bright on the changing hills. There is only One who does not change. All else is ephemerata.

48 miles this hike
Boat Dock Two to Ohio 664
Morgan, Athens, Hocking
    and Perry Counties, OH
1002 miles total NCT

A Nice Walk in the Woods
33 - July 1-12, 1998

We watched the sky for almost an hour before we spotted the tiny black dot. The dot became a dragonfly. The dragonfly became... a larger dragonfly and landed with a buzz on the runway. It looked barely large enough to carry one person into the sky, but the pilot hustled Mathilda into the passenger seat and away she flew to a new life. The pilot, her soon-to-be husband Vint, had no emotional attachment to us. In fact, we had never met him before, and he just wanted to move Mathilda quickly into his world. But we felt the abrupt loss of our long-time hiking companion deeply. At least we had enjoyed her company for the two weeks of this pleasant stroll through eastern Wisconsin. We had no epiphanies, but neither were there any plan-changing difficulties. There were no "exceedingly steep climbs," but the scenery was consistently interesting. The weather was neither too hot nor too cold. We never even had a squabble, except with one cache tree. It was just a nice walk in the woods.

If there was any residual unpleasantness left from the Adirondack trip it has been forgotten and Marie and I eagerly anticipate having Mathilda hike with us this summer. The Wisconsin terrain is sure to have more stable footing, and she decides to come with us despite Vint's anxiety over how close the hike is to their approaching wedding. We are most happy with her decision. She makes another decision that we appreciate too. For this hike she agrees to carry a walking stick. Notice that I did carefully say "carry." Most of the time she just holds it horizontally in one hand, but we occasionally catch her actually using it as an additional support. All of our expectations about the treadway do prove true and we three humans easily hike at the same pace. Chips is ever content to be on the go, with another new path to explore.

Marie comes in her short-bed, red Toyota truck for this trip. With sporty wooden side rails, this vehicle looks much more appropriate for camping than the Chrysler New Yorker ever did. Mathilda takes turns riding with each of us as we make our way to Weber Lake Campground in eastern Wisconsin. The setting is beautiful, a small teardrop of a lake tucked in with trees and low hills. Another good thing about this location is that we can travel on our first hiking day to the Wisconsin/ Michigan border in one car and then walk to our campsite with only day packs.

So on Thursday morning we park our car behind "The Corkscrew" package store. You may wonder that I remember the name of the store, but it's not difficult when there is a 20-foot corkscrew holding the sign to remind you. After just a few road miles, and with some good directions from Bill Menke in hand, we join the Uller Ski Trail where it follows the Gogebic Ridge. Our first day is easy, through dry warm woods, and we return to Weber Lake in time for a relaxing evening.

Friday morning we complete the final vehicular logistics, don the full packs, and begin with Marie's "favorite," a bushwack around the north end of Weber Lake. We cross small wetlands on soggy hummocks and clamber around a few scattered glacial boulders. Finally we are heading westward on the Sullivan Fire Trail, a jeep road of very low maintenance. The sun is bright; small marshy areas near the road are filled with Golden Alexanders, Michigan Lilies and milkweed, surrounded by busy butterflies: large, orange Great Spangled Frittilaries, and small orange skippers with an occasional black-and-white White Admiral. The bed of Potato Creek is lumpy with brown rounded rocks, which suggested its vegetabular name. We pause to put on our sandals in order to ford the stream. Even vehicles must drive through the water here. Marie hollers, "Move now, there's a truck coming!" and we grab packs, shoes and the dog and leap for the grassy edge of the road. A 4x4 truck roars across the ford; we are not sure that the driver even notices our presence. A few seconds later a handsome Chocolate Lab trots through the stream. He is wearing a serious radio collar, and we assume that he is being trained from the truck. Nevertheless, he is at least interested in stopping to say a doggie hello. At our first crossing of Tyler's Fork we wade the edges to cool our hot feet. Startled by tickly nibblings at our toes, a closer look reveals hundreds of tiny pale crayfish in the shallows. There are so many that they can't all get out of the way of our curiosity. We capture some and examine their amusing diminutive claws, feet, bug-eyes, and waving antennae.

Saturday finds us nearing the end of another road and heading into the woods with compass in hand again. At least Marie was warned ahead of time that we would have this one more short bushwack to take us crosslots to the powerline beside Copper Falls State Park. This is supposed to be easy. Bill's notes say: "follow the power line to the bluff, return 300 feet on the south edge, and watch for the narrow trail down the hill." But ahead of us, a hemlock swamp stretches across the right-of-way. We sensibly choose the uphill side to look for a route around, but oddly, the land falls away ahead of us through the trees, lower and lower, and swampier and swampier. Backtracking to the downhill side yields an easy traverse, and we find the trail down to the State Park as the sun is beginning to send its slanting rays into the early evening.

We have reserved one of the two backpacker sites in the park, and we find them easily. The first one near the latrine is occupied, so we proceed to the other designated area, near the east bank of the Bad River. We have read the words "sandstone cliffs" on the map and are expecting some interesting geologic scenery, but are not prepared for the intense beauty of the site that will be our home for the night. In that late sunshine the 100-foot high rock walls glow in tones of red and gold. The river at their base shimmers a deep midnight blue, laced with white riffles. Looking eastward upstream, a point of rock juts into the water, a golden goodbye to the afternoon.

Evening light on the Bad River

We can only speculate that the other backpackers have passed up this beautiful site because they desire to be closer to the latrine. What a mundane choice!

The attempt to hang our cache bag tonight is another good example of the vagaries of life on the trail. We locate an appropriate tree, but I can't find a chunk of stick that I like for throwing the rope over the branch. I had been impressed with an idea we had observed a man use in the Adirondacks, so I decide to try it. He had used a rock in a small nylon bag as a weight. I borrow the bag that holds my compass, fill it with a smooth rock from the riverbank, tie it to the lead rope and give it a toss. It settles nicely in the crotch of the tree that I am aiming for. And there's the problem! It can not be coaxed to fall through the crotch. It can not be pulled back down for another throw; it has snagged on something. Half an hour later I haven't budged the bag, and I grudgingly fetch Marie for help. With both of us pulling together we manage to break the bag's nylon drawstring. A concerted search for a better stick and a different tree eventually leads to hanging the cache for the night. As far as we know the gray nylon bag with the nice rock is still in the first tree, and I'm cured of trying that trick again. Chunks of stick are easily replaced, and a clove hitch in the rope tied to it will always work loose with a few tugs, even if it catches in a tree.

As to that latrine the other campers wanted so badly to be near... it is not that wonderful. Marie's report, after her first visit there, informs us that the entire building shifts like a rocking chair on its foundation!

On Sunday we walk the length of the park[1] at a leisurely pace to take in the many waterfalls and interesting geology of the area. Two billion years ago the sedimentary floor of the Cambrian sea became infused with iron from streams carrying the dissolved mineral. But one billion years ago lava began to ooze from the Mid-Continent Rift. For 1400 miles the North American continent was torn, from eastern Lake Superior to Wichita, Kansas. The iron-rich sediments were locked in place by this volcanic layer, awaiting human treasure seekers with the keys of knowledge to unlock their metallic potential.

Minnesota and Wisconsin might have been an ocean apart if the rift had not inexplicably closed. But before this miraculous healing occurred, enough molten lava had flowed to cover the Lake Superior region with thousands of feet of volcanic rock: in some places 60,000 feet deep. This is known as the Keweenawan "flows and sediments," named for the Keweenaw Peninsula of Upper Michigan. This peninsula is a major feature of the south shore of the present Lake Superior, which is defined by northern Wisconsin, where we are now, and Upper Michigan. Keweenaw is Ojibway for "a landing place;" if the rift had not closed we might have been ending our hike with a happy landing of a cool drink and an ocean swim on a white sand beach of western Wisconsin!

But the rift did close. Cubic miles of lava weigh more than a pound or two, not to mention that they had just vacated a great space below the earth's crust. Their sheer weight caused the region to sag, and thus was born Lake Superior. As the new lake was created, settling lower and lower, new streams and rivers rushed down jagged gashes to join it. They carried with them broken pieces of those Keweenawan rocks, sediments of boulders, sand and mud. As the Bad River and its sisters clawed and hammered their way to the lake, layer upon layer the conglomerate, sandstone and shale were created. Finally, as the Lake continued to nestle deeper into the earth some of the layers succumbed to gravity, cracking, tilting and sliding to fantastic angles.

One more Ice Age, the one humans may have been around to enjoy instead of that ocean beach, left behind more boulders, rocks and thick red clay.

Copper Falls State Park is a showcase of all these geologic marvels. Without the map in hand as we walk through the park it would have been difficult to sort out the tributaries and many twists of the Bad River. The varieties of rock also have various resistances to the rushing water. Thus the river has cut a wildly meandering pathway where the rock was softest. We first pass Little Creek, a caramel stream slipping quietly along in a deep shale glen. It's all too easy to

---

[1] Dogs are no longer allowed in this section of the park.

forget that this 50-foot-deep gash was undoubtedly carved by waters not nearly so peaceful.

We take a side trail to see Devil's Gate, a narrow vertical cleft in the rocks. Dark walls of rock extend toward the middle of the Bad River from each side, indeed like a gate. Vertically tilted beds of conglomerate now stand as lumpy sentinels in the river channel. This sight is not on the main trail because here the river has taken a long westward horseshoe loop, turning completely back upon itself before continuing its northward flow.

Hiking farther upstream we pass Tyler's Cascades, on Tyler's Fork. These falls are low and wide with milky channels of frothy water, streaming over a black volcanic bed. This waterway joins the Bad River just below Brownstone Falls, now featuring a red lava shelf. An odd U-shaped dip in the rock wall beside and below the Falls is an overflow channel scoured by rocks during the Ice Age as Tyler's Fork impatiently strove to join the Bad River. If that description sounds odd, as if the Bad were almost beside Tyler's Fork rather than straight downstream, you have formed an accurate mental image. For here, where the two rivers meet, the Bad is forced into a tortuous turn to the left through a narrow channel with 100-foot walls. It is difficult to grasp, even when you are looking at it, that the main river is the one leaping northward through a small slit in the precipitous hard rock.

Tyler's Cascades

Just upstream (south) from this location is Copper Falls, from which the park takes its name. And here black lava is again the predominant rock. A few more yards of walking and we reach the concession stand where thick red mud banks mark an ancient Lake Superior shoreline. We have enjoyed the park so much that we make a reservation to come back to the same campsite on our last night together, after the planned hike is completed.

By lunchtime we reach the village of Mellen, one of the very earliest trail towns on the NCT. We welcome the opportunity to buy fresh nectarines and grapes for lunch, and cold drinks. And just for an extra ounce of comfort we come upon a picnic table at which to enjoy that meal! A few road miles in the afternoon and we enter the Chequamegon National Forest where we will enjoy off-road trail for the remaining 61 miles of this trip.

There a maze of ski trails presents us with quite a puzzle. The NCT does not seem to be blazed in a way to differentiate it from the other paths, and we have no clue which color code to follow.

"I think it's the yellow squares," Mathilda asserts. But then the yellow trail veers off in a direction unexpected from a careful scrutiny of our route marked on the topographic map.

"It's the yellow stacked with a blue," Marie offers. We follow this combination for a while, but come to a junction where no clear decision is obvious. While we are pondering this, two young men approach us along the westward route. They too are backpackers.

"Hey, can you tell us how to get to the parking lot? This place is impossible to figure out!" they exclaim.

"We sure can," we promise. "Do you know which way the North Country Trail goes?"

"Yup, it's the way we just came, and there is a shelter just about a mile ahead of you."

We explain the route by which they can reach their car, and stretch our legs for the shelter. The sky is becoming increasingly gray and a light rain has begun to fall. Our luck is surely better than the boys', since it was much farther to the parking than to the shelter. Not ten seconds after we step under its welcoming eaves and skin off our packs a torrential downpour begins.

We offer no apologies for setting up the tent inside the shelter. We are warm, dry, and mosquito-free on this very wet night. Sometime in the darkest hours I make a dash to the woods for a potty break. When I return everyone is awake, listening to some critter munching with great gusto on the shelter. It's probably a Porcupine, but we are unable to catch it in the beams of our flashlights. I quickly fall asleep again, but Mathilda and Marie are amused by the chewing for quite a while longer. "We are easily entertained," Marie offers apologetically.

In the morning Mathilda calmly points out that her feet have several "little ouch pouches." She says that she is going to concentrate on them really hard and make them turn into calluses. For our eternal optimist it seems to work; we never hear of her blisters again.

The Chequamegon trail includes sections of pathway which have been in place for several decades. This older trail was known as the North Country Trail, and lent its name to the National Trail. And it is a beautiful mother to her longer offspring. The forest floor is rich in nutrients, supporting unusual, specialized plants. Most plants manufacture their food through photosynthesis, and you probably remember from high school biology that these plants are recognized by their green leaves, colored by chlorophyll. These kinds of plants are classed as autotrophs. *Auto* = self, and *troph* = having to do with nutrition. However, we find example after example of heterotrophs: *hetero* = other. These plants draw their nutrition from outside sources. Heterotrophs are mostly represented by bacteria and fungi; however, there are over 2500 flowering plants which fall into this category. To see more than one or two examples on any hike is rare. But this hike is memorable for such plants.

We come upon whole openings filled with Squaw Root. This parasitic plant looks like slim pine cones growing erect through the brown fallen leaves. It particularly likes to feed on oak roots. Parasitic plants draw their nutritional needs from other living organisms. Saprophytes are a group of plants similar to parasites in that they are unable to meet their energy needs through photosynthesis, but they grow on decaying, rather than living matter. White, leafless Indian Pipes are a commonly seen saprophyte, and we find large glowing clumps of their ghostly stems. It's easy to see why its other common name is Corpse Plant. We also find examples of the similar, and also saprophytic, Pinesap, which might be mistaken for a yellowish Indian Pipe which is turning its multiple heads toward the sky.

On long hikes I always seem to find new examples of mushrooms and fungi. I'm no expert on these variable and diverse organisms, but they are always fascinating, and we find several bright magenta patches of Violet Branched Coral. The deadly but adorable Yellow Patches mushrooms continually tempt us to search beneath them for elvin houses. Many a rotting log sports Golden Fairy Helmet. Less colorful, but interesting are Horsehair Mushrooms, tiny tan parasols waving on fine black "horsehair" stalks. This patch is intriguingly growing from the center of a larger round tan fungus.

Some woodland orchids are heterotrophic and saprophytic; some are not.

Clockwise from top L: Heartleaved Twayblade, Pinesap, Puttyroot, Spotted Coralroot

Spotted Coralroot blooms are maroon and white with no green parts to be seen. Puttyroot also displays no green; we see a yellowish example, although it can also be purplish. Other orchids are autotrophic. We find a beautiful Heartleaved Twayblade in full bloom. *Auto* or *hetero*, orchids all require rich soil, and have blooms with a lip or sac-like lower petal. Their blooming time is usually very short; we feel quite fortunate to see three examples on one hike. Their beauty is stunning.

Autotrophs are the largest group of plants, which is not to say that they are all common. Shinleaf, a green plant with waxy bells, also requires rich soil. We also see Pale Corydalis. Despite its bright pink and yellow blooms it has chosen to grow from crevices in pink granite, rendering it almost invisible.

Some of our favorite plants are late Serviceberries that the birds have left for us to taste. Wonderful! And a whole meadow full of Red Raspberries slows us down for a few minutes. We are not at all intimidated by the footprint which shows that a bear has also been enjoying the berries.

But by far the strangest plants we encounter are the slime molds. Frankly, even though I loved my college Botany class, I had completely forgotten the Myxomycophytes. We had encountered Scrambled-Egg Slime (you can probably guess what that looks like) on earlier hikes. But I'll never forget about slime molds again. Ahead of us on the trail a patch of black mud, two by five feet, is shimmering wetly in the afternoon light. In fact, it appears to be moving, but that must be impossible. We move closer and "welcome to Eerie," Wisconsin, it IS moving, waving tiny stubby arms.

You can be sure that as soon as I returned home I began trying to find out what that patch of mud might have been! It was surely a slime mold, but that information is only moderately informative. Slime molds seem to be sometimes plants, sometimes animals. Even the experts can not agree where to place them. They have a three-phase lifestyle: the resting spore, the sexual stage, and the truly astonishing plasmodium. The resting spores are most like fungi when they grow small stalks or threads, containing spores which are dispersed by the wind. These stalks, threads and spores may have distinctive shapes or colors and are the visible forms we usually see. When the spores germinate they give birth to naked gametes. You may think that you too were once a cute little naked gamete, er... gamin, and yup, these babies grow up and mate with a buddy. But the similarity ends there. As soon as the gametes pick a partner the two fuse to become a zygote. As the zygotes grow they lose their cell walls and become a mass of protoplasm (think of the inside of an amoeba with no definitive outer edge) with many nuclei. Somehow this mass of fluid arranges itself into a fan-shaped network with vein-like branches. This plasmodium flows over surfaces like a Salvador Dali painting, surrounding and digesting bits of organic matter. Waste products are simply left behind as the plasmodium flows on. At some critical nutrition and size the organism again begins to produce spores. Our waving fingers may have been the spore stalks beginning to grow.

How bizarre and rich is the world! God once reminded Job of His vast and varied creation, and Job replied to the Lord, "I spoke of things I did not understand, things too wonderful for me to know!"

Flowers, fungi, molds, blue water, blue sky, gray and red rock continuously stimulate our visual sense. Three more sensory dimensions of this hike's unique memory matrix are filled: with the scent of hemlock on warm, damp days permeating the air, with a light breeze soothing the sweat from our skin, and with the chuckles and screechings of the loons. Finally, our taste buds are never ignored or deprived on these hikes.

I cringe at the trail tales of long-distance hikers subsisting on ramen noodles, rice, mac and cheese, and Snickers bars. It amazes me that AT thru-hikers don't return home with scurvy, although perhaps all the off-trail meals at nearby towns and hostels compensate for the terrible trail diets reported in books and journals. A friend of mine hiked the Pacific Crest Trail on a menu dominated by Doritos. It certainly can be done. However, after reading accounts of many 19th century expeditions ending with sore gums, loose teeth, weak legs, lassitude and death, I'm not sure why anyone would wish to tempt such a fate within a few miles of grocery stores featuring world-class produce sections. Not to mention that these junk food menus sound pretty boring.

Be assured that at home I am no gourmet cook. In fact, I've largely given up the kitchen role. Years of cooking for battalions of teen-age boys and a fussy family have cured me of most of my culinary ambitions. Yet, trail cooking somehow seems different. I enjoy the challenge of planning nutritious, appealing menus and transforming them into compact, lightweight trail meals that are easy to fix in camp. We've always said that on our hikes even if the day is long, hot, cold, wet, painful, horrible, or otherwise less than ideal that we always have a good meal to look forward to. *The Well-Fed Backpacker* by June Fleming has been our bible, and by this time we've also invented a good many recipes and menus of our own.

Generally we fix one hot meal a day. Menus include such things as tuna curry with rice and peanuts, cabbage salad, and lemon pudding for dessert; spaghetti with hamburger, veggie-plops, and cookies; salmon fettucine with spinach and a hot-fruit compote. The list can go on for more than 30 complete meals. Now the challenge has become which ones to choose for a particular hike.

We almost always eat a cold breakfast in order to break camp faster. Usually this consists of a fortified bar or cereal of some kind and a homemade fruit leather. Our favorites include Paul Bunyan Bars (named on the Chippewa hike, with peanut butter and bacon, P.B.B.), Rhubarb Torte, Grandola Bars, Protein Power Cereal, Mountain Cereal, and Peachy Keen. In honor of Wisconsin we have named a sweet treat with a chocolate striped middle Badger Bars. Favorite trail mixes are named Northern Nocturne, Sunny Day, Tropical Storm, and Carnival. My longing for vegetables has resulted in the invention of a number of trail salads in addition to the afore-mentioned veggie-plops. We've created creamy cucumber and onion salad, an olive salad, mushroom sandwiches, and quite a few variations of cole slaw. The classic trail staples, gorp, mixed dried fruits and nuts, peanut butter and cheese, are featured regularly. Fleming's Trail Shakes have become a staple of our snack diet. These are high-protein milk-based mixes, kept in a plastic bag. Add a little water, mix and drink; one is guaranteed to perk you up for the final three miles of the day. We've expanded the flavor list to include chocolate, dark chocolate malt, eggnog, coconut, Gatorade (my favorite), raspberry, cherry, coffee and strawberry.

Key to all these menus is a good dehydrator and a decent scale to weigh portions to the nearest ounce. For a week or so prior to each trip the kitchen becomes a scene of organized chaos with 50 or so meals being prepared simultaneously. Ingredients are in wildly varying stages of chopping, dehydrating, combining, labeling and weighing. The folks who are impressed by our neat and organized meal packs on the trail might have other labels for me, could they watch the food preparation marathon. "Anal" is a word that has come to the minds of some. The weight of each meal or snack pack is entered in a spreadsheet, totaled and divided by the people and the days, crunching out a value of "pounds per person per day" (ppd). The books say this number should be 2 ppd. Well, we soon found that for us gals, this amount is way too much food. But for David, when he joins us, it is not enough. Marie and I are able to hike, feeling comfortably fed, with 1.25 ppd. This amount rides easily on our backs too!

It's a good thing that Marie is used to my idiosyncrasies. She calmly follows my pre-hike instructions to separate the menus into rows by day with the lighter meals clustered into the longer walks between supply pick-ups. To ensure that each pile provides variety, don't pick all the rice-based menus for the first four days. Place menus with items which might not keep well for two trail weeks near the beginning. Then the neat rows of daily meal and snack packs are boxed for immediate placement in the backpacks, or into supply boxes with labels of their own. Other hiking companions have not been so patient, but have been heard to proclaim with despair, "You mean I have to decide right now what I am going to eat a week from Tuesday?" The answer is YES!

But such pre-trip pedantry results in carefree meal preparations on the hikes. One packet pulled from inside the pack provides the cook of the day with everything needed to complete the meal. Instructions are printed on a chit of paper placed in the bag. With the stove, a few utensils and some water, the cook usually has a great meal prepared in under 30 minutes. *Bon Appetit!*

Early in the hike we invent a game. At the end of each day we have to tell each other what was the best and worst part of the day. Things like yummy blueberries, bright red Bunchberry or white water lilies, swimming in warm soothing lakes, or the vistas above the Marengo River feature prominently on the good side of the ledger. We have a lot of trouble with the bad side. The worst thing we can ever think of is that at the end of a day of hiking we are tired. As we've said already, a nice walk in the woods! At Beaver Lake, on our day off, a supply box is delivered to us by Tana Turonie of the Chequamegon Chapter of the NCTA. To the good side of the ledger Marie adds, "The packs are lightest the last day before supply pick-up!"

Mathilda's shy contribution to the list sums up both the joy and the challenge of backpacking. "Wherever we go, at the end of the day, there's a bedroom tent!"

Mathilda

The Chequamegon includes two small designated patches of Wilderness, Porcupine Lake and Rainbow Lake. Such areas are protected from resource extraction, any motorized or even mechanized devices, and from blazes as well. After following the trail into Rainbow for 45 minutes, we arrive back at the sign where we first entered. This is a more time-consuming way to determine which fork in the path to follow than we would prefer, but it does work!

Even though small, the Wilderness areas are much wilder, as their name would suggest. We enjoy a swim one warm mid-day in Porcupine Lake. We pass up Rainbow Lake, holding out for Tower Lake, but the loons inform us that this one is theirs. They chortle at us, swimming close enough for us to see their checkered backs and striped breasts. Small wetlands are edged in Water Shield and spathed Swamp Calla. Large drowned stands of hemlock indicate the long-time work of the Beavers. One *Castor canadensis* has apparently finished his dam and moved on to cutting trees for a log cabin. A freshly gnawed and fallen tree is ten inches in diameter! We doubt that even this largest American rodent can move a tree of this size. What was he thinking?

At Esox Lake the shame of the rope-throwing fiasco at Copper Falls is vindicated. With a rowboat full of boys watching I heave the cache rope over a high branch on the first try and finish hanging the bag with a nonchalant smirk. I hope they are properly impressed.

Water Shield at the wetland edge

The final morning we pass from the cooler hemlock-scented forest into an open sandy region heavy with the scent of Sweetfern in the hot sun. Abruptly, much sooner than any of us expects, we arrive at the car. With a change of shoes, and our packs stowed behind the hatchback we are hardly distinguishable from the many tourists at the A&W Rootbeer stand which is our first stop. Only the observant might notice that we are somewhat different as we each gulp down two large size cold drinks, and buy a full serving of ice cream for the hot but smiling dog as well as for ourselves.

After a shower and change of clothes we capture Tana and take her to Ashland to eat at the Soo Line Depot. This train station has been made over into a wonderful, ornate restaurant with cool, dark wood and leaded, beveled glass window panes. Across the road, railroad Steam Engine 950, a 2-10-0 Decapod, is being restored. As we approach the restaurant an elderly gentleman named John accosts us and begins to tell how he is the last living fireman who actually worked the rails on that engine. Tale after tale of the days of iron ore roll from his memory. Have we seen the ore docks on the bay? Do we know how the hopper cars lined up above the chutes to send their loads tumbling down into the holds of the waiting ships? Finally we manage to pull away, enter the restaurant and order our meal. Sadly, I do not have my tape recorder with me, so John's tales have probably passed into that great sucking vortex of unrecorded and unremembered history.

Only one more night together remains, and one more story from this hike has yet to be told. It could be titled "Mathilda's Revenge." Remember that we have reserved the backpacker site at Copper Falls?

We had listened to John's train stories for nearly an hour before eating. By the time we take Tana back home and drive to the Copper Falls parking lot it is nearly dark. We still have a two-mile walk through the park to reach our campsite. Shouldering our packs one more time we head north along the well-defined park trail. However, the farther north we go the darker the night, and the less developed the pathway. For the final half-mile Marie and I are progressing slowly, the lead person continuously warning the rest of us about roots, rocks, step-downs or ups which we cannot see. Shortly, from behind us comes a soft giggle. "What's so funny?" we demand.

Mathilda's demure but honest reply, "Now you are walking how I walk all the time!"

100 miles this hike
Hurley, WI through
    Chequamegon NF
1103 miles total NCT

Wheelin' @ 3 FPR
34 - August 22, 1998

I have yet to hike the few miles which the Forest Service tacked on to the ones I adopted in my home county, Mason County. Truth be told, I wasn't sure that I wanted to adopt quite so many miles (nine total), but they said that the parking situation and the record keeping would be easier if I take this extra piece, so I have complied. Today I will see the remainder of the piece I have agreed to maintain. And I have the chance to try out another fun activity at the same time: wheeling. But let me explain what has led up to this day when I am pushing a clicking, fluorescent orange wheel along the trail.

This fall I am planning to increase my participation in the North Country Trail Association another notch. Along its length the trail is maintained by local chapters of the Association. The miles near my home "belong" on paper to the large Western Michigan Chapter. But I live 100 miles from their center of activity in Grand Rapids. These are also some of the oldest miles of the NCT. Since the hotbed of early activity in the 1980's was in Michigan, the Forest Service and a number of enthusiastic volunteers created the 120 miles of trail to be found within the Manistee National Forest. Now these miles are 15 or more years old. Treadway and structures are aging. The blazing needs to be refurbished. This northern section is too far from Grand Rapids to receive much attention from them. The Forest Service has neither funds nor the human resources to keep the trail in tip-top condition. Meanwhile the neglected trail needs a lot of love.

Until now I've hiked the Trail when I could, told lots of people about it, and adopted the miles that I want to call my own. But this summer Bob Papp, Executive Director of the NCTA, has asked me to consider starting a chapter to maintain the trail in the area I call home. Knowing that this would move me readily from the comfortable role of occasional hiker to that of volunteer administrator, I groused a bit. But in the end, I knew that it was what needed to be done for the trail. The kick-off meeting, when I hope to convince at least ten people to join the Association and charter a chapter, is just a week away.

Additionally, at the North Country Trail Association Annual Conference last summer, representatives from the chapters were allowed to offer suggestions and then vote on their top priority for NCTA headquarters. The easy winner was to create consistent, quality maps of the trail. Without further ado, Bob Papp began working on the budget to determine how this could be done. Within a few months funding was procured and a cartographer, Tiffany Halfmann, was hired.

Because of the popularity of the section of trail maintained by what will be the new local chapter here, the first official NCTA map will cover 65 miles of the trail in the Manistee National Forest.

Volunteers are needed right away to measure and check the location of the trail against Tiffany's growing database. The National Park Service owns a Global Positioning unit with good accuracy, but for the average person, map, compass and wheel are still a good source of information. Our new chapter will have the chance to collect quite a lot of data, and today I get to try my hand at this new skill. Tiffany has provided me with a four-color topographic map showing the route of the trail according to her current records. It is my job to double-check the location of the treadway, to measure distances between roads and other points of interest, note parking areas, trailheads, services, scenic views, and other important features.

The bright orange wheel looks a bit like a skinny bicycle tire with a handle. The wheel's diameter is exactly three feet. At each linear foot there is a small peg which mechanically advances a five-digit counter, so with each turn of the wheel I have measured Three Feet Per Revolution, 3 FPR. Carrying a notebook and pencil, I record the number on the counter at places of interest. I plan to note the major turns in the trail by their compass bearing in degrees: North is 0 or 360, East is 90, South 180, and West 270. At home, I'll plug it all into a spreadsheet, divide the numbers by 5280, and I will have the mileage from my starting point to each place in my book.

00000, mile 0.000: Freesoil Trailhead. There is parking for about five cars, and an information kiosk. Services are available 9.5 miles east at the village of Freesoil. The trail enters the woods on the north side of paved Freesoil Road.

00555, mile 0.105: Turn to bearing 280, join an old railroad bed which first passes through a hemlock grove and then into a bottomland hardwood swamp. There are five small bridges across streams, and the trail is lined with Musclewood, Ironwood, and Leatherwood.

02686, mile 0.509: Leave the railroad grade bearing 340, and climb a small hill to join a ridge that runs roughly North-northwest. Now the swamp can be seen below and to the right.

05280, mile 1.000: No real landmark at one mile from the trailhead, but the trail continues through dry, mature forest of oak and pine.

10863, mile 2.057: Cross a sand two-track which must lead west to Tyndall Road. The trail is quite close to the road, but unless you catch a glimpse of a vehicle you would hardly realize this.

13077, mile 2.477: Reach the turnoff to Beartrack Campground. This Forest Service campground is located just over a mile to the north of the trail. I will measure that trail later.

13531, mile 2.563: Tyndall Road, a graded gravel road, where there is parking for two cars.

A stodgy Porcupine is there to greet me. We nod to each other, but decline an embrace.

This has been a real learning experience. My notebook contains many more numbers than I've included here. It is slow work to watch the wheel, making sure that it does not bounce too much, to take notes and record the numbers from the counter. The dog thinks this lack of speed is really boring. But I am happy to do it. I feel as if I know this section of trail intimately.

The fine details of the trail and its related data imposed on a topographic grid – a map of utopian perfection – are now forever imprinted on the wish list of my mind. Today I've reached another level from which there can be no turning back.

3 miles this hike
Freesoil Rd. to Tyndall Rd.
Lake County, MI
1105 miles total NCT

Down a Memory of a Lane
35 - October 24-26, 1998

The cement is cool against my stomach and the sun warms my back. The disparity of temperature sensation between my front and back sides is surprisingly satisfying. I am resting – sprawled across the exposed end of a huge round cement culvert along a county road in western Ohio on the final day of this hike, and my head is filled with tidbits of memorable events of these three days. The trip began with a drive on a sunny Friday afternoon that could only be described as "golden." A hard frost had caused large quantities of leaves to fall while still brightly colored, and yellow pools beneath aspens and maples glowed with fluorescent fervor. I watched a farmer harvest the last white-gold square of wheat from the center of a field, and in another field golden kernels of corn sparkled fluidly as they poured from the harvester into the hopper.

In contrast to this serenity, I also passed a terrible accident which had occurred in the opposite lanes of the divided highway, US 23. Twisted metal lay everywhere and a Medi-vac helicopter sat on the roadway awaiting what I can only assume was a badly injured, but still living, victim to be extracted from a vehicle.

The crescent moon has been beautiful at night, with the hoots of a Great Horned Owl, and the clear liquid trill of some other bird for counterpoint.

A not-so-placid memory in the dark: the night I spent at Loramie State Park a family roared in when most everyone was already sleeping. Their truck had no muffler. They jangled their metal poles, loudly discussed setting up the tent, and dragged a heavy cooler, thumping across the blacktop parking area, accompanied by their two barking dogs. Next we all listened to *The Simpsons* on their portable TV, followed by someone's persistent coughing until finally the noise petered out.

Although interesting, these memories are but fragments. My scattered thoughts are beginning to focus on transportation routes: roads, rails, canals, rivers and lanes.

My path has taken me along a magical remnant of a lane between two farm fencerows. Along the narrow lane, ahead of me in the slanting light, Robins and rabbits flit and scurry to lead me deeper and deeper into the enchanted forest. I have entered a fairy tale, the untold destination at the end of the story, a mystery to be explored. Well, at least it feels that way for the brief half-mile before the spell is broken and I'm back on plain gray asphalt. I'm hiking in flat northwest Ohio, through land long tamed for human use. This farm lane is trapped between fences separated by just a few feet. I speculate that two feuding landowners might once have installed the fences to prevent trespassing by the neighbor. The age of the trees guarantees that the lane has been preserved for at least 50 years; its lack of width indicates that it was never intended to be used by large vehicles.

A quick jog on a county road and I'm again following the Miami-Erie Canal, often on the original towpath. The canal operated along 249 miles from Cincinnati to Toledo. Now remnants of the canal stitch themselves through the landscape, appearing and disappearing regularly as I hike along for these three days. In some places preservation has been a priority and the towpath is gated and marked as a trail. In other places where the engineered waterway must have continued there stretches only a cornfield, as if the canal has ducked underground briefly before emerging a mile farther away. Some sections of the canal are filled with water, attractive lawns running down to its straight banks. Other times the canal remains as a dismal and malodorous muddy ditch, or only a dry linear depression lined with brown fallen leaves.

Memorabilia of the canal is seen sporadically along the ditch, like so much litter. Yet a century and a half ago this apparent litter was state-of-the-art transportation machinery, and the ditch was an artificial river, bustling with commerce and travelers. Mile marker 126 still stands beside the trail, a thick limestone block with a rounded top and the number deeply chiseled in the stone. Near Lake Loramie the trail leaves the main canal, but crosses a dry side channel on what looks like a wooden bridge bristling with hand wheels and gears. Lake Loramie was once a source of feeder water for the Canal. This bridge is the access to open the watergates to let that water flow to the main channel.

Wheels to open the feeder canal watergates

Loramie has another claim to canal fame. Despite the conventional wisdom that says a marble dropped on northwest Ohio will not roll at all, if you consider this idea you will realize that it can not be true. The Great Lakes, whose waters flow eastward to the Atlantic Ocean via the St. Lawrence River, border Ohio to the north. But the Ohio River, which flows west to the Mississippi and the Gulf of Mexico, forms the state's southern border. These are two of the major North American watersheds. Somewhere between these borders must be a divide, no matter how flat the state seems. If you have been to the Dayton area you might suspect that divide to be found in this hilly region, but you would be wrong. Much farther north, at Loramie, in the midst of land which appears so level, you reach the Loramie Summit, 512 feet higher than the Ohio River, and 395 feet above Lake Erie. Over 100 locks were required to lift and lower the packets and cargo boats which plied canal waters. Many of these structures, in various conditions – decomposition through preservation – can be seen along the trail.

The canals had their short heyday, from the early 1800's through mid-century, when the railroads quickly captured folks' imagination and commerce. Mules simply could not compete with the speed and towing ability of steam engines. And trains could run all year long; freezing water did not stop their travel.

Rail lines are still important to the region. I slept in my car the first night, pulling into a dim vehicle trace which led back near a double railroad track. All night long, every hour, a train came through, first one direction, then the other. These are now Conrail, Consolidated Railways, tracks, one of the huge conglomerated lines designed to save the entire system from bankruptcy. But these lines were previously owned by the CCCStL, Chicago, Cincinnati, Cleveland and St. Louis Railroad. The CCCStL might be best remembered for capturing the United States train speed record in 1966, 183 mph, with a Jet-Powered Budd engine. This record still stands in the US, where true high-speed rail has yet to become a reality.

A short line, the RJCW, Robert J. Corman Western, also still operates in the area around St. Marys. For much of my walk this line has paralleled both the canal route and Ohio Route 66. Grain, fertilizer, aluminum, rubber, plastics, steel, and tomatoes carried by these trains reflect both the agricultural and industrial nature of the region.

Today I have passed a monument to an even older transport route made by white man. The marker isn't particularly useful for learning anything, but it does serve as a reference point. It says "General Harmar Military Trail – 1790." I am not impressed by this dry bit of information; it needs some details to give it value.

Throughout the late decades of the eighteenth century the native peoples of the Midwest clashed continually with the frontiersmen and settlers from the East. The Miami, Shawnee, Pottawatomi, Kickapoo, Ottawa, Chippewa, Sac, Fox, Winnebago and other nations were constantly pressured by the influx of new and different peoples. Perhaps everyone could have lived in harmony, but greed and cultural differences seem to win out every time. The Europeans would force one tribe to sell or yield the rights to a piece of land, usually a piece that was considered to belong to a different tribe or clan. One Delaware Chief put it succinctly, "I point to a horse in the meadow and say to you that I agree to sell it to you. I even sign a paper to that end. But the horse belongs to another, the meadow is not mine and the land upon which they stand belongs not to me. Can you then claim that you have legally bought [them]?"

But of course the new Americans did claim just that... some through ignorance: "Aren't all Indians alike?" Sadly, we must admit that most of these treaties were conceived in malfeasance and dedicated to the proposition that white men would own the land because they could. Despite the egregious error made by both "red" and "white" that painted all persons of the other color with the same black brush, there was probably nothing that could have stopped that "westward expansion," as Europe burst its population seams.

In 1789, at the first meeting of the Congress of the United States under its new Constitution, Ohio was recognized as a separate Territory, and the way was paved for its statehood. In stark contrast to this inclusion of Ohio, the Indians still were fighting to exclude all whites from the region and to keep them south of the Ohio River. The late 1700's were particularly brutal for anyone attempting to live in or near Ohio. There is plenty of depravity and terrorism to go around without portraying one side as more evil than the other. The Indians were perhaps more likely to torture their victims, but unprovoked hit-and-run attacks by both sides were the norm. "The only good Indian is a dead Indian," was no idle boast.

The young United States was not about to let this situation continue. There was money to be made in land speculation, and the smell of the fear on the frontier wafted even to Washington. That's Washington, as in George, the first President. He sent notice to the newly promoted Brigadier General Josiah Harmar to prepare for a possible expedition to subdue the Indians. Harmar was enjoying the perks of his rank, in hard liquor, at the recently built Fort Washington at the mouth of the Great Miami River in the town of Losantiville, better known to us as Cincinnati, Ohio. Harmar was not the greatest military hero of the Revolution. He hated militia troops, and often said so. His drunkenness was commonly acknowledged. Yet, there he was, and this responsibility would be his.

This invasion was supposed to be kept secret, but secrets were difficult to keep on the frontier. Rumors flew and yet the preparations continued. Harmar was to march up the Miami River into the heart of Indian country to punish and humble the somewhat confederated tribes. The tribes had established a headquarters at Kekionga, "The Glorious Gate," located at the headwaters of the Maumee River, where Fort Wayne, Indiana now is found. Kekionga was no flimsy town of a few bark huts or teepees. Over 3000 people lived there in 800 plus homes.

The outskirts of the town did host stereotypical portable Indian dwellings, but the core of the metropolis was made of sturdy log cabins, furnished with European finery. Many high-ranking Native Americans were not strangers to comfortable lifestyles. Regular streets had been laid out, and the central square was faced with stores fronted with wooden sidewalks. Kekionga was to be the target of Harmar's strike.

Before such a military expedition could be mounted, politics needed to be tended to. There was concern that an attack on the city, which hosted several British trading posts, would be construed as an attack on the British Empire. The last thing the new United States wanted was to re-open hostilities with England. So the British were notified to give the traders time to withdraw, naively thinking that they would not warn the tribes. But the British had always been thick with the Indians.

So Kekionga was warned. Harmer marched in September of 1790. His force consisted of 1453 men, 80% of whom were the militia he so despised. Yet Harmar had on his side more than 10 times the warriors the Indians could muster. He had three artillery pieces with him, two cannons and a howitzer. And they apparently marched past the spot where I am standing today. They marched to Kekionga and found it deserted and already burned to the ground by the Indians themselves. Harmar, apparently not much of a strategist either, split his force and on three consecutive raids sent small groups out to chase down the warriors. Each of these detachments was ambushed and destroyed by Indians waiting for just such a foolish move. On October 23, Harmar finally ordered an all-out assault on the Indians. But he was possibly drunk that day, as he was many days; he never once used the artillery they had dragged those many miles. Under Blue Jacket and Little Turtle the tribes fought fiercely and Harmar ordered a full retreat, back to Cincinnati. Victory this time was with the Indians. The US forces suffered 183 men killed, the tribes only 27.

Yet the remainder of the inscription on the monument at my feet subtly tells of the ultimate victor. "About 300 feet north, Thomas Thatcher, first Shelby County settler built his cabin – 1805."

What was so special about the present location of Fort Wayne that would cause the Indians to establish such a large multi-tribal settlement there? Yet another kind of transportation lane, one extremely important before the time of railroads and pavement, is rivers. Kekionga's glorious gate was a reference to headwaters and portages, which like the spokes of a wheel, led from Kekionga to significant waterways navigable by canoe. The Maumee was a direct passage to Lake Erie; from the Maumee, one could also enter the Auglaize, and reach the Great Miami and the Ohio River via that route. The St. Joseph led northward into the villages of the Pottawatomies and

Ottawas, and a short portage led to another, separate St. Joseph River which fed directly into Lake Michigan. The St. Marys flowed south and east to connect with other villages in Ohio. Other short portages put travelers in the Eel River, or the Wabash, both flowing westward through Indiana.

Rivers were the interstate system of the early travelers. Like a city dweller of today who carries a map in his head of all the major routes out of town, the mental maps of a sojourner in the 1700's featured natural waterways. The Ohio River, not Interstate 80, was the favored route to move into Ohio from Pennsylvania. Important place names were The Forks of the Ohio, the Falls of the Ohio, or North Bend, all riverine nomenclature. Today we know these places by the less picturesque names of Pittsburgh, Louisville, and Cincinnati.

Loramie Creek at the State Park

The natural passageways provided by geological features used to keep us connected to the natural world. Valleys and rivers provided the easiest passages for transport. Trails and then roads also followed these routes. Those roads were built by men with shovels, axes, muscles and mules. The easiest route was truly important. Canal routes were particularly chosen for their most level course, since elevation changes meant costly extra structures. Military roads on our own soil, such as Josiah Harmar's, are barely a dim memory. Muscles, not motors, moved the goods and materiel over those roads. The hiker has the opportunity to be attuned to the heartbeats or hoofbeats of his ancestors, as he matches step for step the throbbing of their collective history.

As I drive Ohio Route 66 home, even I am nearly unaware of the close proximity of the trail that I have just walked. Foot paths seem insignificant when you are moving at 60 mph. I pass over the rivers, unnoticed, the road I am driving imprisoned by cement bridges. For the sake of safety I am barred even from glimpsing the waterways below. Unless I am forced to stop and wait for some train at a grade crossing, it is all too easy to remain ignorant of the presence of the gleaming rails. Roads tame the hills. Even when they follow historical pathways of easy access, the grades have been lessened. Great cuts have been blasted through inconvenient hills, and the smooth curves are designed by engineers, rather than by the flighty cows on their way home from pasture.

We are so out of touch with the pulse of the planet. Why not step out of the car and feel the throbbing of the rails, the cries of "low bridge," the beat of distant tom-toms, thudding hoofbeats, and the crack of the drovers whip. Embrace the earth and the trail, and they will reveal their long-forgotten secrets.

33 miles this hike
Bloody Bridge to Pampel Rd.
Auglaize and Shelby Counties, OH
1138 total NCT miles

Call the Police
36 - November 23-25, 1998

Pre-arrangements for this walk are nearly in place. Earlier this Monday morning I had driven the Canal Road south of Tipp City, Ohio and obtained permission to leave my car at a home near an intersection later in the day. Working my way north I had stopped at a farm just past Troy and arranged to put my tent down in their fence line the next night. A permit to camp at Lockington Dam County Park tonight is already in my pocket. All that remains is to leave my car at the north end for the day until Jerry Starcher of the Buckeye Trail Association (BTA) can meet me and help me move it to the south end. I drive to the house where I had left my car at the end of the previous hike. I had not been able to reach these people by phone, but was hoping that someone would be there, or perhaps I could just leave the car with a note attached. Their dogs are loose, though, and greet me rather too exuberantly. Chips is in the car with me, racing from windshield to hatchback and back, while the other dogs do the same outside. All are barking and snarling. I decide that trying to get our packs unloaded and donned will be too difficult with a canine side show to deal with, so I leave and look for another place to park along this short stretch of road.

The entire east side of this half-mile of road is part of a campground. Jerry had also helped me spot my car on the previous hike and had told me that the BTA had used this facility for a conference one year. Now the camp is empty and locked up. He has heard rumors that someone else bought it and he hopes that the Buckeye folks can form a good relationship. Today I find that the main gate is open, so I decide to investigate. A pickup truck is visible at the waterfront, and sure enough, three men are fishing out on the lake. One of them rows in to talk with me. I explain that I am hiking and ask if I can leave my car at the end of their service drive just for the rest of the afternoon. "Sure, no problem," he says. "My daughter and son-in-law just bought this camp and they want to re-open it for small groups." We chat for a few more minutes about the trail and the camp. As I back the car up to the cable gate I feel a sense of satisfaction that this may be an initial contact with the camp owners for Jerry.

I now have eight miles to hike in the next three hours, so Chips and I get into the business of walking. This hike is to be mostly road miles, not our favorite, but there they are. The weather is mild for November; I know the route; my pack is light – things could be lots more difficult. We reach Lockington with just time to set up our tent before Jerry arrives at 5:00 pm. By 5:30 we are turning on to the road where the campground and my car are located. A county Sheriff's Department car is coming toward us. I joke to Jerry, "They probably called Omer to report an abandoned car. He's getting pretty calm about explaining that all is well, his wife is just hiking." Sure enough, as we pull up to my car the deputy comes back and parks there as well.

"Is this your vehicle?" he asks.

"Yes," I reply.

"Well, these people want to have the car towed and to charge you with criminal trespass."

There was a time in my life when this news would have made me cower and begin feeling guilty like Oliver Twist, just because I was accused. However I'm older now, and either tougher or dumber. Without the faintest twinge of concern I counter, "No, no, no. I have permission to put the car here for the afternoon and I'm just leaving anyway."

"Fine with me," the deputy says, with a somewhat supercilious look that seems out of place.

I begin to walk around the car to unlock it and notice a lady walking up the service drive. "Are you the owner?" I call cheerfully.

"I certainly am." She hammers each word in like a spike through the heart of a vampire.

"I spoke with a man who said he was your father, and he said that I could leave the car here for a few hours."

"Well, I don't have a cell phone. How am I supposed to know that? I thought you were a deer hunter. I haven't seen my father."

"All I can say is that he seemed to feel he had authority to allow me to park here, and I'm sorry. I'm leaving now."

"My father was here this afternoon," she admits reluctantly. She begins lamenting about how other people have trespassed and vandalized the property ever since they bought it, so I am getting the picture. Here is someone (me!) who is finally a potential object of prosecution for all their frustration. Her tirade never slacking, she asks why I needed to park at this spot. I try to tell her about the Buckeye Trail, and the North Country Trail, that pass right in front of the camp, on the road. She says she's never heard of them. Unfortunately that is a common response. She demands to know why the Buckeye Trail people don't provide parking for their hikers. I suggest that this might be a goal, but it is a small group of volunteers and this is not currently possible. Asking permission usually is acceptable. She is calming down a bit, or at any rate, needs to pause and regroup before the next verbal assault. I ask if we can exchange names and if I can give her a flyer about the trail. Jerry is introduced. Her husband has also now joined our cheerless party. At this point the law steps back in. A backup unit has arrived so there are two deputies present. The new arrival says to me, "Why don't you just leave?"

Apparently, today, nothing can daunt me. "No," I stubbornly insist, "We need to have a good relationship with these folks. The trail goes right in front of their camp." Jerry and I are scrambling to find trail brochures, paper and pen.

The supercilious deputy suddenly makes a regrettable comment. "The neighbors don't think much of the way you are managing this property, either." With this provocation, the owner and her husband "go ballistic." The yelling match is under way with both deputies participating. Jerry and I share a furtive look as if to ask,"What is going on here?" Accusations are falling around our ears as thick and brittle as the dead oak leaves under our feet. Sentences overlap in angry disorder making it difficult to distinguish legitimate commentary.

"What neighbors? We haven't talked to any neighbors."

"The neighbors just don't like you."

"They're angry because someone else bought the place."

"What right have you to say that?..."

I purposely block out the words because I am watching the husband. He's built like a pro-wrestler, blocky, muscular, barrel-chested, an aggressive looking guy. He and one deputy are practically chest to chest, and frankly I hope we are not going to progress to fist-fighting. As if underneath the main storm of accusations Jerry and I return with trail information. I get the owner's attention and she and I do exchange names and addresses. We part with a tentative smile for each other, and Jerry and I drive away. The screaming match continues, but we gladly leave it behind. This is one time I can easily pass up knowing the final outcome of a situation since the outcome for me is settled and does not include fines or charges.

Before parting that evening, Jerry and I comment that if we have managed to salvage a positive relationship out of that shaky beginning we have done well!

A chilly night, colder than predicted, means restless sleep for me. The Tuesday miles seem long and weary, and pavement walking is always tough on feet and knees. Little or no road shoulder means that the traffic is constantly in our faces, and I must be ever-vigilant to keep Chips and myself out of the path of cars, vans, and gravel trucks. My last rest stop of the day is a short snack and water break while sitting on the bank of the ditch. Shortly after resuming my walk I am approached by a Sheriff's car.

"Now what?" I wonder.

"Are you all right?" the deputy asks.

"Sure."

"We got a report that there was a lady lying in the ditch who looked like she was in trouble,"

I assure him that we are fine, and mention that I was not even lying down, just sitting there eating and having a drink of water.

"Well, some people really exaggerate, you know." he comments as he waves me on my way.

A few miles later I pass a State Police car parked by the road near an Interstate exit. We chat briefly and I am frankly relieved to find that they are not looking for me. Their prey is speeders. Well, we won't make that category this afternoon.

Yet another chilly night is followed by more bone-thumping road miles on Wednesday. When a Sheriff's car passes me slowly I flinch a little, but this time my activities are of no interest to the law enforcers. I am not sorry. One more episode rounds out this adventure. On state Route 41 there is a brief respite from the traffic at least. Although it is a very busy highway there is a wide paved shoulder so the dog and I can walk without having to concentrate on every approaching vehicle. Thus I am day-dreaming, probably singing to myself, when behind me I hear a shout. I turn and see that a car has pulled off the road and stopped. The driver is beckoning me to walk back that way. Resistance is definitely high to backtracking, but I wave and retrace a few steps, hoping that the instigator of this meeting will take a hint and walk towards me. This tactic works. Within a few more steps I can tell that it is the lady from the campground. "Wow!" she exclaims. "I saw you walking and said to myself, 'I know who that is!'"

I diffidently mention that I had told her I was hiking.

"I know, but, I mean, to really see you.... You do remember who I am?"

My initial thoughts are perhaps unkind. Internally my cynical side declares, "If you think that I could forget YOU after two days you are certainly mistaken." But outwardly I just answer, "Oh yes, you are the owner of the campground." We talk for a while and I do assure her that I also think the deputy was out of line to make the comment he did. This gives us a common "enemy," so with promises to correspond about the trail we strengthen the fragile relationship.

A few more miles, another walk is completed successfully. A long drive home for Thanksgiving is punctuated by a hot shower and a few hours of warm sleep in a bed at the home of some friends in Indiana. A parting thought: how much more pleasant, efficient and less stressful it would be if we could assume something better than the worst when evaluating an unfamiliar situation. If the person who saw Chips and me in the ditch could have rolled down the window and simply called out, "Are you o.k?" the police would not have been needed. If the camp owners could have reserved judgement about my car until they had some information that whole incident might never have involved the police. But fear and defensiveness have built walls that keep us from approaching each other. When the camp owner stopped me on the highway she also asked, "Aren't you afraid to be out like this? I wouldn't feel safe."

My standard answer is, "You are not really safe anywhere." She grudgingly acceded to the truth of this statement.

Instead of causing others to feel threatened and defensive of their own space, how much better if we give people a chance to show us their better side. Instead of reacting to the unfamiliar with fear and retreat, how much better if we embrace new situations, expanding our wealth of experiences. Instead of cowering in our suffocating, musty towers of the familiar, how much better to breathe the fresh air of new worlds. To me, to breathe the air of the new is to live.

38 miles this hike
Pampel Rd. to Old Springfield Rd.
Shelby and Miami Counties, OH
1176 total NCT miles

Spirit of the Woods
37 - February 13, 199

Since last fall my involvement with the trail community has become much more organized. A local chapter of the North Country Trail Association has formed, covering four counties and adopting eighty miles of trail. At our first official meeting we voted overwhelmingly to name our chapter "Spirit of the Woods." Not only does the name have a nice ring to it, but the words themselves are a loose translation of the word "Manistee." All of the miles our chapter will maintain are within the Manistee National Forest.

Once a month the chapter has met to discuss business, and also each month has hosted a hike. We have decided to begin taking a look at "our" miles of trail, and the November and January hikes covered the miles on which I took my first hike on the NCT.[1] This month we will hike some miles that I have not previously seen. Six of us meet on this chilly day. There is little snow cover so we will have no difficulty walking the trail.

It is also Chips' sixth birthday. His enthusiasm rubs off on the hikers in our group; they always welcome him to enjoy our activities. It seems to me that he is beginning to calm down a little bit, to be a bit more manageable even when he is excited. I am looking forward to the years ahead with all of his good qualities preserved as part of his character, but with some of the naughtier aspects toned down.

On Christmas Day he had been very ill, apparently with some gastro-intestinal upset. He lost a lot of weight before he began to feel better, a few days later. His energy and appetite have returned to full strength, but he seems to have remained thin. I keep trying to decide if he really is looking gaunt, or if it's just "in my head." I've even compared his looks to some older photos, but I still can't decide; he's never been anything but bones and muscle covered with fur. Otherwise, he has completely returned to being a vigorous, golden dynamo.

Our chapter has discovered a dynamo of its own in Ramona Venegas, a Recreation Technician with the Forest Service. Ramona loves the North Country Trail, well beyond the limits of her job description. She has actively met with the chapter, teaching us how to work through the complexities of a government agency, to accomplish improvements for the trail. Today she is here with us, greeting people

---

[1] see Chapter 1: "The Kernel."

at the Trailhead, making introductions. She seems to know everyone in the county!

Soon we all set off to explore this section. The trail quickly drops down from the road to the floodplain of the Manistee River, along a narrow bench that is overgrown and crumbling. Several slanting bridges punctuate the obvious need for maintenance here. Soon we are climbing up the bluff, to continue our walk high above the river. With the trees winter-bare, the views of the river meandering far below are grand. After a few miles a set of switchbacks down the steep slope returns us to the floodplain, to an area known as Leitch Bayou, although it is now a wet meadow rather than a body of open water. It is a popular spot with fishermen who like to camp at the Forest Campground named Sawdust Hole. Sawdust Hole is reached by again climbing up, away from the river, and then following a short side trail. The campground was once the site of a local sawmill, and an angled depression chiseled into the cliff marks where logs were skidded down from the forest to the river. A few yards farther and we reach Dilling Road, the end of today's hike.

I recognize the place where I sat and waited for Omer to pick me up after my first NCT hike, seven and a half years ago. A slight shivery thrill ripples my skin. I am making increasing connections with the trail and the Spirit of the Woods.

5 miles this hike
Highbridge to Dilling Road
Manistee County, MI
1181 miles total NCT

A Golden Chip of Sunshine
38 - February 23, 1999

Chips is pulling on his leash with his usual imperative exuberance, nearly forcing me to jog to keep up with him. It's a gray and overcast Tuesday, but we have traveled just a few miles from home to walk some trail that I have not yet seen.

My little golden dog, I cherish the memories of you as a ball of fluff, an exceptionally beautiful puppy. You were just 12 weeks old when I rolled a ball for you and you immediately brought it back. I added the word "fetch," and there was your favorite game! In my mind I see you running towards me, a half-grown puppy, your red rubber ball held in your mouth.

With a "snap" the clip on Chips' leash breaks loose from his collar, and I decide to let him run free for a while. Enthusiastically, he ranges back and forth across the trail, searching for some extra-interesting smell to follow.

You are such a bright light in my life! Your puppy fur was a glistening white gold, the color of fresh split maple chips... and so you were named "Chips." I know you are so attached to me that you cry and pout whenever I am forced to leave you behind on some expedition, whether it's just a ride to the Post Office, or a hike where dogs are not welcome. And I know that I am equally attached to you. When we are together you love to rest your head in my lap, and I welcome your doggy kisses. You abandon yourself in telling me how much you love me.

We reach a downed tree, spreading its branches rudely across the trail. With no problem at all, Chips jumps across the large horizontal trunk.

"Ready for Adventure" is your life's motto. At four months of age you took to riding on the bow of my canoe. When you discovered long hikes with us, you embraced the outdoor life with an intensity equal to mine. Only once in the

Puppy Chips enjoying a canoe ride

more than 1200 miles of North Country Trail that you have hiked with us did you question the request to come have your pack put on. And we could hardly blame you on that 105° North Dakota day! You learned to ride in my pack, and climb ladders with never a look back. Sharing one sleeping bag on cold nights keeps us both warm and happy. You are entertained for hours with nothing but a stick and a human to throw it for you.*

The sun breaks through the clouds briefly, but there is no sunshine in my heart today.

How can Dr. Jim be right? How can what he told me on Thursday be true, that you have only six months to live? I know that Jim is trying to break the news to me gently, so I realize that we've probably only got three months left together. Jim says you have a tumor the size of a football inside your rib cage, that it weighs almost ten pounds. The five pounds you have lost, which prompted me to take you to the doctor, are actually more like ten pounds of muscle and healthy organs. But you seem so normally energetic, just a little thin...

Chips barks eagerly at an elusive squirrel, and we turn around to head back toward the car. The brown leaves are crunchy beneath my feet with only a light dusting of snow – easy walking for me, and easy tracking of interesting smells for a curious dog. We need to return home in time for Chips to eat before noon, so that his stomach will be empty for his surgery tomorrow morning.

Should I put you through this trauma, dear pup? Jim says the tumor is in your liver and that there is really nothing that can be done, but his partner, Dr. Paul, thinks it might be in the spleen. He says spleen tumors can be huge and still be removed successfully. Jim says that the surgery may shorten your life, that you might not even survive it. But to do nothing to try to save you is not a choice I can live with.

At home, Chips eats some dog chow and then I pour the rest of the food from his dish back into the bag. He gives me a look of total surprise at this strange turn of events. "What the heck?" he clearly asks. It's a funny scene, but I wish I hadn't caused him even this minor insult when tomorrow may be his last day. I can see that the mass inside him has shifted back a little, into his abdomen, making him look slightly pregnant.

Wednesday morning at the veterinary office Jim draws blood from Chips to do a liver function test. He puts Chips in a kennel to wait, and lets me sit in the cement and chain-link room with him. We will not tolerate separation now. Chips sprawls, flattening his tummy on the cool cement, shunning a warmer and softer mat provided for comfort.

Are your insides on fire, my Chiplet? You have always been on fire with the joy of life. Remember when I had to walk you eight miles to even tire you out as a six-month-old puppy? Remember all the hours of retrieving sticks thrown in lakes or rivers? You love that even more than your ball. And that ball! How many times have you leapt in the air to catch a ball thrown high before it could bounce even one time? I always thought you would break your teeth catching that hard rubber toy that way, but you never did.
I know that Jim will do everything he can to save you. If you die during surgery, so be it. At least there will be no long sad end.

At last Jim returns and calls us into the examination room. The liver function tests are done. The news is not good. The values are off the chart by which they evaluate such things. Jim explains that this means that the liver is fully involved and there is no way he can survive major surgery, because the liver is responsible for de-toxification after the anaesthetic. "Take him home and enjoy what time you have left, Joan," Jim says gently. This often gruff, but always caring, vet has helped me through the deaths of several dogs, but there has never been a dog like Chips before.

Your middle name may be Houdini, but I don't think you are going to be able to escape this sentence, my furry friend. You can slip any collar or harness. You can wriggle through a car window opened only a few inches. No fence has ever kept you cooped up for long. Remember the day that you escaped Phil's back yard? We wouldn't have believed it if we hadn't watched you pull the pin in the gate latch with your teeth, flip the latch and then open the gate. But there's no latch on this door that is closing today.

Thursday morning, Chips is not nestled in bed with me when I awake. He is spread-eagled on the bathroom floor, trying to cool the hot monster in his belly. When he stands up I can see that the tumor has grown, overnight. He now looks pear-shaped. I give him food and water, but whatever he eats or drinks comes right back up. I tempt him with his favorites, cheese and milk. Nothing stays down. Despite the facts presented to me over the past six days, the finality of the truth that my dog is dying smashes into me, and all I can do is watch and wonder how long it will take.

Baby dog, I wish you would eat just a little bit. If you won't even have some milk you are surely in trouble. You've been my Dairy Dog, the

Parmezan Pup, the Yogurt Yipper. Ice cream, yogurt, cheese and milk have always had you drooling near my knee, your tail twitching with anticipation as you wait for a treat.

Thursday evening, Chips lies on his back on the couch, a favorite position, while I rub his tummy and chin. It doesn't feel right, with that hard lump filling all that space that should be so soft, but he seems to derive some comfort from my touch.

You've always insisted on being close enough to touch me, haven't you? You lie beneath my desk while I work, your head resting across my foot. In the car you know you can't sit in my lap while I drive, but you have to have either the tip of your nose or a paw, just making contact with my thigh across the center console. When you first left your litter-mates, and we made that first long drive to Ann Arbor together, you felt calm and safe as long as I rested one hand on your fuzzy back. Does my touch calm you at all today, when I am anything but calm?

Sharing a special moment

At about ten o'clock Chips begins to wag his tail in an odd manner, not rhythmically, but in a jerking motion. He walks around in a few circles, and jumps on the couch to be held. His heart is racing in an unnatural manner. The look on his face is one of utter surprise. In about five minutes, his heart settles back to a normal rhythm, but the attack has done its work; he's clearly weaker now.

How can you be so weak just two days after our walk in the woods when you must have roamed 15 miles to my eight? You are such a strong dog... pulling with such strength for your 40 pounds that grown men have wondered aloud at your power. Such statements have usually been preceded by teasing me for barely being able to control such a small dog. Then after taking you for a walk themselves they would return and exclaim profound truths such as, "You weren't kidding... this dog is STRONG!"

During the night Chips retches nearly every hour. Each episode is followed by a deep agonizing groan, which sounds as if it is tearing his insides apart. Each groan tears at my heart, but there is nothing I can do except try to keep him comfortable. He now wants only to stay on the floor where it is cooler. I had thought he would become less conscious of what was happening as the end came nearer, but such relief is not to be.

You are looking at me with those wonderful liquid eyes, asking questions I cannot answer. You are clearly saying, "I don't understand." And neither do I, my Baby Dog. All I can promise you is no more leashes, fences, and choke collars. There will be meadows and woods in which to run free in the sun, and to feel the wind in your ears. Remember Heze? He was old when you were a puppy and was grumpy when you chewed on his ears, but now he will welcome you. Get acquainted with Butchy-Boy and Charlotte, Bonnie, Billie and all the others who have gone before you. You find us some good trails to follow, and wait for me.

This can not go on. If Chips is still alive when Jim's office opens, I will take him in, and make the end more bearable for both of us.

At 5:35 in the morning, Chips gives one horrible groan, arches his back, and goes limp. The light fades from his eyes; his heart is not beating.

Goodbye, my golden Chip of sunshine.

4 miles this hike
Freesoil Rd. to 5-Mile Rd.
Lake County, MI
1180 total NCT miles

Puzzled
39 - March 26-30, 1999

I've always loved puzzles. Crossword puzzles, hidden picture puzzles, logic puzzles, puzzles with those interlocking metal twisted shapes: I want to try them all. Two of the first kinds of puzzles we try as children are jig-saw puzzles and connect-the-dot puzzles. But some puzzles are very difficult to solve.

Just days after Chips died I fled to New York, to visit Marie for a few days. No matter that it was a 14-hour drive, I had to get away from the space where every step I took or place I looked reminded me of my missing best friend. I was crying almost constantly and had to find a way to stop. The stress of the final week of his life, followed by the long drive (and without the pup who went nearly everywhere with me) ensured that my first few hours there would be filled with the oblivion of dreamless sleep. Marie had to work the next day, but she too likes jig-saw puzzles and pointed out two new ones, suggesting that I pick one to start. The choices were a fussy European castle or (no fooling) three polar bears in the snow. I chose the bears. There were 990 pieces of white, off-white, gray-white, bright white, or tan-white, and 10 pieces of black. Even polar bears have noses and paw pads. The shapes also had no variation; every piece had exactly two "outies" opposite each other and two "innies" on the other sides. This was going to be a challenge even for us!

I assembled the 10 black pieces into their little groups in about five minutes. Over the five days that I stayed with Marie we managed to complete the edge except for two holes which were either fitting errors or missing pieces (already!), and to connect about 100 other pieces into little groups of two or threes. Not a highly successful endeavor if you count success in terms of puzzle completion! But the time spent with Marie, my best human friend, is always successful in lifting my spirits.

The time spent alone in the car arguing with my best ever friend, my Heavenly Father, was successful in reminding me of His love and care. I'm not one to ask "why" when unpleasant things happen... they just happen. And one of life's seeming injustices is that we outlive most of the animals we love. But I was having a hard time accepting this loss. Chips was only six. We had so many trails yet to explore, balls to toss, and so many warm smiles yet to share. He was in so many ways a unique dog, and so exactly the dog I had always wanted. Knowing with my head that life is unfair did nothing to lift the weight on my heart. I know that the healing process is just that, a process, which takes time. But as I argued, I realized that it takes more than time. Without a loving, merciful God there would be no healing at all, even with all the time in the world. The grief and pain of each loss and hurt would just accumulate, suffocating us. This was surely a reminder to me that life without a compassionate God would be unbearable.

Yet, the jig-saw puzzle remains in obstructive disarray on Marie's dining table.

One month to the day after Chips' death, I am now headed for Ohio, for another hike. Alone. But in that intervening month I have resolved to do a number of things this summer that are not convenient or possible to do with a dog, and to look for another trail puppy in the fall. Thus I carry in my car not only camping gear, but my bicycle. It has been stored for the past several years because Chips and the bike were not compatible. A week of WD-40, and some elbow grease too, has freed the chain and derailleurs. The brakes work. The rest, well – marginal – but rideable. Omer, who has become quite accepting of my risk-taking, suggests that he would feel better about this trip if I would buy one new tire. So, I do. The plan is to ride my bike one way each day and hike the other, back to the car (and then retrieve the bike). My larger goal is to connect two previously hiked sections in Ohio. It's an ambitious, 64-mile, plan but I am looking forward to the challenge. The mechanics of such a hike are like a connect-the-dots puzzle.

It seems as if the connect-the-dots page of Chips' life is complete, and I must turn the leaf and begin a new picture. If you do each connection in the correct order you end up with a picture. Young children will often connect the dots in non-numerical order. This results in some shape on the puzzle page, but not the intended picture. Similarly, I seem to be unable to discern the order for this puzzle. This hike has provided a whole new collection of dots, but I do not yet know how to connect them to form a meaningful image.

Dot: the bike

Biking is both fun and terrifying! Except during the week of preparation for this hike, it has been a long time since I've ridden more than a mile or two. Will my long-standing but out-of-date biking experience cover concerns about fitness, balance, or reaction times? Zooming down the road (compared to walking) at 18 miles per hour is exciting! In all honesty, the back wheel needs rebuilding and the spokes are loosened to prevent them from poking through the rim and causing a flat tire. Thus it wobbles more than it should. Will it last for 60 miles? I'm taking that chance, but the risk of a flat tire or bent rim at any given moment is high. The full range of gears is not working; I choose to have the derailleur locked in the high range for speed. My pride suffers a blow or two. Ohio, south of Dayton, begins to have topography. I have to walk a few hills, but forward progress is more important than my pride. Brakes are functional, but not great, and I sure hope I won't have to stop in a big hurry either! Yet, biking through Dayton isn't as scary as I have anticipated. I somehow manage to pick times and routes where the traffic is not deadly, through the sections that do not have bike paths.

Dot: the bike breakdown

My guardian angel continues to be on duty. I do not say that in a flip manner. With just three miles yet to bike, on the last day of this adventure, my rear axle breaks, locking up the back wheel. If it had happened five minutes earlier I would have been on a two-lane state highway crossing a dam with no shoulders, metal guardrails, and heavy traffic. If it had happened two minutes earlier I would have been riding down a steep hill, traveling at perhaps 30 mph. If it had happened when I had been riding at all, I might at the least have had an unpleasant fall. But it happens just after I have just carried the bike across a set of really rough railroad tracks on a road closed to regular traffic. I am remounting to continue the ride, when the wheel locks. A short walk to a country club gives me a safe place to leave the bike for the rest of the day.

As I approach the clubhouse to make sure it's all right to leave the bike, two men emerge from a posh gray car. One is wearing a suit and tie. The driver has left his suit jacket in the car, and his white shirt would dazzle the eyes of Mr. Clean. I, keep in mind, have been hiking and camping without benefit of shower for five days and have now been playing with a greasy wheel for the past 20 minutes. But these are true gentlemen; they open the door for me! I protest that I'm probably not clean enough for such treatment, but instead of disdainfully judging me for my appearance they ask if they can help. I explain about the breakdown and that it can't be fixed with the few tools I have with me. We enter the pro shop where I ask permission to leave the bike for a few hours. I ask the fellow behind the counter if he knows of anyone who might be driving north in the near future. He does not. But Mr. White Shirt, behind me, asks where I need to go! I explain to him my bike-hike strategy and point to my goal on the map, just three miles away. "No problem," he says nonchalantly, "I'll take you there." In just a few minutes my dirty, greasy self is riding in his plush back seat. He even shakes hands with me as I leave him at the trailhead. Introductions reveal him to be the local Chief of Police!

My Ohio hikes have come to be something of a running joke. When Marie asks me later if I have been picked up by the police this time, I grin and say, "Yes." This is getting to be quite a habit. If only I could report that all the encounters were as positive as this one!

Dot: Tadmore

Tadmore is just a tad of a town, certainly no more: that's "no more" in both size and time. If it had one fewer structure it could hardly qualify as a town. If it had one fewer sign no passerby would now know that it had been a town, important though small, at one time. Just a few crumbling foundation walls and footings still stand near the canal. And the county has provided a small interpretive sign.

Since these stories are being told in the order they happened, I can't cheat and put Tadmore two chapters back, but that is certainly where this puzzle piece seems to belong, with other transportation tales. A store which served as hotel, post office and canal-keeper's house; a grain elevator which also housed the grain dealer; and a depot — these were the buildings. Other structures were a bridge and a sluice gate. Tadmore was a crossroad of every major transportation route through the area until the town was wiped out by the Flood of 1913. Here the Great Miami River and the Miami-Erie canal parallel each other, and the sluice gate connected them, allowing excess water in the canal to be drained off to the river. Year-round transportation was provided by the Dayton & Michigan Railroad, built in 1863. Finally, travelers in wagons, on horseback, and on foot were accommodated on the National Road, the first federally built interstate highway. The Road was begun in 1816 at Cumberland, Maryland and reached Vandalia, Illinois in 1839. For over 60 years the National Road was the primary overland route from the Atlantic States to the interior of the Midwest, and it also passed through Tadmore.

Dot: Dayton

Dayton is not a tad of a town. It is a city of 170,000, yet the concurrent Buckeye and North Country Trails manage to wind their way through the metropolis. Parks, bicycle paths, levees along the rivers, and a few sidewalks connect, most definitely like a puzzle. They provide a foot path which is, for the most part, pleasant. The sun sparkles off the flat water of the tamed Miami River as I walk south from Triangle Park into Island Park at the north end of town. Turning east to follow

Island Park in Dayton, OH

the Mad River, the path is perched at the top of a flood control levee. To my left the view is appealing, but I am set to pondering whenever I gaze to the right. The river is on my left, blue and polka-dotted with white gulls, lined with the green-sloped levees. But on my right I see chain link fences with aging gray or brown blank factory walls just beyond, surrounded by crumbling parking lots. No parks, planned pathways or attractive access points invite people to recreate. I have to wonder why the city has turned a blind eye to the water resource here.

But farther into the city the water is accessible; I pause for lunch beneath a stand of Red Pine within Eastwood Park and watch a pair of nesting geese on the tip of a small island. Just beyond the park I am forced to push my way through a dark, prickly thicket of honeysuckle and Osage Orange that could be a candidate for Sleeping Beauty's protective bramble patch. At the middle of this woods I find, not a castle, but a railroad track. Actually the rail line is what I am seeking, where the map says to pass beneath Harshman Road.

Emerging abruptly on the other side into what appears to be a driveway I am soon face to face with the Air Force Museum, across the Dayton-Springfield Pike. Sadly, I don't have time today to visit this largest and oldest museum of military aviation in the world. There is no way that I can take time to ogle 300 planes and still return to my campsite by dark. I'll just have to come back another time.

At Springfield Road I pass under the railroad, and just for me, a train is crossing at the exact time I am approaching. I wave at the engineer, and he waves back. The friendly interchange gives me hope that the huge conglomerated Conrail may still employ people as good-natured as the crews of the defunct small lines whose names have formerly graced these tracks.

More suited to the time I have today is studying the next piece of the Dayton puzzle. One small, steep climb up the side of a triangular hill and I am standing on Huffman Prairie, at the Wright Brothers Memorial. This flat field is located atop a bluff, high above the Pike. Orville and Wilbur used this 100-acre field to perfect their aircraft in 1904-1905, and later operated the Wright Company School of Aviation here.

The final piece of the Dayton pathway puzzle is a winding, wide bikeway providing safe passage on to the city of Fairborn.

Dot: the feet

Riding a bike on $40°$ mornings results in really cold toes. I often begin walking on feet that I cannot feel until I have stomped along for many minutes. This warming process is painful, although it is satisfying to know that my feet are not really dead!

And for some mysterious reason my heels decide that this is a good trip on which to blister... seriously blister, as bad as the North Dakota hike[1]. By the end of the fourth day it brings me near tears each time I have to begin walking again after a rest stop. Such a bother! Why can't I seem to figure out what set of circumstances brings on this problem? Large, loose gravel is the usual culprit, but I see little of that on this trip until the last day. By then the heels are long gone. Moleskin, duct tape, and sock liners lessen the blow from each step, but they haven't seemed to prevent the condition in the first place.

Dot: the vehicles

This is motorsports country. I wonder if there is a male person under age 76 in rural Ohio who can accelerate a car without spinning tires and throwing gravel. I usually try to avoid sounding sexist, but on this particular trip I encounter no female motorheads. All too often I cringe as some driver near me roars through the gears, spraying small lethal weapons. Near Trebein I munch my lunch to the rhythm of racing motors on some nearby speedway where the boys can play more safely. Later I pass race car trailers, customizing shops, and garages specializing in racing engine repairs which verify my hunch about the source of the sounds.

Dot: nature lessons

Despite the generally urban and suburban character of this hike, and the fact that it is barely spring even in Ohio, I collect a number of wildlife encounters. One of my favorite things about morning (although morning and I are not good friends) is to lie quietly and listen to the sounds of the world awakening. I wake slowly, teasing the tangled noises into the calls of Crows, Blue Jays and Cardinals, squirrelly chattering, tree frogs singing, a tapping woodpecker, Mourning Doves cooing, and assorted unidentified twitterings.

While hiking I catch sight of a soaring immature Broad-winged Hawk. I could not identify this bird on the spot, but good notes helped me puzzle out the answer from a field guide later. An unidentified plant turns out to be Sand Vine. Long pods filled with silky down are a clear indication that it is a milkweed relative, but I've never seen a vining milkweed! Indeed this plant has climbed over nearly every fence along the river, and it does turn out to be a cousin of the Common Milkweed of field and roadside. Glimpses of familiar wildlife are like old friends:

---

[1] See Chapter 6: "Where the Trail Begins"

a Garter Snake, a Kingfisher perched above Taylorsville Dam, the call of a Barred Owl at night, and the bright yellows of Coltsfoot and Lesser Celandine. Although it is too early in the season for most wildflowers, crocus and daffodils are cheerfully opening in many suburban lawns. Sun on young Sycamore bark, broken into its familiar puzzle shapes, inserts bright exclamations into the dreary March landscape.

At the Glen Helen Trailside Museum I am able to learn about more creatures new to me. Red-eared and Spotted Turtles are featured here, as well as the more familiar Painted and Box Turtles. For the first time ever I learn of the Fox Snake. This harmless patterned reptile has the misfortune to be able to rattle his tail, and also to have a coppery head, thus he is often mistakenly identified as venomous and killed. He's actually a constrictor, and would be happy to grab your extra mice and swallow them whole!

Perhaps the best natural manifestation occurs the final night, a blue moon. Technically, just the second full moon to appear in a calendar month, they aren't really blue. At least that's the scientific explanation. But this one hovers in a cloudless, deep-blue sea of a sky, with bare dark branches shifting in gentle patterns across its face. This one seems quite blue; I'm very fond of blue!

Dot: the pavement

Much of this hike is on paved pathways. In and near cities this is expected, but it never will be my favorite kind of walking. South of Yellow Springs is a popular segment of paved rail-trail. It's Sunday when I arrive in Yellow Springs. Fortified by a dish of ice cream, I enter the throng of strollers, bikers, dog-walkers, roller-bladers, skateboarders, and power-walkers. Yikes!

Dot: the Glen

Before I've walked a mile, dodging feet and wheels, I am really hoping for an alternate route. Fortunately, just then beside the pathway, Glen Helen beckons with limestone fingers. The glen is a nature preserve, owned by Antioch College. Although I am too early in the year to see any of the wildflowers for which it is noted, the frequent rocky outcrops do hide the busy pavement from my

Rocky outcrops at Glen Helen

view and hearing. Many enchanting pathways braid their way among the rocks, down through the valley and on to the covered bridge just below John Bryan State Park. This will be another excellent destination to return to some day.

Dot: the campers

I am base camping at John Bryan State Park, and I arrive here on a Friday night. The park has over 100 sites, and they are nearly all filled before dark. Kids are yelling, dogs are barking, doors are slamming, music is blaring. A large Boy Scout troop arrives in the late afternoon and sets up a huge pavilion made of pipes fitted together into a framework and covered with plywood sheets laced to the pipes with ropes. The scouts scurry through patrol chores. It's easy to watch them; their shelter is bright with gas lanterns. Obviously they are here for the weekend.

Saturday morning at 6:30 am the yelling and slamming begins again. The shelter is disassembled and, much to my surprise, the Scouts disappear! Plenty of other people remain. But even with the noisy human activity, when it finally falls quiet at night the Barred Owl can be heard querying the insomniacs.

Dot: the camper

Chris arrives on Sunday in a truck. The park is nearly empty by then, but his clumping gene is activated, so he picks the site right next to mine. All he unloads is a chair and a Black Lab! Soon he comes over and introduces himself, and Ralph the dog. He wants to go to town to get something he forgot, and asks me to watch the dog and his stuff.

I answer, "Sure," although I am not so sure that I want to get emotionally involved with a dog, even for an hour. Chris promises that Ralph won't fuss at all when he leaves. Thankfully, that prediction is correct. Ralph never even seems to notice that his master has driven off and left him with nothing but a chair.

Chris returns with gifts for me, a bottle of water and a frappucino, and beer for himself. He lines up eight bottles on the picnic table and methodically drinks his way through them, while I cook my dinner and enjoy a cup of coffee by the campfire. I am desperately hoping, even praying, that he is not the sort of drunk who needs a shoulder to cry on. Finally he gives an enormous belch, and speaks gruffly to the patient Ralph. He fumbles with the tailgate of his truck. He and Ralph crawl in and are soon snoring. They are gone when I awake the next morning!

Dot: the missing camper

Monday night's excitement revolves around a boy named Chad whom I never meet, but I hear a lot about him. By then I have the north end of the campground all to myself. In the early evening two carloads of teenage boys roar in and drive twice around the loop. I am hoping they don't feel the need to camp close to me. They are swearing loudly, and calling each other filthy names with great enthusiasm. They finally park at the other end of the camp loop, and I pretty much forget about them, enjoying my final evening beside the fire. I fall asleep thinking how much easier this hike has been without an energetic dog to deal with, but wishing that Chips was with me anyway.

At 11:30 pm I am awakened by a teen boy's voice near the latrine calling, "Chad!"

This demand is answered by a loud "What?" from the woods. The sequence is repeated, and then silence follows.

Soon I hear a really puzzling noise, a hollow-sounding, metallic klunk, repeated frequently but not rapidly. After a lot of thought I decide that it sounds like the shaker ball in a can of spray paint, except that those balls don't just make single "klunks." Nevertheless, I wonder if decorating the latrine is on some teen-ager's agenda for the evening. Next a car begins driving slowly around the loop. Adults in the car call, "Chad, Robert!" A motherish-sounding voice adds, "Come on, let's go home. Just forget it."

Robert must have responded to this plea because the next sound bite is a young man walking around the campground yelling, "Chad, just come on back, I'll take the blame, those other kids really screwed us."

Then the whole family piles in their car and begins driving in and out of the campground, through the picnic area and back, continuing to call for Chad.

I decide to peek outside the tent, but I can see only the lighted area near the information kiosk. I have been contemplating calling the police, but a clearly agitated teen is pacing under the light, where the pay phone is located. I have no desire to insert myself personally into yet another Ohio law enforcement adventure, so I decide to remain out of sight in my tent.

The driving and yelling last until 12:30 when Chad apparently is found, because now begins the phase that he was probably afraid of – the wrathful parents. The family seems to feel the need to discuss this loudly, at the kiosk, of course at my end of the campground. Even so, I can hear only enough of the words to make the whole episode even more puzzling, given the emotional level of the confrontation. The issue seems to be whether the boys had seen some other kids drink a can of beer, or if their kids simply had a can with some beer in it. The parents keep threatening something about taking the whole thing to court.

Finally they all get in the car and leave. This seems to be a good campground for leaving at odd hours.

In the morning I tell the story to the ranger. He is frankly uninterested. "I'm just the day ranger," he says, as if this exonerates him from caring what happened last night. He chalks it all off to the fact that it is spring break weekend. "Oh yeah, kids drink two beers, and they think they are really something," is his final word.

It's always hard to break camp

Despite the sore feet and the continuing confirmation that a good portion of the population of Ohio is crazy, I am as sad as ever to break camp in the morning and head for home. I build a fire and have a hot breakfast of tapioca with apricots. I pour the last of the campfire coffee into my travel mug. The taste is tangy from the wood smoke, a flavor oddly out of place in a motorized, metal conveyance zipping along at 60 mph. While driving home I realize that I have strung together enough hikes to make a solid red line on my map from Kings Mills, Ohio, all the way to western Michigan. All the towns I pass, all the miles beneath my tires, I have WALKED! It's beginning to feel like I'm getting somewhere on this quest. The puzzle that is this trail is coming together.

Yet, the "dots" of this hike remain strangely unconnected, refusing to sort themselves into a coherent picture of life without Chips. Every event seems to have ended with a sniffle and a whimper, "I just want my dog."

At home, I call Marie. She tells me that she has nearly completed the bears' bodies, but the majority of the puzzle still lies disconnected on the table.

64 miles this hike
Caesar's Creek to Old Springfield Rd.
Greene and Montgomery Counties, OH
1249 total NCT miles

April Ambitions
40 - April 10, 1999

It's time again for the monthly hike of the Spirit of the Woods Chapter, and we are continuing our trek to explore our adopted trail. This time we will walk west from the Highbridge Trailhead. This section of trail takes us high above Blacksmith Bayou on the Manistee River, a beautiful walk through mature oak forest. Trail work needed here is most notably better blazing. This month we also follow one of our few road walks, west on Chicago Avenue and then south on Michigan Avenue. These pretentious names are definitely not a clue to the real nature of these sandy woods roads! We wishfully discuss possibilities for off-road trail through this private inholding within the Manistee National Forest. Next the trail follows a power line over a hill. Meandering ATV tracks are the notable feature of this piece; we hope that there might be a different solution for taking the trail through here too. One more road walk to take advantage of the bridge over Pine Creek, and we pop back into the woods for the final mile of the hike. This hike ends at Udell Trailhead on route M-55, where I first learned of the trail's existence.[1]

Our chapter does have ambitious plans for the summer, in addition to increasing regular trail maintenance. We are planning a National Trails Day celebration with the focus of inviting young people and families to come hike, and learn about the trail. We are inviting an expert on local history, and a Cub Scout pack will set up an example of a Leave-No-Trace campsite. The American Hiking Society is providing lots of guidance and also cool stuff that we can give away as prizes. This rush of organizational activity is changing the focus of the time I spend working on trail issues, but not my enthusiasm. Promoting the trail to other people is always high on my priority list.

We have also taken on building a 600-foot raised boardwalk through an area with the intriguing name of Dead Horse Marsh. Funds have been secured through the Challenge Cost Share program of the National Park Service. The Forest Service has supplied the plans and the required studies to meet all regulations. The chapter will provide the labor, and we will start marking the route through the marsh in just a few weeks. The project looks like it will be a perfect example of how federal agencies and the North Country Trail Association can work together.

---

[1] See "Introduction to the Trail."

Despite the short amount of time I've known most of them, the chapter members empathize with my grief at the loss of our trail pup companion. I'm no longer crying all the time, but the mere mention of his name is enough to bring on the tears. But in just the few months since we were chartered I've made good, new friends. They ran the March business meeting while I ran away to New York, and at this meeting they voted to honor the memory of Chips in a special way. I am overwhelmed, so touched by their expression of care and their understanding of the special role this small dog played in our lives. The boardwalk we are to build will be dedicated to "the memory of Chips, the hiker pup, and all our four-footed hiking companions."

5 miles this hike
Highbridge to Udell Trailheads
Manistee County, MI
1254 total NCT miles

She Who Builds Fire
41 - May 9-15, 1999

It would really be more interesting to have this chapter's name translated into an Indian language. "Boodaway," for example. That's "she who builds fire" in Chippewa. But the hike took place in Ohio: should not the language of choice be Shawnee? That would make the title "P'kaleena."[1] Since I am she who builds fire, maybe the translation should be to the language of the region where I grew up. That would require translation to Cayuga. Then again, since I mean no offense to any native peoples, maybe it's just as well that the title remains in English. Many Native Americans received a new name which fit their adult characteristics, usually given to that person by others who knew them well. The famous Sakakawea, whose name demarcates the western end of our trail, was known in childhood as "Grass Girl." She later was named "Bird Woman," the meaning of Sakakawea. But most of this trip was over before I was christened with my new name.

Rich Pfeiffer and I are making good on our promise to hike together again. This time we are not meeting in the middle of the night with water rising around our boots. Rather, I drive by day to Rich's house. We sleep in beds, and eat a hot breakfast at a kitchen table, although much earlier than I would normally choose. Then we drive together to spot a vehicle and begin walking from the crossroads where we ended our May 1998 hike.[2]

Rich's dog, Buddy, will join us for this hike, adding the canine dimension to our week together. Like Chips, Buddy's favorite game is fetch, but his name for it is "stick- stick." I'm

Buddy & Rich celebrate a good hike

not sure if Buddy's presence will cheer me, or bring on unbidden tears. Rich and I plan to see some of the most beautiful sections of trail in

---

[1.] Translated by Native Languages of the Americas; www.native-languages.org

[2.] see Chapter 32: "Ephemerata"

Ohio, and he intends to chat with some of the landowners along the trail. And for this trip I have brought my own set of maps. Rich is still in charge, but at least I will know where I am.

The walk begins on roads graveled with the chunky rocks which usually rip and bruise my feet; I am a bit worried by this. Then, around mid-day we reach a closed bridge. I am able to squeeze under the guardrail with my pack, but Rich, being larger, climbs down to cross on the rocky creek bed. I hear a grunt from the troll under the bridge, but it is not until later than Rich confesses to me that he has taken a nasty fall, twisting an elbow and skinning one knee. The next day Buddy gets a scare of his own, although we doubt that he appreciates the potential for disaster. Walking past a creek, we are looking for a spot where Buddy can get down to the water for a drink, and to cool down on this unusually warm day in May. Just as we find an access to the water we also spot two Copperhead snakes swimming in the very location we were about to send Buddy. Fortunately he is a very good dog, and obeys Rich immediately when he is ordered to "Come away." Finally, I take a fall of my own, catching one toe under a root as I am stepping down the very first step to the Grandma Gatewood Trail where we enter the Old Man's Cave area of Hocking Hills State Park. But none of these unfortunate events leads to any serious consequences, and my feet hold up fine. For once all the goblins which seem to haunt my Ohio hikes finish their mischief early, and are banished from the rest of our week.

Perhaps it is the power of Grandma Gatewood's memory that protects us. This section of trail from Ash Cave to Old Man's Cave was her favorite, and that's saying something! Emma Gatewood lived close to the land. She raised eleven children and four grandchildren before she read of the Appalachian Trail, and learned that no woman had ever walked its length. Without further ado, she headed for Maine to correct this condition. This first attempt ended when her glasses were broken, but she did hike the entire AT in 1958 (at age 71), and again in 1960 and 1963. A true believer in ultra-light, but also low-tech, she hiked with only a blanket, plastic sheet, cup, first-aid kit, a change of clothes and a raincoat. She ate dried beef, nuts and cheese, and the wild foods that she knew so well. Her footwear? Tennis shoes. She also walked from Independence, Missouri, to Portland, Oregon, in 1959. Her plan had been to walk with an Oregon Centennial Wagon Train, but she arrived in Independence a week late. No problem! She started walking, passed the wagon train, and arrived in Portland a week ahead of the wagons. You go, girl!

Monday is a perfect trail day, the kind that will keep you hiking and searching for the rest of your life just to capture another. We greet the morning with Flowering Dogwood sparkling in the sunlight. Rafts of dwarf Crested Iris flow down the rocky hillsides near the trail. Cooler, wetter areas are frothy with Allegheny Foamflower, and all are randomly punctuated with red Fire Pinks, and pink Moccasin Slipper.

Grandma knew beautiful trail when she saw it; she was not fond of this section simply because it was near her home. We begin walking above the gorge in the deep green of hemlocks, popping in and out of the refreshing shadow into hot pools of sunshine. Soon we drop to the bottom of the gorge where we follow Big Rocky Branch to a narrow plank bridge which has been installed to replace temporarily a better one which was swept away in the early spring. These gorges formed when glacial meltwater carved tunnels in the soft Black Hand Sandstone (named for a black hand print found by early explorers) of an ancient ocean bed. When the glacier retreated the harder cap rock was no longer supported and the roofs caved in. Instant gorge!

The next section returns to high ground, following a wide bench above the creek, but far below the rim of the gorge. We encounter a personal-size rain shower; beads of water dropping straight into the pool at our feet. Reason instructs us to conclude that this is a small waterfall coming from the overhung rim, far above. But with the source hidden in the trees we can't prove this with our eyes. Perhaps there really is a cartoon rain cloud over our heads! At the next one we are less awed by the odd spectacle, and we cool our hot heads and shoulders under the refreshing droplets.

Cedar Falls

Late that afternoon we reach Cedar Falls, one of the most interesting formations in Ohio. A large shallow pool of water is maintained by a sensuous stream emanating from a narrow cave. The stream splits into two curvaceous branches which flow around a dark point of rock and then rejoin. Softer areas in the Black Hand Sandstone are carved into free-form bowls cradling and cuddling the silky water as it continues downward, ending in a short free-fall into the pool. We have this wondrous playground to ourselves. Buddy asks for and is granted a game of stick-stick. Rich and I wade lazily, cooling our legs and heads. We rest on the rock islands, sampling different ones for maximum view and comfort until the shadows lengthen.

On Tuesday we approach the spectacular Ash Cave, the largest rock wall in Ohio. A chunky, blocky overhang spreads across the head of a gorge, and beneath this overhang, a high and shallow cave defines the end of the declivity. The entire rock face is covered with fine, powdery gray ash. The origins of the ash are lost in the history of the indigenous peoples. Perhaps the ashes come from centuries of fires, lit to warm bodies, cook meals, or host council meetings. Or perhaps the cave was used for less innocent purposes; another theory has it that gunpowder was made there. Nearby are natural saltpeter mines, necessary to make the explosive powder.

Rich and I are an odd hiking couple in terms of body rhythms. In his other life, Rich drives a delivery truck. He rises at 2 am, goes to a local transfer station, loads his truck, delivers the packages, and is done working by early afternoon. Me? I'm often going to bed at 2 am! On this hike, we are using something between the two schedules. Rich shakes my tent to awaken me before seven o'clock. Groaning, I emerge each morning to learn that he has been up since dawn. Breakfast is done, his tent is packed, and he is ready to hike. Buddy tries to help by urging me to play stick-stick. Rich is patient as I stumble through my morning routine, grinning quietly at my groggy clumsiness. And somehow I manage to get moving and packed in time for reasonably early starts. This also means that we finish the day's hiking around 2 pm. Thus we have lots of time for afternoon visiting, resting, or exploring near our campsite.

Today we take a short walk down a rich damp valley, finding dozens of clumps of yellow Mocassin Slipper, and several Showy Orchis. We also check out our route for tomorrow morning. "That way we'll be able to find it by flashlight!" teases Rich with a sly smile.

Showy Orchis

On Wednesday we enter Tar Hollow State Forest. We are welcomed by small butterflies of the same shade of blue as the trail blazes; perhaps their name might be Buckeye Butterflies. It seems as if we also see more than the usual number of yellow Zebra Swallowtails, and the black Pipestem Swallowtails with electric blue trim. Several wildflowers we've not seen before appear. Carolina Cranebill, Tansy Ragwort, and deep purple Larkspur are mixed in gloriously random splashes of color across sunny openings.

This is a special section of trail for Rich. It was here, less than two years ago, that he found Buddy. Remote and little patrolled by law enforcement, this area has a higher-than-average number of unwanted dog drops. One day, doing trail work, Buddy joined Rich's work crew and just stayed. At the end of the day Rich took him home. Attempts to find the owner were unsuccessful, and Rich gained a great trail dog.

Several sections of trail here cross private land and Rich takes the time to chat with as many owners as possible, strengthening those relationships and learning about their concerns. He takes his role of Section Supervisor quite seriously. He also is glad to share tips with me for trail maintenance and marking. My new chapter at home is just learning about this task of caring for the trail. Rich gives me tips about clearing and blazing, including plans for a small blaze painting kit. "Five miles to the quart!" he claims, speaking with the confidence born of experience at toting a paint can to the woods.

Our last night is spent high on a wooded, private ridge with the permission of the friendly landowner. We arrive at the site just before 3 pm, with a rain storm hard on our heels. We just have time to find level spots which are barely large enough for our small tents, to set them up, and dive in before the storm hits. Rich finds it amusing to pass the time by taking pictures of himself with his new digital camera. I decide that my tiny bivy tent is too small even for reading, and hope I never have to spend an entire day cooped up in it! In a couple of hours the rain stops, but the woods are damp and cold.

"A fire would sure feel good!" Rich exclaims, crawling out of his tent. "Too bad we can't get one going."

I am the quintessential "jack-of-all-trades, but master of none." However, there are a few things in life that I am really, really good at: building fires is one of them. "I can do that. Just give me a few minutes," I claim.

"I don't think so. Everything is too wet," Rich counters.

"You wait and see," I reply smugly.

In short order I have collected some fairly dry twigs which have fallen at angles or were protected by other branches. I will confess to using two matches. Nevertheless, in just a few minutes we are squatting around a bright fire holding warm cups of coffee and chocolate. Buddy nuzzles close to enjoy a warming hand on his back. Soon there is a fine blaze going, sustained by rolling three large logs in toward the center of the fire. Whenever their ends crumble to coals I roll them in a little more.

Taking a long sip of his drink, Rich sighs contentedly. "I'll have to give you a new name," he proposes. "I think I'll call you 'She Who Builds Fire.'"

Well, I may not actually be Shawnee, Chippewa, or Cayuga, but my dad always said I was at least half "wild Indian." I hope no one is offended; I always considered it a great compliment. And maybe Dad was right!

62 miles this hike
OH 664 to US 35
Hocking and Vinton Counties, OH
1315 total NCT miles

Rain First, Umbrellas Last
42 - June 13-15, 1999

The rain begins while I am attending church. Pastor Doug knows I am headed for the woods and a hike right after the service. As we shake hands he asks if I am still going. "Of course," I answer. "This just means I'll be pre-wetted."

Several weeks ago, a lady named Elaine Goodspeed called me from Grand Rapids and asked if I would like to join her and two friends on a hike. I don't know any of them, but they want to hike some miles near home that I haven't yet walked, so of course I say "yes." They plan to start hiking north from 16-Mile Road near Newaygo around noon. I can't make it there that soon, but we've agreed that I will walk as fast as I can, and they will wait for me at the 76th St. Trailhead.

"Pre-wetted" is exactly right! The rain is coming down in sheets, and I am soaked through almost as soon as I put my boots on and lock the car. By the muddy tracks, it's easy to see that I am following behind several hikers and a dog, and since that is exactly the description of the people I am chasing I have high hopes that at least my wet misery will soon be in good company. But the afternoon drips on, and although I am walking as fast as I possibly can, I never do catch up with anyone. After seven soggy miles, I reach 76th Street. No one is there. Tacked on the kiosk is a note. "...not sure if we missed you. We're soaking wet and need to get dried out! See you at Benton Lake Campground."

I admit to having a disgruntled thought or three. If they are chilly and wet sitting in a heated car, what am I, standing in the cold rain? Do they think that someone else is planning to pick me up? Oh well, I agreed to this plan to catch up to them. With a granola bar and a sigh, at 4:15 pm I head south again, knowing I have seven more miles to walk. Thankfully the rain tapers off, so my brisk pace is finally having a warming effect on my body. But you can be sure that by the time I reach my car, and then the campground, I am really hungry.

Elaine, Paula, another Joan, and Elaine's Sheltie, Bridgett, greet me cheerfully, glad that I have found them. Wonderful, tantalizing aromas arise from the open containers of food they have spread on the picnic table. "We're stuffed! Can you eat some of this?" they ask. You bet I can!

The long June twilight is spent resting and getting acquainted around a cozy fire, the quintessential camp evening. Fortunately the sky seems to have gotten all the weeping out of its system. The rest of the hike is dry and warm. The moisture and warmth seems to call forth a panoply of plant and animal life. We all seem to notice the ferns. The rain has washed patches of Northern Maidenhair to a clear paint-box green. With its dark forest-green "stockings" marching up the rachis, Christmas Fern is easy to recognize. We come across an entire field of Ostrich Fern, a sea of waving, feathery fronds. Paula and Joan's favorite is the fern that isn't a fern. Sweetfern, *Comptonia peregrina*, is actually a woody plant related to bayberry, but its leaves do look like short, bumpy fern fronds. On warm, damp days such as this its fragrance is released almost without brushing against the foliage. The distinctive sweet and spicy aroma is an aerosol of everything summer suspended in the still air. One pink Pasture Rose provides poignant visual counterpoint.

Creatures, too, are called forth into the warm woods. We meet a beautiful Box Turtle with the bright orange squiggles on its shell arranged symmetrically, looking very much like fireworks exploding on the dark dome of a very small sky. He peeks shyly at us from between shell and plastron, but doesn't find us frightening enough to duck inside and slam the door.

A Scarlet Tanager parallels our path. We only occasionally catch a glimpse of his bright red-orange sides, but his Robin-with-a-sore-throat song is easy to recognize. We also hear the Black-throated Blue Warbler, whose call I have only recently learned. "I am so la-ZEE," he claims from the lower branches of some nearby bush. Warblers are a source of much frustration to amateur birdwatchers (that includes me!), and the female of this species is the textbook brown and olive enigma. However, the male has a beautiful deep blue head and back, with white below. He can't be all that lazy since he's always managed to stay just out of my sight, but his melody is hauntingly appealing.

On the other hand, we have no trouble seeing the Hog-nosed Snake, or Puff Adder. She has claimed a section of the trail and is challenging our right to pass. This harmless reptile is perhaps one of the ugliest in North America. Without careful study, your first impression is that you are looking at a rattlesnake, and that much too closely! The snake is counting on just that reaction. It coils its mottled body, shakes its tail, flattens its head, hisses and strikes. However, if you recognize that it has no actual rattles, nor the triangular head and pit of the viper, you can hold it down carefully with a forked stick, and even pick it up. At this point the cowardly worm will roll belly-up, defecate, and feign death. If you would happen to be bitten, the wound is no more serious than any minor puncture. The snake has no venom.

Warm damp forests are also perfect for the growth of fungi. Several logs have grown the familiar Artists Conk. For many of us this was the first fungus we ever learned; we were shown how to pull it carefully from the wood and scratch primitive pictures of leaves, or of pines along a lakeshore, on its sensitive white undersurface. What woodland lodge is complete without one or two such family masterpieces on the mantel? Occasionally one may even find a true work of art drawn by someone with talent, as well as a handy fungus and a few spare minutes — the camper's scrimshaw.

Much more interesting is a four-inch Jack Pine, circled by a ring of huge flabby overlapping wings. It appears to be a common Oyster Mushroom, but it is so symmetric that we are tempted to believe that it was arranged by some other artist loose in the woods.

Just about a mile before we reach the end of our hike we come upon those umbrellas we needed so badly on the first day. Growing eighteen inches high from the forest litter is a "pile" of Umbrella Polypore. The fleshy tan umbrellas grow from a central stalk, a huge jumble of diminutive bumbershoots warehoused for an army of very small walkers!

Since we are not small and it is no longer raining, the umbrellas are not practical, but no matter. We've had a wonderful excursion in the summer woodland. We can graciously afford to leave the umbrellas for the mice or other tiny nibblers. The umbrellas are reported to be delicious.

Umbrella Polypore

28 miles this hike
16-Mile Rd. to Centerline Rd.
Newaygo and Lake Counties, MI
1343 total NCT miles

Back to the Beginning
43 - July 10, 1999

Since that ambitious April,[1] the Spirit of the Woods Chapter has indeed accomplished many things. On National Trails Day we attracted 62 people to the woods; 17 of these were kids. The framework for the boardwalk was in place by then, and we supervised the kids in setting and screwing decking boards in place. They loved it!

Since then work crews have continued extending the boardwalk, and it looks as if we'll have the project done by the end of summer. Meanwhile, we've decided to hold a training session for painting blazes, and to get going on that project. We have 80 miles of trail to spruce up! Both Bill Menke[2] and Rich Pfeiffer[3] have given me tips, and I'm about to pass on this knowledge to eager members of our chapter. The Park Service has sent us scrapers, brushes and paint, and we've made some painting kits from Rich's plans. The standard blaze is a two-by-six-inch rectangle, but first the tree must be scraped to remove the loose outer bark, dirt, lichen, etc. The blaze is painted with Nelson® blue tree-marking paint. It's supposed to be specially formulated to be long-lasting on trees. For sure it's messy! It's oil-based and thick, and waving a brush high above the head can result in blobbing and blazing many things besides the tree of choice. Such splatters and drips are to be worn as badges.

Today 18 people have assembled who are willing to wear the blue with pride. First we practice blazing a small mountain of cordwood, brought just for that purpose. Crisp, square corners are

Kids line up with their boards on National Trails Day

---

[1] See Chapter 40: "April Ambitions"

[2] See Chapter 13: "Breaking the Chains"

[3] See Chapter 41: "She Who Builds Fire"

tricky to paint, but they are the goal. We talk about the spacing of blazes. Measured distance between blazes is not important; what matters are sight lines. From any given blaze you want to be able to see one more blaze on the trail ahead. Depending on the density of the forest and the meanderings of the trail, the next blaze might need to be nearby or farther away. Turns are marked with two blazes, one higher than the other, with the top one offset in the direction of the turn.

Soon we are done practicing, and divided into small teams we head south from Udell Trailhead, choosing the trees which will be blazed, and painting neat rectangles on them. We learn that this is a project that will take a serious amount of time to do correctly.

Chapter member, Nick Mehmed, paints blazes

Perhaps most appropriately for me, we have chosen to begin this project at the same trailhead where I first found the North Country Trail... and then never did find the actual trail for lack of blazing.[4] Today, we are making it less likely that the next person who stops here to explore will get lost.

7 miles this hike
Udell TH to 9-Mile Bridge
Manistee County, MI
1350 total NCT miles

[4.] See "Introduction to the Trail"

The Song of Hiawatha's Friends
44 - August 11-20, 1999

I. The Song Path

"By the shores of Gitchee-Gumee,
By the shining Big-Sea-Waters,"
Walked three friends
      in summer Heat Moon.

Trod the dunes of Nagow Wudjoo
Where the merry Pau-Puk-Keewis
Danced at Hiawatha's wedding:
"Stamped upon the sand, and tossed it
Wildly in the air around him
Heaping all the shores with Sand Dunes,
Sand Hills of the Nagow Wudjoo!"

"Came they to the rocky headlands,
To the Pictured Rocks of sandstone
Looking over lake and landscape,"
Where the Old Man of the Mountain
Hid the vexing Pau-Puk-Keewis,
Mischief-making Pau-Puk-Keewis.

Where Hiawatha with his mittens,
"Magic mittens, Minjekahwun,
Smote great caverns in the sandstone,
And the crags fell, and beneath them
Dead among the rocky ruins
Lay the cunning Pau-Puk-Keewis."

On the shores of Gitchee-Gumee
Friends of Hiawatha rested,
"Heard the whispering of the pine-trees,
Heard the lapping of the waters,
Sounds of music, words of wonder;
'Minne-wawa!' said the Pine-Trees,
'Mudway-aushka!' said the water."

Maggie, Marie, Joan

Grand Sable Dunes

Grand Portal Point

"On its margin the great forest,
Dark behind it rose the forest"
Where "the melancholy fir-trees
Waved their dark green fans
                        above" them —
Sighing for dead Chibiabos.
He the master of all singing,
He who taught the brook its music,
The rivulet, the Sebowisha —
Sighing for the strong man Kwasind
"Who seized the huge rock in his fingers
Tore it from its deep foundation,
He the very strong man Kwasind."

Fallen rocks along the cliff

Through the leafy woods they wandered,
Over smooth and tranquil streamlets,
Motionless the sleeping shadows
Dream of never-ending summer
Sent by Shawondasee. Fat and lazy
Shawondasee, keeper of the South-wind.
He it is who woos the sunlight,
Sweetens Meenahga, the blueberry,
Scatters mushrooms red and yellow
Through the leaf-mold, beads of wampum.

Passed with Gheezis, the great sun-ball
"From the distant realms of Wabun
From his shining lodge of silver"
At the home of Wabun, East-wind.
"He it is whose silver arrows
Chase the dark o'er hill and valley.

Unidentified mushroom

And the sunshine and the shadows
Fell in flecks and gleams upon them,"
Brake in sun-flecks on their shoulders
"Through the rifted leaves and branches."
To the arms of Mudjekeewis
Gheezis in the eve descending
Set the clouds a-blush with passion.

Sun-flecks on our shoulders

To the Portals of the Sunset,
To the doorway of the West-Wind,
Westward, westward fared the travelers.

Saw the skin of Mishe-Mokwa[1]
Him who Mudjekeewis conquered,
Saw the serpent, subtle Kenabeek.
Were protected from all monsters,
From Wendigoes, loathsome giants,
From the war-song of Suggema,
Fearful warrior, the mosquito,
And from thunder, Annemeekee,
Crying, "Baim-wawa," in anger.

Miner's Castle

II. The Invitation

"Ye who love the haunts of Nature,
Love the sunshine of the meadow,
Love the shadow of the forest,
Love the wind among the branches,"
Come see the grouse, Mushkodasa,
See old Kagh, the sleeping quilled one,
See where hides brown Omakakii[2],
And tooth signs of Ahmeek, the Beaver.

Spruce Grouse

Ye who seek a pleasant pathway,
Seek Chetowaik, the plover's pathway,
Seek that furred and striped marauder,
Nervous Agongos the chipmunk;
Ye who seek to trace the wanderings
of Pau-puk-keena, the grasshopper,
Who wish to learn where Mama[3] feasted,

Grasshopper tracks in sand

Yellow-bellied Sapsucker holes

---

[1] bear

[2] frog

[3] woodpecker

Or play the strings of Subbekashe[4] –
Follow in our pleasant pathway.

So to journey onward, westward,
Become Strong-Heart, Soan-ge-taha,
Follow Kayoshk, white-winged seagull
Through the home of Hiawatha,
Through the haunts of Hiawatha,
Walk now with us through the Northland.

Beginning the westward journey

Apologies to Henry Wadsworth Longfellow[5] if you don't care for my "song," but I can't ignore the fact that we are walking through Hiawatha's homeland. A significant figure in my childhood was a remarkable grandmother. Granny Rowe could, and often did, recite epic poems from memory. I was sometimes tucked into bed with Hiawatha for a companion, and those memories are all pleasant. I've convinced my friends that for our evening reading on this trip we should include the full "Song of Hiawatha." Perhaps they are less enthused than I, but they acquiesce, and the stories are timeless.

Marie, her cousin Maggie, and I are trekking some of the most beautiful miles anywhere on the North Country Trail. We chose this hike for this summer because dogs are not allowed in Pictured Rocks National Lakeshore. Since I don't have another trail dog yet, this seems like a good time to do these miles. We begin far to the east of Pictured Rocks where the trail follows the lonely shores of Gitchee-Gumee, that great Lake Superior. Blue-green water is reminiscent of Caribbean seas, except for the temperature! Miles of sand are strewn with water-rounded rocks: banded red and gray sandstone saucers, flecked granite smoothed into eggs of all sizes, flattened balls of black basalt with angling bands of white or pink. The wind rattles the Beach Pea and gyrates the beach grass, drawing circles in the fine white sand.

[4.] spider

[5.] All parts of the poem on pages 222-224, and 237 within quotation marks are from "The Song of Hiawatha;" by Henry Wadsworth Longfellow; 1855; public domain.

Maggie brings a new flavor to the usual palate of our hiking. She had backpacked many years ago, and now wants to try out the experience again. For footwear she has brought oxfords made by the Caterpillar Company. Their triangular logo is molded into the soles along with the words "Walking Machines." "I'm ready," Maggie announces every day, "I've got my walking machines on!" She is an Artist, zany, always bubbling with a new idea or a new way of looking at things. She arranges designs of the beautiful stones in the sand, builds small cairns decorated with driftwood and whitewashed bones as offerings to the spirits. She forces us to look ever more closely at the beauty of green sun-lit leaves against the orange fungi, to see faces in the rocks, toes on the trees, geometry in the patterns of lichen, colors and textures rampant across the landscape.

No trip of mine seems to be complete without a "missing trail" adventure and we find this one between Muskallonge State Park and Grand Marais. Deep within the Lake Superior State Forest we find a trail of blazes to follow, and I do mean just that. There is no treadway at all, and we wander from blue mark to blue mark along any convenient way. The route we are walking doesn't resemble the line on our map very much, and when we cross the road from Randolph Lake a man in a car stops and insists that the road is not where our map says it is. He claims that we are only a mile from Lake Superior via a ski trail, which he points out. Following the ski trail, the cries of "Baim-wawa" begin to be heard from the skies. Just in time, before the rain, we pitch our tent on a round hilltop so covered with Reindeer Moss that it appears as if we are camped in the snow.

A steady cold rain keeps us in the tent until noon the next day, when we continue the search for trail markers, still heading towards the lake. Plunging down a steep hillside, Marie announces, "Going down! Third floor, toiletries. Second floor, notions." What we really need are towels. Ferns and baby pines retain buckets of water after a rain, and whoever leads our gaggle is soaked to the thighs.

Soon we come to a stake, painted bright orange. I am quite apprehensive at this find, suspecting the end of some management area, and perhaps the end of our blazes, which we are still following without benefit of treadway. Indeed, there is not a blaze in sight. But we follow a line of young pines which look like a natural pathway, and sure enough, one blaze winks at us from a hillside ahead. Next we come to a USGS benchmark. It's a wonder we saw it! The four-inch engraved disk is flat to the ground in the center of a weed patch that might have been mowed once this year. But the information it provides locates us exactly on our map. We cross one more low hill, and suddenly Kabibonok'ka, the cold wind from the lake, slams us as if we have walked into a meat locker. We make our way to the shore, and the lake today doesn't look Caribbean in the least. Gun-metal gray rollers are breaking into whitecaps beneath a dark, forbidding sky. Soon we locate a blaze, but its usefulness is minimal. It is still firmly nailed to a tree, but the tree is lying in the lake at the bottom of the recently collapsed sandy bluff. However, with the lake as a major landmark all we need to do is follow the shore westward to Grand Marais.

After about 100 yards of climbing through fallen hemlocks, and being grabbed by wet blueberry bushes we realize that eleven miles of this terrain are going to make a mighty long day. But the blueberries are large, ripe and luscious! Another hundred yards ahead an elderly lady is filling a bucket with the blue fruits. She can not hear us approaching through the shrieking of that cold wind, and even our attempts to alert her to our presence by calling out, "Hello," are unheard. Not surprisingly, when she finally looks up we fear she is going to faint, but the lady has spunk, and soon recovers from her surprise at being accosted by three women clambering through the timber. She informs us that the trail is all washed away, and that the shoreline is like this all the way to Grand Marais. Her advice is to take the jeep trail, and we do just that.

Some of the best wildlife experiences on my hikes have happened on detours, and this proves true once again. Strutting in the tangled branches beside the trail is a male Spruce Grouse. Red patches on the sides of his head, and white speckling on the edges of his dark breast make him a most handsome bird. Shy and bold at the same time, he lets us approach closely enough to watch him, but always takes one hop, keeping us at a safe distance.

A few miles later, we are quite pleased when we intersect new, properly marked trail. A good end to that adventure!

Grand Marais is hosting a Rock Festival this weekend, and although we have a reservation at the campground, the 127 regular, and 25 overflow sites are filled. Tents are even pitched in the parking lot. The registration lady sighs and fills out a "Parking Area" tag for us too. It seems just too incongruous, to be camping in the midst of so many people who have no particular interest in the outdoors. But the sunset over the lake comes to the rescue of my psyche. The wind has died down, and the lake is a soft, matte black. At the horizon a band of regal purple stretches as far as the eye can see. Above that, the sky burns a deep orange. All the colors and surfaces are flat, with no shadows or variations of light, a landscape cut from posterboard by a child.

———— ✺ ————

By noon the next day we are waiting at the Ranger Station at the east end of Pictured Rocks National Lakeshore to pick up our hiking permit. We have a supply box here to retrieve and sort, and while we are doing this we talk to some giggling college students who have just come off the trail. They might not be giggling if their story had turned out just a little differently. One of the boys left his tent at night to take a leak, and did not take a flashlight. Although he says that he only went over one small hill to obtain some privacy, he was unable to find his way back to their group of tents. He spent the night outside in a t-shirt and shorts, huddled in the lee of a dune trying to keep warm. The night was chilly; my thermometer registered 50° this morning. I hope this group of young people learned something about safety in the woods from the experience of their friend, and will all be a little smarter next time.

Inside the stone building, Ranger Brody is a smiling, bearded patriarch. He is deftly juggling permits, phone calls, sales, and questions. We had been told that our permit was unalterable, whether we liked the campsites or not; and we did not. Based on the sites available we had been forced to accept one fourteen-mile day in our itinerary. We didn't really want to have to hurry so fast through this area where we knew there would be so much to see. Since we aren't anywhere near first in line we listen to a couple ahead of us whine and plead to change their permit, and succeed! We leave out the whining, but we do ask nicely. Brody grins, scoops up the phone, checks with the Ranger Station at the west end of the Lakeshore for cancellations, and just like that, our longest day is reduced to twelve miles! Beautiful!

The shadows are already lengthening before we scoot away from the parking lot, but we arrive at AuSable Campsite with plenty of daylight left. We hang our food on the metal bear pole. A separate, long hook is provided too, so you can lift your bags to the top of the pole. We discover that there is a bit of skill required to leverage a heavy bag, swinging at the end of a 15-foot rod, into position and to then slip it on to a stationary hook! Even so, there is time for Maggie, our socialite, to make the acquaintance of the kids "next door," and for all of us to take a dip in the lake. Swimming in Lake Superior has traditionally been known as "passing the manhood test," no matter what the swimmer's gender. Its normal temperature is closer to 50° than 70°. But this summer the big lake is unusually warm, and we take good advantage of this fact. Most every night we tuck ourselves into bed feeling cool and clean instead of the backpacker's normal sweaty and stinky.

It's cherry shortcake for breakfast, cooked over an open fire. The chipmunks are more of a threat than bears this morning. If you take your eyes off any morsel of food for a moment they will grab it! Too many campers have fed these cute little thieves.

We are taking a day off from hiking to tour the AuSable Lighthouse. It's been non-stop racing for days for Marie and Maggie. They had scrambled to get packed and ready to come to Michigan from New York, and had car trouble on the way. Because of this we changed our beginning hiking date, but couldn't change the entry date to Pictured Rocks, so we had to move our starting location. Then we managed to get a late start from my house anyway since we were trying to do three days of preparation and sorting in two days. Marie has hardly had a breather in a week. With a sigh she announces, "I'm going to stay by the campfire till I'm older."

"Our permit won't last that long," I warn. But Marie is not frightened of me!

AuSable Lighthouse

By afternoon Marie is older and we take the lighthouse tour. What a lonely place this familiar lighthouse once was! For years the site was inaccessible except by boat: supplies, mail, and companions arrived only occasionally. At first just one couple lived at the light; they could split the night shift to keep the lamp lit. However, when fog whistles were added an assistant keeper was required to keep the steam up to power the ear-piercing horns. There's a job that required a true masochist!

When the light was built they dug through 25 feet of sand to reach bedrock, and built the 120-foot spiral staircase first. Then the masons used the stairway as a guide to construct the walls of the tower, first an inner wall of white glazed bricks, and then the outer wall, with an air space between. The four-foot Fresnel lens was imported from France. Fresnel lenses bend the light rays from the flame and concentrate them to create the powerful beams which flash through the night or stormy sky. Muslin curtains cover the open windows to protect the lens from becoming etched by blowing sand. The AuSable Light, flashing once every 2.5 seconds, could be seen for eighteen miles. Each light on the Great Lakes has a specific color and different number of seconds between flashes, so that a ship can "read" which light they are seeing.

Technology may be considered progress, but it is much less impressive to look at. Mounted on the edge of the catwalk railing at the top of this scenic, historic light is a solar panel. Next to that sits a "bubble gum machine," a "K-Mart special" light, in white, about eight inches across and a foot high. This wart on the skin of the venerable tower now sends its beam across fourteen miles of darkness each night. I know it makes perfect sense to place the new light here, but it feels rude, like a youngster thumbing his nose at his elders.

The Song of Hiawatha's Friends

———— ✳ ————

Our mood this night approximates that of a junior-high slumber party. We pass the evening making stupid jokes about how to pee in the woods. Or more precisely, how not to pee in the woods! (For example: don't face downhill or your boots will get wet.) In empathy with our damp topic the sky piddles on us all night, but the morning clears to reveal a clean, bright day. We hike through a moist hemlock forest, our footfalls hushed on the soft peat. The day stirs thoughts of another Longfellow poem, "Evangeline."

"This is the forest primeval. The murmuring pines and the hemlocks, bearded with moss, and with garments green, indistinct in the twilight..." And throbbing through the afternoon, again the cries of "Baim-wawa" are heard from the sky.

At Pine Bluffs, Maggie's artistic soul inspires us to decorate our tent site with clumps of Reindeer Moss, interesting sticks, grasses, and colored rocks. Around 8 pm we head for the beach in our swimsuits, with the water filter, planning to fill all our bottles to save time in the morning. We may be saving morning time, but I can hardly recall a more complicated filtering experience. The air is filled with biting flies! We wade out rib-deep, thus protecting our lower halves. Marie holds the bottles, I pump the filter, and Maggie's job is to fan and slap and blow wherever needed to keep those pesky *Diptera* off all our skins. Every so often the flies get ahead of Maggie, and one of us takes a sudden dip to dislodge a biter.

As we finish the water project, the sun is slipping down toward the lake. We swim out to deeper water, to cover more of our bodies. We spread out, each seeking a private moment with the cosmos. The flies seem to be leaving for wherever flies go for the night, and the sun slips behind a bank of low clouds. I scull out even deeper, and my motions become lazy, providing just enough buoyancy to keep my head above the surface. Each swell rolls toward me, rising to cover the horizon, the mound passes through me, sweeping toward the distant shore. Fully relaxed, my eyes cease to focus on single objects, seeing instead patterns and rhythms. Twisted satin ribbons of midnight blue and baby blue coil and ripple across the liquid surface, braiding and unbraiding around my body, water sprites, the Nee-ba-naw-baigs, dancing a maypole dance. Coral fire burns below the gray cloudbank at the horizon. The upper edges of the gray are teased into puffed cottony balls. Wisps pulled from the puffs shimmer with gold and silver. The sun itself is still hidden behind the gray, but from the center of that dark band white rays of light stream downward to the lake and upward, strong, straight spears shooting out to me and up to the heavens.

All sense of time is lost. Has the sun stood still this evening? The mesmerizing light and motion lasts minutes or hours, till the sun winks through the gray cloud, a suncatcher jewel throwing rainbows with the force of mighty Kwasind.

The spell is broken. I return to the shore, and climb the hill to our campsite. Once inside the tent we hold a killing party for the flies who have made the unfortunate decision to attempt to spend the night with us.

In the morning another camper runs over to our site, exuberantly shouting, "You have to come see this!"

"This" is a large Porcupine, perched in full view on the slanting branch of a Cottonwood tree. I begin taking pictures, inching closer. Kagh perks up, and begins to move her paws. I must have disturbed her; this will surely be the end of any chance for a good photograph. Wrong! She is quite used to campers, and is only arranging herself more comfortably on the branch. She finds a position she likes, lays her head down on her paws and settles in for a nap.

On our way to Mosquito River an awesome pair of Pileated Woodpeckers keeps pace with us for nearly a mile. Hearing their loud hammering on dead trees is fairly common, but to see these normally shy birds flying so close to us is a rare treat.

The trail has been following the coastline, but by mid-day rocks begin breaking from the sandy ground. Next we come to a little rocky cliff sprouting like a fledging wing from the forest. The trail ascends its gentler "feathered" back, and returns to the beach. Before long we climb around another rocky wing, but this time the rock is larger, miles larger! We emerge at the top of the bulwark onto a plateau as smooth as a flagstone courtyard. The courtyard adjoins a porch with four chunky stone pillars supporting a stone roof. The porch fronts on Lake Superior. We are dumbfounded, slack-jawed, stopped dead in our tracks at this odd discovery. Suddenly someone cries "Chapel Rock!"

Somehow we had failed to realize that we would be arriving today at the section of the National Lakeshore known for its interesting formations. How is it that this rocky playground emerges complete from the sand like some *Planet of the Apes* movie set?

Picture the state of Michigan, both the Lower and Upper Peninsulas, and pretend that it is made of soft, sandy clay which will retain an impression made upon it. Take a shallow bowl and center the bottom of that bowl just where the

Chapel Rock seen from the water

thumb meets the hand of the Lower Peninsula. Push hard on the bowl, so that when you take it away the entire state has become shaped like that bowl. Now put that clay state in the kiln of time and bake it for 100 million years. Take it out of the oven and spread a few more layers of sandy clay over the whole thing, but be sure you keep that bowl-like shape. Add one more thin layer of lime frosting (not the citrus kind!) on top, and pop it back in the kiln for another 400 million years. While you are waiting for the timer to buzz throw some light clay and salt on it too. Let a glacier stomp over the whole thing, and then leave again, dropping sand and rocks behind it. Buzzzzz! Michigan's done!

All that loose stuff, and the glacial action, have filled in and around the bowl, but not quite enough to cover the now hard-baked edges of the bowl. One of those hard, angled edges poking through the sand is Pictured Rocks. The clay base, the pre-Cambrian floor of the bowl is mottled-red Jacobean Sandstone. The middle layer is the Munising Formation. This layer is a mixture of conglomerate, cross-bedded, dark Chapel Rock Sandstone, and light-colored Miner's Castle Sandstone. The frosting is a hard limestone layer known as the AuTrain Foundation. This hard crust helps protect the soft sandstone from eroding away completely. The rocks are not only varied in color, but are painted with minerals leaching from the stone by water running and dribbling down the faces of the cliffs.

Seemingly in sympathy with the stark, pre-historic landscape we have entered, a cold wind has begun to blow off the lake. It is strong enough that we are glad it is blowing us land-ward wherever the trail wanders close to the edge. The horizon is gray, fading to black, and the waves break in heavy whitecaps above the deep green water.

Around every curve and headland is a new, startling view of the pied cliffs. Below us, white gulls circle and glide, their screams silenced by the wind. Although the landscape is full of lurid colors – green, orange, tan, black – and fantastic shapes, it is also bleak and empty. A shadow moves, but it is not ours. Is it a gull's? Or does it belong to one of the Puk-Wudjies, the little people of the forest? Legend says that mockers of the old Osseo, Son of the Evening Star, were changed into birds, until Osseo's son broke the spell with an arrow, and they returned to earth as diminutive dancers and mischief-makers.

At Mosquito River we spend a pleasant evening with a lady named Mateo who seems as mysterious as the Chippewa legends. She calls herself a herbalist, and is collecting mushrooms for her meals, and perhaps more mystical needs. Her garb is topped with a Peruvian tasseled hat and a fringed shawl. She shares cups of tea with us, and we share readings from "Hiawatha" with her.

Maggie is usually the one who arises to watch the sun come up, but this morning Marie and I take on that responsibility. For a seat we find a large flat rock jutting into the lake at Mosquito Beach. The sharp arrows of Gheezis strike the rocks and a golden sap pours from the wounds, gilding the cliffs and water.

A long day of hiking brings us to the famous formation at the western end of Pictured Rocks. We reach Miner's Castle at 5 pm, and the lengthening shadows heighten the drama of the site. A tour boat is framed between its two pocked white towers. The cliffs fall sheer to the beach. We read the sign which tells of sailors shipwrecked here who climbed into the caves below the Castle, and huddled in its keep for three days until they could be rescued. The walkway to the towers is fenced for the safety of the people and the protection of the soft rock. The last time I was here, in the early 1970's, there was no fence. I study the rocks and recognize the places where I stood and gazed straight down to the shallows below. It was so much easier to feel close to the history of the place when you were allowed to climb and touch and experience the height and the danger. Even though I understand the need for the fence, spectating from a safe distance just isn't the same.

We spend the night at the Cliffs campsite. There the bear poles are kept greased because the Raccoons have learned how to climb them. Sure enough, in the night, one tries hard to reach our food bags, and makes a terrible racket clanging something against the pole. But in the morning the food is still safe. Score one for the people!

On Thursday we pick up our second supply box at Sand Point, and hike into Munising. At the Hiawatha National Forest Ranger Station they are thrilled to learn that we are continuing our hike westward for a few more miles. Most people hike only through the National Lakeshore, and the trail is little used west of that point. Maggie wanders into town to buy a root beer, and we join her after chatting a bit longer with the rangers. We have a few road miles to do here, and soon a car passes, its driver honking and waving. "Oh, that's the man who paid for my soda," Maggie informs us with a sly grin!

Maggie and Marie thought that since we were leaving the picturesque cliffs behind that perhaps I would begin moving faster than Way-muk-kwa-na, the caterpillar. One reason our progress has been slow is that at every turn of the trail someone cries "Nushka! Oh, look at that!" Then the camera has to be taken out, and we all stand around with our packs on our backs while I fuss with lenses and settings to take yet more pictures. But more speed is not to be.

It's true that we leave the cliffs behind. We are now hiking through the western division of the Hiawatha National Forest. We are away from the lake, surrounded again by deciduous forest. We are within a rich woods where a new and different fungus appears every few yards. Now I am not only stopping and standing, but contorting my pack-backed self into whatever awkward pose is required to get a good shot of the current colorful mushroom. The names tell intriguing stories: Violet Branched Coral, Dead-man's Fingers, Yellow Tuning Fork, Salmon Unicorn, and Turkey Tail. Black Chanterelle arises like a buttery black rose from the ground. We find Gem-studded Puffball, Oyster Mushrooms, Orange Jelly, and yellow and orange slime molds. Not a fungus, but another parasitic plant, the purple Beechdrops sends naked stems upward from the littered beech leaves.

The ones we nick-name "Rear-view Mirror Fungus" because their stems grow from the sides of their oval faces turn out to be Hemlock Polypore. We never have identified the ones with thick stems, having tops that look like perfectly cooked golden pancakes. Everywhere we see a small perfect stereotypical golden cap with a bright red-orange stem. They are so numerous that it is difficult to keep from trampling their lovely fruiting bodies. But this beauty also has yet to be identified! Two expert mycological friends have looked over the pictures, but without spore prints and more information, no one has yet been able to identify them, proof that sometimes the most common item is also the most rare. Maggie and Marie exhibit great patience as I tie myself in knots to get a good angle on the current treasure 'shroom, but I suspect that if I also start taking time to make spore prints and count gills they may object!

Dog Stinkhorn

The oddest of all is easily identified. I've seen its mug shot in the books, the Dog Stinkhorn. This fungus grows like a fat pink or white finger from the ground. Instead of a mushroom "cap" the end appears to be encased in a tight ferrule which has caused the tissue around it to become an inflamed and angry red. Stinkhorns deserve their name, erupting from a small "egg," which looks like it came straight off the set of *Alien*. The egg contains a green slime which becomes increasingly fetid as the horn matures. At least these creatures don't fly through the air and attach themselves to your face! The slime contains their spore mass, and the odor of decay attracts insects. They carry the spores away on their feet and bodies, propagating the fungi.

For our final night in the woods there is no easy campsite. We've been spoiled by the established sites within Pictured Rocks! Marie and I revert to our regular routine like some old married couple. At about 6 pm I mention that we have covered enough miles, and can begin looking for a campsite. "We could check over there in that open area," I mention casually, after a few more minutes.

"Let's go just a little farther," Marie counters.

We both are looking for places where we might tuck a tent in this woods of younger trees and with more understory. "How about that?" I ask, pointing left.

"Let's go a little farther," Marie repeats.

In a few more minutes I say, "Let me check up on that ridge."

"All right, let us know what you find."

I push my way through the shrubby growth and a damp slough near the trail, and reach a fine dry ridge on the other side. "We could fit the tent up here," I announce.

"I'm looking over here," Marie calls.

"O.K., but this will work"

"I don't like the way you got there. Come look at this place."

Maggie and I catch up to Marie and view her selected spot. "This is nice," we agree.

This typical and apparently requisite exchange completed, we shoehorn the tent in between the saplings and a large collection of orb spider webs, and I climb through the thick underbrush with difficulty, up the nearby hill to look for a cache tree. There is no convenient bear pole here. But there are no inconvenient noisy or talkative neighbors either! I find a great, high branch overhanging a lumpy clearing, and by summoning an extra oomph of energy, manage to sling the rope over the branch. Perfect!

However, soon after we retire for the night a terrible caterwauling begins in the definite direction of our cache bag! It's probably just a Raccoon, but why would it be that angry at not being able to get an easy meal? It's our last night, and we are all feeling too lazy to care. Even if something gets the bag there will probably be enough food left for one meal. After ten minutes of yowling, squawking and screeching we hear the creature shuffle off through the leaves. In the morning, everything is fine. The bag is untouched!

"What would cause a Raccoon to make that much noise?" I ask Ranger Ramona after we return home.

"Something trying to get her babies," she answers quickly.

Since this has no connection to our food bags, I dismiss the topic from my mind... that is until later yet, when I ask myself the question, "But what is big enough to be trying to steal Raccoon babies?!"

——— ✳ ———

One more morning of walking, the search for a motel room, showers, and a nice restaurant meal cap the hiking experience. But we have one more activity on our list. Now that we've seen the Pictured Rocks cliffs from the top, we want to take the boat tour to see them from water level. The day is perfect, the sun warm and the breeze soft. Our

The Song of Hiawatha's Friends

captain looks not quite young enough to dream of the Tooth Fairy, but he is a skillful pilot. Not long after we pass Grand Island and leave the harbor at Munising, the painted cliffs appear on our right. We had debated whether to take the boat tour before hiking or afterwards. Afterwards has turned out to be the delightfully correct choice. We continually point and exclaim things such as, "That's where we ate lunch on Thursday." "O m'gosh! We stood right there and waved at the boats," as current hikers wave their hands and hats at us joyfully.

First we cruise past the obvious Miner's Castle, the westernmost formation of the picturesque section. Red kayaks dot the green waters. Such colorful counterpoint is artistic, but I appreciate more the canoes we encounter. I want the scene to be reminiscent of the Hiawatha tales.

From this level, we can see many formations which were not so easily located or even noticed from above. Now the gulls soar above us, along the cliffs stained with black, red, green and orange. Upturned cones of weathered rock guard the entrance to Painted Cove, and a flock of the gulls has settled on one slanted frustum, waiting for their dinner to swim past.

Next we glide past Mosquito Beach. "There's where we watched the sunrise!" "There's the little bridge!" This is followed by a flurry of picture taking of a scene we could not see at all from above, the Caves of the Bloody Chiefs. The cliff is undercut, and dark, suggestive stains have dripped from the gash above that cut.

The water level is low this year, but that is good for our education. The portals in the cliffs appear as ovals, pointed at each end. This shows the normal water level (at the points), and demonstrates how the rock erodes both above and below that level.

Another view hidden from above is Rainbow Cave. We wonder at this name. The rocks are dripping with many black streaks, but are less colorful than many other painted rock faces.

And now we are shown the official "Indian Head" point. We had proposed a different headland for that profile. Many such rounded, irregular cliffs can be imagined into faces. Standing on the Indian's brow are other hikers, taking their turn to shout and wave at us, the *nouveau touristes*.

My favorite cave comes next... and it has no official name! I call it "Sunrise Cave." Surrounding the largest portal shine spreading rays of white and gilded red.

Grand Portal Point looks for all the world like a Way-muk-kwa-na, a huge curious caterpillar. It noses its way into the lake, crawling with its true legs, its prolegs vanishing back into the faceless cliffs. We have wondered why this interesting, but not spectacular formation has been given the name "Grand Portal." At least one other portal along the way has been larger. The answer lies in its history, and is a reminder of how nature and life constantly change. The Portal did indeed used to be grand. Another entire section of rocky cliff used to project from the front of the caterpillar's nose. Through this wall gaped a huge domed opening, the grand portal of its nomenclature. In 1898, this entire structure collapsed. Not even small remnants remain to remind those who pass by 100 years later of its existence.

Just beyond this rounded headland, five points with sharply chiseled bows jut into the lake. This is aptly known as Battleship Row. Our young Captain announces, "It's calm enough to have some fun!" and begins to steer us toward the battleships. He eases our boat, which had seemed fairly large, between two of the rocky ships into a narrow bay known as Indian Drum. (Perhaps for the booming of the waves on windy days?) The cliffs loom over us. The trees growing on the decks of the battleships seem to be directly above our heads! Looking back at the entrance it appears as if our boat is too wide to have entered. No wonder this is not a stunt for rough days! Beside us on one wall, we recognize some familiar bands of weathered copper, with their soft green patina. Once again we are exclaiming, "Nushka! Look, we stood right there. Those ARE the same bands of copper we saw!"

Leaving the battleships behind we progress to the Flower Vase, a formal footed shape filled with a bouquet of trees.

The final formation, at the eastern end of Pictured Rocks, is Chapel Rock. From a distance it looks like a face, even a skull, quite the opposite sentiment from a chapel. Atop the Chapel grows a single, spreading White Pine. It gets no nourishment at all from the rock. One single six-inch root spans the long gap from the rock to the mainland, a living nutrient pipe. When some shifting of the rocks or infamous Lake Superior storm severs the root, the tree will die.

Inexorable time allows no place and no person to remain unchanged. Mighty Kwasind has indeed thrown huge rocks into the water. Pau-Puk-Keewis has danced the sand dunes into great drifts. Megissogwon, the magician of fevers, disease and pestilence has been subdued. Hiawatha was wooed and won by the laughing Minnehaha. Iagoo, the great boaster, spoke of the swift canoes with wings bearing men with faces painted white. No one but Hiawatha believed Iagoo, but it was true. And we, the grand-daughters of the palefaces, walk today along Hiawatha's Big-Sea-Waters, imagining the forest in his time, before the fiberglass kayaks, the tour boats, and the campgrounds. Life here has changed. Life is change.

III. The Singers

Westward Hiawatha ventured
To the land of the Hereafter.
Westward called he our three travelers,
"Pleasant is the sound," they murmured,
"Pleasant is the voice that calls us!"

Through the mist from off the water,
Down the hazy shafts of sunlight,
Sparkling on the pebbled margins
Of the shining Big-Sea-Waters –
Came the voice of Hiawatha
Sounding from the fallen portals,
Echoing in the lonely portals,
A voice from regions of the home-wind,
Whispers of tales told in secret.

On the pebbled margins

'Many moons and many summers
"Will have come, and will have vanished,
Ere I come again" to meet you.'
"And the evening sun descended,
Set the clouds on fire with redness,"
Burned their hearts with pleasant sadness,
Burned their naked hearts with longing,
Sobbed, 'Farewell, but not forever!'

And the evening sun descended

88 miles this hike
Reed & Green Bridge to AuTrain Lake
Luce and Alger Counties, MI
1438 total NCT miles

Big Mac, Michigan Style
45 - September 6, 1999

Mackinac Bridge looking north

If you live in or near Michigan, you already know that I'm not talking about a fast hamburger. "Big Mac" here means the Mackinac (say MACK-in-aw) Bridge. As bridges go, this one is definitely something special. The Golden Gate may be more famous, but the Mackinac is in the same class, and equally beautiful. In fact, depending on how you measure it, some say the Big Mac is actually, well, bigger! The Golden Gate is reddish-gold, the Big Mac towers are white, the cables forest green. I've crossed it dozens of times by car, even by bicycle (groups used to be allowed to ride across), and it never ceases to take my breath away. The bridge is also an official part of the North Country Trail.

The Straits of Mackinac, which the five-mile bridge spans, are where the meeting of Lakes Huron and Michigan is pinched to a "narrow" five-mile waist. This location is naturally of strategic importance. Fort Michilimackinac was built here by the French around 1715, as a link in their system of trading posts. The location was variously controlled by the French, British, Indians and Colonials/ United States several times before the United States took final possession in 1815. The U.S. troops had not managed to capture the fort, but it was granted to them by terms of the Treaty of Ghent.

Today I will hike these five miles. Although the bridge is part of the trail, it can be walked on only one day of the year, Labor Day. On that morning each year, two lanes of the bridge are closed to vehicles, and hordes of walkers, led by the Governor of the State of Michigan, cross from St. Ignace to Mackinaw City. "Hordes" is no exaggeration: there are typically between 20,000 and 70,000 people. Today I have about 62,500 hiking companions. I know one of them quite well.

Omer likes doing things that are a little off-center, and the Bridge Walk, even though it requires walking, fits his criteria. One important priority is that we must be first. This means different things at different times, but for this event it means first in line.

Mackinaw City provides parking and runs shuttle buses to the north end of the bridge, beginning at 2:30 am on Labor Day. We plan to be on the first bus. Since it is a four-hour drive from our home to the Bridge, we don't even bother going to bed, and we do make that first bus. On the St. Ignace side we and the other early crazies rattle around the large open gathering area, in the dark, until more busloads of people arrive. Soon the area is no longer open, but beginning to feel rather close. At least it is beginning to get light. The walk is scheduled to begin at 7 am, only a couple more hours to wait.

The basic needs of thousands of humans in a small space are met on one end by donut and hot dog hawkers, and at the other by a long row of porta-potties. The parallel lines facing these doors are long, very long, and the people in them are not cheerful. I have fought my way from the very front of the crowd, near the roadway, to stand in one of those lines. A man wearing a funny hat, canary yellow rubber gloves, knee boots, and rainbow suspenders flourishes a toilet brush. He works his way down the lines, making each one wait in turn while he enters the door ahead of them. Despite the grumpiness of the people in the lines, the toilet brush captain wins a smile or two, and not a single person yells at him for "taking cuts."

On the way back to join Omer after I finally have my turn in one of the little blue rooms I learn something about the expected etiquette of this event. Despite my repeated explanation that I am trying to rejoin my husband, I receive many dirty looks, and comments ranging from "Yeah, sure," to "Get back where you were." Apparently you are supposed to have a super-bladder if you come early.

At about 6:30, someone checks the microphones on the small stage erected beside the bridge approach, and soon Governor Engler appears in casual slacks and a polo shirt. Twenty minutes later, a select group of advance joggers are allowed to enter the roadway, followed by the Governor, his entourage which includes his triplet girls in a stroller, and his security van. Before long, the rest of us can begin. It is a walk; running is not allowed for the safety of all. Walking fast is definitely acceptable, and this is another of Omer's criteria. If an event requires walking, fast is good. In fact, one of our first common bonds, 30-some years ago, was that I could walk fast enough to keep up with him. We easily pass the casual walkers who have started ahead of us, and soon are in the thick of the serious striders.

Entering the suspended span, walking slightly uphill, we can look down through the open grillwork to see the water below. The mesh is fine enough that there is no danger at all of a foot slipping through, but it is a little disconcerting to glance down and see the water 199 feet below. The expansion joints are quite interesting, seen up close, instead of just heard as a thump of the tires when driving over them. Each side is a large-toothed metal plate riveted to the roadway. The teeth mesh together. When the bridge expands the sections may nearly touch. When the metal is cold the gap may be an inch or more wide.

We pass the center of the bridge and start the long gradual downhill. Before long we pass the Governor, and now the crowd ahead of us has definitely thinned. At the finish line, each person is handed a numbered certificate, indicating their approximate order of finish. Mine is marked #803. Not bad, given the size of the crowd. We have made the crossing in 70 minutes.

Traversing this band of water has always been both important and treacherous. Before powered vessels, birchbark canoes crossed easily on calm days; windy days were a test of the paddlers' skill, courage and strength. In most winters, the water of the straits froze, and the traverse could be walked, but deep currents which break and shift the ice always made this a dangerous hike. Perhaps obviously, the first ferries to cross the water here carried railroad cars. Rail magnates chaffed at lines which dead-ended at water. More recently, ferries carried people and automobiles from Mackinaw City on the southern shore to St. Ignace and back. Waiting lines were often hours long, and only 462 cars could make the crossing each hour. But everyone "knew" there was no way to bridge these waters, although engineers had been dreaming of such a structure for over a hundred years.

These five miles were considered unbridgeable for several reasons. The straits are known for high winds, always problematic for bridges. Located at 45° 49' north latitude, any structure built here must be able to withstand the destructive expanding effects and weight of ice. Another serious obstacle to construction was the 300-foot depth of the double glacial gorges beneath the frigid waters. The straits may be narrow, but they are not shallow.

Additionally, there was strong political opposition to a bridge from the State Legislature. This attitude seems unaccountable, now that the bridge is such a part of Michigan life. Yet it took years for the state to approve the sale of bonds to finance the project. When approval was finally given, a time limit of eight months was set to finance the project fully, or the request would have to be resubmitted. Bridge Authority bond salesmen said that they felt like the bum trying to sell the Brooklyn Bridge, except that the bridge they were peddling was longer, more expensive, and hadn't been built yet!

The overall length of the Mackinac Bridge is 26,444 feet, just over five miles. There are 8,614 feet between anchorages. Those who measure bridges in this way make it longer than the Golden Gate at 6,450 feet. Measured tower to tower, the Golden Gate wins at 4,200 feet, compared to Mac's 3,800. The foundations for the two main towers rest on the brink of the north glacial gorge. Divers in canvas suits descended 100 feet below the surface during construction. The surveying for the bridge was an accomplishment in itself, requiring two years to complete.

Big Mac, Michigan Style

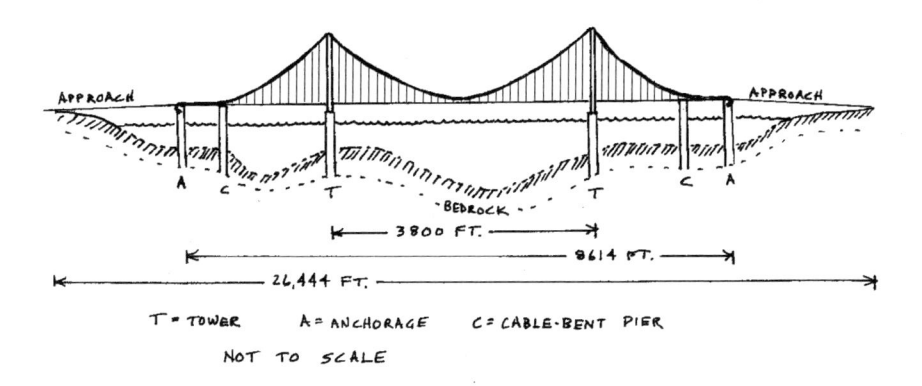

```
T = TOWER    A = ANCHORAGE    C = CABLE-BENT PIER
NOT TO SCALE
```

Dimensions shown: 3800 FT (center span), 8614 FT, 26,444 FT (total). Labels: APPROACH, BEDROCK.

The two Michigan peninsulas had never before been linked by a survey. Without benefit of satellites, the measurements for every pier, span and truss had to be accurate, across the waterway, within fractions of an inch. Many of the bridge sections were built miles away in mills and factories. When brought together, they would have to fit.

Suspension bridges are built in four stages. The anchorages and the towers are built first. Then the support cables are spun. The suspended span is hung on those cables, and finally the approaches to that span are built.

Floating cement factories churned out the "grout" which was pressured into crushed rock in a process patented just for this bridge, to create the deepest foundations ever built for a suspension bridge. The tower piers are as high as a ten-story building; when the towers are added that height rises to 552 feet, equal to a 46-story building. They are the deepest ever laid for a suspension bridge.

Workman with metal spinning wheels, but looking not so very different from the ones their great-grandmothers used, guided loops of wire around those wheels. The wheels traveled back and forth from one anchorage to the top of one tower, to the next tower, to the second anchorage, around "strand shoes" and back, hundreds of times, until 12,580 strands lay on each side. The strands were compressed into a solid mass two feet in diameter, banded and wrapped. Thus were spun the huge cables which support the central span. Barges carried sections of truss across the water, into the shadow of the towers. Workmen standing on catwalks along the huge main cables lowered smaller cables which were fastened to the trusses. These were raised to the proper height and fastened to the adjacent truss sections.

The roadway is a fine open steel gridwork, an innovative design contributing to Mac's status as the most aerodynamically stable bridge in the world. Of the four traffic lanes, two were filled with a lightweight concrete, and in two, vehicles drive directly on the steel mesh. Finally, the approaches to the center span were built from the opposite shores, using more traditional bridge-building techniques.

Remember the expansion joints which spread by a couple of inches, yet provide a level roadbed for driving? These simple-looking devices are the visible evidence of a carefully orchestrated dance prescribed by temperature. When the steel warms, the towers grow, and the cables lengthen. The towers actually lean in toward the center of the straits, allowing the level of the bridge to lower by as much as seven feet! Horizontally, over its five miles the bridge needs to allow for 27 feet of expansion! Even over that distance, it's difficult to imagine where the engineers could tuck up so much space.

Nay-sayers of this bridge claimed that the rock underneath the straits could not support a bridge. Final geologic tests showed that the weakest rock there can bear five times the weight of the bridge. There was fear that no bridge could withstand the local ice pressures. The bridge is designed to tolerate over four times the maximum theoretical ice pressure which can be produced on a frozen body of water. The wild Mackinac storms conjured up worries of a collapse such as occurred to the Tacoma Narrows Bridge in 1940. Thus major attention was given to the aerodynamic stability of the bridge. The bridge is designed to be stable at forces 2.5 times higher than those produced by a 78 mph wind.

On November 1, 1957 the Mackinac Bridge opened to traffic. Instead of 462 cars, now 6000 vehicles an hour can cross the straits. The bridge has proved all the pessimists wrong. The bridge paid for itself, and the tolls were actually lowered. Now we drive between the Peninsulas of Michigan with hardly a second thought.

The designing engineer of this marvel was David B. Steinman, 1886-1960. Steinman grew up in the shadow of New York's Brooklyn Bridge. Living in East Side poverty he dreamed of becoming an engineer for projects like the bridge he viewed every day. In 1948 Steinman's dream literally came true when he was engaged to widen the 65-year-old Brooklyn Bridge from two lanes to six. Other bridges in Steinman's portfolio include the Thousand Island Bridge in New York State, and the Sault Saint Marie International Bridge. His designs were usually innovative, such as the first earthquake resistant bridge at Carquinez Strait, California, and the first eyebar suspension bridge at Florianopolis, Brazil, which is also the longest in that country.

His strong faith served as a basis for his life achievements. This true life rags-to-riches hero recognized the difference between important bridges and vital ones. He wrote:

Help me, Lord, to Build My Span

Anchored firm in solid rock,
On Thy foundation let me build–
Strong to bear each strain and shock,
An arch of dreams and faith fulfilled.

Help me, Lord, to build my span
Across the chasm of the years;
Firm in purpose, true in plan,
Above the drag and doubt of fears.

Help me to build on Thy high road
A bridge to serve the common good;
To smooth the way and lift the load,
A link of human brotherhood.[1]

5 miles this hike
St. Ignace to Mackinaw City, MI
1443 total NCT miles

---

[1] Steinman, David B.; *I Built a Bridge, and Other Poems*; Davidson Press, New York, NY; 1955; p. 15.

Walking Backwards Down the Stairs
46 - October 9, 1999

We start in a foggy fall mist, but the sky quickly clears to become one of those ideal October days. The colors of the leaves are so bright in the sun that they almost hurt the eyes. Four walkers from the Spirit of the Woods Chapter have set out to continue our explorations of the trail we have adopted. Our youngest member also comes along on this hike, but he isn't hiking. Young Forrest gets a free ride compliments of Mom Angie. Not that this is anything out of the ordinary: Forrest has been hiking with us since two weeks before his appearance into the world. And he is aptly named; there doesn't seem to be anything he likes any better than to be outside.

Angie and Forrest

This hike includes a crossing of the Big Sauble River, over the Vince Smith Bridge. We inherited this bridge with our trail. It's a nice planked bridge with railing on one side. Vince was an early promoter and builder of the North Country Trail, and this structure was named for him. We walk the oak ridges and the poplar valleys. Angie clears a big spider web spun across the trail with her face. Thanks, Angie, we do appreciate your helpfulness!

In three brief miles, clutching bouquets of yellow and red leaves, we arrive at the car we've spotted. The trail club has become a source of new friendships, increased trail maintenance, opportunities for exercise and conversation. Simply put, these monthly outings are a lot of fun!

However, there is a line from a Larry Norman song that goes like this: "Walking backwards down the stairs, trying to get higher, how can I get anywhere, walking backwards down the stairs?"[1] That is certainly how I am beginning to feel about my progress on this trail.

When I discovered it, the North Country Trail was projected to cover 3200 miles. That route was originally drawn on an 8.5 x 11 inch

---

[1.] Words and music by Norman, Larry; from "Walking Backwards Down The Stairs;" from the Capitol Records album, *Upon This Rock;* 1969; used with permission.

sheet of paper. At that scale, it was expected that the mileage would actually be longer, but no one suspected just how much longer. Not many years later almost everyone with knowledge about the actual on-the-ground route began quietly admitting that the reality would be more like 4200 miles. In 1994 Ed Talone thru-hiked the NCT, but did not include what would come to be called the Arrowhead Reroute, the northeast tip of Minnesota. His total, 4400 miles. The known length of the Superior Hiking Trail, Border Route, and Kekekabic Trails, plus a return to the center of Minnesota, which parts make up that Arrowhead route, will add 400 miles. Subtracting some extraneous wanderings taken by Talone, one current estimate for the total length of the North Country Trail is 4600 miles.

When I start comparing these numbers to my own total miles, if I subtract the 1446 miles I've hiked to date from 4600, that leaves 3154 miles to go... a net gain on the original 3200-mile estimate of 46 miles! It sure has taken me a lot of years to make that much progress. I'd better start walking faster.

3 miles this hike
5-Mile Rd to 3-Mile Road
Lake County, MI
1446 total NCT miles

Lightning and the Snail
47 - November 4, 1999

Let's clarify this right from the beginning. I am the snail. I've been comparing my progress to Ed Talone's estimate of 4400 miles for years. The completion of this Trail is beginning to recede in front of me to a vanishing point years in the future. 4400 miles divided by 3 is 1467. Despite my persistence in hiking whenever I can, I have yet to cover a third of the Trail. Despite knowing that the total is only a close estimate, that milestone of 1467 sits heavy and just out of reach in my mind. Today I can't even think about the new estimate that places the length closer to 4600 miles. I seem to be crawling, in sharp contrast with the speed my ardor craves along the red thread of miles on my map.

I try to focus on today's distance and to resist the weight of the larger milestone. Today I will fill in the gap left when Pam and I traded the snowy trail for roadwalking in the blizzard of March 1998.[1] Ginny Wunsch has cheerfully agreed to help me spot my car and we spend a while visiting about trail issues. Her dogs, Rajah the Collie and Fudge Mix the German Shorthair, greet me enthusiastically with nudging noses and wagging tails. Their friendliness poignantly reminds me of my continuing dogless state.

Soon my car is spotted and I am stumping resolutely through the sun-cured autumn woods. Oak leaves glow an exceptionally rich caramel brown. The day is truly beautiful, but I miss hearing Chips snuffling through the forest litter, and am painfully aware that this is a section where he could have run free to explore the smells and sounds of duff and crunchy leaves. And even though I am trying not to think of 1467 miles, even though I know that completing this walk will not place my total at 1467 miles, even though I know that hurrying through the woods shortens the time of enjoyment, I continuously find myself rushing as fast as I can walk along the trail. Yet all the while I feel like that snail. Is my goal of completing the trail too large for me to accomplish without dropping everything else in my life? I feel pressed into a snail shell of limitations despite my attempt to hurry.

Ahead of me a White Pine, a foot-and-a-half in diameter, lies dying across the trail. As I reach it and find my way around its shattered stump, the far side reveals that it has been struck and exploded by lightning. The bole, now horizontal, carries a sizzled, peeled and shining wound along its length. The force of that

---

[1] See Chapter 29: "White Lace and a Million Fireflies"

concentrated energy has splintered the broken ends into thousands of white-shining shards of wood, blown for ten feet or more into the brown environs. The stump is shredded, standing, although five feet tall, in vertical and tilting tatters. An overwhelming force of nature has ended this majestic tree's century of snail-slow growth upwards through the forest. Will the overwhelming reality of the total distance of the North Country Trail explode and shatter my snail-slow progress along its length?

White Pine split by lightning

This is too serious and frightening a thought to deal with on this lovely day. I hurry ahead to the car, leaving the portent of shattered dreams behind me with the broken pine.

4 miles this hike
Nichols Lake to Pierce Rd.
Newaygo County, MI
1450 miles total NCT

Look Your Dream Right in the Eye
48 - November 13, 1999

In the same way that I connected with a line from a song to express my frustration with the elastic length of this trail, I have found a song lyric to encourage me to continue my quest. It admonishes me to "look your dream right in the eye, and it will meet your gaze!"[1] That is exactly what I plan to do. No more moaning about how many miles there are yet to hike, and I won't let it bother me when others ask that demoralizing question.

Today will be the last of our Spirit of the Woods Chapter hikes that I'll be able to count towards my total miles. Of course we'll keep hosting hikes, and of course I'll keep attending. But from now on they will all be repeats of trail I've already seen.

Nine of us are hiking past McCarthy Lake, a clear, intimate pond with marshy edges. The trail skirts the lake, giving us views from several interesting angles. We pull down some leaning trees that are threatening to fall across the trail. The wind sighs softly through the branches of a pine plantation as we shuffle through piles of fallen oak leaves. The temperature nears 60°, very mild for November. All the people on this hike are new friends I've made because of this trail.

Hiking near McCarthy Lake

The heartening song continues: "I know that in a million ways, these are the good old days." Well said!

3 miles this hike
3-Mile Road to Centerline Rd.
Lake County, MI
1453 total NCT miles

[1.] Chapel, J and Jennings, B.; "These Are the Good Ole Days;" 1971 Sony/ATV Songs LLC; All rights administered by Sony/ATV Music Publishing; 8 Music Square West, Nashville, TN 37203; all rights reserved. Used by permission.

W2K
49 - December 30, 1999- January 1, 2000

"Where do you want to be on the eve of New Year 2000?" demanded the blaring television announcer. I hadn't really thought about it very much and assumed I'd be staring with glassy eyes at a crowd of people watching a ball drop in Times Square, if I even stayed up that long. With my usual indifference to New Year celebrations, I was thereby busy verifying Newton's first law of motion. "A body at rest tends to remain at rest;" it's called inertia. Inertia rules huge blocks of our lives having a mass too large to be overcome by the force of our dreams. But suddenly I was accelerating with the combined forces of excitement and obsession: the excitement I had felt as a child when I realized I would probably be alive when the century and the millennium changed, and my adult obsession to hike the North Country Trail. Despite the technicality that the new millennium doesn't actually begin until 2001, I knew I did not want to let this New Year slip by without notice. I also knew that where I wanted to be was on the North Country Trail.

Newton's first law clarifies that a body will remain at rest unless "acted upon by an unbalanced force." My unbalancing force became the sum of the dream and the excitement. To most of my friends whom I begin trying to convince to join me in the winter woods for three days, I definitely appear to be an unbalanced force! Most of them charitably accept that I am eccentric but harmless, "harmless" defined as lacking sufficient of that unbalanced force to propel them into the cold. They are secretly glad for family obligations which allow them to decline my invitation to Winter 2K without explaining that they have no interest in shoveling enough snow to build a home, sitting in the cold no matter how cozy a campfire might be, snowshoeing through heavy unbroken snow cover, or huddling in a sleeping bag through the 14 long hours of winter darkness while the mercury plummets to unknown depths. The list of even remotely possible participants dwindles from nine to five to three to settle at two humans and a dog. There is a possibility that the other human is more unbalanced than I! Irene and Gummy must drive for 12 hours just to join me in this mad venture.

Nevertheless, on the sunny afternoon of December 30 we set up camp on the trail at the southwest corner of Five Lake near Alba, Michigan. I arrive first and am shoveling snow into a mound to build a quinzhee shelter. A fox-like dog incongruously wearing a red bow behind one ear approaches me through the woods, barking. Having never met Gummy, I am not certain of my facts but enthusiastically assume this must be the dog who has appeared and begin talking to her. Soon Irene emerges from behind a veil of young Cottonwoods and verifies my identification. Gummy nuzzles my hand, Irene and I hug, and W2K officially begins!

I had arrived in the morning at the site which I had previously scouted, and nearly decided to move the entire venture to a different location. I already knew that a snowmobile trail passes about one-quarter mile from the selected campsite, but I now discover that the holiday ski-doo-ers are loudly and boldly zippering through almost every possible opening in the woods. For some reason which we do not understand, but are thankful for, they are following regulations and not riding the North Country Trail except where it coincides with wider two-track openings. So by moving a bit farther back into the woods we are able to buffer ourselves from their motorized intrusion. The snowmobiles cast the only shadow on our weekend. They give a whole new meaning to the lyric "blue shadows on the trail." We have to pull all our gear three-quarters of a mile back to the campsite on sleds, mostly along their highly traveled tracks. Whenever (whenever being often) groups pass in a whirl and haze of blue fumes and brain-thumping noise Gummy sneezes and rubs her nose through the snow. Irene and I wave them on their way and call to them, but they can't hear us over the whine of their motors. It's probably just as well. They wouldn't like what we are calling.

The sun has warmed the snow so that it packs well, but the goal of building and hollowing the large snow shelter I had hoped for turns out to be a bigger project than two people can handle in a short winter afternoon. The plan is altered to create a snow fort of walls with a narrow entrance curved to block any wind. The roof is created with joists of branches covered with a tarp. Snow is mounded around the edges to hold the tarp in place. It is now so warm in the sun that I have removed two layers of clothing to keep from overheating. Irene takes a shovel and goes to find us "a commodious spot" in the woods. When she returns I explain to her that I've formed the habit of taking out the used t.p. in a sealed bag rather than leaving it for animals to dig up. "Really?" queries Irene. "I've never seen them do that."

"Oh, yes," I assure her and go to inspect our modest latrine. There I learn that Irene from gray-rock-hard-clay New York has begun a tunnel to China. Her enthusiasm for exploiting the ease of digging in Michigan sand has led her to experiment with methods for even tunneling under tree roots. I amend my earlier dogma and admit that no animals are likely to dig up that pit when we are done with it. Indeed, either of us had better be very careful where we step while answering any calls after dark or we might never be heard from again.

Our kitchen area is defined by the other flat open spot not occupied by the snow fort, and we clear it to dig a small fire pit. Soon Irene is warming dinner on the grate in a cast-iron pot while coffee water boils beside it in a classic blue graniteware vessel. Coals glow brightly in the fire ring. The early-winter sun is redly fading and we light the cleaned but rusty kerosene barn lantern and hang it by the doorway of our hut. These points of light reflect in a soft golden gleam from the varnished wood frames of our snowshoes as they stand erect in a handy snowbank. There is some quality of lost treasure, a homely honesty of simple things these objects and their interactions create within me.

Our camp kitchen

Heat, light, nourishment, shelter, transportation, friendship, a sense of well-being at knowing that a job well-done has given us the privilege of a comfortable evening What more could a person require? As much as I love backpacking, finding the lightest and best technological solution to traveling traceless through the woods, the heavy, textured, old and solid camp tools elicit from within me a deep joy. Polished titanium and Gore-tex have never yet brought tears to my eyes or a lump to my throat.

"Hey," shouts Irene as she checks the thermometer, "no wonder we're getting chilly. It's only 7 degrees out here!" My warm sentimental moment is unlikely to keep our body temperatures up all night so we scramble around to clean up and create a nest in the hut. Irene's earlier slip of the tongue, "flannel chipping," while describing a search for something to watch on the motel TV the night before now sounds prophetic. We may need a chisel to remove the ice from our jammies if we don't get busy! Plastic goes down first, then a layer of Therm-a-rest® pads, topped with a Korean War era down sleeping bag. Our own sleeping bags go on top of this, and we cover the both of us with another vintage down bag. Gummy settles between our legs, chilly enough to remain contentedly under the covers. Her trip to the groomer which resulted in the red hair-bow also had shorn her of most of her insulating tummy-fur. The plastic food cooler (or in the winter, the anti-cooler) with a pack on top and a tarp over all is pulled in to plug the entrance.

The predictable first remark after snuggling in with boots and extra clothing removed is, "Oh, Dandy! I have to pee." Ever thoughtful of me, Irene generously completes this camping requirement so that I can make it through the night without having to get up. She struggles back out of her bag, into her boots and coat, over the dog, and removes the door plug, all in a space only five by seven by three and now solidly occupied by two people and the canine.

"That's my tail you're trying to use for a sock," yelps Gummy. Irene disappears into the cold December woods. Eventually she reappears, so I know that somehow she has managed to keep from slipping down the tunnel to China. It's a good thing because from those depths I might not have heard her even if she had blown her emergency whistle. Reversing the whole laborious sequence from cooler to down bag she returns to the warm bed. We check the time. "Oh good, we have only twelve more hours to lie here in the dark."

Irene and I met only this past year, and have never camped together before. Thus she mistakenly believes that I wake up as a human being, the same as I was when I went to bed. She arises cheerfully at sunrise and announces that the clouds have moved in and the temperature is up to a balmy 24°. "Mmmmpfh," I reply with glee and pull the covers over my head so as not to embarrass her with my exuberance. Now it is my turn to be thoughtful. I doze off again, giving her the opportunity to display her camping skills preparing the morning fire. Old Girl Scouts never die; they just lose their fire. When I do arise, and after I gallop back from China, I catch her lighting the matches which won't strike, from her Zippo which won't close and go out. Well, you can't ever say that Girl Scouts aren't resourceful. Those eggs and sausages sure taste good anyway, no matter how the fire was lit.

The day's activity is to be a snowshoe hike. After cleanup we head down the main trail. Fortunately we are able to find the blue blazes as we proceed through the woods. I would like to say "the quiet woods," but the revving of the snowmobiles is ever buzzing through our heads. However, the snow is crisp and unbroken, the blazes lead us on, and we cover about a mile-and-a-half before admitting that we had better turn around if we want to be able to walk at all tomorrow. Gummy bounds resolutely through the deep snow, disdaining the comparative ease she could have of walking behind us in our packed tracks.

Irene knows her trees in winter and we share the pleasures of comparing knowledge of buds, bark and other botanical miscellany. She recognizes Shadbush bark. I point out the Michigan Jackpine. Witch Hazel remains attractive covered with yellow fruit capsules. We discuss how to distinguish Red from Sugar Maple in the winter by their buds. Cottonwood is inferior firewood but dry Bracken Fern stems are good tinder. We both like White Pine better than Red. Ash trees are a poor choice on which to paint trail blazes because the bark splits into an open diamond pattern, but the Shadbush (or Serviceberry) remains smooth to hold the paint well. White Oak is one of Irene's favorites while I favor Eastern Hemlock.

We return to our campsite and start a fire just for its cheering warmth even though it's a bit early to fix dinner. Gummy is limping;

her frivolity in the deep snow has caught up with her feet, and balls of ice have frozen on her paws. "Snow-toes," Irene calls them.

Basecamping always makes me want to build things. I have to mentally stake myself to the ground where I can just sit and play with the fire or I would be cutting down saplings to create lashed tables, chairs, coathangers and washstands. Sharing this outdoor experience with another former Scout, who also lived for the two weeks of summer camp, has increased the power of the Pavlovian reaction to saplings, twine, time and a basecamp. However, I am able with great restraint to resist leveling the forest, and we are able to fix dinner without a corduroy camp table.

We have been smiled upon this weekend. The weather remains mild. The air is calm and there is no wind to chill our bones or remove our tarp roof. The snowmobilers have not invaded our campsite by more than their noise. No city lights intrude on the horizon. The dreaded Y2K bug could infect and annihilate the rest of civilization at midnight and we would be unaffected and unaware. The only bug we encounter is a dopey spider swinging lonely from a twig. We consider staying awake until midnight, but agree that we don't mind sleeping through that overrated moment. We chat beside the fire for a while longer and retire to our snug home wistfully humming "...I'd make two wishes: a winding road that beckons me to roam; and then I'd wish for a blazing campfire to welcome me when I'm returning home." It's old Girl Scout stuff again.

Irene hears midnight come as judged by fireworks being set off both east and west of us. I awake around 2 am and learn that the snowmobiles have not failed to start as a result of some Y2K malfunction (drat!) We both welcome January 1, 2000, after daylight. Irene's campfire skills are again worthy and we feast on hash and eggs. We prolong the sad moment as long as possible, but eventually we have to begin to break camp. We take pictures; we decide to hike another mile after the cars are loaded; we take extra care to cover the fire and latrine sites; we reload the sleds, but the moment of truth arrives and we bid farewell to our short-lived but pleasant snow-home.

We do hike the extra mile, both ways of course. After finding a place to stow the car we expertly

Are you ready for some snowshoeing?

strap on the snowshoes, and our thighs immediately shout, "Hello!" Gummy, on the other hand, seems to be just fine. She pounces through the drifts, hunting mice. The snow is wet and heavy, but we are not to be deterred. We find even greater winter riches. Chickadees twitter and nuthatches "ank" their way through the woods. Irene hears a kinglet, I find a jumping mouse track. We see the trotting tracks of a real fox, and of course many deer paths. Rabbit and an unknown burrower have also left stories in the snow. Today's trail leads over a ridge covered with beech and Yellow Birch then down through a grove of Red Pine. Irene looks for signs of old homesteads but finds little evidence of any. "This tree must have grown up in the open, but I don't see any hedgerows or old orchards, " she ponders.

Soon we are standing at the last blaze we can see on the edge of an opening bristling with angry blackberry canes. "Do we turn around or go on?" we wonder, realizing that we will have to range back and forth when we reenter the woods to find the blazes. But I have no heart for leaving a section undone, and I plunge into the deep wet snow over the protestations of thighs and thorns. I hear Irene moaning something about hip sockets, but I'm sure she is just trying to reassure me that hers are fine. We emerge from the brambles after a time of stumbling, tripping, and loudly calling for the offspring of the canes to be unfruitful, at the very tree where the blazes begin on the other side of the opening. Irene is incredulous, and she effusively charges me with having a blue line for a soul. That sounds so poetic, I hate to tell her it was pure, dumb luck.

All too soon the hike is over and we are back at the cars trying not to say goodbye. Newton's third law works, but slower than it should. "For every action there is an equal and opposite reaction."

"You're the bees knees," Irene claims as she claps me on the back. I am too dumbfounded and slow to find a quick riposte. But eventually I'll get there. You are the cat's flannel pajamas, Irene! Now go get busy chipping while I go lash a table.

3 miles this hike
Five Lake to Bocock Rd.
Antrim County, MI
1456 total NCT miles

Ice is Nice
50 - February 18-22, 2000

Martha B. had a plan. (Yes, she likes to have the "B" included in her name.) She wanted to see the Eben Ice Caves in the Upper Peninsula. She had the maps; she called the Forest Service for more information. She had taken a course about winter camping through SOLAR, the School for Outdoor Leadership, Adventure and Recreation. What she needed was someone else crazy enough to go with her, preferably someone with experience at that form of insanity. Thanks to a mutual friend, we met. In fact we had met the previous summer and had taken some pleasant afternoon walks together. So I was willing to help her chase her dream. When we first made the plans, I did not think that the trip would help me chase mine on the North Country Trail. Obviously it did. More about that later.

On Friday I drive north to a corner just four miles from where the July hike ended,[1] near a bridge that is actually part of the NCT, over the Rock River. We knew that I would probably arrive ahead of Martha B. and her daughter-in-law, Marti. The plan is that I will search out a camping place for us along the river, and begin shoveling snow. Another part of Martha B.'s plan is that we will build a quinzhee hut to sleep in. I'm excited about this idea too. On the W2K hike[2] Irene and I had tried to build this type of snow shelter, but ran out of time. Hopefully with three people, more time and more snow, we'll be able to succeed. We don't expect to finish in time to sleep in it this first night, so we'll shovel out a space for a tent, heaping that snow for the quinzhee. Tomorrow we'll sleep in our wonderful snow dome.

I load my equipment, including my favorite shovel, on my sled. Next I strap on my snowshoes, clip the sled's harness to my waist, and begin hiking along the creek, looking for a clearing. In about three-quarters of a mile I find a space that seems quite workable, with room for both our tent and the quinzhee. Previously, I've claimed to be very good at building fires. Now I'll claim superiority at one more skill, shoveling. The snow is 18" deep, and the perfect consistency for packing. It shovels nicely too, in convenient blocks, not too heavy, but solid enough to stay together for heaving maximum distances. By the time Martha B. and Marti find me, I have cleared a space about 16 feet square, and set up the tent. Next to that space there is the beginning of a great pile of snow for the quinzhee. Martha B. and Marti shovel

---

[1.] See Chapter 44: "The Song of Hiawatha's Friends"

[2.] See Chapter 49: "W2K"

some more after they arrive, and then Martha B. offers to cook dinner. She has persuaded me to eat the food she is bringing rather than to bring my own, and I am more than ready for comestibles after an afternoon of hard labor. Now I will see what Martha B.'s gear look like as she breaks out the cooking kit.

Martha B. has equipment for everything! She has six pairs of gloves: special ones for cooking (I am hopeful when she shows me these), others for sleeping, mittens and two sets of liners for hiking, and another set for wearing in camp. There are blankets for the water bottles and water bottles for the sleeping bag. She has layers to wear in camp and layers to wear while walking. She has a sleeping bag with an air insulation layer that has to be filled each night. She has a stove (I brighten again at the sight of the stove) and an insulator for the stove pans and a stuff sack for each of them. She has each kind of pill in a separate baggie, and extra baggies for her boots and extra socks for her feet and, well, no extra feet.... But, she has them all in one huge duffel bag with no compartments!

Finding one kind of the pills was her immediate goal, and now that she has found them, predictably at the bottom of the bag, she turns her attention to the stove. The too-tall plastic tub that rides in my sled turns out to be just right for a cooking surface. The temperature is dropping, so Marti and I keep warm by shoveling some more while Martha B. cooks. Without too much difficulty and with the correct gloves, despite unfamiliar gear, the cold, and gathering twilight, we are soon sampling some flavor of pasta. It's my first experience with off-the-rack dried dinner packets. I can't promise that I'll run out and buy some when I get home, but it is hot and filling.

We've had a long day, and before 9 pm we are tucked into the tent. Marti and I have extra layers over our sleeping bags. Martha B. is experimenting with her air insulated one. I have to admit that I've never seen one like it before or since. The theory is good, but the practice is more labor-intensive than I would be able to fuss with. A large nylon hood at the edge of the bag opening is used as a scoop. You fill this with air by sweeping it through space, and then force the air down into the bag where a one-way valve prevents it from escaping; 45 minutes later I fall asleep, but Martha B. is still resolutely scooping air.

Did I mention that Martha B. is 72? Did I mention that Martha B. probably weighs 100

Martha B. Has pluck

pounds soaking wet? Need I mention that Martha B. has pluck? In the morning, after some more shoveling to add snow to our pile, we head out on snowshoes in search of the Ice Caves. Upstream from where we have camped, Silver Creek flows into the Rock River. And up Silver Creek high limestone walls enclose the valley. On the south side, an even smaller stream falls over the edge of that wall. In the summer the trickling waterfall is interesting, but not outstanding. In the winter, it's supposed to be another story altogether. We want to check it out! Our plan is to follow the creek until we arrive at the caves.

The sun is bright and the snow is unbroken. We come to a small creek flowing toward the river and turn south to follow it. After an hour of difficult climbing up a steep hill we arrive at a clearing with a cabin and a small pond. Shucks! We have followed a waterway that appears on the map as a seasonal stream, not Silver Creek. Apparently this is its season. So much for today! We head back to our campsite and the quinzhee project.

The pile of snow is getting higher, but it still isn't big enough to make into a shelter. We are determined to complete this project, and we spend the rest of the afternoon shoveling. By 4 pm the pile seems high enough to suit us, but despite the deep snow on the ground (including about nine more fluffy inches that have fallen since yesterday) we have had to haul in snow on the sleds from farther and farther away. The instructions say that the pile must be allowed to settle for several hours before excavating the inside. So we decide to spend another night in the tent. We do find some long straight sticks and insert them into the dome about 24" deep. Now our project looks something like a frozen, studded underwater mine.

I hang a thermometer on a tree near my old kerosene barn lantern. The light is just bright enough to allow us to find our way easily around camp as we prepare for the night, and to see that the mercury is dropping. It falls below zero before we snuggle into the tent, but we have brought even more extra blankets from the cars for tonight. We visit for a few minutes, and Martha B. starts inflating her bag. Once again, she is still collecting air when I fall asleep. I suppose it might be like that maxim about cutting wood, "it warms you twice."

That mercury does continue to creep downward. When I arise in the morning it is huddled and shivering at −19°. Marti is really cold, so we head for Martha B.'s SUV, where it is our turn to huddle with the heater running until we are all warm and dry.

Today we are bent on finding the Ice Caves. We follow our tracks from the previous day, but this time continue past that first stream where we went astray. We find the second stream, Silver Creek, and begin following it upstream. The snow is deep and the hills are steep. We are not breaking any speed records, that's for sure! The snowshoeing is really a challenge, but eventually we climb to where we

Our first view of the Ice Caves

can occasionally see the high limestone cliffs on the far bank. We are tired, and it is getting later and later in the day. The views are interesting, but we want ICE. Finally, we agree that we will continue looking for five more minutes, and then we really will have to turn around.

After just four of those onerous minutes we see groups of people at the top of the near bank. Where did they all come from? Why are they looking over the edge? It is because we have arrived at the Ice Caves. The wall is curved gently inward, making a shallow horseshoe. Great stalactites of ice form a blue, green, and white curtain across its face. People are wandering along the rim, climbing down the sides by means that look completely unsafe, and walking below the wall as well. How did all these people get here? We have seen no other tracks at all on our trip here!

We continue past the top of the ice curtain, pass through a small screen of hemlocks and come face to face with a field full of... snowmobiles! Well, now we know why there is a mini population explosion here. We ask how to get down to the bottom of the wall, and are told that there is a trail just a bit farther. We find it with no trouble, and soon we are standing at the bottom of the impressive frozen formation looking up.

The caves are formed in winter when water from that unimpressive summer waterfall seeps and spreads, freezing as it flows over the ice that has already formed. Where some of the gigantic icicles don't quite reach the ground a person can slip between the ice and the rock, into the ice cave. It's a good thing that by February it's staying light until after 6 pm in the western Upper Peninsula, because now that we've finally found the caves, we aren't about to leave until we've had a good look.

Our experience seems so incongruous with that of the other visitors. We have struggled through the wilderness (and this is in fact the Rock River Canyon Wilderness Area), on foot, in the silence of the winter woods, to arrive at this place so awesome. Others have come from another direction (literally and philosophically), easily, by noisy power vehicles, from some place unexpected. It feels as if we have earned the right to be here, to revel in the loveliness, to be rewarded with translucent vertical jewels. The others are interlopers, burglars of our treasured adventure.

But twilight is gathering around us all, regardless of our motives for coming, or our feelings. We are grateful that following our tracks back to the campsite is much easier and quicker than the outward journey. We arrive just before real dark sets in, and Martha B. cooks dinner for us by the light of her headlamp.

Tonight is not nearly so cold as last night, which is fine with us. However, in the morning, Marti is not feeling well. We drive through the foggy morning to find her a motel. She is content to allow Martha B. and me to continue our adventure as long as she has a warm, dry place to sleep her way through the bug she seems to have caught.

Once we have Marti tucked in, we head back to our camp. While we have been inside, the sun has burned through the fog and every twig, wire, and stalk is frosted with sparkling white hoar. Against a pale blue sky the landscape glitters in the winter sun.

We have one more night to spend outdoors and Martha B. and I are adamant that we are going to sleep in the quinzhee. To do this we need to hollow out the dome we have built, which is sure now to be settled enough.

We begin digging, and we dig, and we dig, and we dig. The first big pile of snow we pull out of the dome we use to mound up an entrance tunnel, for protection from the wind. Soon we are deep enough that we are taking turns at one of two jobs. One person knocks down snow and fills one of the sleds. The other person pulls the sled out, slides the other sled in for filling, and then takes the full sled into the woods to dump it. Yesterday we were hauling snow to the dome. Today we are hauling it away! The shoveling job is easier, but it is really cramped, since there is barely enough room inside yet to maneuver with the shovel.

It seems like this awkward phase takes a long time, but eventually we are able to begin opening up the inner space of the quinzhee. After that we feel less like contortionists, but we begin to wonder if we'll ever encounter the ends of our sticks that we inserted yesterday. Because these were carefully pushed in to a specific depth we know that if we excavate until we hit those sticks the roof will be of an even and safe thickness.

One of the advantages of a quinzhee is that snow is such a good insulator that they are considerably warmer inside than out. Martha B. explains that consequently, to keep the roof from dripping on us, we need to smooth it as much as possible, and ideally, to glaze it. To do this, we need to take a candle and heat the surface just enough so that it will begin to melt and then re-freeze as a coating of ice. We do some of this, but our commitment to adding finishing touches is low, since we'll be here only one night.

Success! We have a quinzhee! We move our tarp and sleeping bags inside and take down the tent. It has taken us all day to finish, but we did it. No one should ever say that even two small women don't have girl power! It's been hard work, but we are all smiles. And we are definitely ready for a good night's sleep. Now that the tent is not in the middle of our cleared space we build a campfire for a relaxing evening. Due to sweating and the warmth inside the dome during construction I'm quite wet, so the hot flames are also welcome for their drying power.

We have one final morning together. Marti is still resting at the motel. We break camp, including the sad task of literally breaking up the quinzhee. All our hard work, and we can't even leave the shelter for someone else to enjoy. SOLAR has instructed its classes that shelters cannot be left in the National Forest.

Martha B. has agreed to spot me to snowshoe through to AuTrain Forest Lake Road on the North Country Trail. But it's a four-mile trek, and with the deep unbroken snow I'm not sure that I can complete that walk in the time I have. Looking at the map it appears that the trail skirts the Wilderness on the north side on a road. It's hard to understand why the trail remains on a road when the public Rock River Canyon Wilderness land is right there. Martha B. and I hike up the road for a mile or so until we run out of time and need to return to the cars. I'm not sure I'll count that short section, but at least I have done some bit of the trail.

The final word on this venture doesn't actually come until the following fall. Sadly, the Rock River Canyon Wilderness management has decided that as far as they are concerned, the mission of National Trails is incompatible with Wilderness. Thus the trail will not be allowed through this wonderful area. The NCTA disagrees with this assessment, but has no real power to challenge the local management authority. There is no viable alternative route nearby.

So for now, since there is no official off-road route, I can choose to travel through the Wilderness, and to count it as *my* NCT route for this section. The actual linear distance I've achieved in these days is minimal. The adventure factor has been outstanding!

1 mile this hike
Rock River Road to Eben Ice Caves
Alger County, MI
1457 total NCT miles

Sneaky Valley
51 - March 31- April 2, 2000

I'm not making it up: it's right there on the USGS topographic map. It doesn't matter that the Wexford County Historical Society has never heard of it. It doesn't matter that an Internet search yields no information except its latitude and longitude. It doesn't matter that the ridges on each side seem to have no names. I know where the real Sneaky Valley is. Sneaky Valley is nestled between the high of bringing home the new baby and that climb up the hill of higher education to the ridge of adulthood.

Angie and I are making our way across that Sneaky Valley. She is 21 years old, and in the middle of the higher education incline. I am not Angie's parent, but we attend the same church and I have watched her grow. From the very first, she seemed to me to have a special spark. With bright, knowing eyes she would watch us all from the safety of her blanket and mommy's arms. At ten months she was ready to take on the world and join the ranks of bipeds. She looked like a peanut on legs!

Angie was one ripple in a wave of children of similar age in our congregation. Most years our small group produces two or three new babies at most. Elementary Sunday School classes are combined, two grades at a time, so that there will be a reasonable number of students in each class. The years that I taught the 5th and 6th grade class, which included Angie, there were eleven children when they were all in attendance. I would not lightly claim that it was a privilege to teach just any group of kids, but there is no other way to describe this particular class. These kids were all above average in intelligence, poised, curious about the world, and most of them were ready to explore what their faith had to do with the rest of their lives.

Angie was one of the shining stars of this group. She internalized lessons as quickly as they were presented. She asked tough questions and expected thoughtful answers. She nearly clapped her hands and danced when she caught a new concept. She easily and eagerly memorized the Bible verses that I asked the students to learn by heart. The anticipation for life that I had seen in those bright baby eyes was no illusion.

Then I went away to graduate school. Angie and her classmates continued their travels through junior high and high school. Now, it seems like overnight, she is a sophomore at John Brown University in Arkansas. I've surely not been around to follow her progress.

She is home for spring break. After Sunday worship service

Angie turns to me and hesitantly asks if I would consider taking her on a backpacking weekend as soon as school is out. My answer is not hesitant; I'm always looking for potential victims to drag to the trail! Thus we begin plans for a three-day hike in the early spring.

Most of our communication is by e-mail. Her quest for knowledge and explanations has not diminished with time. I send her lists of equipment. She counters with questions about details. I send her suggested menus. She replies, "Holy Cow! What a meal plan!" I give her two hike choices, one shorter and one a little longer. She is mature enough to respond, "I would love to say that I am tough, but there will come a very clear point in time where I will have to put my money where my mouth is, so I will say the shorter one."

Some of the necessary equipment Angie is able to borrow. For the rest, we take a day and go shopping together. Angie buys a sleeping bag and some hiking pants. I just have fun getting reacquainted with the bubbling peanut.

I give her a weight limit of 27 pounds of personal gear. I'm determined that this time I'm not going to let a novice hiker start out with too much weight. She packs her borrowed backpack and walks a few miles for practice. I am heartened to learn that I've finally impressed upon a potential hiker the solemn duty of "thinking lightweight."

Finally, on Friday afternoon we park at Baxter Bridge and head into the woods. Our plan is to hike just a couple of miles before stopping for the night. I've had a long, busy day, and, truth be told, I'm ready to find a campsite sooner than Angie. We cook our Spanish rice and I explain that we must look for a place to hang our food bag. The only trees that seem to offer good branches for the cache are on the very steep slope heading down to the river. We choose one to try for, and Angie sets the bag down to ready the rope. Did I mention that the slope is very steep? Our bag needs no Raccoon or bear to help it leave the vicinity tonight. It immediately heads straight for the river, and almost makes it! I try not to crack up laughing; I'm afraid that I'll hurt Angie's feelings.

She is glancing at me, asking with her eyes what we do now. "You probably should go get that," is the flat statement I finally manage to produce. She makes the long descent with some difficulty, and climbs back up with the well-rolled bag.

Before long we have the food hung, and we crawl into bed. I think Angie is trying to visit, but I am unable to stay awake. I vaguely wonder if she is feeling bored being stuck for a weekend with an aging companion who can not even stay awake in the evening. But I am snoozing much too quickly to ponder the question deeply.

In the morning we continue our hike along a high bluff above the Manistee River. There are many places here where old and not-so-old roads have been cut through the forest, ending in braided paths and eroded party spots at the edge of the cliff. I find myself rambling on about the condition of the trail, building and maintaining good trail, and proper blazing. I'm looking for something to talk about, unsure as to whether Angie wants to have a talkative companion or a silent one. She doesn't really give me any clues. Should I shut up, or continue my monologue?

Angie, high above the Manistee River

Soon we drop down from the top of the bluff and enter the cool shadows of a grove of White Cedar along the river. We pause here and I suggest that this is a good place to filter some water. "O.K." Angie says agreeably. Using the water filter is always quite a project for someone who is not familiar with it. I'm quite particular about keeping the parts which are for clean water separate from the parts for unfiltered. Juggling multiple bottles with their multiple caps, those filter parts, and all their various containers, while balancing in some location which never is quite stable make for a challenging camp duty. I finally have all the parts organized and am about to demonstrate their use to Angie. I step off the bank on to a large chunk of concrete which is wedged against the riverbank. Surprise! It's not concrete, it's styrofoam! I perform an animated balancing and juggling act, and now it's Angie's turn to try to keep from laughing. I succeed in regaining solid ground without mishap, and assure her that laughing is definitely called for on this occasion.

Tonight we reach a nice campsite near Wheeler Creek. We have arrived in plenty of time to cook our Salmon Alfredo with spinach in a leisurely fashion on my small stove, and to build a modest campfire. We spend the evening singing, and this activity definitely breaks any ice of uncertainty which might be remaining around the edges of our efforts at getting to know each other better as adults. Angie comes from an extremely musical family who sing together all the time. I don't. But I try to make up for that in enthusiasm. Whenever someone is willing to sing with me, and to put up with my own tuneful efforts, there is no longer any doubt that they are a friend.

The song-fest tapers off into a meditative conversation about the things we each think are important in life. Angie is certainly attaining the heights – her head and shoulders are breaking the plane of that adult plateau.

On Sunday we cross Sneaky Valley, the one on the map. A short road walk takes us across the two-pronged dry dale. Maybe that's why it's sneaky, for deceptively having no stream in its depths. The road wiggles around various humps and bumps of topography as it descends 70 feet, climbs again over the ridge between the two prongs of the valley, dips back down the second arm and then returns to the heights. Even large equipment has not managed to force this sneak into following the straight and narrow.

Angie's dad meets us where the trail crosses highway M-115. He whisks her away to the "real world," and I continue on for five more miles to connect this hike to a previous one.

Within just a couple of weeks Angie begins her summer job, and I've hardly seen her since. Her mom, Gloria, tells me that Angie had a really good time on our hike. In fact, she had such a good time that she has decided to pursue Outdoor Leadership Ministries as her major.

And that is just what she did. For her Senior practicum she took a nine-day hike with minimal equipment. She progressed to leading others on backpacking adventures, and teaching Leave-No-Trace techniques.

Now it's time to hear Angie's side of the tale. She has settled comfortably in the range of adulthood, married to a fine young man named Jeff. I called this week to get some input from her, to round out this story. It was my turn to learn a thing or two!

I had been so uncertain as to how Angie was reacting throughout our weekend together. She was just too busy at the time to let me know. She was completely occupied with having what she describes now as "a watershed experience."

For starters, Angie recounted that she was head over heels trying to assimilate a whole new vocabulary that I seemed to assume everyone knew. Terms like "trailhead," and "spotting a car" meant nothing to her. She wanted to know if "hike pants" meant some special style or fabric. When I told her that she could only bring 27 pounds of personal gear, she couldn't imagine that she would need that much stuff. She soon discovered that even after being very frugal and leaving some things out, that she was still slightly over this weight limit. Her comment, "I've got to tell you that seemed pretty heavy to me. It put 'pack light' into a whole new meaning."

She said that everything seemed strange. She couldn't believe how much planning went into even a short trip, such as this one. The pack felt "really weird."

That first night, when the food bag went rolling away, she confessed that she was really afraid that I was going to yell at her. Perhaps I should have let myself laugh... it was pretty funny, seeing our food going end over end down the hill. Despite the difficulty of retrieving it, she was pleased that there were no other consequences from carelessly dropping the important package.

"There were so many things you talked about that I had never even thought about before," she admitted on the phone. She had wondered if so much fussing and time was really necessary for some things. She had never considered that animals might try to steal our food. The water looked clean enough, but she now realizes that she was really naive to think that it was clean enough to drink without filtering.

The idea that a trail needs to be maintained and groomed was something she had not previously considered. I had chatted on about things like slopes and construction and sight distances between blazes. While I picked up trash and kept our campfire small, Angie's head was spinning with the new concept that there might be a responsibility attached to enjoying the outdoors. She had never before spent so much time outside all at once, and the idea that organization and order could make the difference between an enjoyable experience and a disaster was a novelty.

On Saturday morning, Angie realized that she was tired already. She moaned to herself, "We have all day yet today, and tomorrow too!" But Angie's basic personality came to the fore and she responded to that thought, "I want to like this; I don't want to quit." And so she plodded on.

On Sunday morning, she wanted to be able to put the tent away for me, but she didn't know how. She settled for packing up her new sleeping bag, which stubbornly refused to go back into its bag. I had snapped a photo of her with the bag high over her head. Angie now confesses that she was so angry and frustrated that when she finally conquered it she just had to uplift it in a victory pose.

The silence in the woods was unnerving. To someone unused to spending time outside it seemed too quiet. But now Angie says that this was the first time she had ever been so far removed from the distractions of ordinary life. She used the time to contemplate and evaluate her life. "You learn who you are and who you are not" on a backpacking trip, she continued. "On a scale of 1-10, where 1 is pure comfort and 10 is panic, that trip was a 6 or 7 for me. I wanted to stretch and learn, and I did!"

She had not previously considered the idea that even small actions and choices have a consequence. At first she couldn't understand why we should leave no trace of our passing. "Who cares if we build a big fire?" she thought. But then she saw the scarred, ugly areas where so many people had built fires wherever they like. She realized that if she didn't pay attention to the treadway that she might stumble, and that if the person leading did not warn the one behind of hazards on the trail that it might be unkind or even result in an injury. Even small decisions are more significant on the trail. If one person in a group is grumpy it affects everyone. You can't just go to your room and turn on the radio. If you feel lazy and don't filter the water, you might be able to lie and say you did, but the consequences if everyone gets sick could be quite serious.

After we were done, riding in the car felt as weird as the backpack had at first. She didn't want to tell her dad, but as she headed back to that "real life," it suddenly seemed petty and insignificant.

And that is what she decided that she wanted to help others learn. "So much of what we consider important is insignificant and dumb," Angie said on the phone. "It's important to be outside, to bring people to where their conveniences are taken away. You learn to put away your personal preferences, and your own weaknesses. You become more responsible. If you choose to be selfish, you are miserable like the Israelites in the desert who whined and complained even though God took care of them at every turn.

"On a hike, life is boiled down, in a good way, to what's important."

And there you have it. How did we pass through the valley so quickly from the peanut on legs to the professional camper?

As this book goes to press, Angie and Jeff are standing on the brink of the next Sneaky Valley, with a new baby daughter in their arms.

28 miles this hike
Baxter Bridge to Marilla Trailhead
Wexford County, MI
1485 total NCT miles

Emily, Mama Rita, and Dick Have Their Way with the Regenwürmer
52 - May 7-11, 2000

My excitement level is surprisingly high given the fact that the miles ahead of me are to be on roads and through a major metropolitan area. I've already had to justify my reason for hiking south away from the beautiful Superior Hiking Trail many times. It sounds so ridiculous: "I'm walking through Duluth, from Two Harbors to Jay Cooke State Park." Everyone on the North Shore (of Lake Superior) seems to know that the Superior Hiking Trail extends north from Two Harbors. Everyone seems to know that Jay Cooke State Park has many miles of well-marked foot trails. But here am I, apparently scorning such treasure to root like some senseless worm through the detritus of a city.

Nevertheless, I know that these four days will forge a connecting link between other potentially wonderful walks. I have hopes of bringing friends back with me when I come again to walk those desirable miles. My reason for being in Two Harbors at this time is the NCTA Annual Conference, held jointly with the Superior Hiking Trail Association, a recent affiliate. In a few days we've made new friends, and seen pictures of the remarkable rocky promontories and birch-filled valleys which will now be part of the NCT. This "Arrowhead Reroute" is part of the reason the trail's reputed mileage has jumped to 4600 from the early estimate of 3200 miles. The realities of putting a trail over corrugated landscapes as compared with drawing lines on a planar map account for the rest of the differential.

The conference is winding down on Sunday morning. I've talked with large numbers of people I know, and with too many people I don't know. I've slept too little and eaten too much. I'm tired of the up-scale northwoods decor and ready for some adventure. So here I am – beginning yet another hike – at the edge of another hot parking lot with hot asphalt miles ahead, re-packing miscellaneous pieces of gear into Shamu. But for some reason I'm grinning from ear to ear. Wanderlust is a cheerful taskmaster. A lady neatly dressed in white and gray with silver hair drives up in a silver SUV and asks me where the morning hike group is meeting. When I explain that I don't know (and once more that I'm hiking south into Duluth) her disappointment is evident. "Oh, I saw you talking up front last night, so I thought you would know..." I hope I don't actually roll my eyes. My role as public speaker had been only to present an award to a member of the NCTA. I suggest that she wait for my friend, Ceceilia, who is also planning to go on that group hike. Touching base with Ceceilia is vital to my plans for she will pick me up Thursday morning at the end of my urban miles.

The Silver Lady chatters on with a check-list of items she thinks I may have forgotten. I suddenly realize that she is asking me if I want her to hike with me; am I not afraid to hike all that way alone? If I am like a worm burrowing footpaths through urban neighborhoods I suddenly feel the panic of one whose hole is flooding. I DO NOT want the company of someone I don't know. I don't want company on this hike at all. With great outward calm (I hope, as I wriggle above the floodwaters of intrusion) I assure her that my hike won't be very scenic, all the road miles will be tiresome, and that I will be just fine. Fortunately she accepts my reasoning. Ceceilia arrives, and I give her the maps and times for our meeting later in the week and she and the Silver Lady dash off to find their hike group.

At last I am walking. The sun is warm; Shamu sits easily on my hips and shoulders, and the adventure is begun. One of the appealing aspects of walks on non-certified trail is the challenge and mystery of networking many tiny pieces of parks, less-traveled roads, bridges and bushwacks together into a unified walking route through a landscape designed for automobiles. Thanks to Bill Menke of the National Park Service, I have maps of the proposed route through Duluth. The morning before the conference I had scouted parts of the route in my car and had obtained some local advice, ski trail maps, and made some advance choices of my own. And now, immediately as I leave the conference grounds, I have another pleasant surprise. I will not need to walk the road edge even for the first mile. A snowmobile trail parallels the pavement, so I travel from the conference resort to Burlington Bay on packed earth. At the Bay I make a quarter-mile jog along a street to join the Two Harbors Lakewalk. This is a paved pathway along the waterfront. It will make my trip through town longer, but I have decided that scenic is to be preferred over a shorter walk today. The route curves pleasantly between the trees with the lake gleaming gray and calm to my left. A small fishing boat focused in the bright fovea where sky and water must meet suggests a misty vaporous tunnel from lands uncharted and unknown.

In only 45 minutes I have already utilized three politically separate pathways: snowmobile trail, city street, lakewalk, and have thus reached the Two Harbors Lighthouse. I pause for a lunch of crackers and an apple. There is no cause to hurry on my way and this is as pretty a spot as I am likely to see today. The harbor and some attached area have been converted to a museum where a bright yellow tug, the *Edna*, bobs beside the red-black Cimmerian mass of an abandoned ore dock. Various historical locomotives have been scattered across a lot under cover of roofs just large enough to protect them from a rain polite enough to fall straight down. Cutting cross-lots over an active railroad line and following a couple more city streets I pop back out on Old Route 61 and begin the serious work of walking south. Leaving Two Harbors I am met by a group of ladies who have just left the conference. They recognize me, and I explain my quest once more. Their advice is to be sure to eat at the Scenic Café; "It's on 61, almost all the way to Duluth."

The Duluth, Missabe, and Iron Range Railroad tracks run in a cut to my left. The new Route 61 funnels autos and trucks in haste toward Duluth on my right. Ahead of me is Old Route 61, paved, but labeled as "scenic" for those in less of a hurry. However, I desire the slowest and least engineered of all the land routes (for of course Lake Superior still gleams far to my left). Between the railway and the lake lies yet another road, a dirt one, and this will be my path for the next five miles after leaving town. A side road allows me to cross the historic rail line. Chartered in 1874 the railroad was built with the single-minded purpose of carrying iron ore. Its history parallels that of the US steel industry even as the tracks now parallel three roadways designed for steel vehicles which eventually put many railroads out of competition for commerce. Although it reached its economic zenith in 1953 with record iron ore tonnage hauled by the "Yellowstone," the most powerful steam engine ever built, the company still transports freight along the North Shore. I briefly consider walking along the tracks, but the "No Trespassing" signs are not rusty, and neither are the rail tops, so I cross to the lightly graveled road.

All these transport ways run directly southwest, and the afternoon sun beats uncharacteristically hot for a Minnesota day in early May – directly northeast. By the time I reach Knife River I am hot, heavy-footed, hungry and have lost my earlier sense of charm. My skin is hot and dry, almost sunburned – a condition I've reached only twice in my life. If the river is a knife, it's a dull one. Construction equipment has been busy bludgeoning the edges to conform to a new bridge. In the hot, still air the dust hangs in a visible curtain over the road. But standing coquettishly beside the road in a pastel green coat with white picot trim, Emily lures me to her bosom.

I step onto her green porch and open the screen door which squeaks – singing of bygone comforts. The still air both holds sounds and excludes others as if I were hidden inside Emily's pocket. Past the magic screen door is a world a century old. A high wooden soda counter flanked with wire-backed stools is immediately to my left. On my right a wood-and-glass bakery case displays fresh breads and pastries. The rear of the building contains many small tables of individual design – no two alike – with miscellaneous chairs. I select one which looks comfortable to me: what a nice treat to have choices! Actually Emily has been gone for many years, but her granddaughter's husband, a man near my age, offers me a menu and a glass of water. The current Duluth News reminds me that I've not really been transported to 1890, but the view of the old DM&IR bridge from the window helps maintain the illusion. It seems so odd to be hiking, packing, and yet stopping at a restaurant, reading news of the Kentucky Derby and a computer virus. For me this is most unusual, but for this trip it will be a defining condition. Thick and bubbly white fish chowder and a slab of homemade oatmeal bread, so moist that no butter is needed, do a lot to improve my disposition. I explain to Emily's descendant about my quest for the North Country Trail. He recalls hearing of it once before from another man who was hiking the same trail. Seems that Chet Fromm, a previous end-to-ender, also felt the allure of Emily's charms.

As if Emily's chowder has also worked its magic on the weather, a light breeze has risen, the air is at least ten degrees cooler and the remaining miles of the day glide by with my cheer restored. The stopping place for the night has been predetermined by car. One of the challenges of passing through urban areas is that of finding places to sleep without trespassing. And even though I willingly look forward to several thousand more trail miles, my ganglia jangle in alarm at the idea of walking even a mile out of the way to find lodging.

I slip into the woods above a stream which is well-used by fisher-folk and which does not sport "private property" signs on every tree and post. The woods are full of deer trails, but I finally wedge my tiny bivy tent into a corner made by two leaning trees where no sharp toe-prints have cuneiform scripted the red clay. At 6:30 I lie resting in my tent with the light breeze cooling me through the netting. At 6:40 the rain begins. I began this hike with too little sleep, so I shrug my shoulders, close the rain fly and am quickly asleep: a worm in a small green cocoon.

―――― ✺ ――――

Kaa- raCK! At 1:00 am the thunder and lightning begin. I awake with my hips soaked where the tent has sagged and lies against them. This bivy tent is only good in the rain if it is set up very carefully and if the rain is not too heavy. Tonight neither of these conditions applies. The wind begins to rise, but my position in the woods at least offers protection from all but its wail and an occasional startling flapping of the rain fly. Despite being wet it is warm and I *am* tired. I doze again and begin to dream of small prairie-dog like rodents running at the tent and trying to enter to find my crackers. They assault the tent in squads and unzip the zippers with their tiny hands. I catch them and talk to them. They listen politely, let me send them back into the rain, and then again begin fussing at the zippers. I awake with a start, but all the zippers are closed and no beady black eyes gleam from the corners; only the wind rustles the nylon. Weariness prevails and I next awake in dull morning light with the rain still falling dismally from the sky and dripping from the branches above me. Unaccountably my hips are now dry. I feel of my pajamas to be sure, but it is true. My feet, however, rest in a puddle. Freeing one arm from the sleeping bag I explore my cocoon and learn that my self-inflating mattress is an island in a shallow lake. Only I, or at least most of me, inside the bag is dry. Even though I'm stiff from the long night of inactivity, I spend yet another hour convincing myself to leave the one dry and warm spot I know I'll experience for hours.

By 9:30 I'm ready to walk. Life is full of odd little puzzles of pleasure and discomfort. My underwear is dry, but the hiking pants I must pull on over them are totally soaked. My boots are dry, but have no prospect of remaining so as I stand in puddles of red clay slip which ooze deeper over the edges of the soles the longer I stand in any one location. The plastic-lined inside of the pack is dry, but I quickly fill it with a soaking wet tent and pad, so what use is that liner anyway? I don't even bother to put on the pack raincoat; at this point another layer of plastic would be silly.

At 10:30 I'm facing the Scenic Café where I had hoped to eat a late lunch, close to Duluth, remember? It is a small brown nondescript box of a building, dark and empty-looking. As I contemplate my disappointment a young woman emerges and begins to stack the wet plastic lawn chairs. I cross the road and ask if the café is open yet. "No, not till 11:00," she explains. I decide that I don't want to wait that long, just standing in the rain. "Let me check," she offers. In another minute I am sitting by the heater at a cozy table surrounded by outrageously cheerful carved Moose, fish and Beaver painted in splotches of primary colors. Coffee and juice arrive without delay and then the menu. I select Mama Rita's specialty soup. The young waitress, Dana, brings my bowl and Mama Rita herself, cheerful, poised and not at all outrageous, whisks it back to the kitchen for a final warm-up necessitated by my early admittance. The soup is wonderful, a tomato and pasta affair with spices I can't quite identify served alongside diagonal slabs of squeaky-to-chew Italian bread. It seems that Dana is also a hiker and she sits and chats with me while I eat and explain my quest to follow the Trail. She's seen western trails and many miles of the Superior Hiking Trail. Finally, I must face the rainy day again and as I prepare to leave, Dana demurely mentions that my lunch is paid for. She thinks my hike is so wonderful that she wants to be a part of the adventure. This is a new twist of the tale for me, so the cook appears to snap my picture with Dana and one of the bright painted Moose.

I mention that I had expected the café to be closer to Duluth. "Oh, you are quite close," says Mama Rita, "only seven miles." Now, I KNOW that it is more than seven miles to town. I've walked fewer than three so far and there should be almost 15 miles total to walk, my longest day. I KNOW that people who drive really don't pay attention to actual mileages. But Dana agrees, and I would like it to be only seven miles to the motel room that I know is waiting for me at the end of this wet day. I am unable to prevent myself from considering the possibility that I have only seven miles to go. Unfortunately my original estimate proves to be more correct.

Seven miles would be good given the speed with which I am moving. After only 15 minutes back on the road and still in the rain, the Silver Lady drives up, stopping in the middle of her traffic lane. Thankfully this road doesn't have much traffic, but I have the feeling she might have stopped even if it did! "I know you don't want a ride, you're determined to walk, but are you sure you don't need anything? I can't believe I'm seeing you again!" She is still shiny and crisp. I am spotted with red clay and my pants droop and cling to my legs. Salty water runs from my bangs into my eyes. I assure her that I'm perfectly content and don't need a thing, while watching the frustrated expression of the driver who is trying to edge out of the driveway behind her. She finally waves and eases on towards her shiny life.

About five minutes later my own car is beside me, with Ceceilia at the wheel. Ceceilia is a realist. "Gosh girl, you sure are muddy!" she notes cheerfully, almost gleefully. She also has enough sense to pull off the road. I dash across, glad for a chance to exchange a few items. While telling the Silver Lady that I need nothing is one aspect of the truth, when I am faced with a car full of my own belongings the prospect is a welcome one. I leave a few things, and grab a good book for company at the motel which I'm now convinced I will reach very soon. To paraphrase Erasmus, "When the chips are down, take books, and if any room is left take food and clothes."

The day drags along like a wet rag half caught in a wringer mechanism, not inaccurately also called a mangle. The seven miles should by now be only six, two more "walks" of about an hour each with a short rest. After those two walks are finished, however, the end seems no closer than it had been two hours earlier. I know that there is a section of stately residences and sidewalks north of my destination and I'm not even at the end of Old Route 61 yet. I walk another hour with the rain still drizzling down my neck. Not that it matters any more. I am sustained only by that bright hope known as a heated motel room. My legs and feet ache relentlessly. Day two of any long hike is the worst, and this one is entirely on pavement with no respite. At least I've passed the castle-like Duluth Water Treatment Plant where two workmen, armed with a large wrench, try not to stare at me as I squish by. Engineers control their water with a wrench. The Engineer controlling the water from the sky is on coffee-break.

OK, I admit to myself that I KNEW it was longer than seven miles; now I am wet, grim, longing for the end of this day. At last I reach the residential section which I observe begins at 60th Avenue.

Instead of appreciating a milepost of progress and encouragement, I nearly whimper aloud. My motel is at 25th; these are true one-tenth-mile city blocks; I have over two and a half miles yet to walk. Although admiring the beautiful homes provides some mental relief, these final miles are mostly an exercise in endurance. At 4:30 I reach Valhalla – heaven – the Viking Motel. Only wishing to put down the weight of Shamu soaked with extra pounds of water, to shed my wet and muddy clothes, to dry my dripping hair, to get off my weary feet, I enter the office. The woman there is not the same person who pre-registered me and knows that I am hiking through. But she is not even curious at my appearance. She finds my registration, has me fill out the card, notes that I have left the middle portion blank, and with complete candor asks, "Do you have a vehicle?" I will confess to perhaps feeling just a trifle testy as I retort, "Do I look like I have a vehicle?"

Room 3 is an adequate but small and ordinary motel room for one person. I close the curtains, crank up the heat, strip, and cover every inch of space with wet nylon, plastic, clothing. Next come hot shower, crackers and cheese, soon-dried pajamas and sleep. Oh yes, and a phone call to Marie to tell her what a delightful day she has just missed. She sniggers ruefully and envies me not a bit. What does she know? The adventure is always the reward.

———— ✳ ————

Tuesday morning the sky is clear, the air scrubbed cool and clean. Coincidental meetings continue as I see Nancy Odden, Executive Director of the SHTA also having breakfast at the place where I order my morning juice and coffee and an apple-cinnamon muffin to save for my lunch. I am amazed but thankful that my legs and feet are healed of their aches, and I leave the motel completely dry and comfortable, anticipating this day of walkway puzzles, some parks and potentially great scenery.

The first leg of the day is a four-story switchback stairway which drops me from the level of London Road to the Lakewalk. The Lakewalk is a waterfront renewal project worthy of respect. For over three miles along the shore the city of Duluth has created a strip park with a variety of treadways, artwork, interpretation of historical and cultural features, rest rooms, a stage, a food court. Several re-furbished buildings no longer present blank and ugly backsides to the water, but are now multi-level outdoor cafés with wrought-iron railings and umbrellaed tables. A paneled mural of blue and gray one-inch tiles, perhaps a hundred feet long, pixelates scenes of maritime drama: shipwrecks, commerce, famous vessels and their captains. With so many pleasant diversions to hold the attention, these miles seem to pass quickly even though I stop to read all the interpretive displays.

Reaching the lift bridge at the channel cut through long and narrow Minnesota Point I am reminded that Duluth became a great harbor (at the expense of neighboring Superior, Wisconsin) by hand-digging this canal. The final feet became a race between the workmen and the horsemen carrying a court order to stop the channel-diggers. The shovelers won and the water rushed through, followed over the years by tons of ships who were no longer forced to maneuver around Minnesota Point to reach Superior as their first good harbor.

At the bridge the Lakewalk officially ends. However, I've been informed that in reality it continues under construction for about another mile. The sidewalk leads me across a tiny blue drawbridge decorated with green steel fish dancing on their tails and studded with rivets instead of scales. Restrained in the slip guarded by the dancing fish pouts the *William A. Irvin*, the once proud and fearless flagship of US Steel on the Great Lakes, now a floating museum.

The Lakewalk narrows to a sidewalk skirting numerous construction sites and then ends abruptly at a railing. I cut cross-lots

Green fish guard the Duluth skyline

through a vacant field where exuberant youngsters spill from a school bus. They explode like city grouse in a fan of apparently purposeless directions. A few more steps and the entire character of the walk changes. I'm now treading the edge of Railroad Street which does not even offer a sidewalk. Vacant lots strewn with broken glass and trash alternate with squat crumbly, blocky, industrial brick buildings. Rusty rail tracks thread throughout. The next piece of my pathway puzzle looms, oddly off balance, about three blocks ahead. Rising from this empty, dirty street, directly beside the railroad tracks, is a rusty staircase, at least 30 feet high. Leading inland from the top of the steps is a walkway, covered by chain-link fencing. The complete absence of any humans, vehicles, industrial noises or connections to this stairway suggest that at any moment a wizard may transport me to a world from which there is no return. But the walkway is simply pedestrian, and dead-ends in the edge of the bluff several hundred feet to the west after crossing safely above the terraced strips bearing two railroad lines, and Interstate 35. The strange experience is heightened by a brand new, and completely deserted, connecting walkway which abuts the old. The clean white concrete is wider than a highway lane, and curves downward to duck beneath the interstate. Surely it is a footpath, but its width and placement allow uneasy visions of cars zooming upward to find themselves trapped at the narrower pathway at the top!

Of course, although it appears that I am walking straight into the bluff, MN 23 is benched into the hillside. High above the busier thoroughfare, Glen Place is my next pathway, snaking up the bluff at an angle worthy of old eastern city streets. Puffing my way past apartment complexes whose views probably jack up their rents, I reach another level at 1st Street. Another jog to the southwest and I climb steeply again on 17th Avenue West. (I began the day at 25th Avenue East) beside Central Park. At the end of the street an unofficial trail wanders into the woods of the undeveloped park. Ahhh, earth beneath my feet. Hidden in this poplar haven within the city I shed my pack on a huge, rough, black rock which will serve as today's lunchroom. Although the pre-hike scouting had revealed to me the views I would enjoy, I have hoarded this day's first view, and I now allow myself a look down on Duluth Harbor. The lake and harbor spread smoothly from the foot of the high and ancient volcanic bluff on which I perch. Serviceberry gleams whitely here and there among the bright yellow-green of poplar leaflets whose young green odor fills the warm air. In pleasing contrast, grain elevators, ore docks, and bridges representing many past decades, ships, the lighthouse, central downtown, neighborhoods clearly staggered in age, new roads, and old roads fill the central horizon, all observed from my private pinnacle. I drowse on the warm rock, with bees humming lazy in the Serviceberry blossoms.

Accidentally I have stopped at just the perfect rock, for only 100 feet from my perch I reach the Skyline Parkway. The sound of its traffic had carried away from me, and I had not realized how close to it I was. The Parkway is a vintage, two-lane scenic road which winds along the bluff above Duluth. It has largely escaped the boring safety features of more modern routes. Medium-sized boulders form a guardrail, and the bluff often plunges downward just beyond their dotted protection. Many turnout parking areas are provided for those who wish to gaze across the vast Duluth Harbor and St. Louis River area, and many of its miles have been protected from development which would block or degrade the views. The next four and a half miles along this route are more than worth the 500-foot climb from water level at the Lakewalk. There is hope that the official North Country Trail route will be placed near the Parkway since its right-of-way is wide enough to tuck a footpath alongside the rising hill.

Today I am not weary, wet, foot-sore, chilly, hot or bored! This is proving to be a most pleasant urban walk. A huge but crumbling stone wall perches on the hill above me. It has a large "door" in its lower level, and a large notch one level higher, but offset. These openings are of sufficient size to admit a vehicle, making it look like a remnant of an abutment for some abandoned bi-level road. But where could it have gone? It would sail out into space above the quickly descending bluff. I query a resident of the apartments on the lower side of the road. He glances up in total apathy, as if he's never noticed this spectacular enigma looming above his home, and says he has no idea. I think I would die of curiosity if I lived within sight of such a quizzical structure and didn't learn what it was. I'm still ailing of puzzlement as I write these sentences!

Often when you try to gauge your progress by distant landmarks it appears that you are making no progress at all. For some reason this is not true on the Skyline. As I walk I can quickly see the various bridges, docks, neighborhoods slip past below me. At one of the turnouts which offers wide views I stop to take pictures. I have lugged two extra lenses on this entire hike just for this moment, so I'm not about to let the opportunity pass.

The Parkway hairpins upstream along several small creeks to cross where bridge building was easier. An arched stone culvert and abutment at one turn reminds me more of the Pacific Northwest than of my preconceptions of Minnesota. Yesterday's rain has transformed these small streams into boiling red-mud and frothy torrents which not so much fall over the rocks but storm them, climbing and scrambling to beat out neighboring vectors of clay and foam.

I take a shortcut through the Oenata Cemetery, finding an old barricaded cement highway bridge on which to cross Keene Creek just west of the cemetery to rejoin the Parkway. By this means I avoid following the roadway upstream nearly a half mile before it makes its present crossing. Fishermen keep the old bridge from complete abandonment to the vines.

I had planned to re-cross Interstate 35, US 2, and the railroad by walking through the high gothic culvert which carries Kingsbury Creek beneath them. On my scouting journey, only an inch of water slid smoothly through the 10-foot pointed arch. All day I have been thinking about this plan, realizing that since the rain the creeks are all much different from the day I had peered along the cool cement tunnel and made my plans to splash through the ripples in my rubber sandals. After all, there is a reason the culvert is 10 feet high instead of being an 18-inch-diameter pipe! I am wishing I had spent an extra ten minutes earlier and scouted out an alternate plan. Visions, not of sugerplums, but of dodging vehicles as I scamper across a 4-lane highway between red-lettered signs stating "No pedestrians," and climbing chain-link fences in my full pack dance in my head.

Now I am again staring into the cool, dark culvert. It is not entirely filled with water, but a swift and strong flow, over a foot deep, vetoes my tunnel plan. The civil engineers who hoisted a beer to their success at weaving the DM&IR railway, I-35, US 2, Skyline Parkway, and Kingsbury Creek through this one location never for a moment pondered a pedestrian's fate. But US 2 and the Parkway turn out to be on the same level, and I swing my legs over the guardrail and immediately note the rocks and tumultuous water tumbling down in staggered piles from the mouth of the culvert where I would have emerged.

I begin a short bushwack to connect with the Kingsbury Creek Ski Trail. This proves to be an extremely nasty section, but shorter than expected. I mince along a very steep bank of loose gravel high above the creek, grabbing at blackberry and gooseberry bushes for stability. I need to place each foot carefully to avoid a painful, scraping slide down the ravine. A cracked head or sprained ankle doesn't fit into my agenda. In about 15 minutes I am pleased to find the well-worn treadway of the real trail which parallels the creek and will lead me to the Zoo, and down to the foot of the bluff.

Kingsbury Creek is yet one more delightful episode in this day of almost unbelievable goodness. From multi-level transportation routes I have plunged into a natural corridor of beauty and calm. Trillium and Large-flowered Bellwort, Rue Anemone and violets line the rocky waterway. The path has been improved with rustic steps in its steeper portions and a wooden bridge guides me over the creek, answering my final question about whether I will have to find a place to cross the fast-moving water. All too quickly I drop through this vertical gallery of color, sound and motion and find myself standing at a traffic light on wide, dull and empty Grand Avenue.

Yet across the street are the exact facilities I need: a restaurant and a convenience store. I ask the one human in sight, a shabby young man in a hardware-clerk's red vest, if the Tappa Keg Restaurant is a good place to eat. "Yes, it is, " he immediately responds. That settles it. I ignore the unkempt brown exterior of the building rising from the dusty lot uninhibited by flower boxes, or any other decorative relief. The Tappa Keg is a neighborhood bar with a few scuffed tables along the walls for those who wish to eat. The menu offers "Spaghetti, Dick's Way." Well, I've flirted with Emily and Mama Rita, why not let Dick have his way? Dick likes his spaghetti piled high on the plate with a plethora of mushrooms, green peppers and onions swimming in marinara sauce poured over the whole. Whatever else might be lacking at the Tappa Keg Dick's spaghetti makes up for. What a grand collection of meals I've enjoyed on this walk!

The adjacent and also unadorned convenience store supplies my juice and a granola bar for tomorrow's breakfast. And in a few more blocks I reach Indian Point Campground. It is not yet open for the season, but I've convinced the hosts that I don't require any facilities, if only they will let me set my tent up for the night. So my bivy is the only lodge in a grassy, green sea where picnic tables lurk like an army of gulls. A Palm Warbler trills at me through the warm evening in between chapters of my book. This has been an idyllic day on the trail.

Thursday will be my final day of this trek. For the first two miles I follow the Western Waterfront Trail along the St. Louis River, a path with a crushed limestone surface. Wetlands filled with Great Blue Heron, a migrating Willet, sandpipers, Yellow Warblers, and myriad common birds entertain me. The most common of this hike have been the White-throated Sparrows who fairly scream about Sam Peabody, at a volume which seems impossible from such a tiny syrinx. Soon I join the Willard Munger Trail, a paved rail-trail, not my favorite. Once again I'm forced into thumping along on a hard surface, unshaded from the high sun. I can't understand why such multi-purpose routes can't be made two feet wider and a packed earth treadway added beside the asphalt for hikers. I have ten miles of this route ahead of me. Yet even here, there are a few memorable moments. The woods beside the route are often edged with a white berber of trillium trimmed with Large-flowered Bellwort, yellow, white and blue violets, some wild clematis, and young reddish Sarsaparilla leaves. Several impressive cuts curve through black jagged rock. The valleys are deep, very deep, steep-sided gullies, as they have been all along this coast. Mountains of earth were moved here to create the rail bed grades which cross each of these ravines. I wonder where all this earth came from! An interpretive sign from the previous day celebrated the dredging of the miles of marsh to create Duluth Harbor; could that wetland now be the ridges upon which I am walking? How did they move it here? The number of wagon-loads which would have been required is staggering. A tiny log shelter for resting, complete with bench in its front yard and oodles more trillium, tempts me to take a brief stop. A train whistles mournfully nearby as the Duluth, Missabe & Iron Range Railroad shrills a reminder to its departed cousin line, on which I now walk, that it remains alive and well.

    I have hopes of one more meaningful gastronomic encounter. There is supposed to be one restaurant along this stretch of trail. Reaching its sign, I become leery of the plan. Any billboard on which the beer signs take up 30% of the area, and the word "food" appears only in small letters at the bottom, tends to blunt my enthusiasm. Neither is the name enchanting: Buffalo House. But I decide to check it out. I leave the trail and walk past a field littered with old machinery, lumber, and a line of broken outhouses not meant for use. The driveway curves on... clearly not planned for walkers... too far from the trail. Judging that the destination is designed for snowmobilers my interest falls yet another notch. But now I've committed myself to have a look. More rusting vehicles, a house, and finally a commercial building which must be the restaurant. It is not open. I am not really disappointed. My crackers and cheese will make a fine lunch today.

While I eat, a determined rain begins. Today I will cover the pack; its contents are dry, and I will keep them in that condition. At last I pass the Jay Cooke State Park boundary marker. If it were not raining I would stop for a longer look at Hemlock Ravine, the largest remaining stand of Eastern Hemlock in Minnesota. The rangers have promised me that the park trails which intersect the Munger Trail are well marked, and I'm glad that proves to be true.

I've looked forward all day to leaving the rail-trail and joining the park's more natural pathways. However, just as I enter the woods, the rain begins in earnest; a hard, steady, cold rain which soaks me to the skin. I like to keep walking as long as I can keep warm enough, rather than trying to cover up. Then I switch to entirely dry garments when I stop. But this is a borderline situation; I have to keep opening and closing my hands just to keep the circulation going. I don't want to repeat the situation from a few years ago when I let my hands get so cold that I almost couldn't undo the pack clips.[1]

I am disgruntled at my need to pass by points of interest. The Thomas Hardy power plant, which generates the most electricity in Minnesota, seems tiny in comparison to its reputed output. But I am completely in the open as I cross the dam, and have no desire to stand in the full force of the rain even to sate my curiosity. Greely Creek would be a friendly nook of exploratory possibilities on a sunny day. As I join the White Pine Trail I note that a large area of underbrush has been burned. (I learned later that this was a prescribed burn.) The map shows a shelter along this trail. I focus on reaching it, to trade wet clothes for dry, and wait out the storm. But now I have concerns that the shelter may have been in the path of the fire. All I can do is walk as fast as possible and hope. Finally the burned over ground ends, and I climb to the top of a high hill. The sound and throb of rushing water obliterates all other sensations. And there is the tiny shelter, inexplicably facing away from the trail. I assume that the sound is some waterfall which I will view from the shelter. Reaching the top I am shocked to discover that the immense roaring is from the St. Louis

St. Louis River after a week of rain

[1.] See Chapter 7: "Patches"

River, hundreds of feet below and over a tenth of a mile south of the top of this pointy little hill. The river is an incredible sluice of red-clay and whitewater, many times more violent than any of the rushing but more vertical creeks I have passed in the last few days. Even through binoculars it still looks far from me, yet the sound is so loud that it would force me to raise my voice if there had been anyone to whom I could exclaim my surprise.

The shelter becomes my cozy refuge, a homestead of my imagination. In a few minutes I'm in dry clothes, and am curled snugly in a corner with a snack and my book. The roaring is so incredibly loud that it is difficult to block it out in order to read! And the rain continues. One hour, two hours... it is now 6 pm and I am becoming cool again from inactivity. The impish thought arises, why not just spend the night here? It's not allowed, and I know it's not. I couldn't even plead ignorance. I consider the alternative... I'll have to spend the night in an unprotected, muddy campsite, in a rain severe enough to guarantee that everything will be wet in the morning. I know there is no ranger on duty. It is May in Minnesota; it is pouring rain; it is getting dark. What are the chances that anyone at all will come along this path? I wait till 7:00. Now I am definitely chilly. I will need to get out the sleeping bag to remain warm. That proves to be my Rubicon. Once the bag is out (of the cat? The pack model is "Catskill!") it's only a small step more to pull out the tent which I will need for its insulating warmth. The temperature has already dropped to 45 degrees. The shelters are small, probably designed to keep people from setting up tents inside. But my bivy tent is tiny too, and I spin my warm green cocoon, anchoring its threads in the corners of the shelter. It is becoming too dark to read inside the shelter, and it's too wet outside. So once again, while it's yet light, I crawl into bed. I have delusions of watching dusk settle over the river through the tent's net panel, but once inside I realize I'm too low to the ground. Sighing, I zip myself in and drift off to sleep.

"Hey, dude! You're going to get ____t," proclaims a male voice. A female giggle follows. I thrash my way to consciousness, up through layers of drowse, sleeping bag zipper, tent zipper, rainfly zipper. There is no one there. It is still light, and the rain has backed down to a drizzle. I know I did not dream this encounter, but they are gone, not even visible along the trail. Now it's time to fuss. Did he say "You're going to get wet?" That makes no sense even though it is what I think I heard. "Get caught?" By whom? He's caught me, what's he going to do? Should I pack up and move to the campground? Why? I know there is no one to report to until 9:00 tomorrow morning. "Get hurt?" If he were going to hurt me, he would have done so already. Besides, the girl thought the whole thing was funny. Since he assumed I was a guy, he probably was not issuing a challenge without knowing how big or tough I might be. It is finally getting dark, so I release my anxiety. At the worst I'll probably be facing a fine, except for the embarrassment. I do resolve to leave the shelter early and reach the ranger station well before 9 o'clock!

And so, at 7:30 Thursday morning I am waiting for Ceceilia on the Visitor's Center porch. I know she will not arrive until at least 9:00, but I am ready, and I am dry, and I am protected even now from the rain which has begun to fall again this morning. I have no real regrets for my evil deed. I'll say it again; I AM DRY. I confess to paying for campsite number 51 when the Center opens. Fortunately that site was not already listed as occupied! I hope any Jay Cooke authorities who may ever read this will cast a forgiving smile my way. Ceceilia arrives and scoops me from my damp adventure into the next one. But that might be another story.

I have felt like that aforementioned worm from time to time on this hike. Worms like it wet. Large "nightcrawlers" languished on the pavement with me in the rain. They must have been German worms, *regenwürmer*, "rainworms." I wondered occasionally if I was moving any faster than they. We were often mud-covered, the worms and I. I truly feel like a small worm in my green-bivy-cocoon-prison-tent (but it weighs only two pounds!) And the great value of the humble earthworm is its ability to digest humic matter as it burrows in solitude through the landscape. I have bored a small tunnel of experiences through the Greater Duluth area in these four days. Perhaps these numerous alphabetic castings will prove beneficial to some gardener of the mind or soul.

55 miles this hike
Two Harbors to
      Jay Cooke State Park, MN
1540 total NCT miles

May the Road Rise to Meet You
53 - June 28- July 9, 2000

Marie, Bess and I are walking up Irish Hill Road when Bess comments that the whole day has been a living example of one version of the traditional Irish Blessing:

> May the road rise to meet you,
> May the wind always be at your back,
> May the sun shine warm upon your face,
> And may you find a friend at the end of the road.

The sun has beamed upon us, today we are hiking with only day packs, and the road certainly has risen once again to meet us. I'm not sure that the blessing really had the idea of continually climbing hills in mind, but that is what most definitely comes to our minds when we think of this trip.

The hike began just south of the New York state border, and we will walk to the Genesee River, near Portageville, New York. These miles belong to both the Finger Lakes Trail and the North Country Trail. Bess, a friend of Marie's, who teaches the visually impaired, is joining us for this jaunt. Bess wants to take a long backpacking trip with other women. We qualify as women, if not ladies, and apparently two weeks counts as long enough.

This trip, like "Baby Steps on the Giant Trail," begins with a visit to Marie's Aunt Agnes, a nun living at the retirement home in Allegany, New York. Agnes, Sister Tarcisia, is now 89 years old, and probably weighs about 80 pounds, but she is as spritely as ever. She cares for the flower beds all around the Mother House, and this time she wants to show us her potting room as well as the plants. The building is arranged in a huge square with wings, and unless you know the hallways, you could be anywhere. But as we are quietly padding down one of the cavernous halls Agnes turns a corner into a side passage, whispering conspiratorially, "Let's go this way, I don't want Sister Mary Lourdes to find us." It's great fun, avoiding Mary Lourdes, and we suspect that what she has in mind is to deter Agnes from some aspect of her gardening. The sprite in a white habit has been told to slow down and let someone younger take over a bit of the gardening, but Agnes can't bear to part with her role as Digger of the Soil. The potting room is a merry jumble of crockery, baskets, tools, bags of seeds and supplies. We get the tour and then we head out to see the garden.

Completely surrounding this huge square building is a wide flower border, and Agnes shows us every inch. Sunflowers, snapdragons, poppies, zinnias and many more flowers compete happily with dill, thyme, sage and other herbs. It's weed-free and colorful; Agnes deserves to be proud of her garden. I hope I'm as energetic and cheerful as she when I get to be that age. If a love of gardening is the secret to a pleasant old age, maybe I'm on the right track.

We sleep that night in the small, neat guest rooms on crisp white sheets, the last night we will have this luxury for a while!

The next day, with short stops to watch an Osprey on a nesting platform, and to fill our water bottles, we park at the northernmost road crossing of the trail in Pennsylvania. Marie and I actually hiked these first few miles on that previous Allegheny National Forest hike, so I don't get to count them into my total, but it's the closest we can get to the New York border by car. With our packs full, we head north on the trail climbing up Schoolhouse Hollow. We had not noticed what a long climb this is on that previous trip. That time, we did this stretch with just water bottles and a snack, just so that we could say we began at the elusive border line. The 700-foot hill feels significantly higher with an extra thirty-plus pounds.

When we reach the state line, we enter the Allegany State Park. (Yes, New York spells it differently from Pennsylvania.) This park is a rough triangle, sitting on the state line and jutting north into New York. The area is geologically unique in that the last glacier split and flowed around each side of the triangle, never scouring the hills which are now within the park. Thus the hills are supposed to be steeper and the valleys narrower than anyplace else nearby. We wander from ridgetop to hollow and back, making our way across the park. I surprise a small bear at a creek crossing, but its startled exit is so hasty that Marie and Bess

Ragged Fringed Orchid

don't even get a glimpse of its tail. We all get a good look at the four-foot-tall Ragged Fringed Orchid, not rare, but of rare beauty.

Leaving the park we cross the Allegheny River on a gray, drizzly day and enter the hills of the Southern Tier which have been scoured by the glacier. I've told you the geological history of this area, but now I need to tell you that there is nothing low or gradual about any of these hills, no matter on which side of the line of glacial advance they lie.

This hike is forever defined in our minds by Jimmerson Hill, our next big climb. In a bit over one mile we ascend 700 feet from Sunfish Run to the top of Jimmerson. Before another mile is finished we have plunged back down those 700 feet to Sawmill Run Road. So at least we went up the gentler slope, but it was hard to be grateful, we were panting so hard! Switchbacks seem to be unknown to folks here, and the trail climbs pretty much straight up the fall line (perpendicular to the contours, and most susceptible to erosion). Marie and Bess have the harder time going up. Their technique is to walk 50 paces and then rest for a 50 count. I'm pretty good at going up, but the very steep descents make my knees ache and weaken. I make downward progress slowly, leaning heavily on my walking stick. Thus as a group we manage to move at the slowest possible pace.

The next day we cross three big hills, a 900-footer, a 600-footer, and we end the day with Bucktooth Hill, a mere 300 feet. More than one of the steep downhills is imprinted with deep muddy logging machine tracks, or ATV damage, making the walking positively awful. But none of them feels as bad as Jimmerson Hill! I arrive to hear Marie in the middle of a description of one climb: "...striding up the hill, singing an aria, while being chased by the Germans." Knowing how much Marie likes climbing hills I am picturing some dark Wagnerian opera. We are scrambling for our lives, looking over our shoulders to catch glimpses of armed fat ladies wearing horned helmets, who can sing, wield swords, and also walk fast enough to catch us, all at the same time. Turns out that for once she is not grousing about some steep hill. Instead she is explaining that a vista at the top of a long climb made her feel as exuberant as the VonTrapps at the end of *The Sound of Music*, when they cross the mountains into Switzerland, and freedom.

We are greeted as we eat lunch by a tall, thin man with a very small pack. "Are you Marie, Bess and Joan?" he demands. We confess that we are, and he introduces himself. This is Joe Dabes, on his fourth Finger Lakes Trail end-to-end hike. He's trying to beat the record time now, to hike the whole FLT in 23 days. "So far I'm end-to-ender numbers 2, 8, and 131!" he exclaims. We invite him to lunch with us. "Gotta keep moving," says Joe.

This brings us to Rock City. There is a village by that name, but I refer to the Rock City of the Rocks. This city was founded by that glacier which keeps coming into the story. Having scoured the area down to bedrock here, the water dripping from the

Going down to Rock City

glacier's nose seeped into cracks in the rock. This froze and split the bedrock into immense cubes, separated by streets and alleys of varying widths. The trail approaches a large flat rock surface and vanishes? No, it descends an incline between two of the blocks to the "floor" level. Down in the alleyways the air is damp and the rock walls are decorated with multitudinous lichens and mosses. Trees growing on top of the rocks send their roots down crevices or along the outsides of the cubes making them look like long-legged tree-people.

Our fifth night out we arrive at Holimont Ski Area where campers are allowed to bivouac in a field near their pond for snow-making in the winter. We pitch one lone tent in a sea of grass. The pond is a local swimming hole in summer complete with a raft, and we head over that way for a quick dip. Three boys, about 12 years old, are having a lot of fun on the raft, but we can't quite figure out what they are doing. Suddenly a good sized Bluegill flies out of a hole in the middle of the raft and lands with a plop in a small inflatable pool the boys have brought with them. They are happy to share their new fishing technique with us! They have lowered a t-shirt down the hole, weighted with rocks tied in the corners. Then they wait until a fish swims above the suspended shirt. With a snap they flip the shirt up, and direct the surprised fish into their pool. They are really very good at it! They soon catch their biggest one yet, but much to their dismay it also is strong, and flips itself back into the pond. After a while they tire of the game and release all the fish, and we take over the raft, basking in the slanting sunlight.

The cache "tree" tonight is the end of the ski lift mechanism. It's nice and high, and really easy to get the rope over. We talk long into the night. We are so tough by now that a few hills apparently don't even tire us out.

In the middle of this hike we have made plans so that we will not have to carry the heavy packs for three days. The logistics are complicated, but it seems like it will work. We begin the next morning by leaving our tent on Holimont, and walking away with just daypacks. It feels really strange! Marie comments, "I feel as light as an eagle feather."

"If it's a bronze eagle!" is Bess' rejoinder. Perhaps she's not as certain of our status as seasoned hikers.

Yesterday we had crossed from Hungry Hollow, over McCarty Hill to where the better-fed folks must live in Mutton Hollow before climbing to Holimont. Today we descend to Hencoop Hollow (the population there probably doesn't go hungry either, and go over Plum Ridge (dessert is featured here with cobbler or jam). It's down to Elk Creek for a good drink, but then we climb the very steep Poverty Hill.

Guess these residents didn't know about all the good food scattered so close by around the countryside! Another steep descent on a horrible woods road that has recently been disemboweled by logging equipment Marie describes as "fifty feet wide and six feet deep." Soon we find ourselves climbing Irish Hill in the sun with a Tufted Titmouse singing and Bess reminding us of our blessings. The road has again risen to meet us, and Irene, of "W2K" fame, is certainly a good friend at the end of today's road.

Mid-afternoon, Irene meets us with her van. She whisks us back in a few short minutes to Holimont, and we break camp there and drive to one of Irene's special spots on the Finger Lakes Trail, the Cobb Campsite.

Irene's roles include President of the Finger Lakes Trail Conference, FLT end-to-ender, and trail custodian *extraordinaire*. Folks tease her that she must sweep her trails with a broom, and indeed she fusses and tends the 21 miles of trail in her care with the precision of a government inspector. If you are not a volunteer who maintains any trail, this number will have no particular meaning to you. Trust me that 20-some miles is a ridiculously large collection of miles for one person to maintain, even if that person were not a perfectionist. And of course these are not consecutive miles; oh, no, they are scattered about all of western New York.

The Cobb site includes a side loop trail from the main trail to the road, and also to the top of the hill (where else?) to a nice, neat campsite with a fire ring, lashed table and log benches, all planned, created and maintained by Irene. Irene has brought pork chops for dinner which we cook over a campfire (at road level), and salad too. She also brings lawn chairs to sit in, a nice treat for folks who have spent days sitting mostly on the ground. In return, she enlists our help to lug a steel picnic grill up to the campsite which she will install at a later date. If you pass this way and wonder how that heavy grill got to the top of that big hill, you can thank four girls!

The next day we have planned a day off, and Irene has arranged to take us to see several places of interest. She brings another friend, Pat, who finds plants like *Carex gracillima* and *Apocynum andro-saemifolium* as exciting as I do. Marie, Bess and Irene find other things to discuss, but Pat and I are busy botanizing as we make our way around a small pond. We are all hopeful of seeing an Osprey reputed to live there, but the bird is smart enough to stay out of the rain, which is more than can be said of us. We check out more of the rocks and plants in Rock City. Huge flabby platters hanging from the cliffs are Rock Tripe, supposedly edible in a pinch. New York Fern tapers at both ends. We visit an Art Park in Ellicottville, and enjoy two large meals in a warm dry restaurant, and ice cream at yet another eatery. As days off go, this one is not very restful, although we have lots of fun. Not to mention lots of food, since in addition to all the aforementioned comestibles we also buy subs to take back to the campsite with us.

The next day Irene hikes with us, pushing a measuring wheel and taking notes so that she will be able to bring one of her several guidebooks up to date. Bess enjoys helping Irene with this project. Irene's dog Gummy and puppy Sandy hike with us too. A neighbor drives us back to Irish Hill, and we end the day by returning to Cobb's Hill. Bess has brought sparklers and we light them in the campfire. This is as good and glittery a 4th of July celebration as we need. It's better than any large commercial display viewed by thousands of noisy people and ending with hundreds of noisy rockets.

We have one more hiking day with only day packs from Cobb's to Bear Creek State Forest. We break camp and take the gear down to Irene's van. Hiking once more, Marie notes that it's a good thing we never want a ride: with four gals, three packs, two dogs and a measuring wheel we would need a flatbed truck! Despite a late start we make fast time and by late afternoon we pick a campsite on Bear Creek where Irene had previously stashed a bicycle. She pedals furiously back to the van, delivers our gear to us and heads back to her everyday world.

Once again our crew is just Marie, Bess and I. It seems good to settle back into a familiar routine. We pitch the tent, cook beef-barley stew and an exquisite strawberry-rhubarb cobbler, followed by hot drinks, a little reading, visiting and bed.

The morning light slants in through the pine boughs. A Red-breasted Nuthatch "ank-anks" us awake and two deer approach close enough to the tent that we have a good view of them through the screening. A Goldfinch "perchickories" nearby. Some of the other familiar wildlife is not so well received by members of our group. Bess and Marie aren't fond of the slugs. Every morning there are slugs on the tent, on the groundcloth, on our hiking sticks, and on any items we have left outside. I think they are fascinating the way they can alter their shape so fluidly, or extend and retract their antennae. The other gals just think they are slimy, so slug removal duty is mine.

Bess checks for morning slugs

The challenge for today is to re-acclimate our bodies to the weight of full packs. Taking days off from that in the middle of a hike was not really a great idea. Although we make good time, and even steep hills don't seem to phase us much any more, we feel slower than the slugs. Psychologically it was a bad choice.

Bess has been our early-riser. Often she is outside doing exercises before even Marie is awake. She stretches and bends "to get the tension out." It's fine if it works for her, but if someone tried to force me out of a warm sleeping bag to exercise with the birds I'd be too tense to spend the day with!

She has also turned out to be a companion with a great sense of humor. She adopted a stick with a Kokopelli silhouette and named him George. George had traveled with us for several days until he lost a leg. Knowing that this would make it difficult for him to hike (not to mention making it difficult to distinguish him from the other sticks in the forest), we sadly bid him adieu and gave him a proper hiker's burial.

Tonight, however, Bess proves that her courage is as well developed as her wit. We have set up camp on a hillside, shoehorning the tent into the only nearly level spot. To fix dinner we have trenched small shelves to hold the stove and the pots. The hillside grade is not very steep, but it has just enough incline that a pot carelessly placed may not be stable. We boil water for tea and Bess sets down the small kettle next to her. It begins to tip, she makes a grab for it, and in the flash of an eye she has spilled boiling water on her bare shin. Before Marie or I have time to react she remarks casually, "It's not serious," rubs her hand over the blistering red patch, and layers of skin peel off where she touches. This is the most serious injury we've ever had on one of my hikes. Thankfully we are carrying enough pads, gauze and ointment that we will be able to treat it for a couple of days as long as Bess can handle the discomfort.

The main concern medically is to keep it clean. Marie tends and bandages the leg; we'll have to see how Bess feels in the morning. Fortunately we have only a couple of days yet to hike, and we don't encounter any six-foot mudholes, or deep streams to ford. Bess accepts some Tylenol, and stoically hikes on.

We traverse many more uphills and downhills, none as severe as the ones earlier in the hike, but there is never a complaint at all from Bess about her leg. Near a pleasantly level mile on the old grade of the Buffalo and Susquehanna Railroad, we are entertained by miles of bright pink, purple, red and green tubing strung through a maple sugarbush. No sap is running now, but the tubing can be left in the woods between sugaring seasons.

There are many more farms here than we saw in the western miles. We pass a country corner where a young man on a tractor is raking the hay into windrows. He catches sight of us and immediately sits up straighter in the seat and turns a neat corner, showing us that he is proud of his farm heritage and skill. We also pass a field where two young Amish men are mowing hay in staggered rows, each with a team of two horses. They return our wave, and are also clearly pleased to have us appreciate their workmanship. The young men are from different cultures, and yet so similar. At another farm an entire family, mom, and small boys, as well as the teens and father are working hard to move the hay bales from the wagons to the elevator, to the barn hayloft. The sound of the elevator motors and belts can be heard in the distance late into the night. "Make hay while the sun shines" is no theoretical maxim to farmers.

Today we can see hills on the far side of the Genesee River, farther than we will walk on this hike. With this perspective on the future, we begin to feel that the end of the trip is approaching. Irene and the dogs join us for one more day. Now that the terrain is easier our lungs can consider the possibility of supplying enough air for a song or two, as well as for walking. At one point, Irene and puppy Sandy are far in the lead, and I begin to belt out "The fox went out on a stormy night." Sandy races back to check out this strange phenomenon, poking her nose against my hand and looking at me with alarm, and the question "Are you all right?" written all over her expressive face. Then she races back to Irene for comfort.

Actually, our talents do not end (or perhaps begin) with singing songs. We start to compose a new country tune as we hike. I have taken the liberty of finishing the lyrics. You may decide for yourself if it will make the Country Music Top Forty. We doubt it, but we're having fun, so who cares? Here you go...

>We don't wash our white sink
>Until it turns brown.
>So we left our homes for Olean
>Where the oil seeps from the ground.
>Some folks say we're crazy,
>But we know we're O.K.
>Hiking to the Genesee
>From Allegheny, P.A.

>The hills they are Jim-Dandy,
>Like stairways to the sky.
>We're having fun in the summer sun,
>But we have to wonder why!
>Moaning thighs and aching backs
>Our lungs and knees give way,
>Hiking to the Genesee
>From Allegheny, P.A.

> We greet the slugs at breakfast,
> We race them all day long.
> We hike and smile for many a mile,
> While they just slime along.
> Every night they meet us,
> They sing this ron-do-lay:
> We beat you to the Genesee
> From Allegheny, P.A.
>
> We've seen fantastic sights
> Like the stream where Sunfish Run.
> We heard the Hencoop Holler,
> And the Dogwood bark for fun.
> If you're in Hungry Hollow
> There's Mutton just over the way,
> Hiking to the Genesee
> From Allegheny, P.A.

The last hiking day is an echo of our early day when we crossed the three large hills. The final ridge we must traverse to reach the car is split into three small lobes. We are much stronger; these hills are much lower. Like an echo, repeating a theme, but fainter, our steps seem to be a fitting and fading recounting of the difficult hills. We reach the car just as a hard rain begins. Today we are not sorry to leave the trail.

We spend another day exploring Letchworth State Park, and although this wonderful park is a few miles from the NCT, it can be reached on foot by the purist, via the Letchworth Branch of the Finger Lakes Trail. Therefore I will include a bit about it.

The Letchworth Gorge itself is the deep gash which is home to the central section of the Genesee River. Sometimes known as the Grand Canyon of the East, this valley, 20 miles long and up to 600 feet deep, is flanked with shale and sandstone. These sedimentary rocks are the bed of an ancient Devonian Sea. Before the glacier came, the river followed a shallow valley. But the glacier moved mountains of sediment and rocks, and the river was forced to find a new path around the obstructions. Cutting deeply through the soft layers, the river now features three major waterfalls, one of which is 107 feet high.

Letchworth had been on our itinerary from the very beginning. Along the way we read a book about the life of Mary Jemison, known as the "White Woman of the Genesee." Mary's family was killed and she was captured by Shawnees in 1755, when she was about 12 years old. Her mother had a chance to give Mary some final direction, and told her to do as her captors asked, and she might be spared. Her mother also made Mary promise to practice her English so that she would not lose that language. The young girl determined that she would follow her mother's advice. She was chosen by the Indians to be adopted, and about a year later she was wed to a Seneca Indian. After one more year the teenage Mary, now with a nine-month old baby, walked from Ohio to the Genesee River Valley of New York, her husband's home.

She recounted, "Those only who have travelled on foot the distance of five or six hundred miles, through an almost pathless wilderness, can form an idea of the fatigue and sufferings that I endured on that journey."[1] Our own difficulties seemed insignificant compared to Mary's. The more we read of this survivor, the more we admired the small, strong woman. She was once offered a chance to return to the white man's world, but chose to remain and live as an Indian in the ways to which she had become accustomed. Following the Revolutionary War, she settled in the Ga-da-o Flats in the depths of the Letchworth Gorge. This fertile flat was her home for the rest of her long life. She deplored the cruelty of the Indians, but accepted that they strictly adhered to their own code of justice, living in peace and honesty when that code was not violated. Her own life was filled with the tragedy of wayward sons, and the love of faithful daughters. She was always personally known for her kindness, hospitality, and generosity.

"White Woman of the Genesee"

Within the park is a statue of Mary, and also the preserved cabin, built by her, for one of her daughters. The message of the simple log structure seems to overpower the differences between Colonial and Indian cultures. A rough stone chimney and hearth, a sleeping loft, a dirt floor, a bench. Life was harsh and difficult for anyone living in the wilds of western New York in the 18th century.

Since I grew up not far from here, our family often visited this park. Many times in my youth I gazed at this statue, and felt a bond with Deh-ge-wan-us, Mary Jemison. I would look at her stone dress and instead feel the soft coolness against my skin of the tanned deerskin my dad had given me. I saw her stride and her confident gaze, despite hardships, and sought to make these mine. After many years, and

---

[1] Seaver, James E.; *The Life of Mary Jemison, Edition of 1953*; The American Scenic and Historic Preservation Society; New York, New York; first published 1824; p 53.

many miles, the sense of common spirit is even stronger.

And the gorge was no stranger to 19th century technologies. A decade late and many dollars short, the Genesee and Rochester Canal was begun in 1836 on the east side of the river. By 1841 the canal was navigable from Rochester to Mt. Morris. However, the economic success of the canal was short-lived, because the infant railroads were commanding every commercial dollar available. Eventually the Genesee Valley Railroad was laid on the former towpath. Where the gorge narrows, this route is perched on a rock ledge cut into the cliff. High above the gorge, another railroad, the Erie, laid tracks, and built the highest wooden trestle in the world, 234 feet above the Upper Falls, to carry them over the river. The early trestle burned in 1874, but was replaced with an iron one, which is still in use. At Letchworth State Park you can walk the old towpath, view the waterfalls, and perhaps see a train rumbling high above.

Fourteen miles north, the 20th century wonder of the gorge is the Corp of Engineers dam, completed in 1952. Far downstream, where the Genesee empties into Lake Ontario, lies the city of Rochester. Deep floods buried the city in water and mud an average of once every seven years from 1865 to 1950. One of these torrents built up a water pressure equal to half that of Niagara Falls, causing great destruction. The dam was finally built, and the saving of both human life and property can hardly be exaggerated. During Hurricane Agnes alone, in 1972, it is estimated that over $210 million dollars in damage was prevented by the dam. Pictures after that storm reveal the reservoir filled to the top of the 215-foot concrete structure, with an estimated peak inflow at 7/8 that of Niagara Falls. The water backed up three miles to the Lower Falls. Instead of that water rushing unimpeded through Rochester, the dam allowed for its gradual release, saving lives and the continuity of daily life.

Our days of exploring after the hike have spanned centuries of history. Jimmerson Hill is softened with wraiths of fog as we drive past. Its slopes no longer appear so daunting now that we have crossed them. The sun has returned to shine on us, and we have rested and feasted at the house of a friend. What will the 21st century bring to the Genesee? What road will arise in its future? We hope that many happy hikers will enjoy excursions through its history, its byways, and its forests.

106 miles this hike
NY/PA Border to the Genesee River
1646 total NCT miles

Building Bridges
54 - August 26, 2000

More and more of my time these days is taken up by volunteer duties which are reported to the NCTA under the heading labeled "Administration." As Spirit of the Woods Chapter President I've been pleased to be able to promote good relationships with the chapters both to our south, Western Michigan, and to our north, Grand Traverse Hikers (GTH). Earlier this year some members from Western Michigan hiked a few miles with our Chapter. Today we are joining with the Traverse City group for a hike on some of the trail that they have recently upgraded. This summer they have built twelve bridges in this four-mile section and are eager to show off their hard work. Today we will all build some relational bridges.

So here I am, emerging from a vehicle on this country corner, to become one of a group of 23 humans and two dogs who have turned out to test the bridges, both of wood and of friendships, and sample the trail. Twelve of the hikers are associated with Spirit of the Woods, and the remainder hail from the Traverse City area. To be entirely honest, one of the participants is more of a hitchhiker, a toddler who spends most of the trail time in a backpack. Forrest and his mom and dad, Angie and Mark, are veterans of our jaunts.[1] Hannah the Basset Hound and Kam the Golden Retriever spend a few moments getting acquainted, but their mutual decision seems to be to hike separately. Kam is more interested in jumping in the river anyway. "Dog all wet," succinctly comments Forrest!

Arlen, the GTH trail work coordinator, explains how the crews have met nearly every weekend all summer to complete these bridges. The impatient covey of hikers explodes past the barrier gate at the end of the road and down the trail as soon as Arlen's talk is finished. He and I are the last to leave the parking site. He wants to chat about trail issues... permits, grants, maps, plans. He is also temporarily slowed by the need for a hip replacement which he has scheduled for later this fall. "So you'll be a plastic man," I joke.

"No," he responds, "titanium. I'm going first-class." Those of us who take hiking seriously need to keep the joints in tip-top shape. Arlen has been assured that he'll be able to resume his active lifestyle after a recovery period. He walks with me to the second bridge and then, almost ashamed at the injunction from his doctor to take it easy, he turns back.

[1.] See Chapter 46: "Walking Backwards Down the Stairs"

At the third bridge, a GTH member is pointing towards the streambank and lamenting, "I wish we had someone with us who knows plants." Here is a challenge I cannot refuse, and I call out and trot to meet her, hoping that I won't be embarrassed by my bold claim to knowledge. This time, at least, my pride is preserved. The flower is Bottle Gentian, both blue and white, curving seductively up the creek's steep bank just below the sturdy new bridge.

Bottle Gentian

Before the next bridge, I have caught up with Dick, the GTH President. He, too, has trail issues to discuss. The cost of permits for the bridges is one of his hot topics, as well as chapter relationships, trail maintenance, and program planning. By now we are on a bluff, high above the meandering Manistee River. This is a beautiful section of the trail, freshly blazed and dotted with its new bridges.

Crossing a meadow I overtake a successful meld of the two clubs. Three members from each chapter are visiting and eating lunch. I'm now far behind the leaders, and I do want to reach the next road where we will all turn around, so I hurry on, thankful for those bright new blazes.

I really have no idea of how far I've walked. Hiking with people of varying speeds for varying lengths of time, discussing various topics confounds any attempt to calculate my progress. But suddenly a wave of hikers, the vanguard of the company, washes over me from the opposite direction. "You're almost there," they claim, their voices fading in the surge of their passing.

"Whew," I muse, "do I seem so rushed when I'm hiking quickly?" In another minute I reach Ellen and Scott, members of our chapter. They decide to wait for me and we will walk the return trip together. I reach the crossroad, make a mental note of its appearance for future access, and then begin to backtrack. Usually I dislike walking both directions on a trail, but today I am appreciative of the time to take in the surroundings on the return trip.

And then there are the bridges. I comment to Ellen and Scott that perhaps we aren't working at building bridges with the GTH folks if we are walking by ourselves. They assure me that they spent some time talking with new acquaintances on the outward trek. Twelve Spirit of the Woods hikers. Perhaps twelve small bridges built with Grand Traverse hikers. Twelve small new wooden bridges spanning tiny streams and steep gullies. When bridges are there we callously galumph across the planks, hardly noticing their existence except

Bridges built by hikers

perhaps for the change in the sound of our footfalls. But listen to us when a bridge is NOT available. We moan at the often short but very steep descent down an eroded bank, we whine over our wet boots as our feet slip on the rocks. Deep mud produces deep gutterals of protest, and we are amazed at the extra time required to cross even small rivulets safely. Perhaps we should give more consideration to the existence and value of all the many bridges on the pathways of our lives.

Ellen and I add another 2.5 road miles at the end of the day to allow me to connect this trip to a previously completed section of the trail. It will take more bridge-building, of the kind needed with private landowners, to move this piece of trail off-road. Arlen has promised that will be another goal for another year. More bridges, strong bridges; life is bridges.

6.5 miles this hike
Baxter Bridge to Town Line Road
Wexford County, MI
1652 total NCT miles

Solo, Duo, Triad
55 - October 8-10, 2000

    For the first day of this adventure I am hiking solo. I've decided to explore the shore of the Clarion River in Pennsylvania, in an area which I believe to be State Game Lands. Leaving my car at the end of a township road by the water, I know that I'm in for the possibility of a tough day. There is no trail here at all, and I will have to bushwack through to the next road, and then hike around via road to return to my car. But I'm eager for a challenge.

    Almost immediately I find a large, fleshy growth on the side of a tree. It looks sort of like the tree has sprung a small leak of cave water and has developed a waterfall stalactite formation, except this is soft, not hard. I wonder if it is another slime mold. This past summer we had found two more of those eerie life forms, and neither of them was slimy. One is called Insect Egg Slime. It was arranged on a twig in neat parallel rows of tiny orange teardrops, looking like insect egg cases. The other one I believe to be Chocolate Tube Slime. Each tube was a brown finger balanced on a thin stalk, but they were clustered into neat groups, each clump looking like a tiny pillbox hat. But I am not certain of this identification. And now, here I am in the woods, alone with another strange blobby thing. I'm almost willing to believe that it might pick up its icicle skirts and start crawling down the tree. Where is a good slime mold expert when you need one?[1]

    I am walking high above the river where the going is slightly easier. Before long, much to my surprise I encounter private property signs. I had been told this was all public land. The signs imply that I'm not trespassing as long as I stay near the water. So back down the steep hill I go, straight into the arms of *Polygonum japonicum*. That's Japanese Knotweed, which I call the "Kudzu of the North." Eight-foot tall clumps of this alien plant crowd the banks. The stems look like fat bamboo, and the broad leaves have turned golden for autumn. A patch of this plant here and there might be attractive, but it won't agree to live such a restrained existence. If you've traveled in the southern United States you have seen how the alien Kudzu vine covers and chokes every plant, telephone pole, wall and hillside. Japanese Knotweed is on its way to accomplishing the same things in cooler climes. This beautiful but obnoxious shrub loves to be cut down and abused; it will sprout again from the cut stems with renewed vengeance. Only chemical warfare seems to stop its fearsome advance across the landscape.

---

[1] This turned out to be Bearded Hedgehog, a tooth fungus.

The day began with cool sunlight spilling in white bands across the red and orange October hillsides. But the farther I push between knotweed stands, the longer I scramble down to the river's very marshy edge to avoid "no trespassing" signs, or back up again to find ground on which I can actually walk, the worse the weather becomes. By the time I reach the dirt road that is my goal it's extremely clear that I will have a long, cold, wet road walk back to the car in a sleety drizzle. It is also clear that I've mostly intruded on private land today; it's unlikely that the trail will pass here unless some person makes it his or her mission to forge relationships with landowners. I've not made a great beginning, with my entire day of trespassing.

Later, soaking wet, and nearing my car I do meet one of the landowners who confirms that I have indeed been on private property, and that they are not open to having the trail cross their land. I am torn between embarrassment at admitting my sins, confusion over how I had been so misinformed about this section, and relief that I have actually completed the miles.

At a small restaurant with pictures of schooners on the walls, waitresses in nautical uniforms set plates of hot spaghetti on red-checked tablecloths. It's an incongruous presentation, but a hot and satisfactory dinner.

At the Cook Forest State Park campground, Marie is waiting for me when I arrive, and thus we become a duo. The sleet has become an early wet snow. Winter camping is never Marie's favorite, but we are hopeful for better weather in the morning.

We do not get our morning wish, and we leave in a swirling snow squall from our campsite, on foot. We hike past the Seneca Fire Tower, to Gravel Lick Bridge, and into State Game Lands (today I am sure of the public status). We are looking for trail that is supposed to be flagged, but not completely built. We find markings for a few yards, but all too soon we are guessing at pathways, eventually climbing a steep bank on all fours to emerge on an old oil access road. We saw lots of oil and gas access roads when we hiked the Allegheny, and I accept with a sigh that the oil road scenario is sometimes the quintessential North Country Trail. Marie's sighs are in frustration that once again I'm dragging her through a trackless wood, and in the snow, no less! But later the snow stops and the sun comes out. We follow the road for awhile, then a horse path and a jeep road, and then we find ourselves again closer to the river. The shrubbery here is native, and will be beautiful in another season; the hillsides are covered with thickets of Rhododendron. I have always thought of this as such a southern plant, I'm surprised to see so much of it in the hills of Pennsylvania.

Finally, we follow a rusted oil pipeline for most of the afternoon. It seems roughly to parallel the river, and a trace of a bench in the hillside remains, making the walking easier on our calves and ankles.

We return to the campsite to cook dinner. A campfire is easily started, even in the damp twilight, thanks to a fortuitous encounter. When I had first arrived on Sunday morning, I was approached by three high-school girls. They came from the adjacent site and were just breaking camp. They asked me if I would like some fire starters, since they had made way too many, and were leaving. I accepted the gift and asked them who they were, since it's not every day that you find three girls, and two older women (watching from the picnic table), tent camping in the cold. "We're Girl Scouts!" they answered proudly. I was ecstatic, finding Scouts who still care about camping skills. I couldn't prevent myself from yakking on and on, probably boring the girls to death. But I had to tell them how proud of them I felt, to urge them never to lose their love for the outdoors, to show them my patch jacket with the emblem from the 1965 Senior Scout Roundup. "Come meet our leaders," they invited. I met the older women, and learned that one of them was grandmother to one of the Scouts. I nodded in recognition of the familiar scenario. How many younger women had passed up the opportunity to lead these gals? How many had said that they would not camp out in the cold? My own mother, who was a generation older than the parents of most of my friends, was the one who valiantly took our troop to the woods, sat around campfires on cold, damp logs, and drove us all over the countryside to work on badge requirements.

Tonight Marie comments, "If two old Girl Scouts can't light a fire with an egg-carton-wax-and-sawdust fire-starter and a butane lighter, I don't know who can!" No problem lighting the fire, but meanwhile the sun has set. Cooking in the dark is not too difficult, but our tuna-rice curry seems to have an unusually mild flavor. We soon discover why! Our tiny dishcloth was hiding in the empty pot, and has apparently absorbed most of the spices. I say "apparently," because we did decline to eat the terry-cloth square. We settled for the milder than usual rice, and convinced ourselves that boiling the dishrag must have killed any germs. Never say "bleah" when handed a warm bowl of dinner on a chilly night!

We tuck ourselves into the tent just as a steady rain begins, which lasts all night.

On Tuesday the weather and the hiking are both more pleasant. The air is crisp and the sky is clear. We drive north to the Allegheny National Forest and head south for our campsite in Cook Forest State Park. We cross Coon Creek on a sturdy rustic bridge

Hiking in the rich October woods

and join the Baker Trail. We pass through another State Game Land and Kittanning State Forest. Open hemlock and beech forest surrounds us as far as Maple Creek which we cross on a small suspension bridge. Entering the state park we patch together a route of many park trails, wandering ever southward.

Near the center of the park we enter an area of perpetual twilight. Known as Forest Cathedral, this is one of the largest areas of virgin forest in Pennsylvania. A slice of one of these ancient trees, felled by a tornado, is displayed in the small museum. Historic dates are noted on its concentric rings. Very near the edge of the slice, as big in diameter as I am tall, is marked 1958: first US satellite launched. Moving inward, when the first oil well was dug in Titusville, Pennsylvania, in 1859, the tree was about four feet in diameter. When passenger rail service began in 1828 (on the Baltimore and Ohio RR), our pine was perhaps thirty inches across. Past the Lewis and Clark Expedition, past George Washington's election as President, to a ring which would have been the bark of a four-inch tree. That ring is marked 1776; when our nation was born, this tree was already standing tall in the sun.

Tonight's dinner plan changes soon after we reach our campsite. With uncharacteristic carelessness, we have packed the food in my car... miles away. Well, that's what backup plans and restaurants are for!

Wednesday morning Marie bids me farewell, and now begins the Triad. The reason I have chosen to hike at this place, at this time, is so that I can attend the first of what will be called the Triad meetings. The National Park Service (NPS), the US Forest Service, and the North Country Trail Association (NCTA) plan to meet each fall to discuss issues and seek ways to work together. The Park Service administers the trail. The Forest Service is the landowner which hosts, by far, the most miles, as the trail passes through nine different National Forests and one National Grassland. The Association is the non-profit agency which seeks to build, maintain and promote the trail.

One year ago the Forest Service and the Park Service met and agreed on what has come to be known as the Desired Future Condition of the trail. The agencies have taken the pro-active stance to manage the trail primarily for hiking and backpacking.

This year, the NCTA has been invited to attend, to round out the triad of organizations which have primary interest in the future of the North Country Trail. We spend the day "getting acquainted," hearing about the condition of the trail in the various Forests, and about the goals of the NPS and the NCTA. Discussion items are held for later in the day, and we do make tentative forays into the deliberation of some sensitive topics.

Some differences are not spoken of, but contribute to the sense of disparity between the groups in attendance. The government folks are staying at the upscale Clarion River Lodge, eating very nice meals there, all within their *per-diem* allowance. Some NCTA folks are reeling from sticker shock after joining the agency group for dinner. For the night, the NCTA delegates are huddled in a log cabin provided at no cost by the state park. There is only a fireplace to heat the large, drafty building. We spread our sleeping bags on bunks with brittle plastic covers over the matresses. Our bath facilities are in a separate building thirty vertical feet away, and there is sure no elevator for us!

On Thursday we take a field trip into the Allegheny National Forest (ANF), seeing first hand what some of their issues are. Those pernicious oil and gas wells that so intrude on a natural experience are always an issue in the ANF. But today we hear about the reality of the law. Although the ANF owns the forest, the rights to the minerals under the forest floor are privately owned. Users of both resources have legal standing, and an effort must be made to meet the needs of all parties.

We are shown a section of nice hillside trail recently rebuilt by a very small backhoe. We discuss the merits and the deficiencies of this method. We also see a marvelous stream crossing created by the machine. Three boulders with flat tops have been placed in the water to create an easy crossing. Only the most violent of spring floods would dislodge this natural-looking bridge. We learn that the bridges such as the sturdy, rustic one Marie and I crossed at Coon Creek cost $20,000 each because the timbers were brought in by helicopter. It's hard to believe that they couldn't have been built more economically with volunteer labor.

At the end of the day we all agree that the Triad meetings will definitely be a valuable forum for cooperation between the organizations, and will serve to make the trail experience better for all.

In just a few days I've sampled many aspects of creating a trail. I've explored a route across private land, and talked with a dissenting landowner. I've hiked through state-owned land where the basic policy for trails is multi-use, and the pathway is not yet completed. Within the state park, there is actual trail, but it is not marked as a route of the NCT. I've learned more about the layers of cooperation which are required to apply consistent management to a trail which crosses multiple federal land units. In short, my concept of trails is maturing. Never again will I naively think that making a trail is as easy as one, two, three.

25 miles this hike
Allegheny NF to Miola Rd
Forest and Clarion Counties, PA
1677 total NCT miles

Moon Over My U P
56 - February 5-8, 2001

Some quirk of the wiring in my brain compels me to create stupid parodies of titles such as "Moon Over Miami" and to head north to the Upper Peninsula., "the UP" (say the letters, not the word "up") of Michigan in frigid February. The 90-plus inches of snow that have fallen on the Lower Peninsula have sent the "snow-birds" scurrying to Florida and other points south to find 80-plus degrees of temperature. There they may be gazing up at the same full moon as I, while we both experience traces of precipitation. However, I doubt that they are hunkering around a small propane stove in the dark, cuddling a warm dinner bowl to let no wisp of its heat escape to the air. They probably aren't wearing wet boots, or the same clothes they've had on for three days. The precipitation they are experiencing is almost certainly not falling in soft white flakes, and they probably are not planning on spending the night in a double sleeping bag with their clothes stuffed in the bottom to keep them from freezing overnight. There is no way on earth that they could be as happy as I!

Approaching despair in January at not lengthening the red line on my master map of the Trail since October, I was delighted when an e-mail arrived from a young man, Steve Smith of Indiana. He sent a general inquiry to lots of trail folks looking for a winter hiking partner. Much to his surprise the one response he received was from this middle-aged woman with the quirky brain. Mustering great trust, his wife agreed to the hike. Omer has accepted my willingness to hike with nearly anyone in order to be able to add more miles toward completion of the Trail. Thus we begin to plan. Steve had winter-hiked a section of the NCT in the UP the previous year and he wishes to continue from where he had left off. This fits in fine with my goals since this is a section I have not yet covered. With just a few e-mails and phone calls to feel out each others' capabilities and preparedness we are organized.

But back to the moon... We have just begun our four days and three nights on the trail. Two-and-a-half miles of snowshoeing on Monday afternoon have brought us to an oval clearing just off the trail on the bluff above the Pine River. Two tall and pointed Balsam Fir split the gray, luminous curtain of twilight hung beyond the edge of the bluff. The clearing itself is ringed with black-green hemlock, every branch and twig weighted and coated with glazed snow. We are a ceramic Christmas village scene come to life... except instead of quaint brick buildings, gas lamps, and cobblestones our village consists of my small blue tent, a trench to protect Steve (who will sleep with no tent, but only in his super-warm bag), a dug-out "kitchen area," a candle lantern, and myriad snowshoe prints. I have walked away from the campsite to scrub the traces of stew from our dinner bowls. Now I turn to retrace my steps to our village, guided by the glow from the tiny lantern. Startled at a motion ahead of me in the snow, I find myself face to dark face with my hard-edged shadow! I turn quickly, alarmed at the sudden light. The near-full moon is risen above the hemlocks and aims its borrowed fire with precision at our campsite. Chagrined at my initial jittery reaction to the shadow, I now absorb comfort from the blue moonlight, and saunter back to camp, grinning.

Tuesday's challenge turns out to be one of map-reading. Off to a slow morning start, we are nevertheless making steady progress and have covered three miles along the river before we stop for lunch. We follow a sandy ridge which snakes its way along the north side of the trail. There are very few trail markers, but we are sure of our path for now, as we simply need to follow the river. A snowmobile has used the trail recently. Although this is an illegal use of the path, we find it hard to be annoyed since the packed snow is much easier to walk on. The sky continues gray, but there is almost no wind and the temperature remains near 32°, certainly pleasant weather for a winter hike. Coming down off the ridge after eating, the snowmobile tracks immediately turn south. Steve goes to investigate. Sure enough, he finds a footbridge, but no trail markers... No trail markers on the bridge, no trail markers south of the bridge, no trail markers north of the bridge: well, what else is new? Studying the map we can clearly see the location of this bridge, where a footpath crosses the river. However, on two different maps that we have with us the trail is shown as continuing north of the Pine for one more mile and then turning straight south to cross the river and continue on Forest Road 3375. Thus we conclude that we must leave the ease of the snowmobile-packed track and venture east through the unbroken snow. Dozens of three-striped blue paint splotches on the trees sing siren-songs, luring us eastward. I suspect they are timber-boundary markings, but Steve entrusts himself to their leading, having had good luck following them the previous year. The bluff widens to an open plateau covered in three-foot-deep soft drifts. Steve is a solid 6'2" column of perfectly fit manhood carrying a 40-pound pack; he sinks over a foot deep with each step. I follow along with my lighter pack, pulling the sled. His alternating widely-spaced deep prints don't fit my short and stubby gait! When we switch and I lead, my shorter stride and the longer tails on my snowshoes make a more level track, but I am so much lighter that he still sinks deeply with each step. The moral of the story? It is very difficult walking no matter how we order ourselves! We awkwardly plunge eastward for 30 minutes, 40 minutes, an hour.

Where is this stupid bridge? I keep detouring to the edge of the bluff, trying to spot the crossing. All I can see are meanders and oxbow swamps with banks becoming more steep the farther east we travel. Comparing this with the topo map, it is becoming all too clear that we are past the place where the expected bridge should be. Steve hates to abandon his trail of triple-paint-splotch blazes, and we continue east yet another quarter-hour. Beginning to accept that we have passed the location of the anticipated bridge, Steve leaves his pack with me and explores eastward a few more minutes. He also goes down to the river edge to determine if we could possibly cross. No real trail blazes. No possible river crossing without getting wet, a condition we both know would be foolish, if not actually deadly, in the winter. No certainty of which way to turn if we could cross the river...

Once we accept the reality of needing to backtrack we set out with determination. At least we can now follow our own nicely packed trail. So what was beaten out with huffing, puffing and panting in two hours of eastward travel we fairly race over, westward, returning to the footbridge in 30 minutes! It is now 5 pm, and just south of the bridge is an established campsite with a wire-spool table and campfire circle. Our six miles of walking this day have netted us only three miles of progress on the trail. But at least we are on the correct side of the Pine.

Some quick work with shovel and saw provide us with a cleared campsite and stack of firewood. Steve has brought a lightweight poly snow shovel with the handle separated from the blade. The pieces can be reassembled easily with one bolt and a wing nut. When not in use they fit neatly in the bottom of our plastic sled. I had been skeptical of the need for a full-size snow shovel, but there is plenty left for me to learn. The shovel's worth can't be overstated. He clears my tent site, the kitchen area, and digs himself a snow cave while I gather firewood. Our treat for this evening is a warm blaze with a pot of slow-cooked 15-bean soup for dinner. While I start the fire and set the beans to simmering Steve disappears into the brush with the saw. Several miles of difficult walking and several cubic yards of snow removal are not enough for this guy; he returns with half of a dead pine tree, ten inches in diameter!

We don't actually burn that huge log, but we do use up most of the smaller wood we have gathered. The day has been mild enough that we are quite wet, and drying gloves, hoods and knees over the crackling conifer branches brings a satisfying close to the second day.

Wednesday morning we make a better start. Only two small matters delay the morning chores. First of all, Steve hates a stubbly beard. He hates it so much that he is willing to shave with rapidly chilling water standing in the icy morning air! Secondly, my boots had indeed been wet. In fact they were so wet that they are frozen stiff. In spite of inserting new, dry liners it takes a half hour of repeated stomping and allowing the heat of my feet to soften them before I can get the boots on. And even then they feel tight, boa-constrictor-swallowed-an-elephant tight.

Within a few hundred yards we discover the trail marker we needed so badly the day before. The maps had been wrong. This bridge is indeed the official trail crossing of the river and the path follows the south side of the river before turning due south on the Forest Road. Thankfully all the roads have been traveled by snowmobiles, packing the snow. This allows us to make quick progress, needed today to make up for that lack on Tuesday. After only a couple of hours I realize that despite being new and dry, my boot liners are not providing relief but are creating a new problem. The boa apparently cannot digest this elephant. The new liners have a seam on the top side which is rubbing my toes raw. It only takes about thirty seconds to opt for wet and frozen liners that fit instead of dry but raw and bleeding toes. As awful as frozen boot liners sound, the reality turns out not to be bad at all. My feet are so warm that they quickly thaw the polar fleece. And although my feet remain wet, the boots are good enough that they keep my feet warm, regardless. Besides, the sun appears for an hour or two this morning to warm our spirits as well as our shoulders.

Steve Smith in the Hiawatha National Forest

Around noon our packed and easy path ends. Crossing Biscuit Creek on a road bridge we find true blazes directing us into unbroken snow through a dense forest of hemlock and sapling birch on the south side of the creek. Within a few minutes we determine the strategy which we will use for most of the rest of the hike. The trees are so close that with the weight of ice and snow they hang over or are bent across the trail. I lead, slowly breaking trail and knocking the wet masses to the ground with my walking stick. Even so, occasionally we still are salted with wet crystals falling on our necks. Steve follows, pulling the sled. In many spots the birches have completely filled the pathway, woven in ice-sheathed wattling across the linear clearing.

Sometimes we are able to break these free and push ahead through them. Other times we must find a path around the obstruction and then return to the treadway. There are also a large number of huge trees down across the trail. There is no way to clamber over them with snowshoes and sled, so we must find alternate paths around these as well. Perhaps this doesn't sound too difficult. Perhaps you should try it for five hours! Blazes are infrequent. Our main confidences in being on the trail are the topo map and compass, and that we are seeing a slight depression snaking ahead and behind through an opening in the dense woods. Twice we follow that set of criteria to a complete dead end in the hemlocks. Fortunately, it turns out each time that we have not left the true path too far behind. By five o'clock we are congratulating ourselves when we can continue for twenty minutes at a stretch without taking a breather.

"Remind me why I think this is fun," I demand as another spray of ice chills my neck and my snowshoe catches in the sun-softened snow.

"So we can look back later and know that we did it," Steve replies, panting. "And it will sound great when we tell our friends!"

We are completely agreed that we want to make the Wisconsin Central RR crossing before we stop. For one thing, there are no openings large enough for a campsite in the darkening forest. For another, we just need the milestone. We need to know that we have only two miles to do on the final morning.

A few minutes after 6:00 we convince ourselves that we can see open sky beyond the trees ahead, and at 6:15 we finally stumble up the railbed berm into what might be a Siberian landscape from *Dr. Zhivago* as easily as the Michigan scene we know it to be. The rails vanish at the horizons, ruler straight in either direction, with snow packed tight at the level of their shiny tops. On either side, ranks of snow-caked hemlocks, and the trail on the south side of the berm plunging again into their dark arms. Rather than being dismal and enervating, somehow the simplicity of the white planes, dark lines and oblique boughs energizes us. It is the first open view we've had for hours. In short order our final night's campsite is prepared. We tuck ourselves into an irregular clearing thrust inward from that sea of snow, like a small bay into the black forest.

There, over my shoulder, over the tips of two hemlocks which have tiptoed from the forest, holding hands, to stand hushed at the edge of their world, shimmers the moon. The full moon. A moon muted by fairy dust and ice crystals, yet its cold light has tunneled through 238,857 miles of nothing and clouds, since bouncing off its dusty surface. Thousands of miles, just for this moment. Just for me.

Thursday morning we rise early and with determination stump on down the trail. Even this short walk is not without its follies. The blazes completely disappear. After yet another fall into one of the cleverly concealed hollows under the surface where leg-grabbing gremlins reside (which capture each of us regularly), Steve pragmatically suggests, "let's head straight south!" We locate Trout Brook Pond entirely by compass. Predictably, as soon as there is a natural feature to follow, the edge of the pond, the blazes reappear and are spaced no more than 25 feet apart! Just as predictably, they disappear again as soon as we must find our way through a patch of wattled birch as thick as the hairs on a dog's back. We avoid the "dog" and take to the compass again, skirting the marshy area. The vehicles are retrieved on schedule, without incident, and abruptly another trail adventure is complete. Steve and I agree that we have enjoyed each other's company and would do it again. Another year, perhaps another winter hike together.

You have to keep a friend who agrees that if you can't be the ideal temperature you'd rather be too cold than too hot! And then there's the moon... my moon, over my UP, over my Trail.

13 miles this hike
FR 3141 to H40
Chippewa County, MI
1690 miles total NCT

Eye of Elk, Shade of Toad
57 - April 29- May 7, 2001

> Eye of elk, shade of toad,
> Wernwag truss, winding road,
> Slither snake and spot of newt,
> A silken path for larval foot,
> Spider scurry, shadows murmur,
> Ohio cauldron boil and spatter,
> Burp and burble, ooze and mutter.

By now you may have noticed that many of my Ohio hikes seem to include slightly more unusual tales than those from other states. I can only promise that I did not make up the stories. You will have to draw your own conclusion as to the cause of the uneven distribution of strange happenings. Now I find myself hiking again along the southern reaches of the NCT, wondering what magic potions will spill from the cauldron of Ohio.

Organizationally, the trip was another complicated puzzle of maps, people, roads, trails, and management authorities. I hiked for one day with Rich and Kaye Pfeiffer through Burr Oak State Park, then backpacked alone for two days, mostly on roads. Then Marie joined me, and with two cars we were able to day-hike for two more days, carrying lighter packs. Then we completed the trip with a four-day backpacking trek through the Wayne National Forest in the southeast corner of the state. But these details have nothing to do with the magic.

The first memory that comes to mind from this trip is the riot of spring wildflowers. Entire hillsides in Burr Oak State Park are covered with the familiar White Trillium. Their beauty is always impressive, yet I'm forever searching for the unusual, and I am rewarded with two red trillium cousins. The Red Trillium, or Wakerobin, looks much like the familiar white one, but the flower is a deep maroon, and smells bad. Another dark red trillium I find on the slopes is Toadshade. Its flowers do not have any stalk, but grow close to the three familiar leaves. The Toadshade leaves are mottled, supposedly looking like toad skin, and the red petals remain closed and bud-like.

Blue is the cool theme of meadows pied with blooms, sunlight and shadows. Blue Phlox can vary from blue to light purple; these are consistently blue, and provide the backdrop for highlights of richer tones. Wild Geranium and Appendaged Waterleaf sprinkle pink-purple accents throughout. Deep, royal purple Larkspur fill and create shadows. Occasionally patches of the nodding true-blue bells of Mertensia hover above their broad leaves.

Soon after departing from the company of Rich and Kaye I encounter multiple trails crossing my trail. Thousands of Tent Caterpillars are marching from a 15" diameter White Oak on my right side to an equally large tree on my left. Each caterpillar is crawling along one of six silken pathways which begin high in the oak, cling to the bark till they reach the ground, traverse my trail, and climb again up the opposite tree. Although I've been familiar with the harmless (to humans) Tent Caterpillars since childhood, I've never seen them do this! But it turns out that they are not behaving out of character at all.

Apparently as the caterpillars grow they become restless at home, and in the final stage before adulthood they may seek out new sources of excitement. When teenage humans exhibit this behavior there are parents around to wring their hands and fret; at least the larvae have only themselves to worry. Also like genuine teens our caterpillars are always hungry. Eventually one of the bigger kids on the block will begin searching for something else to eat or new sights to see. But only the most daring will venture out without a silken trail to follow. The explorer will spin a trail of silk from specialized mouthparts and coat the thread with a stable pheromone, a scent which attracts other caterpillars. Pheromones are usually associated with sexual attraction, but caterpillars don't get to indulge themselves, only the adult moths mate. Most moths and butterflies are much better known in their adult, winged phase, but the moths in this case are so seldom seen that they are known as Tent Caterpillar Moths. They are light brown with two diagonal white stripes on their wings, and like most moths, they mostly hang out at night.

That scent trail laid out by the caterpillar leader does attract the other crawlers who are too timid to venture out on bark and fallen leaves or dirt. Wiggling quickly in single file along the silk they follow their buddy to the next full refrigerator in the neighborhood. These teens are more likely to crave cherry leaves than pizza, but that protects the pepperoni for your kids and mine.

I'm trying out a new one-person tent on this trip. Just after I bought it I was told that it has a condensation problem, so I'll have the chance to find out if that's true. It certainly is more spacious and stable than my green bivy cocoon, and it weighs two ounces less. I like its colorful profile as I make camp on a scenic hillside.

I wake uncharacteristically early, and am hiking by 7:30. Even with my foggy morning brain I am able to appreciate the beauty of the early light on layers of Flowering Dogwood blossoms.

The next animals I meet in the trail are much larger, but they aren't doing anything very strange. An Amish man has parked his team of four horses on a bridge, because it's the only spot of shade nearby. He lets me photograph the horses, but declines to join them in the picture. Horses can be so skittish; they don't like my shape with a backpack! I cross a safe distance away, and continue in the sun, leaving the cool shadows to the team.

The magic cauldron bubbles; and the next surprise to burst forth is a pink frog. With a black "robber mask" it looks like a Wood Frog, but pink? Of course I don't mean fluorescent hot pink, but neither do I mean pinkish brown. This frog is PINK! Sure enough, the guide book says the Wood Frog has "pronounced variations in coloration... from pink... to almost black."

Buckeye in bud

The Ohio state tree is the Buckeye, named for its large brown nuts with a tan spot, reputed to look like the eye of a buck deer. The Buckeye leaf is palmate, with five fingers (the Horsechestnut usually has seven fingers). But the most spectacular feature of the Buckeye is its springtime bloom. Above the new leaves rises a stalk of yellow-green tubular flowers 6"-8" tall. Before they open, blushes of red and pink mark the buds.

By 2:30 I've reached the creek where I plan to camp. Upstream is an overhung rock with swallows nesting in its shadows. The valley is narrow there, but just before that is a broad dry floodplain where I set up the tent on a carpet of Wild Geraniums, and Spring Beauty. I am trying some new menus on this trip including cheese biscuits baked in a reflector oven, and there is plenty of time to build a good bed of coals, mix the batter, and allow it to bake slowly in a shallow pan with a tinfoil reflector. Dinner is relaxing, but the book I've brought jangles my nerves. I'm reading *Great Heart*, the story of an ill-fated expedition across the wilds of Canada in 1903. Reading of one disaster after another, most of them set in motion by poor planning, does not calm my campfire evening!

At first light a cacophony of song and sound awakens me. Deer are snorting, squirrels chattering. Turkeys are gobbling from the ridge above. I hear the distinctive ping-pong-ball-on-a-table rhythm of a Field Sparrow's song. Every available crevice of the streamside morning is stuffed with twitterings, rustlings, squawks and whistles.

I lie still, soaking up the sound. What a way to wake up! Turns out I've been soaking up more than sound. The new tent sure does need more ventilation. My sleeping bag is very damp, just from my moist breath collecting on the ceiling, and dripping back down on the bag. I guess I'll have to add an extra mesh panel when I get home.

I hate to leave this lovely spot, but hikes are about moving, not about staying in one location.

By early afternoon the air is hot and still, at 84° a very hot day. My enzymes are still accustomed to Michigan's cooler spring days, and I stop to cool my hot feet in a creek. I rest in the shade of a bridge for nearly an hour, but dark mumblings from beyond the span call me into the sun to look skyward. An ominous black band across the western horizon motivates me to get moving, but there's no way I can outwalk this storm. Ahead of me on the road is a long curving uphill, completely in the open. Behind me I can hear the cracks of lightning and the continuing rumbles. The hill is steep; the wind picks up. At the top of the hill is a lone house with a porch wrapped around the front. A man is trimming the hedge in the yard, and watching my approach. "Come up on my porch!" he calls as the storm and I arrive at his property.

From the shelter of the broad veranda we watch the rain sweep up the hill. The day is suddenly violent, young leaves are torn from the trees, the hedge trimmings are lifted and thrown into the road, skittering down the pavement. A bird feeder swings in dizzy arcs. But just as suddenly the storm passes. As the rain eases, the homeowner and I watch the birds return to the feeder. Goldfinches, bluebirds, Cardinals, sparrows and a Killdeer appear under the limbs of the budding maple tree. And then, tapping on the bole of the tree, we see a Red-headed Woodpecker. On this hike I've seen Hairy and the smaller Downy Woodpeckers, a Red-Bellied, and also a Pileated Woodpecker: five woodpecker species in just three days!

An hour after the rain began I'm back on the road. The brief storm has not cooled the air, and the final three miles are a misery of forcing hot, heavy air through my lungs, and hot, heavy feet along the road.

I'm happy to reach at last the Wolf Creek Community Center where I have permission to camp, and happier yet to see Marie drive in before dark. We retrieve my car, dry my damp equipment on the engine-warmed hood, and grab some dinner, all before night falls.

On Wednesday, Marie and I are again walking side by side, catching up on the news of friends and family. The heat has returned with no recollection of yesterday's cooling rain. Glancing to our right we see a Black Rat Snake slithering across the roof of a bird house. Mesmerized, we watch the snake enter the birdhouse, its body undulating as it disappears through the hole. Soon the nose of the large dark snake reappears. Is that a smile we see? The English Sparrow screaming in alarm from a nearby bush is not smiling. Thus, the life of one creature is sustained by the death of another.

Right on the edge of the Wayne National Forest is a free campsite known as Lane Farm. That fits our plan perfectly. I should have known it was bound to lead to another of those people conflicts which seem to haunt my Ohio hikes. We pull in on Thursday evening, and are pleasantly greeted by a young man who is a local Scoutmaster. He and his wife say that they are only staying through dinner, and we can have their site, and their extra firewood in just a couple of hours, since the other two sites are already occupied. We think this is a great plan and drive into town to secure dinner the lazy way.

When we return, we become the keepers of the campfire, and settle in for what we hope will be a quiet evening. But camping means different things to different people. The group next door to us is already drinking heavily, playing loud music, and yelling. Marie decides that they are doing their neighborhood a favor by moving the party outside of town! I honestly don't understand the appeal of spending an evening with people who call themselves your friends, but who continually call you and everyone else filthy names while guzzling refreshments which will give them a nasty headache the next day. I guess I'll never be a party gal. At 1:30 am a truck leaves, and with it the music, but the people continue talking loudly enough to disturb us until after 2 o'clock.

Unbelievably, at 6:30 am a woman emerges from their tent and begins swearing. We have no idea who she is yelling at, but it might as well be us, since we are now wide awake. At least it guarantees we'll get an early start for today's walk, but we have plans to camp here one more night. We wonder how that will go.

Today we walk through Marietta, located on the Muskingum and Ohio Rivers. Marietta was founded in 1788, the oldest city west of the original thirteen colonies. It is named for Marie Antoinette, infamous for her callous attitude toward people. She was guillotined during the French Revolution, but before that sad ending she was venerated for the aid the French gave to the United States during its war for independence. Veterans of the Revolutionary War were granted tracts of land in the Northwest Territory, which included Ohio. The Ohio River had always been the highway to the West. To the native people, Ohio was the "Great River," and for pioneers it was the primary way to travel from Pittsburgh to the Mississippi. The other major waterway, the Muskingum, "Elk's Eye River," drains all of what is now the east side of the state. Elk were once so numerous in these hunting lands that the river was named for them. Deer, bear, wolves, Mountain Lions and small Bison also roamed the area, and Muskellunge and 80-pound Shovelhead Catfish were found in the river. The riverbanks were lined with dense stands of Paw-paw trees.

Settlers built mills, and steamboats soon plied the rivers. Pioneers on rafts had been content to drift down the Ohio in the spring; even the great river often dried into disconnected puddles in the hot summer months. But steam power brought on the desire for regular navigation and consistent depth. Locks and dams began to tame the water level as early as 1841.

The confluence of these rivers has always been a natural place for human settlement. Both round and square prehistoric mounds and earthworks found here were surveyed and preserved by the first white inhabitants. It is now known that these were built by the Adena and Hopewell Cultures; some are nearly 2000 years old. Thousands of these ancient mounds existed in the Ohio Valley at one time. Most were destroyed by the advance of civilization. Marietta's attitude of preservation seems to have set the tone for the centuries. Strolling through parks, as we make our way across town, we find monuments to all those who have shaped the city's history. Beauty and care for the land are being balanced with the needs of a population center. The city is filled with old, beautiful homes that were built by those who made fortunes in oil, coal, gas, and boat building. Marie and I are always ready to look at interesting houses.

Despite Marietta's early prosperity, both the National Road and the major rail lines were routed farther north through Ohio. Thus Marietta has remained a relatively small town with a lot to offer.[1]

We make the decision to call the local Sheriff Department about the noisy campers. We aren't sure we can do another full day of hiking tomorrow if we manage only three hours of sleep again tonight. It's another blistering day, but we walk into the Lane Farm campsite at 3 pm. The lady from the next site comes over to introduce herself. She is twig-skinny, with no front teeth. "I'm Tina," she says. "The police were here. They had a report of someone shooting nearby, and wanted to make sure everyone here was all right." The officers must have decided that was as good an excuse as any to check on the situation, and we didn't volunteer the information that we had called them!

A little girl (who must think that the events of last night are a normal lifestyle) flits by and announces that she is Jamie. "I like your sweater," she jabbers. "I like your hair. I like your pants. I like your shirt." Marie manages a civil conversation with them, while I find something else to do, anything, to avoid interaction. Marie is always the better of us at human relations. Before they are done talking, Tina has apologized for keeping us awake, and has promised to be more quiet tonight. She is.

"Wernwag Truss," I confess, is a term that had never entered my head before. Now, Marie and I are standing by a covered bridge at

---

[1] Since the 2004 Annual NCTA Convention, which was held in Marietta, the city has embraced the idea of becoming a real "trail town." The new Ohio Valley Chapter there is building an off-road route through the city, and there are plans to create a hostel in the old Armory.

the southern end of the Wayne National Forest. An interpretive sign explains that covered bridges had various arrangements of their posts and timbers, usually named for their designers. Thanks to the diagrams, we recognize that the bridge we crossed two days ago used the Wernwag design, having angled uprights, with an arched timber truss bent from one foundation to the other. The load is carried by the arch in compression like an upside-down suspension bridge. The bridge we are looking at now uses the Howe design, with posts criss-crossed into diamonds. Other designs used nearby in Ohio include Long, Smith, and the Multiple Kingpost Truss design. Before stresses could be analyzed mathematically, bridgebuilding was learned by trial and error, and the lessons and traditions passed from fathers to sons. Ohio once had over 2000 covered bridges, more than any other state! The early engineers covered their bridges to keep the timbers from getting wet and rotting, but young folks liked their dark interiors for a different reason: their other common name was "Kissing Bridges."

Wernwag Truss bridge at Wolf Creek

    To be honest, there are parts of our trail experience in the Wayne that we would be glad to see changed. The area is still actively producing oil and gas, and the companies who service all that equipment care little about hiking trails. We often see roads bulldozed over the top of former treadway. We joke that one phrase would do for the entire guidebook. It would be: "Descend to a creeklet, climb to road past oil storage tank, turn left on gravel road, proceed to oil access lane, find blazes in back of storage facility, descend to a creeklet..." Just substitute "left" for "right" occasionally, or "paved" for "gravel," and you'd be all set. The trail here sees few hikers, while the biking community is active. Some steep places are badly eroded, and most of the paths on hills are much too steep. But even these drawbacks can not hide the natural beauty of the forest.

    One of our best experiences in the Wayne is a few hours spent exploring the Natural Bridge. Above a narrow dry gorge flies a stone pathway so covered with earth, moss, and even a good-sized tree, that you might miss it if it were not for a small identifying sign. Our pictures are inadequate; it's too difficult to find a good angle from which to frame the scene. We walk across the bridge, we scramble up and down the steep valley which descends below its deck. Above the bridge the gully is truncated. Perhaps the water which blasted away the stone came from a spring in the hillside. The entire slope is a maze of odd little holes and shapes. I find a narrow space between two rectangular stones, that looks like a door to a stone house. But when I climb down and stand in the space it is revealed as being 15 feet tall, the entrance to a magical maze? We'll have to check that out on another day. The shadows lengthen; we shoulder our packs and hike on.

Spring is sweeping across the countryside. When I began hiking, not quite a week ago, the trees were still fuzzy with yellow, light green and red. Now in the moist heat, everything is almost in full leaf. You can almost see the cauldron of life bubbling and teeming with changes. We come face to face with a huge Box Turtle on the trail, and he is not shy about meeting our gaze. A large, hairy Wolf Spider joins us for lunch one day. She has crawled from between some flat rocks near a stream, and remains motionless in the sun. Perhaps she is contemplating where she will capture her lunch. We see a Red-spotted Newt, before it becomes a Red Eft. Today it is an olive green, but shows the characteristic spots which help to identify this changeling, who looks so different in its various phases. Huge limestone boulders, pocked with holes like a petrified boiling pudding, line the trail. Three stacks of Dryad's Saddle Fungus protrude from a large dying maple. Are the spirits of the tree getting ready to ride away on a Horsechestnut or a Horseradish? The Long-Fruited Snakeroot is opening leaves wrinkled like the face of an old green hag, topped by its blossom – a snaky ball of white hairs. We pass a field filled with Lousewort. How curious that people believed that sheep kept in fields with this plant developed lice, thus its name. Its other common name, Wood Betony, is a more appealing moniker for this attractive flower with feathery leaves and yellow and maroon flowers. Wild Columbine, also adorned in yellow and maroon, tumbles down the sides of moist rocks lining the trail, and Allegheny Foamflower foams in the low, wet niches. Another entire opening in the woods is filled with Wild Pinks, a hot magenta blanket whose flaming color is surpassed only by the Fire Pinks. Fire Pinks are indeed a fiery red; their flames rise, the cauldron boils, and we are burned with magic memories of the Ohio springtime.

100 miles this hike
Boat Dock Two to Ring Mill
Athens, Morgan, and Washington
                              Counties, OH
1790 total NCT miles

Milk Train
58 - August 11, 2001

It's NCTA Annual Conference time again. This year it's being hosted by the Finger Lakes Trail Conference (FLTC) folks, at Cazenovia, New York. I'm busier than ever with the Trail Association, since I was recently hired to be their web site manager. So much for the years of graduate school in Environmental Engineering. I seem to be turning out like the husband of my high school librarian. George could never seem to last at any job for more than a couple of years. Hometown folks would sigh and glance sympathetically toward Dolores. "Poor women, such a burden," they thought of this man who would not settle in to real life. But here am I, like George, living proof that you can bumble through life without ever deciding what you want to be when you grow up. I'll never get rich this way, but I'm pretty happy. Maybe George was too.

At the conference I'm too busy to think straight. A board meeting, committee meetings, questions from myriad people, I scarcely have enough time to enjoy the company of friends. Marie is there too, and fortunately she enjoys spending time with other people as well as with me. Irene, as chair of the weekend's activities, is busier than anyone, but we all manage to join an afternoon hike on a newly created segment of trail.

The famous and popular feature of this section is known as Nelson Swamp Unique Area. A boardwalk loop has been built over a freshwater marsh at the edge of Chittenango Creek, and most of the hikers in our group find this fascinating. It's not that I don't appreciate the plants and the wonderful walkway through their neighborhood; it's just that I'm familiar with most of what's there. I become the tour guide for plant identification, and that is a role I always enjoy.

But the outstanding memory of the hike for me is a tumble-down shed beside a piece of trail placed on the abandoned Lehigh Valley Railroad bed. Railroad history, especially of the "fallen flag" of the Lehigh Valley, is another of my favorite topics. And here I have just been surprised by Mary Kunzler-Larmann, our able tour guide, with the information that I am walking on a section of that defunct line.

Milk transport has always been a serious component of the economy. When towns grew in population, small dairy herds kept in the occasional open lot could not possibly produce enough milk for the masses. Many people actually kept cows in their basements, fed them waste mash from breweries, and produced enough milk for their families. Those urban cows probably lived short, unhealthy lives. Most of this liquid commodity needed to be brought in from the country.

The freight trains which ran here stopped each day to pick up milk from farms along the way. Have you ever thought of the logistics of this? Did the farmers assign a hired hand or family member to wait for the train? How did they keep the milk from spoiling as they waited in the hot sun by the tracks?

In this instance, here's how it worked. Near the tracks the farmer dug out a wide spot in a creek. This pit was about two feet deep and a concrete pool was built for the creek to flow through. The sides of this cistern also served as a foundation. A small shed was built on this base. Milk cans could be placed in the cool water, in the shade of the shed's roof. To signal the train, the simple expedient of hanging a flag outside would alert the trainmen that they needed to stop and pick up the cans.

Today the shed is caving in, the water is stagnant, and there is no milk can. There are no shining rails on the level grade I tread, and what economy of today would bother with one or two cans of milk from some poor farmer? Hardscrabble, the name of the nearby road, probably tells the story of his toil on the land.

Yet from somewhere in the distance I can almost hear the lonesome whistle of a steam engine. Near at hand I'm sure I hear the soft nicker of a cart-horse, the clink of a heavy can being bounced over the rocky ground, and a splash as it settles in the cool water. Milk train coming!

3 miles this hike
Holmes Rd. To Stone Quarry Rd.
Madison Co, NY
1793 total NCT miles

Erie Canal
59 - August 12, 2001

I've got a guide and his name is Al, just for a mile on the Erie Canal. That's Al Larmann, who with yesterday's guide, Mary, form the dynamic duo of the Central New York Chapter, co-hosts of this conference. Al and Mary have fallen in love with the idea of the North Country Trail, perhaps as much as I have. And when these two get an idea in their heads, there's no stopping them! Their chapter has taken on the task of connecting the NCT from the Finger Lakes Trail to Rome, New York, which is the jumping off point for some future route into the Adirondacks. I think Al and Mary must know every person in the county who might have a critical slice of land, a piece of equipment, authority to grant some permit, or a means to promote the trail.

The chapter's first big task was to negotiate a peaceful resolution to a problem the NCT never anticipated. There were two logical and potential routes north from the main Finger Lakes Trail to the general vicinity of Cazenovia, and both routes had vocal advocates. Instead of begging for any possible way to connect point A to point B, the NCT now had to select one of two without antagonizing people whose support we desired. This tricky task was accomplished with much research and input from Al and Mary. The final route used pieces of both proposals.

Once this was settled, Al, Mary and their cohorts began with a will to turn the selected route into trail on the ground. The route includes many land owners, old railroad rights-of-way, city parks, cemeteries, and more. There are structures to be built. Steep hillsides spilling onto roads need stairways; there is no room to build gradual switchbacks. Culverts on the railbed have become clogged or damaged. The resulting drainage problems have led to the washing away of sections of the potential treadway. But wherever there is a problem, Al puts his engineer's brain to work and in a soft-spoken manner brushes aside all the difficulties as if they were cobwebs, and presents us with safe, clear trail!

Well, Al might not agree that the problems are cleared as easily as a spiderweb, but that's how it sometimes looks to the rest of us! Today, Al will show us a section of his chapter's handiwork.

I've chosen this group hike because after seeing all the trail miles along the Miami-Erie Canal in Ohio, I'm more than ready to hike a portion of the famed grandmother of them all, New York's Erie Canal. Yup, that's the "Albany to Bu-uff- a-lo-oh" canal.

Our afternoon begins with a visit to the Chittenango Landing Canal Boat Museum, where one can easily imagine the busy waterway, the mules, the passengers, the merchants, and all their baggage. The museum is located at a former repair drydock for canal boats. Several slips off the main canal have waterdoors, just like a lock. The floor of the slip has supports on which a boat would settle when the doors were closed and the water drained out. This would leave the boat perched high and dry, ready to be worked on. Inside the museum we learn how important it was to keep the hulls of the grain packet boats absolutely watertight. The grain was loaded loose, completely filling the bottom of the boat. If the grain got damp it would swell, and the packet would explode! We tour a building filled with strangely shaped tools, interesting lanterns, and other artifacts of an industry totally foreign to modern transportation.

Finally we are hiking! There are actually almost 20 miles of Erie Canal Towpath Trail that the NCT will follow, but today we will sample just a smidgen of that total. Soon we arrive in downtown Canastota where we visit another small museum which features historical displays of local importance.

Hikers along the Old Erie Canal

Heading south out of town we rejoin the Lehigh Valley railbed, and veer west through a cemetery. As we go, Al explains the political contortions which were required to connect all these pieces into a connected trail. And we also descend one of the long, long stairways which the chapter has built so that the trail can safely change levels. Thanks for choosing to hike in this direction, Al!

The famous Erie Canal truly deserves its reputation. Picture the United States at the turn of the century, the 19th century, that is. In 1800 the young nation was huddled in the narrow strip of land between the Atlantic Ocean and the Appalachian Mountains. Natural waterways there generally flow north or south, and the mountains stretch nearly unbroken from Georgia to Maine, as any hiker of the Appalachian Trail will be happy to verify. The single greatest exception is found in the Mohawk River of northern New York State. In fact, the native peoples' name for the river was Te-non-an-at-che, "the river flowing through mountains." The Hudson River provided easy passage from New York to Albany, and the Mohawk was the best hope for transportation routes from there to the west.

Canals not over two miles in length, some with locks, were built as early as the 1790's to connect lakes and rivers in the Mohawk Valley. However, exploiting the full length of this natural passage became the focus of proposals in the first decade of the new century. Reaction both at home and in Europe was mixed at best. Never had such a long and difficult canal been built. The new Federal Government declined to finance the project. But DeWitt Clinton was determined to see the canal built, and it is his name that is forever wedded to that waterway. It was called Clinton's Folly, Clinton's Ditch, even the Governor's Gutter. The $6 million price tag was considered outrageous, the task nearly impossible. But Clinton was not to be deterred. He convinced New Yorkers to cough up the money, and agreed to an additional connecting canal from the Hudson to Lake Champlain, just to gain the support of the northern counties. The first shovel of earth was turned on July 4, 1817, at Rome. European engineers predicted it would take 32 years to complete the 363 miles of canal, with all of its structures. But Americans were eager to prove their technological prowess to the world, and in just eight years the waterway opened. The Grand Ditch was four feet deep, required 18 aqueducts to carry it over inconvenient valleys, and boasted 83 locks to overcome the 573-foot elevation difference between Albany and Buffalo.

Throwing extravagant celebrations is not something Americans have just recently learned. On October 26, 1825, the *Seneca Chief*, loaded with dignitaries and symbolic cargo, left Buffalo for New York City, towed like Cinderella's carriage by four white horses. Governor Clinton supervised two kegs of Lake Erie water, to be poured into the Atlantic Ocean. Logs of Red Cedar and Bird's-eye Maple made the trip. These were later crafted into boxes to hold commemorative medals. Some live Whitefish and a canoe built by Lake Superior Indians were carried from the Great Lakes to the ocean. The *Seneca Chief* was followed by *Noah's Ark* carrying bear, deer, a fox, a pair of eagles, assorted other birds, fish, insects and two Seneca Indian boys. Next in line was the *Superior*, also carrying two fawns. Whereas the overland trip from New York to Buffalo had previously taken up to four weeks, the canal would shorten that travel time to nine days. Not satisfied with even this amazing speed, Clinton determined that he would immediately notify Manhattan that the canal was open. To accomplish this pre-telegraphy feat a series of 32-pound cannons was set up along the 425 miles of the route. And they were not just any guns. These cannons had armed the ships of Commodore "We-have-met-the-enemy-and-they-are-ours" Perry during his Lake Erie victory, so important to the US success in the War of 1812. In one hour and twenty minutes the signal had been relayed across the state, and was then sent back again to Buffalo.

And the reverberations might be said never to have died away. The "West" almost instantly leaped, well, westward. The economics of this new nation were changed forever. Businessmen could afford to ship all kinds of goods, even perishables. A family might live in Rochester, but serve oysters for dinner. Mail delivered to New York could reassure a mother that her son living on the frontier was healthy while the message was still recent enough to be meaningful. Even more astounding, a visit was not out of the question. Although the canal was built with freight in mind, people clamored almost immediately for passenger service. In our age of instant everything, a nine-day trip sounds uselessly slow. But at that time, the effect was so profound that it might be compared with the invention of the airplane.

Some welcomed the change with open arms and pocketbooks. Others decried the negative impacts of technology upon their lives. But no matter how people felt, the canal was here to stay. By 1837 the entire cost of building and financing the canal was recouped through tolls!

The first canal was rebuilt, beginning in 1841. A 36-mile angled section of the Old Erie Canal was abandoned in favor of a shorter route just to the north. And a 20th Century version, known as the New York Barge Canal still is used to transport goods across the state. The cut-off section of the Old Canal is now a linear state park, and is the route followed by the NCT.

In 1862, when the first rebuilding was completed, young people had no memory of life without the Erie Canal, and the event passed almost unnoticed. Railroads were pushing the "West" past the Mississippi River, and shortening distances even more. And today, there is no one yet alive who can truly understand how extraordinary was the opening of "The Great Western Canal."

4 miles this hike
Canastota to Nelson Rd.
Madison Co, NY
1797 total NCT miles

Philomathic Deipnosophists
60 - August 15, 2001

Three days later, Irene and I are sitting at her dining room table, packing away some delicious rice, hamburg, sour cream and black olive concoction she has made. We are also reading the dictionary. Why, you ask? Just because we like words, of course. Actually we are trying to remember the word for evergreen cones which need fire in order to germinate. I think it's "serotinous," but Irene disagrees. The dictionary only informs us that the word pertains to delayed development, but nothing more specific. We decide that we need Robert[1] to help us out with this puzzle, but he's not available. We are suddenly overcome with the desire to remind ourselves which plant pods throw their seeds. Is it the dehiscent ones, or those which are indehiscent? From "dehisce" (the throwing kind) it is only a short slip of the eyeball past "dehydrate," "deicer," and "deign" to a word neither one of us has previously met: "deipnosophist – one who discourses learnedly at meals." Guffaw! We are not likely to forget this one again!

But I've come here to Irene's, following the conference, not to play with words, but to play on the trail. So in the morning Irene takes me to the Genesee River, to connect with the "May the Road Rise to Meet You" hike. Two more hikers will join me for the day. One of those hikers you've met: Irene's growing puppy, Sandy Fe. Irene has convinced me that Sandy won't be any extra trouble, and that she will love to walk with me. It's not that I doubt that, but I am not sure I want to take her because my other hiking companion is also a dog, my "new" dog.

Meet Maggie, aka the "Red Worm," aka "Sweet Potato Pie." Maggie has spent the weekend with Sandy under the care of a neighbor, while we humans attended the conference. I'd known Maggie since friends brought her home from the pound, a very sick little puppy. But she recovered from pneumonia, and grew to be more than her owners could handle. They wanted me to adopt her, but I had reservations. I suspected that her hips were bad, and she didn't ride in cars well. But finally it came to the point where Maggie would be mine, or she would go back to the pound. What could I say but "yes?"

She's not destined to be a real hiking dog. Her hips, indeed, are very bad. She can't carry a pack. But she can take car trips on roads that don't curve and wind, so long interstate trips are fine, and she likes day hikes. Thus I've brought her east to meet all my friends. Now

---

[1.] See Chapter 22: "Great Scot! The Ugliest Mile in Army Boots"

we're ready for the day hike. So with hopes that the two dogs will be manageable, we hop in the car and head toward Whiskey Bridge over the Genesee.

We have one easy mile to do on the west side of the river, and Irene waits with the vehicle to carry us all across the bridge. Major construction is underway and to walk it is not possible today. (Yes, I returned here on another trip and walked the bridge.)

East of the bridge Maggie, Sandy and I leave Irene and climb a long hill. So here I am, trolling along behind a double leash with 110 combined pounds of red dog at the ends. It occurs to me that if Maggie and Sandy take a mind to chase something, that I outweigh them by only a very few pounds, and they have six more legs than I! One squirrel in the bushes could turn me into nothing more than an inconvenient anchor. The mastery which I intend to portray to any passing motorist, being the human standing upright, controlling the animals securely tethered to my belt, is a pleasant delusion. Any passing motorist with any sense is sniggering behind his hand at the obvious impending result of a doggie decision to bolt.

But on this warm and splendid day the dogs don't hurtle into the ditches and soon we reach trail where they can run free. We are tiptoeing along the edge of a steep sand bluff which overlooks the Genesee, 300 feet below. Also below me on the steep hill is a stand of American Chestnut. Although these majestic trees were nearly wiped out before the 1950's by a blight, a few pockets survive. Irene says that I'm about a month late to be able to see the tree tops in bloom. From the opposite direction comes the whistle of a locomotive. On the Norfolk Southern line (once the Erie) a train is headed for the Letchworth High Bridge.

Mid-afternoon, we three companions descend to shady, dappled Keshequa Creek. The Keshequa roughly parallels the Genesee River, and both flow northward. While the Genesee owns the Letchworth gorge, the Keshequa follows a valley one ridge east of the river. Just east of the village of Mount Morris it joins Canaseraga Creek, and in another mile these waters do flow into the Genesee, which continues north to Lake Ontario. Both Keshequa and Canaseraga come from the Seneca language, and both mean "a spear." Because of the resemblance of a spear to the head of a viper, the words also signify "rattlesnake." Timber Rattlers can still occasionally be found in these woods. Just east of here is Rattlesnake Hill Wildlife Management Area. One can easily assume that the reptiles were much more common to this locale in earlier centuries.

The snake image also fits these streams in that they wiggle oddly through the landscape. Both streams originate west of Rattlesnake Hill. At one spot they are barely three miles apart, but at that point the Keshequa is flowing north, and the Canaseraga south.

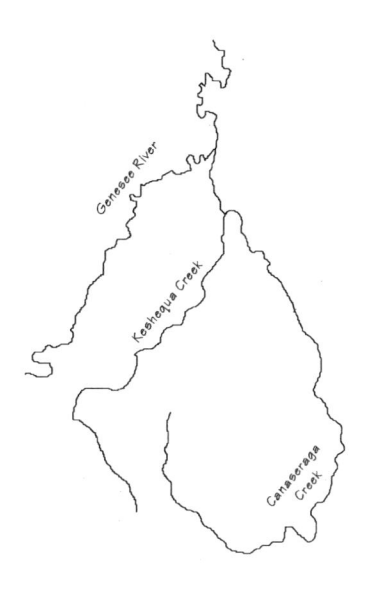

The Keshequa takes a western detour and then pretty much heads directly NNE, up the glacial valley. But the Canaseraga continues south and east, around Rattlesnake Hill, till it too finally bends northward, really NNW. Looking at a map showing only the water features, the two creeks seem to form the outline of a triangular viper head flicking its tongue at the Genesee. Could the Senecas have discerned this interesting coincidence?

With no trouble at all we meet Irene at the appointed time, at the top of the next hill. From a corner with a long, long vista Irene points northward. "You can see Rochester from here," she indicates. "Right there, just over that shoulder of a hill." Of course I tell her I can see it, and maybe I can, but I don't perceive it. I have no idea what I'm supposed to be looking for.

Well, it turned out that I was right about one thing. Serotinous cones are those which require fire for their seeds to burst forth and germinate. But two dedicated philomaths aren't likely to stop discussing sesquipedalian words. I recently told Irene that she shouldn't use the word "pixilated," and expect most people to know that it means excited. In fact they might think that it means blurred, because a digital image that has become the homophonic "pixelated" is one that has lost focus. "Nerts," she responded, "another good word ruined by technology."

But she gets the last word. Thanks to her expert editing, you are being spared from split infinitives, too many commas, and misplaced modifiers.

12 miles this hike
Portageville to Fox Hill Rd
Wyoming and Livingston
                        Counties, NY
1809 total NCT miles

Super-Duper
61 - September 22- October 4, 2001

Super Expectations

Ever since the inclusion of the Superior Hiking Trail (SHT) into the Arrowhead Reroute of the North Country Trail we've heard nothing but rave reviews. The beauty of the area is renowned, particularly in the fall, and we want to see it at its best. Marie is no longer teaching full time, so an autumn hike seems possible. For the first time ever, no one else is joining us on our major hike of the year. Despite the fact that it is probably safer to have a third person along, we are looking forward to the extended time alone together. As usual the maps and names fascinate me as I prepare for the hike. Reading of Mystery Mountain and the Devil Track River sends a thrill through my bones, while Temperance River and Pincushion Mountain sound much more tame. Names run the gamut from mundane-sounding Onion River to ethereal Crystal Creek. The Superior Hiking Trail Association (SHTA) provides maps which already have an elevation profile of the trail. Saved the time of doing this on my own, I code each day's projected walk. From North Bally Creek Pond to Big White Pine campsite I note: d-u-D 4-3-8, meaning "down 400 feet, up 300 feet, Down 800 feet. Sure, we could hike without this information, but I love the anticipation.

Super Lake

That's Lake Superior, to be precise. 1.1 billion years ago, give or take a day or two, the Equator ran through Minnesota, and North America tried to split in two, from Canada to Kansas! The continent got a little hot under the collar over this and oozed a whole lot of lava out to the surface. The lava cooled into black basalt and red rhyolite. The cooling lava harbored pockets of minerals, and even floated huge blocks of rock high above their natural locations. As the lava spread out over the land it was heavy, and it had also left a big empty space where it used to be. So it began to sink, forming the Lake Superior basin. That basin is five miles thick and 200 miles across!

Mysteriously, the rifting ended and tropical storms carried sediments from the new high rocks to the lower places. Just when you thought it was safe to grab your beach towel and sunglasses again, along came the Ice Age, changing the region once more. By the time all this was over, the Equator had wandered south and Minnesota was left with bogs, swamps, cold rivers, big rocks, and Lake Superior.

Although smaller than the Glacial Lake Duluth, the current lake is nothing to sniff at. The lake received its name because of its most northern position among the Great Lakes, being "superior" to the others on maps oriented to the north, and as the highest in elevation. As an adjective meaning "superlative," the word works well for this lake too. Lake Superior is the largest freshwater lake in the world, with a surface area of 31,280 square miles. (But if you measure by volume, Lake Biakal in Russia wins.) Superior's deepest spot is 1,279 feet below the surface, and it contains so much water that if it were drained it would take almost 200 years to refill. If those numbers are difficult to grasp, this should help: if the lake were to spill over and be spread out it would cover all of North America with three feet of water.

Super Trail

Some people seem to think that the "Superior" Hiking Trail is trying to sound uppity. Of course, the name is taken from the Lake, the primary feature that it follows. In the mid 1980's a group of visionary people conceived of a hiking trail from Duluth, Minnesota, to the Canadian border. Businesses, government agencies, and hiking buffs quickly endorsed the idea, and a route was selected by an employee of the Department of Natural Resources, Tom "Never-met-a-hill-I-didn't-like" Peterson. The trail was officially opened in 1987, and a "Halfway Party" was held in 1990. In 2004 the trail was extended north from Hovland to join the Border Route Trail, and work has begun on a beautiful route through Duluth. I roughly followed this course on my walk through that city.[1]

There is a sense, however, in which it is a superior trail. The views from those hills that Peterson climbed are indeed wonderful, and for 200 miles a hiker can imbibe vistas until completely intoxicated with blue water, blue sky, forests and multi-colored rocks. Because of the

Marie hikes the rugged SHT

[1.] See Chapter 52: "Emily, Mama Rita and Dick Have Their Way with the Regenwŭrmer"

natural beauty of the area, and the close proximity of many resorts, all within easy driving distance of a large city, the trail has a large group of supporters.

In 1994 the North Country Trail Association began to talk to the SHTA about the possibility of the NCT following the Superior Trail route. Naturally, a group so enthusiastic about their own trail wanted to be sure that they would not lose their identity if they agreed to this plan. But eventually consensus was reached. Now, joined with the Border Route and the Kekekabic Trail, everyone is waiting for Congressional approval of this Arrowhead Reroute. It just makes sense. Not only is this route more beautiful than a straight line path from Duluth to the middle of Minnesota would be, it's actually the easier. The direct route traverses sixty miles of cedar swamp. Building that trail would be quite a challenge!

The Superior Trail is a rugged footpath. Slopes are often steep. Since the trail is well-used this would usually result in serious erosion problems, but the trail is also rocky, so that may help prevent the degradation. Interspersed with the rocky hillsides are low areas, usually cedar swamps where the trail has no stable treadway, and the hiker will need to step from one exposed root to the next. We called it our "root route." We were more often footsore than tired. We joked that we never got blisters because we never touched any one spot on our feet or ankles to the ground more than twice a day, but that we did touch every spot twice. We said that if this trail didn't teach us to pick up our feet, we'd never learn. Once, when Marie asked me how far to our next stop, I checked the map and started to tell her the distance. In the middle of that project the arch of one foot came down hard on a root, and I announced the mileage as "one point OUCH." The SHT offers strenuous day hikes, and a definite challenge for the backpacker.

Super Rocks - Big Ones

The North Shore of the present day Lake Superior is a geologist's dream come true. Lumps of hard volcanic rock still protrude above the sediments which have been deposited near the lake. Some lumps – we call them mountains! The weathered bits of these lumps have been carried to the valleys and beaches. Whole books have been written on the great variety of rocks, crystals, and semi-precious stones which can be found, often in very specific locations, along this shore.

Our route takes us up several of those mountains. We are hiking from north to south (the angle of the shore is such that it's really more like east to west). The mountains are not like other ranges we've seen. Usually when you are in valleys you can't really see anything more than the bases of the nearby hills. But here, because they were formed so differently, the hard unweathered peaks are separated by various distances, and stick up from the sedimented plain. So as you hike you can watch the next mountain grow ahead of you.

We have watched Pincushion Mountain since yesterday afternoon. Its name obviously comes from its low, rounded profile. Now Marie puts on her long legs, and away we go! She always claims that I hike faster than she does. Today she is saying that I need an anchor to slow me down, but she is in the lead and I'm panting too much and working too hard to keep up to tell her that it's not true. We reach the base of Pincushion and decide to take the side trip to the top. This is our first sampling of the heady elixir of Superior views. Whereas down below we could easily see the next hill ahead, from up here we can see our routes past and ahead for miles. The actual cut of the trail is not visible, of course, being too narrow, but it's easy to compare the landscape with the topographic maps, and to see where the trail must be hidden in the trees. The top of Pincushion is bare black rock with just a few stunted trees. The view is panoramic, and we spend many minutes just walking around sampling each of the angles. Beneath our feet, growing from every crevice is Three-toothed Cinquefoil, a leathery low plant with three tiny teeth in the end of each leaf, which loves rocky mountain tops. About half of the plants have already turned bright scarlet, stunning against patches of white Reindeer Moss.

Three days later the main trail takes us to the edge of Lookout Mountain. Lookout is roughly the same height as Pincushion, but the shape is completely different. While Pincushion was a rounded dome popped up from the surrounding countryside, Lookout on its lake side is just a continuation of the steep, but evenly ascending hill from the water. However, on the northeast, the landscape begins to break into a fan of steep streams flowing into the deep-sided gorge of the Cascade River. And above that mile-wide fan the eastern slope of Lookout falls nearly sheer for 300 feet. It's a great spot to take the kind of photos which look as if you clambered up to really dangerous places. I clamber, and Marie takes pictures of me looking completely satisfied. We don't take any pictures of Marie looking anxious.

Next day, we take another side trip to White Sky Rock. Making this detour is a serious decision, because the Rock is nearly a mile off the main trail. But the name is intriguing and the guidebook says that on the way is a staircase cut from a single log, so we have to go look. And we are not disappointed. Like a set from *The Swiss Family Robinson*, sixteen steps have been sawed into a large log which is wedged into the slope and against several convenient trees. A rustic handrail has been added. It seems odd to be going down into a valley of cedar swamps since our goal – and that not so far away – is a pointy little peak. But of course, first we have to come down off the pointy little peak that we are already standing on! White Sky Rock is indeed magnificent. From its steep eastern side we overlook convoluted Caribou Lake. The day is perfection in blue, red and gold. From the south edge of the lake a narrow band of land connects the shore to what would otherwise be an island in the center of the lake. Its low hump, covered with blazing leaves, is reflected in the calm blue water. It feels great sitting on the warm rock. The thermometer attached to my belt pack claims that it's 75° in the sun. I admit that the air is probably only 65°. "Nope," says Marie, "only 62°, my ears are still cold."

Next we head up the back side of the hills of the Lutsen Ski Area. Looking north we have long views of the Poplar River which seems to be a lost old man in this world of steep, rushing rivers. Meandering from the north for miles, down a long flat valley, the river is headed for the declivity between Eagle (not the one of highest Minnesota peak fame) and Moose Mountains. Aptly named, the odor of poplar leaves and wood rises from the yellow valley as we walk by. The bridge over the Poplar River has been built directly above the point where the wide, flat water is pinched and hurtles down a black wall of rock. From there it continues in cascades, rapids and deep torrents till it reaches Lake Superior. The old man is reborn an exuberant youngster.

After a night at Mystery Mountain campsite we head up the steep slope of Moose Mountain. Moose is a long, steep-sided oval of dark-colored diabase magma. If it weren't for that River gorge it would be kissing noses with Eagle Mountain to the northeast. Such topography suggests technology to alpine-minded entrepreneurs, and a gondola has been strung across the divide. However, the main trail heads southwest along the ridge of Moose. The views are all away from Lake Superior, but by now the colors are peaking and even without the sparkling blue water for counterpoint, the red and orange hillsides are breathtaking. Today's perfume is essence of hemlock.

We had passed up taking a detour all the way to the gondola in favor of having time to climb the square lump facing us across the next valley, Oberg Mountain, also volcanic diabase. The trail winds around the inland edge of Oberg, close in the shadows of its steep sides. This is Saturday, a perfect Saturday in September, and dozens of day hikers have come out to take a short walk from the parking lot right at the western foot of the mountain to any one of the many views from the top. We meet people walking alone, as couples, with babies or children, and a variety of pets. One couple is hiking with a Great Dane named Daisy and Yorkshire Terrier named Moose. We

Looking back at Moose Mountain from Oberg

meet a Black Lab/ Basset Hound cross, a Lab with four-inch legs. Unique among them all is a lady hiking with an African Gray Parrot tethered to her shoulder. She tries to get him to talk to us, but he offers us only a beady eye as he cleans a claw and kneads his owner's shoulder. "He's shy with strangers," she apologizes.

Sunday morning we pass up Leveaux Mountain for a short, very steep, hand-over-hand climb up to Cedar Overlook. It's hardly big enough to qualify as a mountain, rather more like a pimple, but from its sunny top a glance northeast reveals a row of peaks behind us, Leveaux, Oberg, and Moose in the distance. It's so unusual and satisfying to be able to see how far we have walked in just two days!

But our primary goal for this morning is Carlton Peak, which will be our last mountain of this hike. Carlton is not black like most of the rocks we've climbed. Carlton is white rock, anorthosite. Being lighter weight than the molten rock of the more recent lava flow, the chunks of anorthosite were torn from the earth's crust and floated, yes, I said floated, to the top of the magma. From this point south along the shore there are many such white rocks, er, mountains. The trail traverses steep and rugged terrain, with white cliffs rising above our heads. We've anticipated spending a private Sunday on Carlton, and even though there are still many weekend hikers on the trails, the top of this mountain is so broad and open that we get our wish. Rows of trees have grown from cracks and divided most of the crest into private rooms, many with a private view. Our Sunday agenda includes lunch, basking on the sun-warmed rock, gazing far into the flaming birch and maple distance, chuckling at a tiny chipmunk, and singing hymns. As a worship service, this one was hard to beat!

One additional geographic high spot doesn't merit the label of mountain on the map, but it makes our list of memorable moments. Just east of Manitou River the trail follows a semi-circular formation known as Horseshoe Ridge. For more than a mile we circle around, but on the outside of the curve. Only at the beginning and end of the arc do we pass through saddles where we can see the inner curve of the ridge. The ridge ends at a completely symmetric conical hill, which apparently has no name.

Super Rocks - Small Ones

Hardly a hiking day goes by that we don't find some new color or shape of stone or crystal to marvel at. Before the first day is past we take in what the guidebook describes simply as the Lakewalk. It is a section of beach about 1.5 miles long covered with small pebbles instead of the usual large rough black rock. The pebbles range from red to white in color, but the overall effects is definitely red. Beaches with small flat weathered pebbles seem just fine to Marie and me. This is the typical beach of the Finger Lakes in New York, where we grew up. However those beaches have black and gray stones. Quite oddly, these red stones squeak with our steps. We are used to more of a crunching sound. Later I discovered that this beach is a strip of a remnant of volcanic rocks, not covered with the sediments which have filled in most areas along the shore line. This narrow band extends inland to connect with the higher, wider region of volcanic rock called the Duluth Complex.

Lots of the rocks have vesicles. This is the term for those curious bubbly holes in so many of them. And bubbles is exactly what they are. As the lava cooled, gases expanded and left holes in their place. Next, mineral-rich water flowed over the rock and the holes were often filled with minerals, forming amygdules. Some of the prettiest amygdules we see are a blue-green prehnite in black basalt. More commonly we see quartz, calcite, and other white or pink crystals or aggregates in the red rhyolite.

South of Carlton Peak we cross the Temperance River. This was supposedly named by someone with a sense of humor, because it is the only river on the North Shore which does not have a sand bar at its mouth. Next we begin to encounter strange crumbly rocks. Each rounded rock seems to be composed of small spherical cinder-like pebbles cemented together. They obviously weather faster than the other kinds of rock, and in places there is so much of the loose rubble that the trail looks as if someone has carted in loads of gravel. That turns out to be "rotting" lava! Well, it doesn't smell as bad as the description sounds.

Super Rocks - the Other Ones

Sugarloaf Cove is not exactly on the trail, but it is so unique that we make a stop there after the hike. The cove is created by what was a small island, now connected to the mainland. We learn another new word, "tombolo." That is the triangular strip of sediments that connect the island to the shore. Tombolos are usually wetlands, my favorite! On the south side of the point the rock slopes toward the water, looking pretty much like all the other sloping rock beaches along here... until you look closely. If you pay attention to the cracks in the rock surface you will begin to realize that the cracks have created a regular hexagonal pattern, with each hexagon about two feet across. Columnar joints! This is another volcanic feature, showing that the rock crystalized from hot magma, cracking as it cooled. If we could see a cross section below the surface it would look like a collection of hexagonal rods fitted together and standing on end.

Temperance River is one of the few places in the United States outside of Hawaii where there is Pahoehoe (say puh-HOE-i-HOE-i).

The word for it definitely comes from Hawaii! Pahoehoe is a term for a basaltic lava flow which advances in a series of small lobes and toes that continually break out from a cooled crust.

At Crystal Creek we discover the source of its name. Huge bands of calcite crystals line the rocky banks of the creek just above a collapsed mine shaft. Early miners often suspected there were ores to be found wherever the crystals were located. Broken chunks, like sharp-sided gumdrops, sparkle in the sunlight.

But our favorite rocks of the trip are at Cascade River State Park. We take a rest day there, hiking down to the information center to pick up one of our supply boxes, and checking out all of the waterfalls and other noted points of interest. On a whim we decide to continue down as far as the lakefront. What a plan! We are greeted by a landscape from the game of *Riven*, one of our favorites when we are home in computer country. Polished, exotic, black and rounded humps of rock arise from a silent shoreline. Not a gull wheels or cries. We expect any moment to see the Sunners, the dinosaur-like creatures of the *Riven* beach! The sun is high and warm, the air still. Even Marie is comfortable in shirt-sleeves. I gambol about searching for crystals and new plants. I find Alpine Goldenrod, and a short sedge which remains unidentified. The Three-toothed Cinquefoil grows profusely here, and some crevices in the rocks are lined with Wild Strawberries. Occasionally a nodding blue Harebell still flowers. The colors are riotous. A lichen, the color of Halloween pumpkins, spreads in interlocking splotches with one of pure white. Not many feet away a kelly-green algae coats the smooth rock like wet paint. And I do find crystals, vein after vein of them. Red ones, white ones, and aqua-green ones. Sometimes all three colors are jumbled together, filling cracks several inches wide in the rock surfaces. Sometimes there are amygdules polka-dotting the basaltic landscape. The waves lap at the edges. On the north edge of our imagined world a larger rock shelters a hidden cove where the miniature cliffs are reflected perfectly in a green and blue mirror. For over an hour we revel in the fantasy, and we do leave before the light, wind or temperature changes. For this one time there will be no sighing that things must inevitably change. The memory of our beach world will last forever in the September sun.

Super Weather

We knew we were taking a chance with hiking so late in the season. But we really wanted to try to catch the autumn colors at their peak. That meant accepting the possibility of rain, snow, wind and all those other northern signs of impending winter. The first night, as we hike into the West Fork Kadunce River Campground it does begin to sprinkle. But we are content to go to bed a little early.

Predictions of rain or snow keep arriving by the tele-hiker network, but they never materialize. Only on a couple of nights do we arise to find that it has rained in the night, or that there is a touch of frost on the ground. A long, perfect Indian Summer reigns over our weeks in the northwoods. My reputation for taking hikes in terrible weather is ruined! But I can live with that loss.

On the final morning we rest and enjoy a snack in the warm sun, surrounded by the red, orange, yellow, and blue that have become our constant companions. Referring to our non-hiker husbands, Marie suggests, "If we could transport Omer and Ed here for just this morning, they would love it."

Super Campsites

The Superior Hiking Trail folks have created established campsites along the length of their trail, and campers are supposed to use these sites. The designers have done a good job of providing enough choices so that backpackers are not locked into one itinerary once they've chosen a starting location. Each site has multiple tent spaces and at least one fire ring. Usually the fire ring even has benches around it. A latrine is provided, often the kind which is an open toilet over a pit located at the end of a short trail leading away from the tent sites. One can endlessly debate the merits of dispersed camping versus designated campsites. On trails which see a lot of use, like this one in the summer months, perhaps keeping people who may not all subscribe to the Leave-No-Trace ethic herded into specific areas is a good one.

At any rate, we don't mind at all having benches to sit on in the evening. At the sites which are near bridges over those steep-sided gorges we simply sling our food bag beneath the bridge. Instant cache! I like the relaxed pace of cooking over a fire rather than using the stove.

Our only complaint about the camping areas is that we don't think that the tent pad sites were planned by anyone who sleeps in a tent! Of the three to six cleared spaces in each named camp, we are lucky to find one that is level enough to sleep on comfortably. At this time of year there aren't too many backpackers, so we almost always are able to claim a space where we won't slide into a pile or wake up with kinks in our backs. But I kept thinking it would be nice to return with some tools and level those tent pads.

Super Bog

Minnesota has a knack for growing northern spruce bogs, but not many of them are located along the SHT. The delightful exception to that is Alfred's Pond. Bogs are wetlands which are acidic, and because of that acid particular plants thrive there. Alfred's Pond has a rather large area of open water for a bog, but it is circled by a typical fringe of Black Spruce. A thick mat of Sphagnum Moss extends into the pond from the edges, and a short boardwalk has been provided so that people can enjoy the botany close at hand. Bogs are some of my favorite places, but I've never seen one at the height of the fall color season before. It's awesome! Flaming behind the ring of dark green spruce are endless hillsides of Red Maple. An occasional Larch adds its spiky texture, and these deciduous conifers have not yet dropped their needles. On my side of the blue water, the Sphagnum mat is partially the typical yellow-green, but also mottled with a deep burgundy, or faded to nearly white. Leatherleaf and Bog Cranberry have retained their dark green. But the breathtaking scene-stealer is the prolific Pitcher Plant. This insect eating plant is growing in large groups, and almost all of the specially adapted tubular leaves have turned bright red.

Pitcher Plant

As if inspired by the unique nature of the bog, even the more common plants nearby have adorned themselves in especially bright colors. We photograph a baby Red Maple, making the origin of its name obvious against a rock covered with a solid mat of grass-green moss. A Marsh Fern has faded to a pale greenish-white, and contrasts nicely with its backdrop of brown fallen leaves. A Cinnamon Fern also explains its name with green Leatherleaf behind it. Even the grasses have joined the celebration with textured, off-white seed heads glowing in the afternoon light. Scarlet shrubs and white Paper Birch bark announce an early Christmas. Baby hemlocks join in the holiday theme by decorating themselves with small red and yellow leaves which have fallen from above. It's tempting to stay till Christmas, but we suspect that even the abandoned Trapper's Cabin would not provide us enough shelter, even if we could manage to feed and clothe ourselves.

Super Supporters

In the middle of this hike, we spend an evening with the Minnesota Parks and Trails Council. John Leinen, NCTA board member, had asked us if we would attend this dinner and meeting. The topics of the evening are celebrating several land swaps to help preserve sections of the North Shore, and working together to find a route from Ely, Minnesota back to the middle of the state to complete the Arrowhead Reroute. As much as I hate breaking the mood of a backpacking trip, John convinced me that Marie's presence and mine would be a great show of support from the North Country Trail.

We meet John at the Oberg Mountain Trailhead right on time. A fast shower at the park (it's easy to make it quick, the shower is cold), and a change of clothes makes us look like any ordinary person. I always hate to give up that "something" that makes me feel special as a long-distance hiker. Dressed in clean clothes, with clean hair, no pack and no hiking stick, I could be anyone, someone with only a wish to be a hiker. With my pack on my back, and a week of hiker's perfume clinging to my body and clothes, my credibility is unquestioned.

But the evening seems productive, and everyone thanks us for attending. We hope we are making friends for the trail.

Super Ambience

Despite how close this trail is to some aspects of civilization, the sensation for a hiker is often one of being in remote and wild places. Before we had walked an hour on our first day we encountered Moose tracks and bear scat. Camping at Jonvick Creek we would have seen the whole Moose, except it was dark... but the Moose was very close to our tent, crashing and splashing and snuffing and snorting. We decided to stay in our tent rather than confront our midnight visitor.

One morning the largest Ruffed Grouse I've ever seen walked across our path, and another day a grouse strutted for us with his tail fully spread and his neck ruff all fluffed up. Fantastic! In Ohio I had seen a pink Wood Frog; here a beautiful chestnut red one sat on my hand, then jumped to my elbow before taking a big leap into the green grass.

The forests varied in different valleys. At Cascade River the light itself seemed to be layered yellow, orange, and green, although we knew it was the way it filtered through the leaves. Near Carlton Peak the trees were all birch, similar in age. Their white trunks were spotted with black, and the yellow leaves were high above our heads. A low understory of maple had turned orange. As we walked we seemed to be floating in the gap between the warm colors.

We enjoyed the familiarity of commonly seen wildlife: woodpeckers, chickadees, and a chipmunk so precocious we named him Pipsqueak. "If you turn your head for one second, I'll have your dinner," he said! We watched a Beaver swimming for his lodge, and heard a Great Horned Owl. But we also saw an elusive Wood Thrush hopping through the leaves. And at Onion River a Gray Jay, not a common visitor in these woods, strutted along the length of the fire ring bench, pecking at each of our stuff sacks which I had lined up there before packing my pack.

Super Size It

Sonju Lake

Every sensory experience on this hike was heightened. Scents, such as balsam, hemlock, or aspen hung in the warm air longer than we expected. Textures were richer — carpets of moss, rocks both rough and smooth, riffled water in the swift streams. We noticed the sounds — some days the leaves underfoot crunched, other days they were quieter, more of a "schwick, schwick." Intense colors were the standard every day — blue water and sky, red and yellow leaves against green conifers and white birch, with a background of black, red or white rock. And we won't leave out tastes either. Some of our favorite meals turned out better than ever. Our day-off favorite, 15-bean soup with cornbread, was cooked to perfection. We savored our hot drinks around the fire each night in the cooling air. And best of all, Marie and I had lots of time alone together.

On the afternoon before our first day off we had hiked fast and skipped a break so that we could reach White Pine Campsite early. We set up camp, cooked dinner, read, and discussed the day, all the usual stuff. But on that occasion we had the luxury of spending five hours doing what we usually accomplish in two. It was super-duper!

106 miles this hike
Judge C.R. Magney State Park to Finland
Cook County, MN
1915 total NCT miles

Fisher Settlement
62 - April 30- May 4, 2002

I am standing at the edge of an unmarked dirt road, an unremarkable trail crossing in the Middle of Nowhere, New York. Marie is here too, as is Maggie the dog, but they see only another plain gray road, like any of the thousands we've seen before. But as I look south, down the valley, I see generations of rugged pioneers, farmers and their wives, soldiers of the Revolutionary and Civil Wars, fearless women, merchants, a druggist, a sailor, a nurse. My ancestors. I am standing at a crossroad of my present with my past.

Because I have been keeping track on the map, I know that this is Fisher Settlement Road. It would lead me if I followed it, in just a few miles, to the corner once known as Fisher Settlement, just north of Spencer, New York. Spencer itself is no longer a thriving community, although it once was home to a station of the Lehigh Valley Railroad. But villages were much closer together when New York was truly wild. General George Fisher and his brother Thomas, a former sailor, arrived in the area from Albany in 1810, bought 7000 acres, and established a settlement two miles north of Spencer. George opened a general store in Spencer, and family legend has it that he brought the first kerosene lantern to that community. Thomas brought his wife, Olive White Hodges Fisher. I give you her whole name, because I have previously mentioned being related to someone whose last name was White.[1] Olive's direct ancestor was Susannah White, who traveled to North America on a very small ship known as the Mayflower. As brave as this was in its own right, I am even more impressed by the knowledge that she was pregnant as she rode all those waves. Her baby, Peregrine "Pilgrim" White, was born on shipboard in the wintry Plymouth harbor. He was the first European child born in the new world to survive.

Olive's genetic grit has not become diluted over the two intervening centuries. It is recorded that she was the first person to drive a horse and buggy alone through the woods from Fisher Settlement to Spencer. This was no project for the timid a mere 30 years after General John Sullivan's march on the Indian villages of western New York. Her granddaughter describes Olive as a woman with "great poise... and a wonderful friend of 'hard sense.'"

One of Thomas' and Olive's daughters was my grandmother's grandmother, Lucinda Cornelia. Her husband, Hervey Smith Hall, came from sound stock as well. One of his sisters, H. Rosamond Hawley, with her husband, was a founder of the village of Rosamond,

---

[1.] See Chapter 6: "Where the Trail Begins"

Illinois. And another sister, Susan Hall, was the first person to answer the call for volunteer nurses in the Civil War, one day after Abraham Lincoln requested troops. My middle name is Hall, in memory of this branch of the family tree.

My grandmother's mother, Catherine Louisa Fisher (she married a distant cousin, bringing the Fisher name back into the line), was described as a "social, generous woman of marked ability and good sense." I own a quilt made by her which won State Fair awards for its intricate embroidery.

Emily M. Fisher, Granny, on Mt. Marcy 1904

And my grandmother, Emily Marguerite Fisher, grew up on the historic family farm in Fisher Settlement. This is my mother's mother, the grandmother who recited "Hiawatha," and other epic poems by heart. Of course, I remember Granny only as a rather stout older lady who was always working on some needlework project. She provided me with books, art supplies, and other wonderful childhood pleasures. And she saw to it that we traveled, visited many historic and cultural sites. I should probably blame her for causing at least part of my case of terminal wanderlust. It was not until Granny was long gone, and I was older, that I began to hear what kind of person she was in her younger days. In the 1890's, when nice young women stayed home and gave teas, Granny was beating her brothers at goat cart races, playing tennis in bloomers, rowing boats on the lake, and otherwise adventuring. One of my favorite finds, among the photo albums I inherited after my mother died, is a photo of Granny. In 1996, the year we climbed Mount Marcy in the Adirondacks, I discovered a snapshot of Granny on that same mountaintop, taken in 1904!

You've already met my own mother on your journey through this book. Mom tolerated my caterpillar collections in egg cartons, torn school clothes (little girls were supposed to be quiet and demure in the 1950's), and piles of unfinished projects. She did, however, put her foot down at the garter snakes in a bucket under the bed. She taught me to snowshoe, helped me to look up the many plants, bugs, fossils, moths, and feathers I brought home, and I never remember being scolded about mud. She encouraged me to follow my dreams, but sighed at my inability to decide which of my many dreams that would be. I think she would be glad to see that I've finished this book.

This mystical moment at the edge of Fisher Settlement Road lasted but a few thumping heartbeats in the midst of several days of springtime hiking.

―――― ✳ ――――

For this hike, we are basecamped at the Chestnut Hill Lean-to. The shelter is surrounded by tall chestnut trees which are large enough to make one believe that they might be resistant to the blight. We will sleep here and drive to day-hike each day.

Nights are chilly and we are learning that Maggie does not like sleeping out in the cold. We have carried our gear three-fourths of a mile in to the lean-to, and we also lug in Maggie's dog bed and an extra blanket to keep her happy. Irene has given her a bright orange neoprene vest, designed for hunting dogs, and she is a handsome pup when she wears it! It's also warm, and her not so secret desire each evening is to have her vest put on, to curl up on her padded bed, and to be covered with the blanket.

One morning we stash Marie's car at our end point, and all pile in my Subaru to drive to our starting location. I am driving and Marie navigating. It's not her favorite role. It's well known to people familiar with western New York that you can't drive east or west except along the pathway taken by the Erie Canal. And we aren't anywhere near there. Ridges, rivers, streams, and lakes run north and south, and to travel cross-wise usually requires zig-zagging and tacking along valleys and ridges to reach your destination. But as we are zigging along a north-west course while Marie studies the map, she exclaims, "That road, right there, goes straight over the hill." So I make a quick right and we climb quickly away from the pavement up Eastman Hill. The "road" becomes rockier and rougher, but I like a little fun in my driving, so Marie grips the dashboard, and I navigate around rocks and holes till we have crested the hill. Then things get interesting. Full across the road, at windshield height, is a tree. It's not a fat tree, but it does have a lot of branches, and there is no way we'll be driving around it. Even the two of us together can't budge the fallen maple. But just a few weeks ago I added a dollar store purchase to my car tool box, a tiny hand saw. It's a poor excuse for a saw, but in about 30 minutes, we are able to continue down the hill, and begin our hike. Despite knowing that we've cleared the road, we think we'll skip the rocks and ruts and take the usual zag to get back to camp tonight.

The hills afford many long vistas of New York's Southern Tier. This area is all just south of where I grew up, not in Fisher Settlement, but 30 miles north. From my house we could see the long Cayuga Lake, and the profile of hills on the far shore. Here, there is no lake of that size to see, but the ridges and long hills speak to me and say "home."

The trail on one steep hill is maintained to perfection by Alex Gonzales. His care is so obvious that he received the Clar-Willis Award from the Finger Lakes Trail Conference. First of all, we must climb down from the road into a deep ditch, and then up the far side even to begin the hill climb. Since the local road commission keeps the sides of the ditch steeply graded, Alex has fastened a rope, with knots in it for a grip, to a nearby tree. This simple solution makes it easy to walk up the far side of the ditch! Then begins a series of nicely laid out long switchbacks, working their way up the hill. The paths are benched, the corners do not "jump" ten feet at the turn. And along the edges of the trail, Alex has laid out rock or log borders, just for fun, to define the pathway. Thanks, Alex; we love your work!

It rains off and on for most of our time together. An extra layer feels good in the chilly air. But the sun shows up for a reasonable amount of time too. One sunny afternoon, after a rainy morning, we are walking down the edge of a field with hemlocks for a fencerow. The sun shines warm on the left sides of our faces. But from the other side, a light breeze spritzes our cheeks with tiny, cold drops of water retained by the trees!

Waterfalls, railroad beds, ponds, vistas, and old foundations of homesteads long forgotten fill our days as the miles pass beneath our feet. We eat our last dinner of this hike by candlelight at the Chestnut Hill shelter, a warm and homey conclusion to a rather chilly week.

But we are not alone. It had only taken a few seconds to cross Fisher Settlement Road. We re-entered the woods. Nothing unusual apparently happened, but I know better. Following us are Susannah, Olive, Susan, Rosamond, Lucinda Cornelia, Catherine Louisa, Emily, and Catherine, even as I am following after them.

58 miles this hike
Sand Bank Rd. To VanDonsel Rd.
Tompkins, Tioga, and Cortland
Counties, NY
1973 total NCT miles

Thousands of Miles
63 - April 24, 25, May 6-8, 2002

Tuesday afternoon, and it feels more like a good title would be "Thousands of Gnats," maybe "Thousands of Rocks," or "Thousands of Screaming Toes." The gnats are so vicious that I have given in to wearing a head net. How can so lightweight and airy an item feel so hot and grimy? Ah well, it keeps the bugs from my eyes and ears. I can't bear the heat of long sleeves, so am getting some extra exercise slapping the gnats that land on my arms and hands. It's a game: can I kill each one before it bites? (The final score: I lose to about six of the little villains, but many more of them lose to my heavy-handed tactics!) The trail wanders through an area noted by guidebook author, Irene Szabo, as "uncharacteristic of New York." That's putting it mildly! A field of boulders stretches for about two miles. Trees are blazed, but no one could ever say that this is a treadway. I only hope I can navigate it without breaking an ankle. And for the final ignomy, on my day of glory, I am so tired I can hardly put one foot in front of the other. My toes ache and burn; there must be at least a thousand of them in the boots. But every time I remove the socks to check, 990 of them run and hide, leaving only ten to take the blame.

2002 miles in 2002 for Joan, 85 for Maggie

Nevertheless the pivotal moment of the day is quietly reached at an unassuming point of interest along the trail. No one is there to celebrate with me. No sign is there to note the divide in the trail. The trail passes along the berm of a small pond. On my left a tiny creek runs through a culvert under the berm, from the pond, and flows away to the north, to Slader Creek, the Genesee River and the St. Lawrence. To my right, the pool shimmers flatly a few hundred feet before falling away to an unnamed creek on the south, to the Canisteo, the Susquehanna, and finally to Chesapeake Bay. But here, in the year 2002, I am completing 2002 miles on the North Country National Scenic Trail. No high ridge with a far-reaching view at the top of this watershed, no fanfare for a foot-sore hiker. Just that quiet bubbling from some hidden spring keeps the water flowing. Like that unseen spring, long-distance hikers need secret sources of motivation to keep putting one foot in front of the other.

The plan for this hike has been convoluted even by my standards. I hiked two days prior to the weekend on which the Finger Lakes Trail Conference (FLTC) celebrated its 40th Anniversary. The North Country Trail Association Board of Directors decided to join them for the weekend, and that is what has brought me to New York.

Board members from each state brought containers of soil and water from their home locale. The soil and water, with flowers, is ceremoniously deposited in a planter at the base of a signpost in front of the new FLTC office. To go on the post, Irene has painted a rainbow of a sign. At the top, a blaze-blue signboard directs hikers east across New York, or west to North Dakota. White is for the main Finger Lakes Trail, Pennsylvania to the Catskills. Boards pointing in other directions are orange for the Conservation Trail Branch of the FLT, and yellow, for the Letchworth Branch Trail. Green stands for the Genesee Valley Greenway. From this point, you can pick a direction and hike... forever! Well, maybe not yet, but it is the goal of many trail organizations to connect long trails in such a way that forever might almost be possible. The theme for the weekend is "40, and Over the Hills." You've already heard about those New York hills in many tales, and with 40 years of experience in all things trail, the FLTC leads the way for the NCTA on many fronts.

I can not "waste" a trip to some region where there is trail I have not hiked, so I have imposed upon several of my friends again. Irene has spotted me to hike before the conference. After the weekend, Marie joins me for a few days. That hike is reported in "Fisher Settlement." After a day visiting another friend, now I am continuing the miles I began on Thursday and Friday, again with Irene's help.

This is Maggie's first overnight hike. Sleeping outside is certainly nothing this comfort-loving dog has ever longed for. We reach Burt Hill Lean-to early on our first day; the woods are warm and quiet. To entertain myself I carve a spoon. It turns out to be harder to cut a chunk from the maple branch than it is to carve the spoon itself, but it occupies my time productively. Maggie is nervous, she chases the Woodchuck, ignores the whistle of the Tufted Titmouse, and doesn't see the turkey, but she is not at all happy about the hammering of the Pileated Woodpecker. She woofs and paces and is happiest when we finally snuggle in to the sleeping bag for the night. She is bigger than Chips was, leggier too. She would like to be inside the sleeping bag, but there isn't room for the both of us. So the compromise is that she curls into my chest as I lie on my side, and we pull the flap of the unzipped bag over both of us. It's not ideal... I don't think either of us is really warm enough, but neither are we too cold to sleep.

After the days with Marie, Maggie is a veteran of the trail. And she does like the hiking, as long as it is not raining! But she is making it abundantly clear that she does not like to be wet or cold. She does not like to sleep on the ground. She's always ready to get in the tent as soon as it is pitched, and as I have mentioned, unfamiliar noises make her nervous. Not that it's any big surprise, but Maggie won't be a "real" hiker dog.

The "Bermuda Triangle" of the FLT is located just north of Swain. Irene swears she's measured these seven miles three times, but experienced hikers continue to observe that there are several lost miles in there which only pop up when a human with no measuring device appears. I, too, am captured by the Triangle. For over four hours I hike resolutely along those miles, before I escape to a bluff and set up camp just in time to also escape the more tangible threat of a heavy rain. Irene's guidebook insists that these miles are "more arduous than average," and that we are all just hiking slower than usual. Balderdash! If you are missing any hikers, I know where they are.

One of the most interesting features of this hike requires either foreknowledge or a really observant and curious nature. Coming from the north through Swain I pass close to two tall concrete abutments, which no longer support anything. Just after this the trail crosses the ski area and joins an old railroad grade. That's not so difficult to realize. But it is difficult now to follow the line of the old railroad embankment through the maturing woods, and to connect it in your mind to those abutments. It is also difficult to believe that your brain is not playing tricks, for the grade seems to turn right around on itself. And it does! This was once a famous horseshoe curve of the Pittsburg, Shawmut & Northern RR. From Route 70, you can still see a wonderful stone viaduct over Canaseraga Creek, which was built into the embankment.

Spring hikes always mean wildflowers. I am delighted that I continue to find new plants that I've never seen. An entire opening in the woods is filled with the coarse, ribbed leaves of False Hellebore. Now that I've finally learned to identify these interesting leaves, I hope some year to see it in bloom. The Hobblebush is covered with clumps of white flowers. Only the edge petals of each clump are open, and the heart-shaped leaves droop. I recognize it as a viburnum, but have to look up which one. Its name comes from the fact that its branches bend to the ground and take root, leaving loops of stem that "hobble" the inattentive hiker. But the red summer berries are edible, supposedly making wonderful jam. Also new for me this trip is Dwarf Ginseng, but not the famed medicinal "Manroot." This one is smaller, lifting its white umbel bloom above the leaves, with a bulbous root. Barren Strawberry has a yellow blossom, and ragged, blunt leaves. The fruit is reported to be inedible, whatever that means. Is it poisonous, too dry, too small, nasty tasting? Sometimes field guides are frustratingly insufficient.

Two thousand miles. That definitely qualifies as thousands, plural. But there are even more miles to declare. Admittedly what I'm about to report occurred on the hike with Marie just a few days ago. But these two hikes have been intertwined, and mixed in my head anyway, so I might as well mix them up on paper too. Thematically, it fits here, so here it will be. At the Tamarack Lean-to, 600 feet up the side of Danby Hill, Marie passed her one-thousandth mile on the North Country Trail. She is always claiming that she simply follows me around. She forever downplays her accomplishment. But she has now seen more of the NCT than any board or staff member. Fewer than a dozen people that we know of have hiked this many miles of the trail. We have to wonder why. Sure, there are sections which aren't completed, but by now I hope I've convinced you that plenty of adventures await anyone willing go out and look for them.

1000 NCT miles for Marie

As we panted and puffed and hauled our selves up to that thousandth mile at the Tamarack shelter, Marie blustered, "If we'd stop going up the sides of cliffs, I'd be happy about it. I'm ten years older."

50 miles this hike
Fox Hill Rd. To Hughes Rd.
Livingston, Allegany and Steuben Counties, NY
2022 total NCT miles

Sheyenne
64 - August 20-30, 2002

The North Country Trail in North Dakota is defined by the Sheyenne River. For over 250 miles the NCT more or less follows the river's winding course from its headwaters in the Lonetree Wildlife Management Area to just east of Lisbon, ND. There the river turns northeast, toward Fargo, while the Trail continues straight east to Fort Abercrombie. The Sheyenne is an old river, and most of the time a lazy one. It originated as an overflow from Glacial Lake Souris in the west to Lake Agassiz, the largest of the Glacial Lakes, which once covered more area than all the present Great Lakes put together.

"Sheyenne" rings in our ears like the dinner bell on a western ranch. Say the word, and you can almost see cowboys and Indians, wagon wheels, steers, tumbleweed and jackrabbits. In fact, you hardly need to look into your imagination for this vision. North Dakota's prairie is still ranch country, and the culture as well as the scenery differs from anywhere else along the North Country Trail. The word "Sheyenne" is a corruption of a Dakota word "Sha-i-e-na," meaning enemy. They called the river "Shaiena Ozupi Wakpa," the river where their enemies planted.

Most of this hike, with a few exceptions, was on roads. Instead of being separated from civilization within the banks of the McClusky Canal,[1] we visited regularly with local people. Despite its sparse population, compared to our previous North Dakota hike, this time we were practically overcome by interactions with people. Folks were open, friendly and helpful; the flavor of the adventure was completely different from our isolated canal hike.

The Trail Association took its own mini population boom to Valley City in August. For the annual conference, over 100 people decided to see what the western end of the Trail had to offer, and they liked what they saw. Marie and I were there, of course. Also attending were Irene, and her friend Lois. The new local Sheyenne River Valley Chapter treated us all to buffalo burgers, buffalo jerky, and accordion music. We took a bus tour to view portions of the trail farther west that Marie and I had seen a few years ago. Another highlight of the conference was a visit to the city park's new Medicine Wheel, a reconstruction of a Native American calendar. The spokes of the wheel point in the directions of the compass, the solstices and the equinoxes. Parti-colored gravel filled the spaces between the lines. We all posed

---

[1.] See Chapter 6: "Where the Trail Begins"

around the neat rows of rocks, while photographers snapped pictures from high in the bucket of the fire department's ladder truck.

From the Wheel, representing the sun, a paved pathway meanders through city land. Dotted along this pathway are rocks marked with the name of each of the planets in our solar system. Their distance from the sun is in proper proportion, putting Mercury, Venus, Earth and Mars near the Wheel, and Pluto about a half-mile away.

Following the conference, all four of us girls drive to Fort Ransom State Park. Irene and Lois take the campsite next to us for one night before they embark on a whirlwind tour of North Dakota and Minnesota. Marie and I plan to base camp here for most of our time together. The one exception will be three days of backpacking through the Sheyenne National Grasslands. We like our campsite, shielded from the parking area and neighboring sites by a screen of brush and Woodland Sunflowers. Soon we have the tent set up, a rain fly over the picnic table, and a decent wood pile. We pool our resources with Irene and Lois, and sit down to an eclectic and huge dinner.

In the morning we bid them goodbye as they head off on their adventures, and we take the day off. In between extra naps, we drive to the nearby town of Fort Ransom to learn some local history. Most obvious, on a pointed hill just outside of town is a huge metal Viking. Local legends have deep ties to the Scandinavian explorers. No one we meet will quite admit to believing the legends, but they are more than

Viking Hill at Fort Ransom - round hay bales show perspective

happy to tell us about them. First of all, the pointy hill on whose tip the Viking forever stands was supposedly built by the early sailors, who sailed through Hudson Bay, up the Red River, and then the Sheyenne. The next claim is that there is a pair of mooring stones set where the Viking ships were docked, but since they are on private property we aren't able to check it out. And in case there is any doubt that they were here, these Norse visitors left a written record of their visit on a rune stone. Of course, the skeptics and realists say that these have more natural explanations. The pointy little hill is simply eroded from the prairie plateau, similar to hills in southern Ohio. The mooring stones do have holes drilled in them, but there is no reason to believe that the holes predate early settlers with blasting powder who desired to clear their fields. The runes are glacial striations and chattermarks, left by the glacier scraping small stones over larger ones. But as we check out a nearby cemetery another day, we can certainly understand why settlers named Skrukrud and Hegseth would wish for evidence that their ancestors were here before them.

Our next stop is the local museum. The admission is only $2.00. We aren't sure what we can expect from a town with 105 residents, but never underestimate the power of someone with a sense of history who has even a modicum of support. In a large, crooked, white building which used to be the mercantile we meet George. His grandparents ran the store when it was still viable, and now he tends the collections which fill every nook and cranny. The displays are well presented and extremely varied and complete, from 1884 when the town was founded, on to more recent history. There are fossils, cavalry and other military displays, needlework and clothing, looms, folk art such as a chair seat carved of elm, farming relics, including a complete collection of styles of barbed wire. Famous local people are featured, along with a model of the town, furniture, photographs, books, toys, and some random collections of interesting unsorted stuff. Upstairs there are three rooms arranged as would be typical of an early 20th century farmhouse. Dozens of household appliances and tools are mixed with accouterments which might have come from the mercantile. Marie and I give each other a sidelong glance, recognizing that we are having one of those moment-of-truth experiences. These museum pieces are a perfect cross-section of our early lives. We sure don't feel old, and we did grow up in a rather non-progressive section of the country, but it still gives one pause to think of your lifestyle as museum vintage.

We joke with George about this and he pulls a sheet of paper from under the counter. "Bet you've never seen one of these," he challenges. On the paper is a picture of a spidery looking baby-buggy kind of thing with large metal wheels. Suspended below the body on an angled bar hang several plowshares. I have to admit I've never seen anything like it. George chuckles. "That's because there were only about 200 of them ever made." It seems they were made in the nearby town of Enderlin. The inventor talked his friends into buying them. Those friends soon discovered that the plows worked fine when the ground was dry, but (here George stamps his foot on the floor) "there's hardpan underneath, hard like cement, and they dug themselves in. Couldn't get 'em out!"

Of course we have to explain why we are in North Dakota. When we tell George that we are planning to hike through the Grasslands he begins to share his personal recollections of the area with us. "I used to ride my bike there when I was a kid in the 30's," he began. The whole region was bare sand back then. It wasn't just the Southwest that was a Dust Bowl. The wind blew across that sand and in the east it raised small dunes and lumpy hills. For some reason, the western section was just blown flat. Later the rains returned, the vegetation grew again, and the Grasslands began to look the way they do today. All in one man's lifetime an area of 114,000 acres has completely changed!

Just before we leave we look through a pile of paperback books on the front windowsill. We buy a few, total cost, $3.00. George is trying by this means to raise enough money to re-wire the building. We wonder how long that will take.

Tuesday, we are awakened at 6 am by Coyotes yipping not so very far away. At 7:30 we knock on a farmhouse door which is opened by a very young and surprised mother. But when we explain that we are hiking and we'd like to leave a bike in her yard today and a car tomorrow she cheerfully agrees, although she retains a slightly skeptical expression. We drive on to Fort Abercrombie where there is a stockade with some interpretation. This was the first U.S. military post to be established in what is now North Dakota and we want to learn more, but the museum is closed. We grab our day packs and sticks, walk east across the bridge over the Red River, to be sure we have really begun at the Minnesota border, and then turn our steps westward. Before we have gone a half-mile, an elderly man calls to us from his yard, "What are you doing with those canes? Who are you going to hit?" We reply cheerfully that we are just hiking. We think he was joking, but we really aren't sure!

Before we've gone another half-mile a man loading a small bulldozer on a truck yells, "Did your car break down?" We tell him that we are walking the North Country Trail to Valley City (over 100 miles away), and he responds incredulously, "Get OUT!" As we pass through Abercrombie we attract quite a few more gawkers, but everyone is friendly and willingly returns our waves. It's a promising beginning.

The first two days of this hike will be on terrain that is what Easterners expect of North Dakota – flat. This is the ancient bed of Lake Agassiz, now rich farmland with only an artificial hump to take a road over the Interstate, and one small creek valley for relief. We walk forever past corn, soybeans, and sugar beets. It's a land of big space, big fields, and big tractors. Sadly, we find a Great Horned Owl dead in the road. We reach my bike just after 3 pm, and I pedal back to retrieve the car. This will be our *modus operandi* for our one-vehicle trip.

Back at Fort Ransom the local restaurant, the J&S Corral, is having "Buck Night." Marie and I have already been adopted by the townspeople, and we are told that we should not miss this weekly treat. So after showers (yes, showers after just one day of hiking!) we return to the Corral and discover that everyone in the county must eat here on Tuesdays. The $1.00 burgers and taters are top notch, and extra-economical tonight. We meet the owners, Jim and Shirley. Shirley leads the Girl Scout troop, which is soon to take a trip to New York. Their daughter is one of the Scouts. Shirley is thrilled to hear that we are former Scouts, and that Marie is from New York. Somehow, it makes the distant East seem a little closer.

The next morning we repeat the car and bike dance, but today's special birds are alive. We spot a whole flock of Prairie Chickens, and I ease the car to a stop. I slowly put the telephoto lens on my camera, and cautiously approach the skittish creatures. The longest lens I have is not really long enough for serious wildlife photography, but sometimes if I am extra stealthy I can get close enough. I am almost at a reasonable distance to begin to focus the lens when, WHOOSH, another car blasts down the dirt road, the chickens explode in a flurry of wings and tails. No pictures for me today!

Viking Lutheran Church is five miles away from the corner where we begin hiking and we plan to take our first rest stop there. As soon as we start it seems to me that I am actually able to see the steeple of the small church. There isn't much else to fixate on, since we don't know enough about sugar beets to discourse intelligently on variations in the appearance of the fields. We try to judge when cars are even with the white point we are watching, and to time how long they take to pass us, but the results are inconsistent. Sure enough, after a while the white point is revealed to be attached to a white rectangle. Then we can begin to make out the shapes of the windows, and soon we are indeed resting on the cement stoop. I've often watched the grain elevators as I approached a prairie town, from even farther away than five miles, but they are both large and tall. To track our progress visually to this small guiding steeple seems fantastic, even in this flat land.

The next three days, as we backpack the Grasslands, are everything we had hoped for. Indeed, we enter a region of small regular hills, covered with grasses and some clumps of trees. Armed with our knowledge from George it's easy to see that these were bare sand dunes a mere 70 years ago. There are posts with the blue blazes on them placed every so often to demarcate the trail.

Bright purple spikes of Rough Blazing Star shine amid the yellow Leafy Spurge. The Spurge should probably be renamed "Scourge." This alien plant is a serious problem on the prairie. It invades and crowds out everything else. Cattle won't eat it, and cattle is what North Dakota ranching is all about. There has been some success at curtailing its spread with goat herds, since they don't seem to mind the bitter plant. In fact, we meet a large flock of the goats, being herded by men on horseback. I recognize three kinds of white-leaved *Artemesia*, and Spiderwort with its distinctive three-armed leaf division. Hard-leaved Goldenrod, and purple Leadplant with fern-like leaves is also in bloom. Big Bluestem Grass shows its purplish "turkey-foot" heads. But we also encounter plants that I do not know at all. Showy Milkweed is a new variation on a familiar theme. The flowers are held in fuzzy pink clusters above broad leaves, similar to the Common Milkweed. But each blossom has long pointed petals, like a star, on twisted, recurved stalks. A huge white blossom is easy to identify as an evening-primrose with its cross-shaped stigma, but which one? It turns out to be Nuttall's Evening-Primrose. The plant with naked stems and delicate, scalloped pink bells remains unidentified.

Showy Milkweed

With a late afternoon start, after repacking gear and spotting the car, our plan is to get across Iron Spring Creek before we stop. We reach the creek at 6:15 pm. Since it has been raining steadily for hours, we are so wet that we don't even bother to remove our boots before wading across. There's no point! But just as we pick a tent site, the sun comes out. Dry clothes, and a good meal in the warm sunlight are always successful at reviving our spirits.

We are sung to sleep by the cows tonight! The Grasslands are actively used for grazing, and although they seldom come close, neither are the cattle ever very far away.

An opaque white fog hangs behind every little hill when we awake. We wait till it lifts to start hiking, thinking that we can't hike if we can't see the next post with a blaze. It's not long before we discover that we can indeed hike when we can't see the posts; it just takes longer! Twice, with no fog, we find ourselves standing at a post, longing for another blaze. Thankful that I have brought the binoculars, I search the landscape for a telltale splotch of blue until it is located. The third time that we reach the end of the visible blazes it appears that we might have a real problem. We have considered ourselves lucky to find this blaze, since it is lying on the ground, surrounded by curious cows. A swift search of the horizon does not bring any blue into view. We ask the cows where the next blaze is, but they don't know... or at any rate, they aren't telling. Now a *careful* search of the horizon still does not bring any blue into view. So we begin hunting behind clumps of trees and shrubs. Still no blaze. Finally, I find one far to the right, but I suspect that this blaze defines where we have come from rather than where we want to go. I'm nearly ready to go check it out, when Marie calls from the far side of some trees, "Come over here, and bring the binoculars." Sure enough, from this new, higher location, she has spotted one, far across a valley. We have no idea how the trail is supposed to reach it, but we bet it is not by the straight but uneven path we take. The cows are probably still laughing at the practical joke they have played on the silly bipeds.

This afternoon we reach the western, flat portion of the Grasslands. Here the Forest Service, which oversees National Grasslands, has built a treadway just for the North Country Trail. For miles and miles, there is now a graveled path marked with branded posts which are eight feet tall. There is no chance of losing the way here!

Life with the cows is interesting, yet never frightening despite their large size. There are occasional fences, and whenever the trail needs to pass through one there is a gate which lifts, with a counterweight system

Water from an artesian well

which automatically closes it behind us. Water is provided for the cattle by wells with storage tanks beside them. There are two kinds of these wells. Most are pumped by traditional farm windmills. But a few of the wells are artesian, with water bubbling free from a standpipe in the middle of a concrete tank. We filter the water from the windmill tanks. But at the artesian wells, I wade out to the pipe and fill the bottles directly from the flowing groundwater. The water is so cold that my hand is numb before the bottles are full! The cows themselves are certainly not the friendly beasts of small-herd farms. Mostly they cast a wary eye our way and collectively wander just a bit farther off. Only a few times, including when the group stole the trail markers, are we approached with what I consider typical bovine curiosity.

As much as we complained about the rain on our first day, we complain about the sun the rest of the time! The temperature soars to over 100° both of our remaining days among the cows. On this flat western section, there are very few trees as compared to the east. We take our rest stops where we can somehow rig Marie's bright orange plastic poncho to serve as an awning. Taking it out at each stop and devising a way to suspend it between ourselves and the sun is a bother and requires a lot of creativity from overheated brains, but we keep doing it because it's astonishing how much difference there is in temperature immediately after placing that thin plastic between ourselves and the sun. Sometimes, when it's time to get out the plastic, which Marie keeps in the top pocket of her pack, it is so hot that she can hardly touch it. At one stop Marie crams one corner of the poncho into a crack in a post, and braces another corner on her hiking stick. We huddle beneath it, holding the front corners. We have to hold them, because there is a good breeze (hot, of course). We feel as if we are sailing a ship with an orange mainsail across the prairie!

Much to my delight we actually have to wait for a long Soo Line train to rumble across our pathway. On the other hand, I am disappointed that the Western Prairie Fringed Orchid has already completed its blooming for this year. This is an endangered plant, and the Sheyenne Grasslands are home to the largest remaining population. I'll have to come another year to see the showy white blooms. We do find Purple Prairie Clover, Blue Vervain, the Gray-headed Coneflower which is yellow, and Red-top Grass – a veritable rainbow of plants.

Wildlife encounters of note are a Sandhill Crane with six babies, and a White-tailed Jackrabbit.

With such a clear pathway to follow now, we fairly dance across the prairie. Our dance steps? The Cow-Pie Sidle, The Poison-Ivy Swing, and The Mosquito Swat. We are highly motivated by thoughts of tall glasses of ice tea, with which we reward ourselves in Lisbon.

Also as reward is a motel room for the night, because we want to attend church in the morning and then go to the Ransom County Fair. Just as we are getting settled in our room, cars begin arriving, lots of cars! People are pulling out chairs and setting them up beside the road. It must be a parade! And it is just that, a genuine, homegrown parade. Most of the floats are celebrating 100 years of 4-H Clubs, and 50 years of Ransom County Fairs, with various cardboard birthday cakes. It would be easy to characterize these displays as amateurish and unsophisticated. But that would not only make me a snob, it would also be evidence that I have lost my small-town roots. What I see in reality is a parade as parades were meant to be. The local dignitaries, people who have the courage to try to lead their neighbors and relatives, are at the front. Behind them, most of the town's children enthusiastically celebrate their interests and talents. The school band plays with gusto. Kids have worked hard to represent things which are important to them: farming skills, crafts, gardening, safety and reading. Their parents and grandparents wave and cheer from the curbs, encouraging the next generation to find an identity in their Ransom County heritage.

Marie wakes me in the morning with the offer, "If you have your pajamas off by 8:00 you can have them washed." That's hard to pass up, even from a comfortable bed, and at 7:58 I manage to get into some clothes. Church and laundromat occupy the early morning, but then we do head for the Fair. First on our list of events to see is one called Team Penning. We have had to admit sheepishly that we don't have a clue as to what kind of activity this might be. This admission gets us a bit of an explanation from a shopkeeper, but the reality is much more thrilling. Team Penning is such a familiar part of life in the Dakotas that people have a hard time explaining it to strangers. So we have to go see it for ourselves.

We head for the corral, and take seats on a set of wooden bleachers in the full sun. Pretty soon, eight people arrive carrying an awning stretched on a frame. They plop it down over the bleachers, and we all have a good laugh because now we are in the shade, but the front of the awning is so low that we can't see across the corral. The eight people disappear again and return with cement blocks to prop up the front legs and lift the obstructing canvas.

Over the next few hours we watch 17 rounds of Team Penning, so I'll try to explain it here, in case you are not from ranch country. The teams are groups of three people. We first assumed that these people knew each other and entered the event together, but that is not the case. Each person enters the event individually and the teams are chosen at random within the various divisions. Each team member must be dressed in a cowboy shirt with no ragged seams or cut-off sleeves, a cowboy hat, and western boots. Pants are not optional, but are apparently not so strictly regulated. And each team member is mounted on a horse. In addition to the team members, there are two other mounted individuals, the handlers. At one end of the corral the three mounted team members wait. At the other end the two handlers keep 21 calves huddled into a tight herd. Each calf wears a large number on its side. There are three of each of the numbers from 0-6.

When the calves are tightly herded, on our side of the corral a man sitting in the back of a pick-up truck raises a flag. At that point the announcer declares, "Flag's up; you may advance." The riders begin riding toward the calves. When they are about halfway, the announcer calls out one of the numbers, 0 through 6. (If any rider has lost his or her hat before the number is called, that person is disqualified!) Once the number is called, the action begins! The handlers quickly retreat, and the team must separate out the three calves with the announced number. These calves are to be chased back to the other end of the corral where there is a small pen with a gate. The three calves, and only those three, must be shut into that pen. And this is to all be done in the space of 90 seconds!

We watch beginner divisions, youth (many of whom are definitely not beginners), and some more experienced contestants. Not all of the teams manage to get all three of their calves in the pen. Some do. The best time, up until we get hungry and wander off to find food, is 43 seconds. See how much can be accomplished in less than a minute! It's a fascinating view of life in cattle country. This is not a sport which is played for its own sake, such as basketball or soccer, or most other sports we enjoy. These are skills that people use in their everyday lives, rounding up and cutting out cattle from the herds.

We are thinking that in beef country we'll be able to enjoy a good beef barbeque sandwich. Much to our

A Team Penning contestant

surprise, every food concession is selling pork. Pulled pork on a bun, pork barbeque, sliced pork, but no beef! Maybe ranchers are sick of beef, and want something different at the Fair.

The exhibition hall is filled with beautiful displays of vegetables, sheaves of wheat, massive sunflower heads, pickles, pies, cookies, canned peaches, needlecrafts and more. The 4-H and Future Farmers of America have entire sections exhibiting the education of the younger generation in the prairie way of life. Photography, basic welding projects and crafts are interspersed with displays comparing various grains and their uses, or results from test plots of new seed strains.

And we can't pass up the barns. First we check out the small animals. Cages of geese, ducks, rabbits and chickens of all colors and varieties line the walls. One girl, about sixteen years old, is holding an odd-looking hen. The chicken's feathers are all curly, twisting every which way, including feathers on its legs and feet. "It's a Frizzle Hen," the girl explains. "You can't let them stay outside in the winter because their feathers freeze, and they die." She tells us that about 20 of the animals there are hers, and we note that many of the cages she points to sport blue and red ribbons.

In the large animal buildings we check out the pigs, goats and sheep. Three silly sheep refuse to eat the food provided for them in the building, but have stuck their heads through a loose board so that they can eat the green grass outside the building. They know that grass is greener on the other side of the fence! I'm always interested in cattle, or beef as they seem to be called around here. Most are Simmental, Charolais, Black and Red Angus. We come to a whole line of cows that are marked like Hampshire pigs... the black ones with the white band around their middle. I've seen a few of these cows in my lifetime, but never knew what they were. Most of them are being exhibited by members of the Beuling family, but I can't find the name of the breed. At the end of the line of stalls is a skinny teenager with a pitchfork. I ask him if this is his cow, and he replies affirmatively. So I ask him what kind of cow it is. He says some word that doesn't compute, so I have to ask him again. Suddenly, I get it! "That's your name!" I exclaim, as my brain finally processes the word Beulingo (byou-LIN-go).

"Yup," he replies, looking almost shy. "My great-great-great grandfather developed the breed."

We've observed quite a bit of pride in the local ranching culture this weekend, with participants of all ages. It looks to us like Ransom County will not lose all its young people to the big city.

After the Fair we head back to Ft. Ransom State Park to set up our basecamp again. We also stop at the grocery store. One of our purchases is lefse (LEF-suh), a thin round bread, very much like a tortilla, but made of potato. We really like finding regional foods to sample, and neither of us has seen lefse before. There are even suggestions on the package as to how to use them. Number one on the list is to stuff with lutefisk (LOO-te-fisk). Now, no offense to my Scandinavian friends, but I don't think I could eat lutefisk if I were being held at gunpoint. In the first place, I'm not all that fond of fish. In the second place, I know what lutefisk is. No one really knows how it was invented, which mostly means that it's open season for fantastic speculation. The most famous tall tale has it that the Irish sabotaged and ruined the Norwegians' fish, but the Norwegians ate it anyway, and stole all the Irish potatoes to go with it. St. Patrick damned the Norwegians to hell, and it worked, because they all moved to Minnesota! The actual recipe is no help at keeping the conversation rational, either. Take several pounds of dried fish, soak it for four days, add lye (yes, as in drain cleaner and rat poison), soak three more days, then it is ready to cook. Boil the rotten mess until it is a gelatinous mass that can be eaten – lutefisk. I just can't do it!

Marie says, "I don't think they use rotten fish any more." Doesn't matter, I can't do it. Fortunately the list of suggestions continues with hamburger, wieners, cheese, fruit, etc. We buy bacon, cheese, and cherry tomatoes for our stuffings, which turn out to be a tasty selection.

On Monday, we are back on country roads again. Our first encounter is with a friendly, black, mixed-breed shepherd dog who comes out to see if we need herding up. We don't, but the owner, a wrinkled man in the ubiquitous plaid shirt and cowboy hat, hollers, "Are you out for a jaunt?"

"We're walking to Lisbon," we reply, already anticipating some unusual response.

Our cowboy doesn't quite roll his eyes. He's a man who puts good solid rural pauses between his sentences, so as to be sure that he's not being hasty. "Taking the other bridge, I guess?"

"Yes," we acknowledge.

A long pause, "It's shorter on the highway."

We admit that we know that, but we want to take the back way. He wishes us well, and calls the dog. We have to give him credit. He never once asks us why we are walking, or even why we want to take the long way. Maybe he has already decided that women are just too difficult to fathom anyway, so there is no point in asking.

After we cross the bridge and turn the corner to the west, in another mile we are passed by a man on a tractor pulling a manure spreader. We wave, and he waves back. Soon he comes back, having left his load on some field behind us. This is repeated, and a third time he heads out with a full load. It's getting to be lunch time, and we would like to find some shade to rest in. We've been watching where the tractor turns in; it's the only farm for miles around, and thus the only shade, where some trees flank the driveway. We decide to take our break along this edge; surely the friendly farmer won't mind. So when he returns again, he finds us spreading out our lunch underneath his trees. He stops the tractor to chat with us. And he is as friendly as we had suspected, even more so! His wife pops out on the porch of the house, far up the long driveway. She is wondering why he has stopped. He waves for her to come. She practically runs down the drive; she has seen us in the grass and thinks that someone is hurt.

It turns out that the reality, in her mind, is even worse than any injury. We are about to eat PEANUT BUTTER for lunch! This is totally unacceptable. We have to come in and have lunch with them. I protest; we always lose so much time when we allow ourselves to be swept off the trail. But she tempts us with "hotdogs, fresh tomatoes, homemade pickles, and applesauce. I just made the applesauce this morning." That does it; we are about to be well-fed.

We enter the kitchen and Shirley immediately apologizes. "The house is a mess! I'm in the middle of cabbage." Of course, the house is spotless, but there are ten cabbages the size of basketballs stacked neatly on the kitchen counter. The table is already set for two. Our hosts, Shirley and Larry Baarson, make it a regular habit to sit down at the table for lunch, so with the speedy addition of some plates and silverware, they are ready for us to join them.

The hot dogs turn out to be some kind of quality sausage, not just cheap picnic fare. The fresh tomatoes from the garden are scarlet, ripe, and Shirley has even peeled them. She apologizes once more, this time for not having buns for the sausages. Instead she offers homemade bread! We certainly don't mind that exchange. The applesauce comes in a bowl the size of half a beach ball. That was her morning project. If you have ever made home-made applesauce you will realize how many apples she must have peeled to fill this bowl with sauce, which is bigger than any bowl I even own! "Oh, these are just the 'drops.' We haven't even started picking good apples yet," Shirley mentions casually. I am mightily impressed with anyone who can cheerfully work through a morning full of applesauce, invite company in for lunch, and still face ten cabbage basketballs in the afternoon.

Larry describes himself as "just a hobby farmer," meaning that his ranch is smaller than one that would be self-supporting. He also owns one of the four hardware stores in town. For a town the size of Lisbon to be able to support four hardwares tells you a lot about life here, in case you had missed noticing the fields of corn and beans. Yet his forays with the manure spreader had taken him more than a mile from the barn. Some hobby!

Larry cares for about 80 head of beef. "How often do you need to check on them?" asks Marie.

"About every three days we go to check them for hoof rot and pinkeye," Larry explains. He tells us that if they find either condition in a cow they must give it a shot of medicine. The syringe is mounted on the end of a six-foot pole. A long string is attached to the frighteningly large needle. To use the contraption, you must get within six feet of one of the semi-wild animals. Then you poke it in the rump. Of course the critter bolts, and the 20cc syringe, which is spring loaded, injects the medicine. The needle pulls off, remaining in the animal, but then the string, which you have also held on to tightly with the stick, pulls the needle out and you can retrieve it. It sounds pretty complicated, but Larry says it's quite easy... once. The problem is that the dose for hoof rot is 40cc's. Even cows are smart enough to try to avoid that injustice twice!

After an hour, filled with wonderful food and farm tales, we admit that we really have to leave. Filled as well is the extra space in our day packs. Shirley has begged us to take as many of the remaining Yellow Transparent Apples as we are willing to carry.

Tuesday we join the Sheyenne River National Scenic Byway, which we follow for the next four days, and about 60 miles, all the way to Valley City. Although this is a road walk, it is a beautiful route. As I have said, the Sheyenne is old, and meandering. Hills, 100 feet high, rise to the level of the prairie on each side of the waterway. Occasional homesteads and ranches, both busy modern operations, and abandoned, weathered failures, dot the valley. The flavor is Western; we keep expecting to see Roy Rogers and Dale Evans ride over the crest of every hill.

We eat lunch one day at the Theodore P. Slattum cabin. Slattum came to the Sheyenne Valley from Norway in 1836 with an ox team and $40. He built this cabin in the Scandinavian style with squared logs and neatly dovetailed joints at the corner. Slattum worked hard, never borrowed money, yet eventually become the most extensive landowner in the valley. He also married and had nine children. The most amazing part of the story to me is that he never built another house or an addition on the cabin. All eleven members of his family lived in a one-room log cabin with a sleeping loft. The children were probably glad to go work in the fields or barn, just to get some space in which to breathe!

For a few miles the trail leaves the Byway, but still follows the course of the Sheyenne, as there are a few off-road miles through the village of Fort Ransom, and the State

Theodore P. Slattum cabin

Park, on the west side of the river. We are amazed to find a ski area there too! Well, if that river bluff is the highest hill, and you have lots of snow in season, why not? Within the park the trail passes the Sunne Demonstration Farm, a working homestead in the historic Scandinavian tradition. Just past the park a friendly property owner allows the trail to continue on his land and it's a rip-snortin' good thing he does, because a hiker needs some way to cross back to the east side of the river. The rancher has built his own sturdy suspension footbridge, no cheap cobbled-together weekend project, but a bit of an engineering marvel for a private endeavor, to return us to his driveway and then to the Byway.

Monuments to the sod-buster's way of life, atop ridge after ridge is parked an antique reaper, looking much like some prehistoric sniffer of the plains.

Kathryn, ND, is a town that the railroad has abandoned. But the grain elevators and accompanying outbuildings along the tracks occupy a footprint almost equal to the rest of the village. This must be the local collection point for miles around. So the elevator still operates, but now all the produce of the plains is moved by truck. A small café still serves wonderful food, and we are there so often that we get to be friends with the regulars, after they get past that initial shock of two women walking through their ordered lives. The café also sells homemade lefse. The homemade version, like good bread, is infinitely better than the packaged kind. They are larger and softer, and they come with better suggested fillings. Although the dreaded lutefisk is at the top of one lady's list, we are also told "the Waldheim Lutheran Church is serving them this weekend with turkey." Another woman says her favorite is to spread them with butter and sprinkle that with sugar, and the next volunteer favors just butter.

We pass another historic cabin that had been the recreation facility for the men who worked in the nearby mill. A field of alfalfa in bloom scents the air with its glorious sweet fragrance, a nice counterpoint to the primary theme of curing hay. We speculate on the size of the individual ranches. One layout includes a field of about 20 acres which is used exclusively for storing the large round hay bales. By their colors we can chronicle four years' history of the bales. Trucks are bringing additions to the rows of fresh golden rounds as we hike by. How many acres of hay are required to fill this much space with bales? How many beef would that much hay feed? How many more acres are needed to pasture those beef in the summer months? We don't know, but we bet the answer is somewhere in the vicinity of "lots."

We continue northward. On our left, not crossing the river, but spanning some small tributary is an unusual through-truss bridge. We try to get to it for a closer look, but it turns out to be on private land – odd for such a highway-sized structure.

The former King School has been bought by a woman who was a student there when it was a two-room schoolhouse in the not so distant past. She has made it into a nice craft store, and the entrance hall is a mini-museum of school history.

We see a hawk I never have identified, and hear a small owl. A six-inch salamander scurries across the road. I thought this one would be easy to find in a field guide, since it appears to be a distinctive blue. But long-distance ID's never work well, so there are still mysteries of the zoological variety to be solved.

People are very friendly. We invent a game to award one person a day with the "Motorist Congeniality Award." Winners include the driver who slows way down as he passes us on the loose gravel so that no stone is projected as a lethal weapon by his tires. Another day a man puts his whole arm and shoulder out the window, waving violently as if we are his long-lost relatives. I personally am happy to grant the award to a road grader which does not run over me as we meet at the crest of a gravel hill while I am bicycling. We learn that the people least likely to wave at us are little old ladies. We wonder if they are frightened of us, or if they think we should be home making pickles and applesauce. But one day, a small gray-haired woman wins our award for waving at us before we wave at her.

Thursday afternoon Marie is waiting for me to return with the car when a woman pulls her car up and declares, "I have to know what you are doing!" Marie goes through the explanation again.

This lady, whose name is Norma, immediately calls the local newspaper, and then emphatically urges us to visit her on Saturday. "You have to come see my Indian Calendar!" she exclaims. Marie is struggling to make sense of this invitation, envisioning a paper wall calendar with photographs of Indians, and wondering why it is so special that we would want to come see it. Norma talks on, speaking of solstices and equinoxes.

Suddenly Marie understands that Norma is speaking of stones laid on the ground, and exclaims, "We saw the one in Valley City!"

"Yes, but they had the help of astrophysicists to lay that one out. Mine is real," Norma continues. "Come on over." Extracting a tentative promise from Marie that we will consider this offer, Norma drives away.

Three men and a teenage girl are working hard to clear a field a half-mile long of the fresh round hay bales before a rain storm hits. A tractor lifts the bales to the back of one truck. The girl drives to the next bale, as does the tractor, and they load that golden cylinder. Just then the second truck arrives, back from its trip to the storage location. Apparently the girl is not licensed to drive on the road, because she quickly hops out of the full truck and switches to the empty one, while the other driver heads for the road with the full one. These four people had been working on this field when we spotted the car in the morning, and they are just finishing as we hike past, hours later.

Most of the Byway is lumpy large gravel. We are happy but footsore, and our minds turn to the tales from the Baarson farm. We had asked Larry how he gets close enough to the cows to tell if they have hoof rot. "You don't have to get close," he explained. "It makes them limp." Maybe we have hoof rot too!

Friday, we reach the planet Pluto, in Valley City, where we connect with the city trail miles which we have walked during the conference. We have completed the hiking miles of this adventure.

But on Saturday we search out Norma and her calendar. Much to our surprise, the truss bridge we had noticed is on her property. It's one of the three remaining Pin-connected Pratt through-truss bridges in North Dakota. Formerly it was the highway bridge north of Kathryn, and when that structure was replaced Norma's family bought it rather than have it destroyed!

"Can we get to the calendar in sneakers?" I ask.

"No problem," Norma cheerfully exclaims, "we're driving." More quickly than we can react, she leaps on a four-wheeler, and heads down a farm lane. We follow in the car as soon as we recover from the surprise. Before many minutes have passed, we are driving over the very bridge that I have been curious about. Then we turn and climb the hill on the west side of the Sheyenne River; now we are just driving off-road – it's fun!

At the top we stop and walk to the middle of a broad flat hilltop strewn with rocks. Marie and I are not sure what to think. We don't want to act skeptical, but it's hard to imagine that these scattered boulders and cobbles mean anything. Then again, we certainly don't know what an ancient Indian calendar should look like. Looking around, we first realize that there are only two hills anywhere within sight which have such rocks, and they are the one we are on, and a small adjacent one. Norma says, "I've spent a lot of time up here, over quite a few years, trying to figure out if these rocks have any meaning." She suggests that we sit down and just look around for a while. Soon we do begin to realize that many of the rocks are aligned. One might believe that three rocks could naturally appear to be in a straight line, but soon we realize that there are sets of five, six, or even eight aligned stones. Some of them alternate large rocks with small ones. Several large boulders have smaller stones placed part way around them, looking very much like stone paw prints.

Norma points out a long line, oriented north-south. This feature is clearly obvious with almost 20 rocks. She indicates another line which she says marks the summer solstice sunrise, and another for the winter solstice sunset. "I haven't figured out some of the lines, even yet," adds Norma. "But it's a mystical place. Can't you just feel it?" She continues, telling us that she has had the site assessed by experts. They have not been willing to go so far as to call it a calendar, but have labeled it as an "Ancient Rock Alignment" (probably the term for a calendar discovered by an amateur). A grave and skeleton, holding an atl-atl, a dart thrower, were also found on the property, verifying Native American settlement of the area. These have been attributed to the Woodland Period, 1500-2000 years ago, predating the cultures that built the medicine wheels. One of the lines seems to point to the adjacent hill. "I haven't even begun exploring that one," Norma concludes. We spend almost an hour on the hill soaking in the history of the place. I begin to discern the silhouette of a buffalo outlined by the rocks on the far hill. A light breeze rustles the grass and prairie flowers, or is it the moccasined feet of a dark-haired, young girl?

We have promised to return to the J&S Café for a breakfast appointment. One of Shirley's Scouts has applied to be a part of Wider Opportunities, a backpacking adventure in Yosemite. The girl's name is J.C., and she also works as a waitress in the café. So between customers, at Shirley's request, we demonstrate all our gear, and talk with them about backpacking. Of course, this means that everyone else who has come to J&S for breakfast is also getting a lesson on backpacking. We hope they enjoy it, because there is no escaping our piles of equipment and J.C.'s enthusiasm. When we are finally done Jim makes us promise to stop in one more time before we leave to say goodbye.

On our last morning in camp we get up at our leisure and cook a huge camp breakfast of bacon, eggs and toast.

There is yet one piece of nearby off-road North Country Trail. North Dakota has one State Forest, and it has 1.5 miles of trail which is not connected to any other piece of trail, but we want to see it. It's a nice walk, over an oak ridge, through a refreshing island of trees in this landscape of long fields, with long views of the now familiar Sheyenne Valley. We've learned some history, heard some legends, seen the culture, experienced the weather, and made some friends.

Back in camp we enjoy an afternoon nap. Marie builds the cooking fire, and drags the cook out of bed. Dinner is our favorite slow-cooked bean soup with cornbread, followed by a quiet evening of mulling over the events of the hike.

Morning comes all too soon, and we begin the always depressing task of breaking camp and leaving. "Strange how that comes immediately after the first day of the trip," sighs Marie.

131 miles this hike
Fort Abercrombie to Valley City, ND
2153 total NCT miles

The Princess and the P's
65 - December 9-11, 2002

The first "P" is people; that would be Irene and I. "P's" two and three are Irene's dogs, Pearl, and Perfect Sandy Fe. The Princess is Maggie whose pea under the mattress is camping.

Since she's not supposed to carry a pack with her bad hips, it's just as well that she doesn't really like camping out. That way I don't feel guilty when I leave her behind on long trips. She likes day hikes, but none of this getting wet and cold, please and thank you, and she especially doesn't want to stay outside at night. Most of my friends aren't fond of camping in December any more than the pup, so Irene has offered to pay for a motel. We can all sleep in comfort but still walk some miles during the days.

Maggie and Sandy are friends from former trips,[1] but now there is also a large young upstart, Pearl. Three happy dogs in one space can be a little overwhelming.

We leave from my house on a Monday morning after a weekend of NCTA duties, Board and committee meetings. Irene gets Pearl and Sandy loaded in her truck, and Maggie settles in to her favorite chair. She's ready to have some quiet time after a day of wrestling with two Golden Retrievers. I clip her leash to her collar and pull her out of the recliner. She takes one step on the floor and leaps to the couch, spilling the water dish that I am holding in my left hand. I pull her off the couch and she races to the other chair. Finally, I pull her out the door to my car. But she doesn't have a clue that the other dogs are traveling parallel to us, and is quite surprised and grumpy when they suddenly appear at our destination.

Of course, once we are on the trail they all just run around like crazy things and apparently have a wonderful time.

Irene has made a reservation for us at "The Whimpering Thighs Motel" in Manton, MI. She claims this is a huge chain of establishments and there is one to be found in every trail town. This one allows dogs, with which we are amply blessed.

The snow is about six inches deep, not deep enough for snowshoes, but just deep enough to be annoying to walk in. Driving through it seems to me to be no big deal; every road we follow has been heavily snowmobiled, if not plowed. Irene, however, gets nervous on snow-covered roads and now claims that my memory is faulty. "Baloney," she later blustered, "that was no road at all." She quit smoking 20 years ago, but as we drive in to the US 131 Campground

---

[1] See Chapter 60: "Philomathic Deipnosophists"

(through white and crunchy well-packed ruts) she keeps claiming, "I need a cigarette."

For the first part of day one, we follow the high banks of the Manistee River. Small ice floes are riding high on the water and it is easy to see how fast the water is moving. It probably moves that fast in the summer too, but with nothing for the eye to follow I've never observed it before. The sun comes out and sparkles on the water. At one point we can look upstream and see three meanders of the river all at one time. We pass through a field of baby Balsam Fir, all about waist height, regaling us with their sharp aroma.

We have worked out a plan so that Irene can walk shorter days than I. She has a sore hip, and is content to walk four or five miles and leave the insanity to me. So we spot one car where she wants to quit each day, and then she and the dogs (who also don't need long, long walks in wet snow) later go to where I will finish for the day and wait for me there.

The crisp odor of cold autumn duff, lightly scuffed under the snow, with a hint of wood smoke, recalls for me, with a sweet pang of times long past, my dad's hunting clothes when he came in from a morning in the woods.

Not knowing quite how far I might make it this afternoon, I tie a colored string on a bush whenever I pass a road crossing. Irene checks the crossings until she is ahead of me. I walk nine miles even with a late start and the snow.

The next day is mostly on back-woods roads of varying use levels. Again, Irene hikes half the day and then waits for me. By this method she misses the most beautiful section, along Twenty-Two Creek. The trail approaches the steep-sided ravine, then angles down to water level with the sun shining on the snow and trees across the way. The temperature is mild enough that I need only a long-sleeved shirt on my upper body.

Wednesday is the prettiest day of hiking. The topography is small, rolling, wooded hills. The weather is so warm that the snow is heavy and difficult to walk through, but it's hard to complain since we are more than happy to leave the mile-square roads behind. We pass by a wetland just below us on the right. Growing there are oddly mixed conifers, Black Spruce, White Pine, White Cedar and Balsam Fir. Soon we pass through an old clearcut, filling in quickly with maple and aspen saplings.

I end the day on a long straight road walk, but it includes passing by Manistee Lake. The lake is frozen, and there is a light dusting of fluffy snow on its surface, a large crêpe sprinkled with powdered sugar. I finish with a section of the Shore-to-Shore Riding Trail, finally reaching a mile closed to vehicles, and lined with cedars, balsam and aspen. Occasional clumps of the red seeds of Virginia Creeper, and the silky puffs of Old Man's Beard dot the brushy edges.

Irene is waiting for me just at the west side of the Boardman River. This is where Marie and I began "The Kernel," now so many years ago. That hike began here, rather than farther east, because there was no bridge. Today I will end with that crossing; if I have to wade, at least there will be a warm vehicle waiting for me. But since 1991 a bridge has been built, and I'm not sorry. I can pass up an adventure of the wet, cold variety.

Pearl, Princess Maggie, and Perfect Sandy Fe

Nights at a motel made this a perfect trip for a Princess and her entourage. The humans were not forced to bed by darkness at 5 pm like naughty children. Maggie recovered from her grumpy start. She and Pearl playfully wrestled and wrestled and would stop only when we people finally said, "Enough." Perfect Sandy Fe watched the frivolities, but chose to act more dignified. The four-legged girls lined up at the storm door waiting in anticipation when we loaded the vehicles. The picture is lousy, but their eagerness is hard to escape. At night, the Princess slept well, taking up as much of the bed as possible. I guess there was no pea under the mattress.

30 miles this hike
Townline Road to Brown Bridge
and Starvation Lake Road to
Darragh
Kalkaska and Grand Traverse
Counties, MI
2183 total NCT miles

Non-Coin-Operated Amusement Devices
66 - May 10-17, 2003

As an inventory item, the city of Ann Arbor, MI, lists canoes as "non-coin-operated amusement devices." This hike has nothing to do with Ann Arbor, but it has a lot to do with canoes. In fact, it has a lot more to do with canoes than hiking, but I did cover some new miles of the Trail. I can't even claim to have hiked all of them. Some of them were crawled, while pushing a heavy pair of loppers ahead of me.

Well-meaning friends keep telling me that the Kekekabic Trail is incredibly remote. They warn me that I'll need to be unusually prepared to backpack through the Boundary Waters Canoe Area Wilderness (BWCAW). There is no way I can assess their concern versus my ordinary preparations and precautions. Do I need somehow to increase the level of advance planning, or are my eager advisors projecting their own fears?

The American Hiking Society (AHS) runs a program known as Volunteer Vacations (VV), which plans trips to many locations around the country. People sign up with AHS to participate and work on trails. There is one VV planned for work on the Kekekabic Trail in early spring, aiming to be late enough that the ice is out of the lakes, but early enough to beat the black fly hatch. I figure that several days on the trail with other people and an experienced guide should give me a lot of valuable information about the reality of conditions in the Minnesota northwoods of the Superior National Forest. Most Volunteer Vacations are ranked as easy or moderate. This one is moderate to difficult, which appeals to me as well.

When we receive our participant list I discover that there is one other person from Michigan who is going, and that I've actually met him. That person is Lyle Bialk, of the Tittabawassee Chapter of the NCTA, and we agree to meet and drive to Minnesota together. Trail people always can find things to discuss, even if they are just getting acquainted. I think that I am starting out after very little sleep, only four hours, but Lyle is an Emergency Medical Technician, and he was called out twice during the night just past, so he wins with only one hour. We are a great pair to be driving!

Nevertheless, we arrive safely at the Ranger Station in Grand Marais, Minnesota, on Saturday afternoon. We are a little late, and everyone else is diligently struggling to turn new leather gloves wrong side out. "They are more comfortable if the seams don't rub on your fingers," explains Derrick Passe, our group leader. Each pair has a 3"x4" warning tag attached, proclaiming in small print such interesting information as: "These gloves approved for use in helicopters." Or,

"These gloves are approved for firefighting only if the user is aware that they will not protect if the hand is placed in an open fire." To the best of our knowledge we aren't planning on needing either of these kinds of protection; we just hope that they are approved for grabbing berry bushes and hand tools.

After a hearty pizza dinner at the famed Sven & Ole's, we all head north on the romantic-sounding Gunflint Trail. This former backwoods "trail" is now an ordinary paved road leading to upscale resorts, and in fact we are headed for one ourselves, Gunflint Lodge. The genuine backwoodsman might find modern visitors to the forest a bit difficult to fathom. The first guest I spy is a woman wearing purple stretch pants and a knee-length, fake leopard-fur coat, holding a fishing rod and smoking a cigarette.

We settle in the lounge which is decorated with mounted Moose and deer heads, Ojibway dolls, a Voyageur diorama, and logging tools. There are large overstuffed chairs and sofas, but they are spread a little too far apart for easy dialogue. We are seven strangers thrust into each other's company, with only our disconnected histories to offer. Bob is a lawyer from Virginia. Paul, from Pennsylvania, is an instrument technician at Three-Mile Island. Julia, also from Pennsylvania, is retired, and Claire is a book buyer for a large Canadian chain store. Lyle you have met, and Derrick our leader is an engineer from Minneapolis. After basic introductions we seem to find it difficult to proceed down any conversational road.

Eventually someone suggests that it would be good to have time to check our gear, and Derrick shows us to our bunkhouse. In addition to the comfortable, expensive rooms for the tourists, the resort also has more rustic accommodations which they are letting the work crew use for free. Neither the screen nor the outside door of the girls' quarters closes properly. Although we are fortified with knowledge when Derrick tells us that a rogue bear has been raiding the trash cans, Julia is not calmed!

Sunday morning we gather at Round Lake where we will enter the Boundary Waters. No one has thought about who will canoe together, so we begin to sort ourselves by experience level. By this method Bob and Julia make a pair, bow and stern, also Paul and Lyle, then Claire and I. The weather is gray and ominous with misty rain. Forest Service rangers have brought our tools. One ranger goes over more safety rules with us, in addition to the advice we received from the glove tags, and then announces, "The wind is supposed to gust to 45 mph today, and there are small craft advisories posted. Have fun!"

We put in, and paddle easily across to our first portage. Derrick has told us that he wants to move quickly over the portages, because we have nine of them to do today. Some of us did not yet appreciate just what he had in mind. What he wants is for us to accomplish each crossing with only one trip. One real advantage of canoe camping is that usually you do not need to pack so lightly as you do for backpacking. I knew ahead of time that there were a lot of portages, so I chose to pack light anyway, and bought a new, bright yellow dry bag with shoulder straps to stuff it all in: total, 35 pounds. Claire, my canoe partner, had signed up at the last minute. Unable to borrow a small tent, she packed the one she had and everything else she wanted in a huge pack, about 60 pounds worth!

However, we are now standing at the beginning of a 130-rod portage, four-long-tenths of a mile, and we need to decide how to get everything to West Round Lake in one load. Claire's pack is a normal one which sticks up above her head so that it can't be worn while carrying a canoe. Thus, the obvious solution is that one person will carry my pack and the canoe, and the other person will take Claire's pack, the life vests, paddles, and a small dry bag which holds cameras and snacks. I take the first turn with the canoe. With the yellow bag on my back, Claire lifts one end of the overturned canoe. I duck underneath, ease my shoulders into the yoke, and lift with my legs. It's a pretty hefty load for someone my size, 75 pounds or so, but as long as I don't lose my balance I should be o.k. Claire manages to get all the oddments strung on her appendages and we head down the portage trail. Everyone else has had to resolve essentially the same sorting dilemma that we did, but we all arrive at West Round Lake, shaking only slightly. Derrick breaks his own rule, but we forgive him, because in the same time that we all make one trip, he makes two. First he carries over his own canoe and gear, then returns for the bags with all the heavy tools and the group food.

We are looking forward to a nice paddle for relief from the portage, but we quickly notice that West Round is about the size of a swimming pool, so we barely wet the paddles before we are back out, switching roles, and portaging to Edith Lake. I have visions of the trip with Claire's pack being easier, but with so many loose items to juggle, it's really just as difficult as carrying the canoe. By 2 pm the weather has become downright nasty, with a wind whipping up choppy waves and a cold rain. I can't speak for everyone else, but I am starving, having had only a small granola bar since breakfast.

On Bat Lake, after seven portages, we stop at a campsite for lunch. We are protected some from the wind, but if we hadn't been so hungry we might have preferred to keep moving. Someone asks Derrick what it means that the wind is changing. "It's going to snow," he replies.

After lunch, the rain lets up, but the wind rises, and we have to paddle directly into it to round a point of land. For a period of time that seems much too long, Claire and I paddle as hard as we can, but we haven't moved at all compared with the tree I have been watching on the shore. Claire is only a little larger than I am. She and I are absolutely the two smallest people in the group. I am no wimp, and Claire is as strong as I was at her age, which is saying something. But we just don't have enough weight to keep the canoe in the water. At one point the wind lifts our entire canoe and moves it sideways about six feet. We persevere, and eventually we do turn the corner and take a different angle to the wind. At the next stop, Derrick suggests that we move the pack weight forward in the canoe, and that helps a bit.

From linear Bat Lake the next portage drops us into Gillis, 50 feet lower and rounder. Suddenly the wind is calm, there are no waves or whitecaps. Claire remarks in wonder, "It's like we walked over the hill into a different day!"

Claire goes up the stairs on the return trip

In a wilderness area low maintenance is the norm, so the portages are rough and narrow. We have to walk carefully on turns to maneuver the prow of the canoe between trees which are close to the trail. Some of the portages are relatively flat, but two have bad hills. Claire takes the canoe on the worst hill, but I carry it down a stairway and through a snowbank which remains in a shaded spot. She does the longest portage, but I do five and she does four. We decide that overall we have had equally difficult days. Every time I walk with the canoe and the Chubby Canary, which we have named my pack, I can't wait to take the next trip when I don't have to balance so carefully. But every time I carry the Monster Mother (Claire's pack) and all those loose items, I can't wait to trade them in for the canoe!

You can believe after this day that the bare rock on the edge of French Lake, which will be our home, looks quite luxurious. It's challenging to wedge seven tents into the area, but with four tents in regular sites, Paul behind the open latrine (with promises not to peek), Derrick practically tethered on a hillside under a tarp, and my small tent parked in a pathway, we create a tiny city. Campers in the BWCA must use designated sites, and it's not hard to comply because there are no other openings which are large enough anyway. Each site has a fire ring, and a pit toilet.

Derrick will be our cook as well as our leader, and he fixes pasta with sauce, and rice pudding, on his stove. As the shadows lengthen and the temperature drops, we all realize that a fire would feel good. Bob comments that everything is too wet, and we can't do it. Does this sound familiar?[1] Trying not to sound smug I offer, "Oh, I think I can. Let me try." Soon we are all snuggled around a warm blaze. The sun is low and the clouds begin to break up. Gradually the birch trees on the far shore commence to reflect the pink light until the entire hill is bright with alpen-glow. The loons laugh, and the peepers peep. An Osprey is fishing out over the lake, and the White-throated Sparrows sing a twilight song. Tonight there are no awkward pauses, no too-far distances between seats. We joke easily about our adventures with the wind, rain, canoes and portages, sitting side by side to soak up the warmth of the fire and of new friendships.

Monday is our first work day. After breakfast Derrick puts out a bag of granola bars and tells us to help ourselves. Thinking that we are supposed to take a morning's ration, most of us take one small bar. Travel is by canoe, of course, and we have just one short portage alongside a waterfall to enter Seahorse Lake. I am fairly amazed to discover that I am not sore from yesterday's exertions. We canoe up the eastern arm of Seahorse and beach the canoes at an access point for our goal, the Kekekabic Trail. This 38-mile trail was originally created in the 1930's for fire protection; it has always been maintained only minimally. However in 1999, fierce, straight-line winds blew through the BWCAW, felling tens of thousands of trees. Trunks were stacked like pick-up-sticks; no one could get through the pathway. At first, speculation had it that the trail would never be re-opened. But lovers of the Kek could not bear that outcome, and so the speculators were reduced to betting on how many years it would take to clear. Now the trail is open, but in the sudden sunshine saplings and berry bushes grow with the vigor of well-fed teenagers. So each spring, the Kekekabic Trail Club tries to make sure that the trail is cleared at least once. That's why we're here.

The method for the day is "leapfrog." Derrick sets down his day pack, and directs Julia to walk 20 paces up the trail, and put her pack down. Lyle goes beyond Julia, and so forth. Each person will clear to the next pack, go back and get his or her own pack and then leapfrog to the front of the line. Paul takes a large bow saw and strides ahead to find larger trees which may have fallen during the winter. The rest of us are each given a pair of long-handled loppers. They are short enough that I must bend over slightly to nip the brush off at ground level, but long enough that they are very heavy to hold out ahead of me if I squat down. Very quickly, I decide that squatting and then scooting ahead after I clear everything around me is the better choice; stooping brings on a sharp and instant backache. I long for a pair of hand-held nippers, but there aren't any to be had.

---

[1] See Chapter 41: "She Who Builds Fire"

The sun rises higher; Minnesota in May is known for hot days and cold nights. The sweat rolls down my temples and back, I clip and toss brambles and crawl forward a few feet to reach the next patch. Breakfast is long past, and the granola bar is long gone. Everyone else is feeling equally hot and empty. Derrick points out some wolf scat along the trail. Paul's handiwork is evident in fresh-cut branches. We leapfrog and lop and bend or skootch and clip. Finally, at 2 pm we reach War Club Lake. Paul has cleared several larger trees, and added logs to a small bridge. All together, the rest of us have cleared about one mile of trail.

The cool water of War Club Lake feels mighty good on hot heads and faces. Derrick mixes black bean dip in a ziploc bag, cuts off a corner and extrudes the gray result on tortillas. Everyone sniggers, and immediately gives it the slightly naughty, but absolutely accurate name of "Wolf Shit on a Shingle." Without the slightest trace of disgust we gobble down every one of those shingles. Sure tastes good! And as we hike back to the canoes we are amazed by the result of our back-breaking toil. Where there had previously been a strip of nasty brambles, now there is a wide, inviting pathway.

Claire tries her hand at paddling stern today, and with her natural strength, does a great job, even on her first try. We see a Moose, which we name Larry, grazing along the shore. For contrast, after dinner a tiny mouse scampers from the cedars, and cleans the crumbs from our boulder dining area.

Bob asks Derrick, "What does that ring around the moon mean?"

"It's going to snow," replies our leader knowingly.

Lyle and Bob clearing trail

Next day, I am smarter. I take two snacks from the grab bag, one for morning and one for afternoon. We begin with the same technique, working from Seahorse Lake to Howard Lake. Paul, Derrick and Bob spend a long time carefully cutting out a twisted tangle of trees which has fallen across the trail. But by 12:30, we've only covered a third of our hoped-for two miles of clearing, and we've noticed that Larry the Moose has been here. We all hike ahead to Howard Lake to lunch in some shade, planning to work our way back in the afternoon. Julia strikes up a conversation with some young fellows who are fishing on Howard Lake and we become the proud owners of a good-sized Perch to take home for dinner.

Most everyone else is appalled by the ticks. Me, I've done ticks before.[2] Even when Derrick claims to have found 29 of them crawling on him, I'm unimpressed.

"What do those cirrus clouds mean, Derrick?"

"It's going to snow."

For the afternoon we switch to a technique which is promptly named the "drive-by-shooting." We walk in a staggered line, facing alternate sides of the trail. Everyone clips whatever they can as they go by. This works pretty well, but forces us all into the stooped position, because we can't move quickly enough if we squat or sit. And the people at the end of the line discover that they have very little to do. While I am the caboose I just carry the loppers and spend the time picking up the clippings and getting them out of the trail.

Derrick had taken a swim the night before, and tonight he first dares the rest of us to try it, and then tries to shame us into it by telling us we stink. Several of us give it a try. We are assuredly cleaner, but "refreshing" doesn't begin to describe a northern Minnesota lake in May. Bob checks the water temperature; it's 52°. Claire makes fried falafel cakes to go with our fresh fish this evening. The food is consistently good, but I'm always hungry for more. I wonder how the big guys are getting along. Perhaps they have brought some extra food with them; I wish I had.

On Wednesday we begin by moving camp. We need to cross French Lake, paddle the length of Peter Lake, and then around a point

Campsite on Lake Gabimichigami

to the north end of the large Lake Gabimichigami. One portage, of course one on which I have the Canary and the canoe, has four large boulders as part of the trail. You are supposed to step from one rock to the next one. I manage the first two steps, but here, although my heart

---

[2.] See Chapter 6: "Where the Trail Begins"

is stout my legs are too short. I absolutely can't balance the canoe and bridge that final gap. Derrick comes to my rescue and helps me set the canoe down. I deliver the Canary, and come back for the canoe.

It takes until noon to find a campsite at the north end of Gabimichigami. This site is larger; we all have a comfortable space for our tents, and there is a wide flat rock for a landing place. The morning is a picture of Minnesota perfection with deep blue water, clear skies, and comfortable temperatures. We are getting more efficient at the trail work, but we still haven't done any today. This new site is very near the trail, and after lunch we split into two groups, each taking half of the 1.25 miles we want to cover yet this afternoon. The drive-by-shooting method using fewer people is great, even if painful; there is something left for the last person in line to do. Today Paul, Bob, Claire and I are together. This is a section that hasn't been worked for two years, and Paul earns his sawyer's dinner clearing a lot of deadfalls. He earns it, but he doesn't get any more to eat than the rest of us! The trail is hillier here than where we previously cleared, and although it is beastly hot, and we are hungry, sore and tired, this breaks the monotony a bit. We spot Larry again in a lush green wetland below the hill, but on the other side of the trail, dead gray tree trunks are jumbled like matchsticks, many layers deep. The experts say there's no doubt that the area will burn, the only question remaining is "when." Some controlled burns have already been done in an effort to prevent unchecked wildfire from devastating the area.

We ask Derrick what the hot, dry wind means. "It's going to snow," he promises.

Thursday is awesome. It begins with bacon and all the pancakes we can eat! We are facing our longest work day, 2.5 miles, and the most difficult logistics. We begin by putting six people in two canoes and paddling to the top of Lake Gabimichigami again. Four of us, Claire, Paul, Lyle, and I stay there and start working westward. Bob and Julia return to the campsite, and then, with Derrick, begin a long paddle across this lake and the entire length of Agamok Lake, towing the two empty canoes. Once there, they will work east, toward us, until we meet somewhere in the middle. Each group has its own lunch, so we have more control over our stomachs' destiny. I've hardly seen Lyle since the trip began, and he and I now seem to naturally separate into a sub-group, comparing notes of our experiences. The day is cooler, the trail is hillier, and thus more interesting without being particularly difficult. Also, a bit of a slope allows me to stand downhill from the brush I want to cut, so that I don't have to bend over.

We meet at 2 pm, and all hike west to Agamok Bridge. Every work trip should end at an Agamok Bridge! High above a rocky gorge with tumbling waterfalls is a sturdy but rustic bridge for the trail. The wood was brought in by dogsled in the winter of 1982, and the

Kekekabic Trail Club assembled it in the summer, winning the Forest Service Primitive Skills Award for wilderness construction. We dunk our heads, soak our feet, peel off the ticks, eat snacks, filter the cold water and drink our fill. We take pictures of all of us on the bridge using every camera which has a timer. We congratulate ourselves on seven total miles of cleared trail, and then Derrick confesses that he didn't think we would actually finish that many miles in just four days. We have proved our mettle. Finally, we leave a note for the work crew which will begin here next week, and start the long paddle back to our campsite.

Tonight there is to be a full lunar eclipse. How could there possibly be a more extraordinary conclusion to this week? A little after 9 pm, with a multitude of loons eerily calling across the dark water, a small sliver of moon disappears. Our company, now completely relaxed together, watches, whispering quietly so as not to break the mood. By 10 o'clock the moon is gone. "What does the eclipse mean, Derrick?"

Friday, we are so tough that we opt to canoe all the way out to get back to Gunflint Lodge. Several people need to leave for the airport at 9 am Saturday, and they would rather not have any canoeing to do early that morning. It's a perfect day on the water, and we seem to have wings. We take a slightly different return route, with a stop in Gotter Lake on a high rock for lunch. Even with 12 lakes and 11 portages we reach the lodge in time for showers and a large restaurant dinner. Derrick has been a good leader, but I have to report that he was wrong about one thing. It never did snow.

My conclusion about the trail? It is rugged, and a backpacker should be carefully prepared, but it doesn't seem extremely dangerous.

We can testify that we have certainly been amused. And no coins were required to operate those devices, just paddles, muscles, and a passion for the Kekekabic.

7 miles this hike
Seahorse Lake to Agamok Bridge
Boundary Waters Canoe Area, MN
2190 total NCT miles

Quothe the Raven, "Walk, Walk!"
67 - August 4-18, 2003

"Creek!" Marie calls over her shoulder.

"Are you referring to the water feature ahead, or your joints?" I retort.

There's no denying that we are 12 years older than we were when this adventure was begun. We feel old and slow today, but that's a hard thing to judge near the end of a hot and hilly hike. We do seem to have as much enthusiasm as ever, and much more knowledge. We can pack a backpack quicker than a snow flea jumps on a warm winter day, and discuss ill-marked corners or breathtaking vistas with aplomb. We seem to have fallen into a rhythm of taking our longest hike of the year in conjunction with the NCTA Annual Conference. This year that event is in Marquette, Michigan, in the Upper Peninsula, and we will hike the westernmost UP just after the conference.

Rob Corbett, the new Director of Trail Management, has offered to help us place our supplies, and spot our car so that we need only one vehicle. One of those supply points will be a new trick, even for us. Doug Welker, of the Peter Wolfe Chapter, has promised miles and miles of trail with no sign of human activity, and we are really looking forward to that. But the down side of that promise is that there is no place to leave one of our supply boxes. The solution (we hope) is to find one really great cache tree near a road crossing, and hang our supplies for pickup a week later.

We are armed with extra cables and ropes. Our clean clothes and food are triple-bagged to keep them dry and to contain the appealing odors which might emanate from them. For this caper, my standards are higher than for an overnight cache, but without much trouble we find a potential site. An ash at one end of a clearing in the woods has a nice fork about 25 feet up. Rob and I compete, 10 tries per turn, while Marie cheers us on. I'm on my third set of throws when we all win... the rope goes right where we want it to be! We throw another rope over the limb of a tree at the other end of the clearing, and attach it to a second cable clipped to the bag. First we pull the bag up high toward the crotch of the ash. Then we haul on the rope from the other tree until the bag is pulled away from the ash, and is hanging about 15 feet above the ground, and well clear of any tree trunks or sapling runways. It looks great; we'll know in a week how well it succeeds in its purpose to protect the contents.

We walk east from the Wisconsin border on a rail-trail of the former Chicago & Northwestern RR, and the best feature is where a truss bridge of the Wisconsin & Michigan line weaves above it at an oblique angle. We pass a 20-foot fiberglass skier sweltering in the sun at the entrance to Powderhorn Ski Resort and turn north. Sweltering is on our agenda too, but a friendly young girl comes out from her house and offers us glasses of cold lemonade.

At "The Narrows" campsite on the Black River we scramble down to the water and iridescent damselflies, the ones with aqua-green bodies and black wings, light on our arms and wash their little faces. A cluster of an unfamiliar species of water strider with black bodies attracts my attention. I manage to scoop one up, and it hops! The water is a perfect cooling salve to our bare feet, and little fish gently nibble our toes. It would be perfect but for the Pan-size Mosquitoes with Poison Ivy on the side!

Wednesday morning we are awakened by a Gray Jay whistling and "chuck"-ing above our heads. But the day's, perhaps this book's, outstanding wildlife sighting is made at the corner of a country road. Marie glances up, and with a sharp intake of breath announces, "It's a bear." Ahead of us, not 100 yards away, a large black shape is standing at the edge of the road. Somehow it doesn't look quite bear-ish to me, but it is certainly big. Before we have time to ponder this, the black shape takes a step, and a long feline tail is revealed. Another step, and it turns toward us. We can clearly see the triangular face and pointed cat ears. A black cougar! The cat moves smoothly and calmly across the road and disappears into the woods. There was never enough time to even think about getting out a camera, or to even be concerned. We just observe each other and go about our business. Incredible!

Spotting the wild cat is not the high point of the day, because that comes next at the Copper Peak Ski Jump. This is the tallest ski flying slide in the world, right on the trail! Off season, tourists can ride the elevator to the top and enjoy a panoramic view of the rugged terrain.

We spend the afternoon puttering our way past a series of eager waterfalls on the Black River, leading us downstream to Lake Superior. Rainbow Falls remains in memory as the prettiest, but perhaps that's only because we have to work

Marie & Joan, Porkies for a backdrop

the hardest to see it. There are 195 steps from the trail to the overlook. When we reach the sandy Lake Superior beach, the jet-skiers and the rock-throwing teenagers already own it, but we find a semi-private spot in which to tuck our tent.

This trip seems to be one of remarkable awakenings; Thursday morning's surprise is several Ruby-Throated Hummingbirds sipping from the Common Evening Primrose surrounding our tent. We hike south away from the lake, turn west and are welcomed to Chickadee Creek by a chickadee! Porcupine Mountain Wilderness State Park offers more waterfalls on the Presque Isle River. We pass through a grove of Eastern Hemlock whose trunks are as much as 30" in diameter. The geology here reminds us a great deal of our childhood playgrounds. Layers of shale are everywhere, and deep gorges with smooth round holes in the rock scoured by whirlpools. But instead of the gray rocks of New York, this shale is red.

We follow the park's designated route for the North Country Trail, beginning with the Lake Superior Trail, which has almost no views of the Lake. Numerous small creeks have cut extremely deep, narrow valleys through the clay. At each and every one the trail plunges straight down the fall line, and right back up the other side. Not only is this terrible for hiking, but is causing severe erosion of the steep banks. At one crossing we can see the head of the valley just yards away. The trail could have simply been routed around that bend, rather than taking the hiker down and up the ridiculous slope.

We spend another night on the beach, and this time we are reminded of the pebbled shores of Cayuga Lake, and evenings spent at Camp Comstock. Last night we had spent an hour in the warm lake; tonight the water is so cold that we dip our bodies only briefly... and loudly. We look so fetching in swim suits and hiking boots! But the rounded beach gravel has retained the warmth of the sun, and I stretch out, easing my hips and shoulders back and forth to mold the soft, dry bed to my shape. When I was a girl my mother would often take me to the lake to swim on summer evenings. After we returned home I would lie on the solar-heated slate slab outside our back door until I was dry and warm. Dreamy tactile memories mingle with the "glug-glug" of the gentle waves, and the smell of wood smoke. The root sections of several broken trees have washed up on shore, bleached and dried. With very little effort they can be imagined into long-nosed faces with tangled, windswept hair.

As the sun slips, the waves cease and the water becomes mirror smooth. The entire surface of the lake, as far as we can see, begins to glow an astonishing electric blue, while Gheezis becomes a molten orange ball. I find a "lucky stone," one with a hole completely through it, and hold it to the sun where it becomes a fiery orange jewel in a rocky setting. Evening falls; the water fades to aqua-green... our blue tent a gem of a refuge in a Superior setting.

On Saturday we move inland. The Little Carp River Trail, and Lily Pond Trails are pretty, but nothing spectacular, although we do find a Downy Rattlesnake Plantain orchid. We have to wonder why this route was chosen for the NCT. Just north of these trails is a park trail that follows a sheer escarpment to Lake of the Clouds, and some of the most spectacular views in Michigan, reminiscent of the Adirondacks.

We recommend this plan to future hikers; it adds a few miles, but every one of them will be worth it.

We do see a Whitetail Deer. Such a sight is so common in North Country Trail territory that I hardly remember most such encounters, let alone choose to write about them. But this little doe is standing quite near the trail, so I carefully pull out the camera in hopes of taking her picture. She continues to munch on some low plants while I capture her on film. I decide to try for the telephoto lens, and ease it from my belt pack, trying not to make any noise. My foot does rustle the leaves, but the doe doesn't bolt. I would like to have her lift her head for her portrait, so when I am ready and focused we cluck our tongues at her. She ignores us. We whistle, and she pays no attention. We take a few steps, and yell "Hey, deer" at her. Finally she casually glances our way. "Click," got her! We aren't trying to control our noise or actions now, and she continues to graze with never the slightest concern at our presence or absence. We have to admit that although she didn't move much more, this deer is in better shape than the one we saw on the trail yesterday which consisted of a spine, a pelvis, and two legs!

Crossing the West Branch of the Big Iron River we are required to wade since the large wooden bridge is lying in broken pieces on the east bank. Doug Welker had warned us of this, so we are not surprised. What does surprise us is meeting a bulldozer in the trail a little farther along! The operator is diligently filling in a small creek valley, making a pathway for the machine which will bring in the new bridge in just a few days. It is to be the standard issue, rusty metal, Forest Service bridge. These bridges are brought to their sites fully assembled, by a special vehicle, and plopped in place!

At the East Branch of the same river we cross the twin of the broken bridge. This one is scheduled to be replaced, too, since people who know have decided that its collapse is also inevitable. Apparently the designer forgot to allow for the weight of several feet of winter snow![1] It is certainly a design I've never seen anywhere else. The bridge curves steeply upward, and is braced underneath across its length by a chord of cable. The arc is shocking, like something from a fairy tale that should be made of stone, with several blocks fallen from the middle where the sojourner on a white steed can gaze downward to dizzying depths, and dragons soar through a steep-walled canyon.

On the far side of the bridge we do meet four strange creatures with humps on their backs. They are a grubby as we are, but they don't have scales or wings, so we know they aren't dragons. They are that rare and jovial species known as backpackers! We trade bits of information about the trail since we have seen where they are headed

---

[1.] Doug reports that the cost of replacing these two bridges was $240,000.

and vice-versa. It's nice to see some people hiking on out-of-the-way sections.

At 12:30 we reach the road marking where we should find our supply cache. Will it be intact? The answer is "yes!" Relief is a great emotion, and it goes well with lunch. If our food had been taken we'd probably be shortening our hike by some method involving activities like hitchhiking, which is a lot more dangerous than backpacking. We take the bag down carefully so that we can refill it with our dirty clothes, and haul it skyward again. We'll return and take the whole rig down after the hike, but we are a lot less concerned about the future of smelly t-shirts than we were about our broccoli soup and gorp.

Fortified with lunch we climb the steep Bergland Hill in the shimmering dry heat and enter the Trap Hills Area. We have planned to camp after another down, up, and down. But when we reach this valley there is nothing we can see that resembles a flat space. "We'd have to pound in our hiking sticks and tie the tent and ourselves to them," predicts Marie.

"Then I suppose it will be difficult to hang the cache with the same ropes?"

The tape recorder has new batteries today, but we don't. "One more hill," we groan.

We do make the top of the hill where there is not a flat space to be found, but we nestle the tent between two humps so that our hips will rest in a shallow trench. Throwing the rope for the cache tonight feels a lot like standing two feet from a needle and throwing the thread at it, but eventually the needle is threaded and our food is hung. We are pooped. The air is hot and dry, the plants are withering. The moss on the rocks is so dry it crunches underfoot. Even the wildlife is stilled. The only sound tonight is a Robin annoyingly "cheer-up"-ing nearby.

The days continue hot and dry. But even as enervated as we are, it is impossible to miss the beauty of the Trap Hills and eastward through the Ottawa National Forest. The trail tracks behind crenelated cliffs through a thick maple and birch forest, but every so often it approaches the edge and breaks out on a rocky promontory. Usually this is accomplished by a steep scramble up to the open rock, but the woods are so dense and closed in that we have no sense of what kind of vista will present itself until we are out on the rock. At one of the very first, we arrive panting on the outcrop and gaze outward expecting a long vista. Instead, hardly more than a stone's throw away, we find ourselves face to face with another of the rock cliffs. It's so startling that we audibly gasp at the nearness of the other precipice. Other times, we are rewarded with a long, long vista, and a fresh breeze. Then it's downhill, back into the hot woods, cross a valley, climb to another promontory, and emerge to learn what surprise is in store at this opening. It's difficult trail, but so rewarding!

Mid-afternoon we come upon a dead chipmunk in the trail. Swarming over its body are half-inch long American Carrion Beetles. Although they look alarming, and in fact can fly and buzz, similar to June Beetles, they are harmless as long as you are alive. Each beetle is black, with a yellowish pronotum (that shield-like structure across the shoulders). In the center of the pronotum is a large black spot. Supposedly the beetles are content to eat decaying vegetation and fungi, but obviously today they are proving themselves to be omnivores. Although somewhat gruesome, it's fascinating to watch one natural pathway by which decaying matter is recycled.

We camp just past an unnamed creek among some old slash piles, but we find a comfortable flat spot. One Red Squirrel is convinced that we are in her space, and she spends the entire evening chittering angrily, launching herself between the skinny saplings, and even throwing things at the tent. A Hairy Woodpecker taps its way around the site. Tonight it's a classic cache – one high horizontal branch above a clearing with the rope slung over it.

"Walk, WALK!" someone screams from the treetops. It's a rude awakening, being ordered to do what we are already planning! The insistent raven continues his tirade, but never does let on what he has in mind if we don't comply with his orders. With the raven's help we leave early enough that I'm nearly comatose for the first two hour-long walks of the day. But after that we enter an area which had been previously clearcut, and this gets my full attention. Now the clearcut is a wetland, grown tall with grasses, and hummocky underfoot. A sign informs us that it's 1.7 miles to the Beaver Pond. After 500 feet I am able to estimate confidently that we will reach the Beaver Pond sometime tomorrow. The grasses and rushes are taller than Marie. Every time we put one foot forward we have no way to predict where it will come down. It might be high on an unstable hummock, low in a ditch, hard on a rock, or rolling on a length of slash. In the full sun we are sweating buckets, and the mature Woolgrass seeds adhere to our sticky bodies like bugs to flypaper. Of course the blazes have disappeared, and I am tentatively following a pressed-down track of bent grasses which could have been made by a deer just as easily as by some previous hiker. Much to my surprise we find a blaze and arrive at the pond long before tomorrow, but it's no longer a pond. Long abandoned by the Beaver, the oval is now a meadow filled with blooming Boneset and Spotted Joe-Pye Weed. The scent of mint rises off the meadow, almost oppressive in its hot intensity.

Leaving this level extension of the Ontonagon valley we climb again to a second ridge of cliffs similar to the previous one. At a wide granite shelf the vista opens to 270° with not a single man-made feature in sight. That settles it. Here we will camp and take our day off tomorrow. Ahhhhh! We spend the entire day walking as little as possible. With the exception of two trips to a creek to filter water we do nothing but relax and take turns reading aloud from Jenkins' *The Walk West*. Although we've both read it before, it's a timeless tale for addicted walkers. At the end of this much-needed day of rest, after 18 straight hours of blowing, the hot wind finally dies. The sky changes in an hour from cumulus clouds to a mackerel sky, to clear. Ten minutes later it looks as though thunderclouds are building in the west, but then they stretch out and become high stratus clouds. Pick a weather forecast from that hour!

During our day off we discuss a possible plan to overcome an inherent fault of this trip; it isn't quite long enough to allow me to cross the 2300-mile mark. Now that I've settled on that number as a halfway-done goal I can hardly bear the reality that this trip isn't quite long enough. But we are hiking to my car, and Marie has agreed to let me hike through to the next road after we finish, while she drives around to pick me up. It seems to be unfair to her, but she continues to insist that the quest for the whole trail is mine, not hers.

Saturday we are renewed, the weather is cooler, and small details catch our eyes instead of the wide horizon. Delicate, triangular Rattlesnake Fern fills a sun-puddle, while a nearby stump mimics a large snail crawling through the underbrush. Luscious clusters of Wild Black Cherry glow in the sunlight near a creek crossing. Bearberry's thick succulent leaves edged with white contrast with its bright red berries. Every trickle of water must be lined with frogs, for as we approach there is always a frenzy of leaping and splashing. We watch them kicking their cute little frog kicks as they all hunt for rocks under which they can hide.

Maidenhair Spleenwort

Doug Welker had sat with us at the conference, drawing confident lines on our topographic maps. He knows this trail better than his own thumbprint, and he marked a special spot to watch for today. The directions involve crossing two talus slopes. I'm not sure just what a talus slope in Michigan might look like; I've always associated them with high western landscapes. But sure enough, on our left we see a huge tumbled pile of raw black rocks, at the foot of a cliff. What a novelty! And the trail is routed right across it. Someone, probably Doug himself, has carefully arranged and laid in certain stones so that there is a smooth pathway through the jumble, with neat cairns for markers. Just past these slopes we are to watch for a small valley, and then follow it up to a saddle, climb to the top of that rock, and we will be rewarded with a 360° view.

We leave the packs in the close air at the bottom of the valley, sitting in a thick swarm of mosquitoes. With our lunch we climb to the top of the hill, and it is worth the trip. We can see four miles back to the hill where we camped the night before, and once again far across the Ontonagon valley to the south. But it's too hot to stay out on the bare rock, so we crouch under the branches of one small oak tree, with no view at all, to eat. Marie is hopeful that the mosquitoes have grown to Sherpa size, and have carried away our packs, as long as they carry them to the campsite. Sad to say, our packs are waiting for us along with the skitters. So we carry the packs ourselves to Cushman Creek. The mosquitoes are on their own.

The water is clear and clean, running over smooth pebbles. We've been sampling an occasional Thimbleberry that is not over-ripe, but here there is a huge patch of the delectable, fragile fruits. Marie filters water while I pick a half cup of red berries for each of us. The map indicates gentle topography near the creek, thus we think that there will be a nice level place to pitch the tent, but there is no clear flat space. Oh well, "one more hill!"

This climb puts us part way up Lookout Mountain, above the Victoria Reservoir. We can't see the surface of the water, but in the morning the dense white mist sitting in the next valley over clearly indicates where it must be. Down off the hill we come, taking time to study a new fern with lacy round leaves climbing up a dark stem, Maidenhair Spleenwort.

Soon we are walking through the remains of the Old Victoria Copper Mine settlement. We pass broken down cabins which once were lively with children playing, the sounds of women chatting across their backyards to the sweet rhythm of dulcimer music, and the smell of dinner cooking on the wood stove. But today it's not just a memory. Several of the cabins are being restored and once a year a craft fair and festival is held at the site. We have walked into Old Victoria on just that very day!

We spend most of the day there, way too long, but who could resist the temptations? Honoring the Finnish heritage of the region, bowls of Mojaka (MAH-huh-ka) are served, a traditional soup of beef, potato and carrot, seasoned with cloves and peppercorn. A solid man in a sleeveless muscle shirt, arms covered with tatoos, and a shaved head spends the entire day smiling at everyone and roasting ears of corn over a long bed of coals. Tall glasses of ice tea, fresh oatmeal bread, and finally huge cinnamon rolls can also be had, all prepared on the wood stoves in the cabins. We wander through and talk to the chef. He is happy, covered in flour, and sweltering in the small cabin with three fired-up wood stoves. "I'm writing a book," he confides.

After we are sufficiently stuffed, we wander around to the booths looking at quality leatherwork, paintings, wood crafts, pine-needle baskets, clothing, toys, beads, the dulcimer musician and more.

Another of the restored cabins is tended by a man who is no spring chicken himself. This is the very cabin where his mother grew up in the mining camp, and he has decorated and arranged it with belongings of her own. He shows us a thick scrapbook of information about her life. "I'm writing a book about her," he explains.

By now, since we have retrieved and are sorting a supply box we had stashed here, almost everyone has learned that we are hiking through. They've also extracted the information that I'm trying to hike the whole trail. "Are you writing a book?"

Although I've been shy of admitting that I am indeed working on such a daunting project, this seems to be the day for writers. "Sure!" I respond with more confidence than the twenty-some completed chapters sitting in my computer can justify.

Much too late in the afternoon we lift our packs and head back into the woods for what we expect will be a push to reach the car yet tonight. The terrain is flat, and our only challenge may be the crossing of the river below the dam. Of course, as you may have noticed, things don't always work out the way we plan.

First of all, we lose the trail almost immediately. Finding it again involves wading through verdant Poison Ivy. Next, due to heavy floods this past spring, when we reach the river what we see bears no resemblance to the written description we are using. We follow the blazes to the edge of the river bluff and gaze 15 feet straight down from the top of an undercut bank with large boulders below. So we backtrack till we find a place where we can scoot on our behinds down to water level. Crossing the river isn't too difficult, but we spend extra time washing down our legs to remove the ivy oil. Then we have to find a place on the far side to climb away from the water, and locate the trail once that is done. Turns out, we've now completed the easy part.

The terrain is indeed flat, but it's covered in second growth forest and wetland after a logging operation. No two consecutive footfalls land on similar surfaces. Rock, root, ditch, hump, stick, step over a log, root, hump, ditch, rock... we are footsore almost immediately, and slowed perceptibly although we are trying to hurry. And this is the speedy part.

Next we enter an area of serious blowdowns. We can see the blazes, but no treadway connects them. The downed trees are large, and we either have to climb over or walk around their ends. Sometimes they are tangled with adjacent fallen trees and it's hard to decide which is the best route. The mosquitoes are thickening in the warm evening.

We look at each other and simultaneously cry, "Let's get to the CAR!" I look up at one point and see Marie, in full pack, striding along a tree trunk as if it were a balance beam. This is not the cautious hiker I know. She must be really annoyed! But walking as fast as we can under these conditions is not fast enough.

At dusk we come to the final forest road crossing; it's just 2.5 miles to the CAR. But here is an open flat space, labeled as NCT parking. "We're NCT, and we're parking," says Marie. Brushing another mosquito from my ear, I fully agree to the plan. As fast as a pair of backpackers with 12 years of experience we have the tent set up and dive inside. We are bitten and bruised, but content. The plan for me to hike the extra miles at the end are scrapped; I'll walk my 2300th mile some place else, some other time.

Pawing through the gear that night Marie asks for the 236th time, "Which bag is first aid and which one is repairs?" I tell her again that the one with the red cross is first aid, and the one with the band-aid is repairs. "I never can remember what the pictures mean," she sighs. "Maybe if I use them enough years, I'll get it."

"Well, I thought it might help that I wrote 'fix-it' on the band-aid bag." I answer with a chuckle. I think it's hilarious that the symbols apparently mean nothing to her. "And we've been using the bags for 12 years and you still can't remember."

"Fine," she responds with a flounce. "You can write it on my crutches!"

And in the pink light of early morning quothe the raven, "Walk, walk."

108 miles this hike
Hurley to US 45
Gogebic and
    Ontonagon Counties, MI
2298 total NCT miles

Halfway, or Not?
68 - October 7, 2003

As an ending to a book, halfway is certainly a milestone, but an anticlimactic one at best. As a hike, this one is as unsatisfactory as is that uncertain mid-point for closure of this manuscript. But, like an unripe fruit which has grown so large and heavy that it may break the branch, it must be picked. 2300 miles: that mythical halfway point has been hanging, just out of my reach since summer. I need only two new miles, but I do need to travel to a section I've not previously walked.

The whole project comes together with the realization that there are four orphaned miles between two other hikes in the Upper Peninsula, and that I need to meet with leaders of the Grand Traverse Hikers Chapter. Traverse City is not anywhere near the UP, but it is two hours in that general direction, and I decide to combine the two needs into a hike.

I wanted to take several days, basecamp, try new campfire recipes, putter around the fire and listen to the sounds of evening. Maggie is coming with me, and I hope that she will learn to enjoy a more relaxed camping experience. But for hikes to be special, you have to plan for them to be special. Rather than time for planning, what I have is a very busy week with this hike crammed in the middle. I pack haphazardly, throw some left-over food in the cooler, and leave so late that I'll have to set the tent up in the dark when I arrive at AuTrain Campground.

Instead of a leisurely campfire dinner, I eat at a restaurant with a southern theme, not very appropriate for the "North Country." Instead of the hoot of a lonely owl, or the sweet song of a Vesper Sparrow, I get to listen to *Fear Factor* on the TV over the bar. Hearing semi-naked girls screaming while they try to swallow African spiders just isn't what I had in mind.

It turns out that I don't need to worry about setting up the tent in the dark. I had never even thought to check with the Forest Service about their campgrounds. Much to my surprise, although the leaves have not even turned, the sidewalks are rolled up for the winter. The campground is closed, and they do mean closed... a bright yellow gate with heavy padlocks blocks the road. Maggie and I sleep in the car, another new experience that she doesn't understand.

In the morning we are up almost as soon as it is light, which is not very early in the western UP in October. I know that we need to set a fast pace, since we need to hike both directions on this section, and then drive back as far as Traverse City for the dinner meeting. Almost immediately I discover that to connect the two previous hikes the distance is closer to five miles, rather than four. Thus a round trip is ten miles, not the eight I've been assuming.

We begin pleasantly enough, among rolling hills, with one stretch on an aromatic balsam ridge above a wetland. A raven blasts out of a tree, and Maggie tucks her tail between her legs, yips, and scurries to my side. I guess this raven has noticed that we are walking, and doesn't feel the need to order us along the trail. I'm pretty sure that I'm almost at my goal, Rock River Road, when the trail enters a clearing filled with ferns. The blue blaze and the treadway are clear going in. I search for where the trail leaves the clearing, and finally find a faint trail leading out, but there are no blazes and it quickly joins a dirt road heading straight east... the exact opposite of what I want. I return to the clearing, eat a snack and check the time. And there's the problem. I am completely out of time. Sitting quietly, I even think that I can hear a car over the ridge to the west, but I must leave now, right now, and walk briskly if there is any hope of making the meeting on time and somewhat clean.

Time... this inescapable dimension of life has completely controlled the parameters of this hike... pressured planning, hasty packing, scheduled walking. Yet in contrast, this book has removed, or at least diminished the passage of time. What you may have read in a few days has spanned 12 years. All of the people and places are truly no longer the same.

T-shirts which I bought as souvenirs on early hikes have already worn out. Children have grown as they walked through that Sneaky Valley. The lizard-lady café is closed, and the vibrant Tom Beirele has died of cancer. In fact, several people I met along the way have since passed away. People's roles have changed; Wes Boyd no longer edits the *North Star*, and he's moved on to the joys of sea kayaking. The weathered Orthodox church, which to me so typified the plains, has been razed... no trace of its existence now appears on that bleak Dakota corner. Ceceilia, reasonably enough, wiped the smudges from the passenger side window of my car, and removed one more evidence of Chips' presence. I hadn't been able to make myself do it. Marie finally threw away the uncompleted polar bear puzzle. Time, and the participation of two Siamese Cats made it seem less likely that it would ever be completed in the ordinary way. Surely many other things are different as well.

Omer and I are comfortable together again, we've found that our similarities outweigh our differences. Like old cheese, we are either aged or moldy, depending on how well you like it. Either way, we definitely have a unique flavor and identity. Perhaps we have re-acquired our college nickname of "cutest couple on campus."

In some places where I walked, the trail has been re-routed. Chapters have worked hard, and some road walks have been replaced with off-road trail. The Buckeye Trail Association has indeed marked their trail better with a huge "Go to Blue Blazes" painting campaign. Hopefully no sections of good trail have been lost to the wilds, but I can't guarantee anything!

The Ashland Soo Line Depot Restaurant where we ate following "A Nice Walk in the Woods," was gutted by fire in 2000. Ceceilia and I were shocked and sickened to discover its burned-out shell after the "Emily, Mama Rita and Dick..." hike. Yet, on the way to North Dakota in 2002, Marie and I were heartened to find a painted community placard measuring donations toward restoring the historic structure. And in 2003, on the way to "Non-Coin Operated Amusement Devices," I made Lyle take a detour to check out the progress of this fund. To my delight, the painted pyramid was red all the way to the tip: the monetary goal had been attained. Perhaps the next time I visit Ashland the onetime railroad station will once again be roofed, lighted and welcoming travelers, no matter what its new purpose will be.

Although this landmark is not located directly on the trail, it is forever linked with many of my travels to the trail. It has seemed to me symbolic of all that is good about important causes. A significant historic building, a new use and people once again filling its rooms, a setback, volunteers who cannot bear to see it lost, and perhaps in the future there will be a beautiful, completed edifice.

The North Country Trail, in some ways, is like that old station. After the demise of the railroad, the empty building needed a new life; the NCT meanders across the landscape looking for an identity. After the early push to establish many miles of the Trail across public land it was hard to find people to maintain those miles. Some older sections nearly faded into the underbrush before the North Country Trail Association finally began to grow in membership and ability. Overgrown trail has been cleared. Blue blazes are being painted. New trail is being built. Although the project has seemed overwhelming at times, the volunteers have stepped up to meet the challenge. But like the Soo Depot project, we have yet to see what the future will bring.

Some people have even accused the NCT of not being a trail in its own right, but simply a collection of previously existing routes. However, I believe that this Trail is an ideal example of what a nationally significant trail should be. Indeed, the NCT does wander. But in those wanderings the trail embraces literally hundreds of unique and interesting natural features, sniffs out historic sites, and wiggles its bare toes in the culture of mid-America.

It will be years before the NCT is fully completed off-road. This is a long trail, a big trail. It is the longest foot trail in the United States, twice the length of the Appalachian Trail. Sometimes it's difficult to envision what kind of "community" such a long trail could engender. To date only five people can be labeled as North Country end-to-enders.[1] But the stories of people, historic and current, are what will make or break this Trail. We do not have the continent's highest peak, or the oldest structure. We do not have one geographic focus, or one cultural theme. What we do have are connections with America's past and future. As the Trail traverses the northern United States it stitches together a patchwork of the history of the early days of our country, memorable evocative natural features, and the present-day keepers of the land. It is...

The North Country - - - Trail of America's Dreams

Of course I want to finish the second "half," and join that special group of achievers, er...obsessed characters, the end-to-enders. But my trail is not your trail. No one expects that very many people will hike the entire NCT. You might go out tomorrow and hike some small section of the North Country Trail. I hope you do! But your experience will not be the same as mine, and in some cases, I'm sure you will be very glad of that! You will find your own adventures, and I have more adventures waiting for me too.

This hike has been incomplete, and the larger quest is unfulfilled. Yet, perhaps this is actually the perfect halfway pause. As I am driving home from this unsatisfactory hike a Bald Eagle soars between the trees ahead of me, lifting my thoughts on its broad wings. Its sharp eyes capture a landscape wider than what I can discern from the tunnel of today's road. Perhaps my eagle can see the whole North Country Trail.

5 miles this hike
AuTrain Lake almost to
                             Rock River Rd.
Alger County, MI
2303 total NCT miles

---

[1] Carolyn Hoffman, 1978, followed the proposed route, bicycling many of the road sections (therefore some people do not count her effort as a "hike")

Peter Wolfe, 1974-1980, hiked the trail to celebrate being cured of alcoholism

Ed Talone, 1994, first to thru-hike the NCT (all in one season)

Chet Fromm, 1991-1995, attempting to hike every National Scenic Trail, and he has completed four of them to date

Andy Skurka, 2004-2005, hiking the Sea to Sea route this year, which includes the NCT. He completed the NCT between October and April, hiking through the winter! He is in Montana as this book goes to press.

Two other people are also ahead of me in miles: Sue Lockwood and Don Beattie.

Apologies and Acknowledgments

It has been said that good writing consists of knowing what to leave out of a story. Certainly, whether the writing is good or bad, some things are inevitably omitted. Only the most dedicated of enthusiasts really wants to read a log book or journal of any adventure. But leaving things out of a book such as this creates the possibility, even the probability, that some favorite locale in your neighborhood has been overlooked. Many readers of these tales will be people who hike and care for sections of the North Country Trail where I have journeyed.

"Why didn't she talk about the history of Chief Baw Beese, or even mention Tinker Falls? Why did she discuss covered bridges in Ohio, but never the adorable suspension bridge in Dayton's Triangle Park? Where is a description of the virgin Drummond Woods, or even a salute in passing for the sad history of the Kinzua, relocated by the building of the Allegheny Reservoir?" you may be asking.

The answer, of course, is that this is not a guidebook. If I have passed your way and yet failed to include your favorite spot (or even you) I hereby apologize. Although a guidebook is badly needed, this is not it! I offer a collection of personal stories, and only some of these. At times, I regretted leaving out interesting sights, snippets of history, or encounters with individuals. But this book is plenty long enough as is, and chapters headed in one thematic direction strongly resisted being dragged, kicking and screaming, in another just for the sake of a large tree or an historic monument.

Thor Heyerdahl, one of my favorite seafaring adventurers, wrote "as sails and waves can only be of interest to the viewers for a few moments, our eleventh man [the film crew] had his orders not to miss the moment when we began to punch each other's noses."[1] Similarly, descriptions only of trees, rocks, hills, lakes and rivers might never lead you to explore the North Country Trail on your own. While these create the matrix of the trail, trails are about connections... with places and people. You may protest and say that the forest itself is the important element of your hike, but that is probably as a relaxing contrast to the rest of your structured world. Perhaps you go to the woods to escape interactions with people. I often do. But few people go to the woods and stay; they emerge renewed, after a hour or a decade, to face relationships. And those who have shared the trail with us always seem somehow akin. As David Lillard recounted in his foreword to this volume, even a "non-hiker" recognizes that the bonds forged in meeting

---

[1.] Heyerdahl, Thor; *The Tigris Expedition*; Doubleday & Company; Garden City, NY; 1981; p 76.

Apologies and Acknowledgments

the basic needs of shelter, warmth and food are deep and lasting.

Many thanks are due to all the friends who have agreed to let me tell their tales, with seldom a chance to give their own side of the story. Take away conveniences, kitchen and bathroom, a soft mattress, and a shower, add a 40-pound pack and a blister, and it's suddenly surprisingly easier to consider punching someone in the nose when a disagreement arises. But my friends are patient and we've not yet come to blows. They've even agreed to being dragged along into this book.

And this tale could not be told at all without the many volunteers who give of their time to build and maintain the NCT. In the early days of these hikes I was always critical of poorly marked and cleared trail. It still makes me sad to encounter these conditions, but I've learned how much effort it takes to build and protect such a resource, and I try to be patient, or even to pitch in. Many thanks to all of you who volunteer for trails.

No trail of mine is traveled without the premier guide, Jesus Christ. I pray only that I will follow in His steps. I Peter ~~3:21~~ 2:21.

Several people deserve special mention for their specific contributions. Early on Janet Payne and Werner Veit urged me to keep writing, when five lonely chapters were a very meager beginning. Their suggestions have probably made your reading more enjoyable. Steven Newman was the first person who did not know me to see some text, and his ideas were valuable. Jen Tripp offered advice through computer and brain farts as we struggled to format files for the printer. Throughout the hikes and the writing, and indeed my life, Marie Altenau forever sticks by me, encouraging yet also giving me a good poke when it's warranted. Omer continues to put up with a house covered with piles of projects, which have become much deeper than usual as the printer's deadline approached. He reads the stories, but still prefers to experience the trail from his chair, rather than in a pair of boots. That's O.K., Om! Three other people must be mentioned. Ester Lamb has been Keeper of the Red Line. Each time I returned from a hike she would humor me, and stand by my desk at the Matthaei Botanical Gardens while I colored in one more small fraction of an inch on a map of the trail. She would exclaim, "That's totally cool!" somehow catching my excitement while seeing only a red felt-tip marker line. Irene Szabo, whom you have met in these chapters, has edited the text, pulled no punches when paragraphs "don't work," and corrected my favorite mistakes over and over again. Finally, only because his were the last eyes but mine to scan the pages, David Michener proofread the copy, checked botanical references, and encouraged me greatly in the final hectic weeks.

Of course, in the end, any mistakes are mine. But perhaps after this many pages you are too tired to notice them.

Joan H. Young, May 2005

Geographic listing of hikes - East to West

Space between lines indicates hikes which are geographically disconnected.

Chapter	Title	Page	State
15-	Forever Wild..................................	71	NY
59-	Erie Canal.....................................	317	NY
58-	Milk Train.....................................	315	NY
16-	The Ghosts of Rose Hollow...................	95	NY
23-	Enjoying the Classics	115	NY
62-	Fisher Settlement	336	NY
4-	One Crystal, Sunlit Moment	13	NY
2-	Twilight Trail	8	NY
63-	Thousands of Miles..........................	340	NY
60-	Philomathic Deipnosophists	321	NY
53-	May the Road Rise to Meet You..............	282	NY
5-	Baby Steps on the Giant Trail	15	PA
55-	Solo, Duo, Triad	296	PA
57-	Eye of Elk, Shade of Toad	307	OH
32-	Ephemerata...................................	156	OH
41-	She Who Builds Fire	211	OH
13-	Breaking the Chains.........................	56	OH
26-	On a Roll.....................................	126	OH
14-	Buckeye Buck	66	OH
39-	Puzzled.......................................	199	OH
36-	Call the Police	187	OH
35-	Down a Memory of a Lane	180	OH
28-	Linger, Linger	144	OH
10-	Losing the Way	42	OH
11-	Incident Report	50	OH
12-	Defiance	55	OH
9-	Buckeye Beginning	45	OH
8-	Connecting to Ohio	44	MI
7-	Patches	42	MI
17-	West, Wes, Wet...............................	99	MI
18-	King Relish to Kentucky Fried	102	MI
19-	Chips Tells the Truth	104	MI
20-	Set Your Compass for Adventure	106	MI
21-	Hale-Bopp and Other Fading Dirty Snowballs	109	MI
22-	Great Scot! The Ugliest Mile in Army Boots .	112	MI

24- Testing in 3-D	119	MI
30- A Trail of Her Own	151	MI
25- Rocky and the Rock	123	MI
47- Lightning and the Snail	246	MI
29- White Lace and a Million Fireflies	147	MI
42- Rain First, Umbrellas Last	216	MI
48- Look Your Dream Right in the Eye	248	MI
46- Walking Backwards Down the Stairs	244	MI
38- A Golden Chip of Sunshine	194	MI
34- Wheelin' @ 3FPR	177	MI
31- A Trail of My Own	154	MI
43- Back to the Beginning	219	MI
40- April Ambitions	209	MI
37- Spirit of the Woods	192	MI
1- The Kernel	5	MI
51- Sneaky Valley	261	MI
54- Building Bridges	293	MI
65- The Princess and the P's (part)	362	MI
3- Shamu	10	MI
65- The Princess and the P's (part)	362	MI
49- W2K	249	MI
45- Big Mac, Michigan Style	238	MI
56- Moon Over My U P	301	MI
44- The Song of Hiawatha's Friends	221	MI
68- Halfway, or Not?	296	MI
50- Ice is Nice	255	MI
67- Quothe the Raven, "Walk, Walk"	374	MI
33- A Nice Walk in the Woods	164	WI
52- Emily, Mama Rita and Dick Have their Way with the Regenwürmer	267	MN
61- Super-Duper	324	MN
66- Non-Coin-Operated Amusement Devices	365	MN
27- Tales from Paul's Woods	130	MN
64- Sheyenne	344	ND
6- Where the Trail Begins	28	ND

Index

4-H Clubs 351, 353
Abercrombie, ND 347
Abraham 110
Addington, Angie 244, 293
Addington, Forrest 245, 293
Addington, Mark 293
Adena Culture 312
Adirondack Forest Preserve 71
Adirondack Loj 90, 92
Adirondack Mountains 5, 71-94, 156, 161, 164, 166, 317, 337, 377
Adirondack Park 71
Ahmeek 223
Agamok Bridge 372, 373
Agamok Lake 372
Agongos 223
Air Force Museum 203
Alba, MI 249
Albany, NY 317, 318, 319, 336
Alder 138, 140, 141
Alfalfa 357
Alfred's Pond 333
Algae (unspecified) 26, 331
Alger County, MI 237, 260, 387
Algonquin 25
Algonquin Mountain 85
Alien 233
Allegany, NY 17, 282
Allegany State Park 5, 283
Allegheny Foamflower 158, 212, 314
Allegheny National Forest 5, 15-27, 42, 283, 289, 290, 297, 298, 300
Allegheny Reservoir 18, 21, 388
Allegheny River 283
Allen County, OH 146
Alpine ecosystem 85, 86
Altenau, Marie 7, 8-9, 10-12, 13-14, 15-27, 28-41, 71-94, 95-98, 115-118, 130-143, 164-176, 199-200, 201, 208, 221-237, 273, 282-292, 297-299, 307, 310-314, 315-316, 317-320, 324-335, 336-339, 341, 342, 343, 344-361, 374-383, 385, 386, 389
Altenau, Ed (Marie's husband) 33, 332
American Hiking Society 209, 365
Amish 289, 308
Amygdules 330, 331
Ann Arbor, MI 15, 29, 30, 41, 45, 53, 55, 72, 73, 99, 102, 144, 365
Annemeekee 223
Anorthosite 329
Antioch College 205
Antrim County, MI 254
Appalachian Mountains 21, 62, 318

Appalachian Trail 3, 212, 318, 386
Apple 47, 109, 116, 356
Apple River Canyon, IL 13
Applewhite, Marshall 111
Arden, Bess 282-292
Arrowhead Reroute 245, 267, 324, 326, 334
Artemesia (unspecified) 348
Artists Conk 217
Ash (unspecified) 252, 374
Ash Cave 212, 213
Ashland, WI 175, 385-386
Aspen 140, 180, 335, 363
Aster, Smooth 2
Athens County, OH 163, 314
Atlantic Ocean 42, 181, 318, 319
Atlantic Watershed 181
Auglaize County, OH 146, 186
Auglaize River 47, 48, 146, 184
Aunt Agnes (Sr. Tarcisia) 17, 282-283
AuSable Campsite 227
AuSable Club Mountain Reserve 76, 77
AuSable Lighthouse 227, 228
AuSable River 90
Autotrophs 170
AuTrain Formation 231
AuTrain Lake 237, 384, 387
Avalanche Mountain 85
Baarson, Larry & Shirley 355-356, 359
Babe the Blue Ox 130, 139, 140, 141
Bacteria (unspecified) 26, 170
Bad River 166, 167, 168
Badlands 28, 40
Baker Trail, 298
Ballast, Paula 216-218
Baltimore & Ohio RR 299
Barry County, MI 105
Basalt 224, 324, 331
Bat Lake 367-368
Battle Creek, MI 102-103
Battleship Row 235
Baxter Bridge 262, 266, 295
Baw Beese 186, 188
Bear (unspecified, but any bear encountered on the NCT is likely to be a Black Bear) 1, 19, 81, 84, 171, 223, 227, 262, 283, 311, 319, 334, 366
Bear Creek State Forest 287
Bear Track Campground 178
Bearberry 380
Bearded Hedgehog 296
Beattie, Don 387
Beaver Lake 174
Beaver Pond 379
Beavers & Dams 90, 141, 156, 160, 161, 162, 163, 175, 223, 334, 379

Beech 26, 232, 254, 299
Beechdrops 232
Beierle, Tom & Alma 32-33, 35, 38, 41, 385
Bellwort, Large-flowered 59, 277, 278
Bemidji, MN 138
Benton Lake Campground 216
Bergland Hill 378
Betony, Wood 314
Beulingo (cattle) 354
Bialk, Lyle 365-373, 386
Big Iron River 377
Big Rocky Branch 213
Big Sauble River 244
Big White Pine Campsite 324
Biking 42, 119, 200-208, 287, 313, 344-361
Billings, Jack 144
Birch (unspecified) 78, 267, 304, 329, 333, 334, 369, 378
Birch, Yellow 254
Birch Grove School 152
Biscuit Creek 304
Bismarck, ND 29
Bison 311
Black River 375
Blackberry 254, 277
Blackbird, Yellow-headed 38
Blackburn, Vint 144, 164
Blacksmith Bayou 209
Blazing Star, Rough 348
Block, Brody 227
Bloodroot 115
Bloody Bridge 144, 146, 186
Bloye, Robert 112-114, 320
Blue Cohosh 115
Blue Jacket 47, 184
Blue Jacket Festival 67, 128
Blue Mountain 73
Blue-Eyed Marys 158
Bluebead (Clintonia) 115
Bluebells 59
Blueberry (unspecified) 25, 174, 222, 226
Bluebird, Eastern 310
Bluegill 285
Bluets (Quaker Ladies) 59
Boardman River 363
Boat Dock Two 157, 158, 163, 314
Boneset 379
Boodaway 211
Border Route Trail 5, 245, 325, 326
Boy Scouts 91-92, 206, 209, 311
Boyd, Wes 99, 100, 102, 151, 385
Brachiopod 21
Bradford, PA 26
Branch, The 27
Bridgett 216
Brooklyn Bridge 240, 242
Brownstone Falls 168

393

Buck 68-70, 127
Buckeye 309
Buckeye Trail 5, 45-48, 49, 50-54, 55, 56-65, 66-70, 126-129, 144-146, 156-163, 180-186, 187-191, 202-208, 211-215
Buckeye Trail Association 49, 187, 385
Bucktooth Hill 284
Budd Engine 182
Buddy 211-215
Buffalo 344, 360
Buffalo, NY 317, 319
Buffalo & Susquehanna RR 288
Bullfrog 113
Bulwagga Bay 75
Bunchberry 174
Burlington Bay 268
Burr Oak Reservoir 157
Burr Oak State Park 307
Burt Hill Lean-to 341
Bushwacking 106, 138-141, 147, 163, 165, 225, 277, 296-297, 304-306
Butterflies (unspecified) 214, 308
Cache 1, 19-20, 81, 84, 87, 137, 166, 175, 262, 265, 285, 332, 374, 378, 379
Cadillac, MI 2
Caesar's Creek, OH 66, 208
Calcite 330, 331
Cambrian Sea 167
Camp Comstock 10, 144, 376
Canaseraga Creek 322, 323, 342
Canastota, NY 318, 320
Canisteo River 340
Cannon Cliff 91
Canoes 240, 319, 365-373
Cardinal 127, 204, 310
Caribou Lake 327
Carlton Peak 329, 330, 334
Carquinez Strait Bridge 242
Carrion Beetle, American 379
Carroll, Lewis 102
Cascade River 327, 331, 334
Cass County, MN 143
Castro, David 13, 15-27, 28-41, 72, 130-143, 173
Catfish, Shovelhead 311
Catskill Mountains 341
Caves of the Bloody Chiefs 235
Cayuga 211, 215
Cayuga Lake 338, 376
Cazenovia, NY 315, 317
Cedar, Red 319
Cedar, White 263, 326, 327, 363
Cedar Falls 213
Cedar Overlook 329
Celandine, Lesser 59, 205
Central New York Chapter 317
Central Park 275
Challenge Cost Share 209
Chanterelle, Black 232
Chapel, J. 248
Chapel Rock 230, 236

Chapman, John 47
Chappel Bay 21
Chequamegon Chapter 174
Chequamegon National Forest 5, 168-176
Cherry, Wild Black 25, 380
Chesapeake Bay 340
Chestnut, American 322, 338
Chestnut Hill Lean-to 338, 339
Chetowaik 223
Chibiabos 222
Chicago & Northwestern RR 374
Chickadee (unspecified, but any encountered on the NCT is likely to be a Black-capped Chickadee) 254, 334
Chickadee Creek 376
Chicago, Cincinnati, Cleveland & St. Louis RR 182
Chipmunk (unspecified, but any encountered on the NCT is likely to be an Eastern Chipmunk) 18, 20, 95, 223, 225, 329, 334, 379
Chippewa (also see Ojibway) 131, 182, 211, 214, 231
Chippewa County, MI 306
Chippewa National Forest 5, 131, 139, 173
Chips 13, 15-27, 28-41, 42-43, 44, 45-48, 50-54, 55, 56-65, 66-70, 71-94, 95-98, 99-101, 102-103, 104-105, 106-108, 112-114, 115-118, 119-122, 123-125, 126-129, 130-143, 144-146, 147-150, 154-155, 156-163, 164-176, 177-179, 180-186, 187-191, 192-193, 194-198, 199-200, 208, 210, 211, 246, 341
Chips destroys pack 29, 67, 73, 141
Chittenango Creek 315
Chittenango Landing Canal Museum 317
Chorus Line, A 67
Chrysoprase 25
Cincinnati, OH 181, 183, 184, 185
Cinquefoil, Three-toothed 327, 331
Civil War 129, 336, 337
Clar-Willis Award 339
Clarion County, PA 300
Clarion River 296-297
Clark, Bob 365-373
Clearwater County, MN 143
Clemetis (unspecified) 278
Cliffs Campsite 232
Clinton, DeWitt 115, 319
Clintonia (Bluebead) 115
Clover, Purple Prairie 351
Cloverdale, OH 50
Coal Mine Lake 34
Cobb Campsite 286-287
Colden Mountain 85
Coltsfoot 59, 205
Columbine, Wild 314

Columnar Joints 330
Condon Lake 148
Coneflower, Gray-headed 351
Conglomerate 21, 167, 168, 231
Conrail 182, 203
Conservation Branch of the Finger Lakes Trail 341
Conway, Joan 216-218
Cook County, MN 335
Cook Forest State Park 5, 297-300
Coon Creek 298, 300
Copper 236
Copper Falls 168
Copper Falls State Park 165, 167, 175, 176
Copper Peak Ski Jump 375
Copperhead 160, 212
Coralroot, Spotted 171
Corbett, Rob 374
Corkscrew, The 164
Cormorants 38
Cornplanter Bridge 27
Corps of Engineers 292
Corpse Plant 170
Cortland, NY 115
Cortland County, NY 98, 339
Corydalis, Pale 171
Coteau 30, 35
Cotton-grass (unspecified) 87
Cottonwood 13, 38, 230, 250, 252
Cougar (see Mountain Lion)
Coyote 367
Cranberry, Bog 24, 333
Cranberry, Small 86
Crane, Sandhill 351
Cranebill, Carolina 214
Crayfish 165
Crocus 205
Crooked Lake 106
Croton Dam 119
Crow 23, 204
Crowfoot Pond 75
Crown Point, NY 2, 72, 74, 94
Crowned Clavaria 8
Crystal Creek 324, 331
Cumberland, MD 202
Curfew Must Not Ring Tonight 100
Cushman Creek 381
Cuyler Hill 118
Dabes, Joe 284
Daffodil 116, 205
Dakota 344
Dakota Hymn 37
Dali, Salvador 172
Damselfly (unspecified) 375
Danby Hill 343
Darragh, MI 10, 12, 364
David (Psalmist) 136
Dayton, OH 201, 203
Dayton & Michigan RR 202
Dead Horse Marsh 209
Dead Man's Fingers 232
Decapod 175
Deep Cut 146

Deer (unspecified, but any deer encountered on the NCT is likely to be a Whitetail Deer) 24, 27, 138, 254, 270, 287, 309, 311, 319, 366, 377, 379
Defiance, OH 45, 46, 47, 48, 49, 50, 55
Defiance County, OH 48
Deh-ge-wan-us 291
Delaware (tribe) 183
Delphos, OH 49, 50, 54, 146
Denali National Park 71
Desired Future Condition 299
DeSoto, Hernando 139
Detroit, MI 128
Devil Track River 324
Devil's Gate 168
Diabase 328
Dog Stinkhorn 233
Dogs 42, 50, 68-69, 105, 151, 165, 187, 206, 214, 246, 293, 328, 354, 362-364
Dogwood, Flowering 212, 308
Dorn, Don & Brita 17, 25
Douglas Lodge 133, 134
Downy Rattlesnake Plantain 376
Dr. Zhivago 305
Drummond Woods 388
Dryad's Saddle 314
Duck, Black 161, 163
Ducks 38
Duluth, MN 267-281, 325, 326
Duluth Complex 330
Duluth Lakewalk 273-274
Duluth, Missabe & Iron Range RR 269, 276, 278
Duppler, Norma 358-360
Dust Bowl 347
Eagle (unspecified) 319
Eagle, Bald 139, 141, 387
Eagle Mountain 328
Eagle Scout Trail 139
Eagles, Julia 365-373
Eastman Hill 338
Eastwood Park 203
Eben Ice Caves 255-260
Edith Lake 367
Edna (tugboat) 268
Eel River 185
Elk (unspecified) 307, 311
Elk Creek 285
Elk Lake 131
Ellicottville, NY 286
Ely, MN 334
Enderlin, ND 346
Enfield Glen 8
Engler, John 239, 240
Erasmus 272
Erie Canal 115, 317-320, 338
Erie Canal Towpath Trail 318
Erie RR 292, 322
Esox Lake 175
Evangeline 229
Evening Primrose, Common 376
Evening Primrose, Nuttall's 349
Fabius, NY 98
Fairborn, OH 203

Falls of the Ohio 185
Falls of St. Anthony 139
Fargo, ND 6, 30, 344
Faul Campground 30-31, 41
Fear Factor 384
Feighner, Paul 365-373
Feild, Lance 152
Feldspar 72
Fern (unspecified) 24, 26, 160, 225
Fern, Bracken 6, 10, 252, 385
Fern, Christmas 217
Fern, Cinnamon 333
Fern, Marsh 333
Fern, New York 286
Fern, Northern Maidenhair 24, 216
Fern, Ostrich 217
Fern, Rattlesnake 380
Finger Lakes 330
Finger Lakes Trail 5, 8-9, 13-14, 95-98, 115-118, 282-292, 317, 336-339, 340-343
Finger Lakes Trail Conference 113, 286, 315, 339, 341
Finland, MN 335
Fir (unspecified) 86, 140, 222
Fir, Balsam 74, 92, 301, 335, 363
Fireweed 142
Fisher, Catherine Louisa 337, 339
Fisher, Emily Marguerite 224, 337, 339
Fisher, Lucinda Cornelia 336, 339
Fisher, George 336
Fisher, Olive White Hodges 336, 339
Fisher, Thomas 336
Fisher Settlement, NY 336, 337, 338, 399
Five Lake 249, 254
Fleming, June 172, 173
Fletcher, Colin 23
Flies (unspecified) 85, 229
Flies, Black 365
Florianopolis Bridge 242
Florida, OH 46
Flower Vase 236
Food Preparation 172-173
Fool's Creek 27
Forest Cathedral 299
Forest County, PA 300
Forever Wild Provision 71
Forks of the Ohio 128, 185
Fort Abercrombie 344, 347, 361
Fort Ancient 67
Fort Custer Recreation Area 102-103, 105
Fort Defiance 48
Fort Michilimackinac 238
Fort Ransom, ND 345, 347, 357
Fort Ransom State Park 344-361
Fort Washington 183
Fort Wayne, IN 146, 183, 184
Fox (tribe) 182
Fox (unspecified) 37, 254, 319

Franconia Notch 91
Freesoil, MI 178
French Lake 368, 371
Frog (unspecified) 77, 281, 23, 380
Frog, Gray Tree 161-163, 204
Frog, Green 113
Frog, Wood 309, 334
Fromm, Chet 270, 387
Fudge Mix 151, 246
Fulton County, OH 48, 44
Fungi (unspecified) 8, 27, 170, 171, 172, 217, 222, 225, 232, 233, 379
Future Farmers of America 353
Ga-da-o Flats 291
Gale, Angie 261-266
Gardner Lake, MN 143
Garnet 71
Garrison Dam 35, 40
Gatewood, Emma 212
General Harmar Military Trail 182
Genesee River 282, 289, 290, 291, 292, 321, 322, 323, 340
Genesee & Rochester Canal 292
Genesee Valley Greenway 341
Genesee Valley RR 292
Gentian, Bottle 294
Geranium, Wild 307, 309
Gheezis 222, 231, 376
Gillis Lake 368
Ginseng, Dwarf 342
Girl Scouts 10, 42, 124, 151, 152, 252, 253, 298, 348, 360
Gitchee-Gumee 221, 224
Glacial Lake Agassiz 30, 344, 347
Glacial Lake Duluth 325
Glacial Lake Souris 344
Glacier 72, 86, 146, 165, 167, 213, 231, 240, 283, 290, 323, 324, 346
Glacier National Park 71
Glen Helen 205
Glorious Gate, The 183
Gnats 340
Goats 348
Gogebic County, MI 383
Gogebic Range 165
Golden Alexanders 165
Golden Fairy Helmet 170
Golden Gate Bridge 238, 240
Goldenrod, Alpine 87, 331
Goldenrod, Hard-leaved 348
Goldfinch 287, 310
Goldthread 24
Gonzales, Alex 339
Goodspeed, Elaine 216
Goose, Canada 160, 203
Gooseberry 277
Gooseberry Mountain 85
Gothics 85
Gotter Lake 373
Grand Canyon 71
Grand Canyon of the East 290

395

Grand Island 234
Grand Marais, MI 225, 226
Grand Marais, MN 365
Grand Marys Lake State Park 50
Grand Portal Point 221, 235
Grand Rapids, MI 177, 216
Grand Sable Dunes 221
Grand Traverse County, MI 12, 364
Grand Traverse Hikers 293-295, 384
Grandma Gatewood 212
Granite (unspecified) 71, 92, 171, 224, 379
Grass, Beach 224
Grass, Big Bluestem 349
Grass, Red-top 351
Grass, Squirrel-Tail 34
Grasshopper 223
Gravel Lick Bridge 297
Great Heart 309
Great Miami River 183, 184, 202
Great Spangled Fritillary 18, 516
Grebes 38
Greek Peak 118
Greely Creek 279
Greene County, OH 208
Gridley Creek 118
Griffis, Pam 147-150, 246
Ground Pine 116, 161, 163
Grouse, Ruffed 24, 334
Grouse, Spruce 223, 226
Gulf of Mexico 181
Gull (unspecified) 34, 47, 203, 224, 231, 235, 277, 331
Gull, Bonaparte's 38
Gull, Little 38
Gull Lake 105
Gummy 249-254, 287, 289
Gunflint Lodge 366, 373
Gunflint Trail 366
Hale-Bopp 109
Halfmann, Tiffany 177
Hall, Hervey Smith 336
Hall, Susan 337, 339
Harebell 140, 331
Harkuf 110-111
Harmar, Josiah 182, 183, 184, 185
Harrison, William Henry 128
Hartley, Jim & Shirley 347-348, 360
Harvey, ND 31, 41
Hawk (unspecified) 358
Hawk, Broad-winged 204
Hawley, H. Rosamond 336, 339
Haystack Mountain 85
Hayward, Danny 106
Hazel Lake 142
Heal-All 18
Heart Lake 90
Heart's Content 27
Heaven's Gate 111
Hedgehog Mountain 76, 77
Hellebore, False 342
Help Me Lord, to Build My Span 243

Hemlock, Eastern (all hemlock in this range) 13, 25, 26, 63, 78, 81, 95, 153, 165, 172, 174, 175, 178, 213, 226, 229, 252, 258, 279, 299, 301, 302, 304, 305, 328, 333, 335, 339, 376
Hemlock Ravine 279
Hemlock Run 24, 25
Hen, Frizzle 353
Hencoop Hollow 285
Henderson Lake 93, 94
Henry County, OH 48
Heron, Great Blue 278
Heterotrophs 170
Heubner, Ceceilia 267, 268, 270, 281, 385, 386
Heyerdahl, Thor 399
Hezekiah 15-17, 198
Hiawatha 221, 222, 223, 231, 235, 236, 237, 337
Hiawatha National Forest 5, 232, 254-260, 301-306
Hickory 24
High Peaks- see Adirondack Mountains
Highbanks Lake 147
Hillsdale, MI 100
Hillsdale County, MI 43
Hobblebush 342
Hocking County, OH 163, 215
Hocking Hills 212
Hodenpyl Dam 6
Hoffman, Carolyn 387
Hoffman, Charles Fenno 91
Holimont Ski Area 285, 286
Homer, MI 101, 103
Honeysuckle (unspecified) 203
Hopewell Indians 67, 312
Hopewell Lodge 67
Horsechestnut 309, 314
Horsehair Mushroom 170
Horseradish 314
Horses 10, 42, 57, 59, 66, 152, 159, 289, 308-309, 348, 352-353
Horseshoe Ridge 329
Hovland, MN 325
Howard Lake 370
Hoxie Gorge 118
Hubbard County, MN 143
Hudson Bay 84, 345
Hudson River 73, 318, 319
Huffman Prairie 203
Hummingbird, Ruby-Throated 27, 375
Humphrey, Clarie 365-373
Hungry Hollow 285
Hurley, WI 176, 383
Hurricane Agnes 292
Hurricane Bertha 76, 77
Hurricane Isabel 82
Iagoo 236
Ice Age 167, 168
Independence, MO 212
Independence Dam State Park 46
Indian Calendar 344, 358

Indian Drum 236
Indian Head 235
Indian Lake, NY 73
Indian Pass 91, 92
Indian Pipe 24, 170
Indian Point Campground 277
Indiana and Ohio Scenic Railway 67
Indians (generally referring to Native Americans) 48, 64, 183, 184, 211, 238, 291, 319, 336, 344, 360
Injuries 38, 68-69, 133, 159, 204, 212, 288
Interlaken, NY 8
Interstate 71 Bridge 67
Interstate 81 Bridge 117
Irish Hill 286, 287
Iron 71,167,175, 269
Iron Spring Creek 349
Ironwood 178
Iroquois 25
Island Park 202, 203
Ithaca NY 8, 9, 13
Jack-in-the-Pulpit 59
Jackrabbit, White-tailed 344, 351
Jay, Blue 204
Jay, Gray 334, 375
Jay Cooke State Park 267, 279, 281
Jemison, Mary 290, 291
Jenkins, Peter 380
Jennings, B. 248
Jimmerson Hill 283-284, 292
Job 172
Joe-Pye Weed, Spotted 379
John Brown University 261
John Bryan State Park 206
Johnny Appleseed 47
Johnnycake Run 18
Johns Brook Loj 79-80, 86
Johnson, Scott 294
Jones, Bill 144
Jonesville, MI 99, 100
Jonvick Creek 334
Judd, Lois 344-345
Judge C.R. Magney State Park 335
Junction, OH 50
June Beetle 379
Kabibonok'ka 225
Kadunce River, West Fork 331
Kagh 223, 230
Kalamazoo County, MI 105
Kalamazoo River 103
Kalkaska County, MI 12, 364
Kathryn, ND 357, 359
Kayoshk 224
Keene Creek 276
Keene Valley, NY 72
Kekekabic Trail 5, 245, 326 365-373
Kekekabic Trail Club 369, 372
Kekionga 183, 184
Kenabeek 223
Kent County, MI 111, 114
Keshequa Creek 322, 323
Keweenaw Peninsula 167

Keweenawan Flows 167
Kickapoo 182
Killdeer 310
King School 358
Kingfisher 205
Kinglet 254
Kings Mills, OH 128, 208
Kingsbury Creek 276, 277
Kinzua 388
Kinzua Watershed 21
Kissing Bridges 313
Kittanning State Forest 299
Klondike Brook 88
Klondike Shelter 90
Knife River 269
Knotweed, Japanese 296
Korean War 251
Kunzler-Larmann, Mary 315, 317
Krummholz Zone 86
Kudzu 296
Kwasind 222, 229, 236
Labrador Hollow 96
Labradorite 72
Lake Audubon 40
Lake Biakal 325
Lake Champlain 71, 72, 74, 75, 319
Lake County, MI 152, 153, 179, 198, 218, 245, 248
Lake Erie 146, 182, 184, 319
Lake Gabimichigami 371, 372
Lake Hudson State Park 43, 44
Lake Huron 238
Lake Itasca 131, 133
Lake Loramie 181
Lake Michigan 185, 238
Lake of the Clouds 376
Lake Ontario 71, 292, 322
Lake Sakakawea 2, 6, 35, 40
Lake Sakakawea State Park 33, 41
Lake Superior 156, 167, 168, 224, 225, 227, 230, 236, 269, 324, 325, 326, 327, 328, 375
Lake Superior State Forest 225
Lake Superior Trail 376
Lake Tear-of-the-Clouds 73, 80
Lakewalk 329
Lamb, Ester 389
Lane Farm Campground 310, 311
Larch (Tamarack) 63, 333
Larkspur 158, 214, 307
Larmann, Al 317, 318
Laurentian Watershed 181
Law Enforcement 46, 53, 123, 125, 188-191, 201, 207, 312
Leadplant 349
Leaf Lake 148
Leary, Catherine (Mom) 8, 13, 14, 15, 28. 291, 298, 337, 339
Leary, Ray (Dad) 8, 28, 291, 363
Leatherleaf 333
Leatherwood 178

Leave-No-Trace 79, 124, 209, 264, 265, 332
Lefse 354, 357
Lehigh Valley RR 315, 318, 336
Leinen, John 333, 334
Leitch Bayou 193
Lenawee County, MI 43, 44
Letchworth Branch of the Finger Lakes Trail 290, 341
Letchworth Gorge 290, 291, 322
Letchworth High Bridge 292, 322
Letchworth State Park 290, 292
Leveaux Mountain 329
Lewis and Clark 156, 299
Lichen (unspecified) 26, 86, 225, 285, 331
Lick Brook 14
Lightle, Ellen 294
Lillard, David - forward, 388
Lily, Michigan 165
Lily, Trout 59
Lily, Water 174
Lily, Wood 41
Lily Pond Trail 376
Limestone 181, 205, 230, 231, 257, 258, 314
Lincoln, Abraham 337
Linear Pathway 102
Lisbon, ND 344, 354
Litchfield, MI 100
Little Carp River Trail 376
Little Creek 167
Little Miami Rail-Trail 126
Little Miami River 68
Little River Café 127
Little Turtle 184
Livingston County, NY 323, 343
Lockington Dam County Park 187
Lockwood, Sue 387
Lonetree Wildlife Management Area 6, 30-34, 36, 344
Longfellow, Henry Wadsworth 224, 229
Lookout Mountain, MI 381
Lookout Mountain, MN 327
Loon (unspecified, but any encountered along the NCT are likely to be Common Loon) 142, 172, 174, 369, 373
Loramie, OH 182
Loramie State Park 180, 185
Loramie Summit 182
Losantiville, OH 183
Lost Nation State Game Area 100
Louisville, KY 185
Lousewort 314
Lower Falls 292
Lower Wolf Jaw 72, 77
Luce County, MI 237
Lutefisk 354, 357
Lutsen Ski Area 328
Lycopodium 116, 161, 163
Mackinac Bridge 5, 238-243
Mackinac City 238, 239, 240, 243
Mad River 203

Madison County, NY 316, 320
Maggie 321-323, 336-339, 340-343, 362-364, 384-387
Mama 223
Manistee County, MI 7, 193, 210, 220
Manistee Lake 363
Manistee National Forest 5, 6, 147-150, 151-153, 154-155, 177-179, 192-193, 194-195, 209-210, 216-218, 219-220, 244-245, 246-247
Manistee River 193, 209, 263, 294, 363
Manitou River 329
Manton, MI 364
Maple (unspecified) 9, 20, 26, 81, 86, 117, 120, 138, 141, 144, 145, 146, 180, 310, 329, 334, 338, 341, 363, 378
Maple, Bird's Eye 319
Maple, Red 252, 333
Maple, Sugar 252, 288
Maple Creek 299
Marengo River 174
Marie Antoinette 311
Marietta, OH 311, 312
Marilla Trailhead 7
Marquette, MI 141, 374
Marsh Cinquefoil 140
Marsik, Theresa 45
Martin, Pat 286
Mason County, MI 2, 154-155, 177
Mateo 231
Matson, Arlen 293, 295
Matthaei Botanical Garden 99, 144, 145, 389
Maumee River 46, 47, 48, 146, 183, 184
Mayfield 10,12
Mayflower 28, 336
McCarthy Lake 247
McCarty Hill 284
McClusky Canal 35-37, 344
McConnells Mill State Park 5
McLean County, ND 32
Medina, MI 42
Meenahga 222
Megissogwon 236
Mehmed, Nick 220
Mellen, WI 168
Mena Creek 124
Menke, Bill 56-65, 165, 219, 268
Mercer, ND 32, 41
Merganser, Hooded 161
Mertensia 308
Miami 182
Miami County, OH 191
Miami-Erie Canal 46, 50, 145, 181, 202, 317
Miami River 183, 203
Michener, David 389
Mid-Continent Rift 167
Milkweed (unspecified)165, 204
Milkweed, Common 349

397

Milkweed, Showy 349
Miller, Paul & Shirley 52, 73, 74, 79, 80, 94
Miner's Castle 223, 231, 232, 235
Minjekahwun 221
Minneapolis, MN 30, 139
Minnehaha 236
Minnesota Parks and Trails Council 333
Minnesota Point 273-274
Mint (unspecified) 379
Mishe-Mokwa 223
Mississippi River 128, 130, 142, 156, 181, 311, 320
Missouri Coteau 35
Missouri Escarpment 30, 34, 35
Missouri River 28, 35, 40, 156
Moccasin Slipper 212, 214
Mohawk River 71, 318, 319
Mojaka 381
Montgomery County, OH 208
Moon - unusual 107, 148, 205, 302, 305, 373
Moose 130, 334, 370, 372
Moose Mountain 328, 329
Moosewood 25
Moraine State Park 5
Morgan County, OH 163, 314
Morgan's Raiders 128
Morning Has Broken 22-23
Morrison Lake 139
Mosquito Beach 231, 235
Mosquito River 230, 231
Mosquitoes 16, 37, 39, 134-136, 223, 375, 381, 382
Moss (unspecified) 26, 86, 161, 285, 333, 334, 378
Moss, Haircap 86
Moss, Reindeer 225, 229, 327
Moss, Sphagnum 25, 79, 154, 333
Moth (unspecified) 309, 337
Mount Jo 90
Mount Marcy 72, 80, 82, 84-87, 91, 337
Mount Morris, NY 292, 322
Mount Roderick 116, 117, 118
Mount Tego 118
Mount Washington 82
Mountain Lion 311, 375
Mountain Sandwort 86
Mourning Dove 204
Mouse (unspecified) 218, 253, 370
Mouse, Jumping 148, 254
Mudjekeewis 222, 223
Mullein 142
Munising, MI 232, 234
Munising Formation 231
Musclewood 113, 178
Mushkadosa 223
Mushroom (unspecified) see fungi
Muskallonge State Park 225
Muskellunge 311
Muskingum River 311
Mutton Hollow 285
Mystery Mountain 324, 328

Myxomycophytes 171
Nagow Wudjoo 221
Nance, Mathilda 28-41, 50-54, 71-94, 106-108, 144-146, 164-176
Naperala, Dick 294
Narrows Campsite, The 375
National Forest Service 160, 192, 209, 255, 299, 350, 372, 377, 384
National Forest Service Primitive Skills Award 372
National Park Service 5, 56, 178, 209, 219, 268, 299
National Road 202, 312
National Trails Day 209, 219
Native Americans 64, 184, 211, 213
Natural Bridge 313
NCTA School House 152
Neebawawbaigs 229
Nelson Swamp Unique Area 315
New Straitsville, OH 156
New York Barge Canal 320
New York City 318, 319, 320, 348
Newaygo, MI 216
Newaygo County, MI 122, 125, 150, 153, 218, 247
Newman, Steven 389
Newt, Red-spotted 307, 314
Niagara Falls 292
Nichols Lake 149, 247
Nile River 110
Noah's Ark 319
Noonmark Mountain 72, 77
Norfolk Southern RR 322
Norman, Larry 244
North Bally Creek Pond 324
North Bend 185
North Country Trail Assoc-iation 5, 42, 99, 151, 152, 177, 178, 192, 209, 267, 293, 299, 312, 315, 326, 333, 341, 344, 362, 374, 386
North Star Magazine 99, 151, 385
Northrup, Martha B. & Marti 255-260
Northwest Territory 311
Nuthatch (unspecified) 254
Nuthatch, Red-breasted 287
Oak (unspecified) 18, 24, 146, 154, 170, 178, 209, 244, 246, 248, 360, 381
Oak, White 252, 308
Oberg Mountain 328, 329, 334
Odden, Nancy 273
Oenata Cemetery 276
Og 31
Ohio River 57, 181, 182, 183, 184, 311, 312
Ohio Valley Chapter 312
Ojibway (also see Chippewa) 167, 366
Old Man's Beard 363
Old Man's Cave 212
Old Victoria 381-382

Olean, NY 289
Olmstead, Bob 37
Olympic National Park 71
Omakaki 223
Onion 114
Onion River 324, 334
Onondaga County, NY 98
Ontonagon County, MI 383
Ontonagon River 379, 381
Oort 110
Opalescent River 72
Orange Jelly 232
Orchid, Ragged Fringed 283
Orchid, Western Prairie Fringed 351
Oregon Centennial Wagon Train 212
Oregonia, OH 67, 70, 127
Osage Orange 203
Osprey 283, 286, 369
Osseo 231
Osseo, MI 42, 43, 101
Ostberg, Angie (see Gale)
Ottawa 128, 182, 184
Ottawa National Forest 5, 377-383
Owl (unspecified) 358, 384
Owl, Barred 57, 124, 153, 162, 205, 206
Owl, Great Horned 180, 334, 347
Oyster Mushroom 218, 232
Ozawindib 139
Pacific Crest Trail 172
Pacific Ocean 42, 156
Pack Weight 12, 66
Pahoehoe 330
Painted Cove 235
Painted Desert 21
Painted Lady 161
Papp, Bob 177
Parrot 329
Passe, Derrick 365-373
Pau-puk-keena 223
Paul Bunyan 130-143
Paul Bunyan State Forest 5
Paul Bunyan State Forest 130, 139, 140
Paulding County, OH 54, 55
Paw-paw 311
Paw-Puk-Keewis 221, 236
Payne, Peter & Janet 102-103, 389
Pea, Beach 224
Pearl 362-364
Pecos Bill 130
Pelican, White 37
Pembina Escarpment 30
Pennsylvania State Game Lands 296, 297, 299, 300
Perch 370
Perry, Commodore 319
Perry County, OH 163
Peter Lake 371
Peter Wolfe Chapter 374
Peters, G. Moore 128
Peters Cartridge Company 128
Peterson, Tom 325

Pfeiffer, Kaye 307-308
Pfeiffer, Rich 156-163, 211-215, 219, 307-308
Phlox, Blue 158, 307
Pictured Rocks National Lakeshore 5, 221-237
Pike County, OH 65
Pike Lake State Park 56, 65
Pincushion Mountain 324, 327
Pine (unspecified) 6, 11, 122, 153, 178, 221, 225, 287, 303
Pine, Jack 218, 252
Pine, Red 107, 203, 248, 254
Pine River 301, 302, 303
Pine, White 160, 236, 246, 363
Pine Bluffs Campsite 229
Pine Creek 209
Pinesap 170
Pinks, Fire 158, 212, 314
Pinks, Wild 314
Pitcher Plant 333
Pittsburg, Shawmut & Northern RR 342
Pittsburgh, PA 128, 185, 311
P'kaleena 211
Planet of the Apes 230
Plover (unspecified) 40, 223
Plum Ridge 285
Plymouth, MA 336
Pohl, John 175, 176
Poison Ivy 67, 375, 382
Polypore, Hemlock 233
Polypore, Many-colored 8
Polypore, Red-belted 81
Polypore, Umbrella 218
Pontiac 47, 169
Poplar (unspecified) 244, 275, 328
Poplar River 328
Porcupine (unspecified) 16, 179, 223, 230
Porcupine Lake 174
Porcupine Mountain Wild-erness State Park 376-377
Porcupine Mountains 5
Portageville, NY 282, 323
Portland, OR 212
Potato Creek 165
Pottawatomi 182, 184
Poverty Hill 284
Powderhorn Ski Resort 375
Prairie Chicken 348
Prehnite 330
Presidential Range 82
Presque Isle River 376
Pritchard Brook 118
Puff Adder 217
Puffball, Gem-studded 232
Puk-Wudjies 231
Puttyroot 171
Quaker Ladies (Bluets) 59
Quartz 330
Quinzhee 249, 255-260
Rabbit (unspecified) 9, 180, 254
Raccoon 95, 160, 232, 234, 262
Racemed Milkwort 12

Ragwort, Tansy 214
Rail-Trail 67, 127, 205
Rain 18, 24,38-39, 42-43, 46, 56-57, 67, 76-79, 88, 100, 115, 121, 215, 216, 225, 270-275, 279-280, 286, 290, 297, 298, 310, 332, 339, 342, 349, 359, 367
Rainbow Cave 235
Rainbow Falls 375
Rainbow Lake 174
Rajah 151, 246
Randall Hill 118
Ransom County, ND 351-354
Raspberry, Red 171
Rattlesnake Hill 323
Rattlesnake Hill Wildlife Management Area 322
Raven 379, 383, 385
Red Bridge 21-22
Red Eft 26, 161, 163, 314
Red River 345, 347
Redbud 58, 59, 63
Reed & Green Bridge 237
Renville, Joseph 37
Revolutionary War 25, 74, 182, 183, 291, 311, 336
Rhododendron 297
Rhubarb 154
Rhyolite 324, 330
Ring Mill 314
Riven 331
Riverdale 40
Robert J. Corman Western RR 182
Robert Treman State Park 8, 9, 13
Robin 120, 180, 378
Rochester, NY 292, 320, 323
Rock City 284-285, 286
Rock House State Park 63-64
Rock River 255, 257
Rock Tripe 286
Rodgers, Roy & Dale Evans 356
Rogue River State Game Area 112-114
Rome, NY 5, 317, 319
Rooster Comb Mountain 85
Rosamond, IL 336
Rose, Multiflora 160
Rose, Pasture 217
Rose Hollow 95-97
Ross County, OH 65
Round Lake 366
Round Mountain 77
Round Pond 76-77, 81
Rowe, Emily (Granny) 224 also see Fisher, Emily Marguerite
Rue Anemone 59, 277
Ruppen, Pat, Jane & family 56, 61-65
Rush, American 161
Rush, Soft 161
Sac 182
Sakakawea 211
Salamanca, NY 5
Salamander (unspecified) 18, 161, 358

Salamander, Tiger 142
Salmon Unicorn 232
Sand Point 232
Sand Vine 204
Sandpiper (unspecified) 278
Sandstone (unspecified) 21, 59, 63, 64, 166, 167, 221, 224, 290
Sandstone, Black Hand 213
Sandstone, Chapel Rock 231
Sandstone, Jacobean 231
Sandy Fe 287, 289, 321-323, 362-364
Saprophyte 170
Sapsucker, Yellow-bellied 223
Sarsaparilla 278
Sassafras 57
Sault Saint Marie Int'l Bridge 242
Sawdust Hole 193
Scheid, Maggie 221-237
Schoolcraft, Henry Rowe 131
Schoolhouse Hollow 283
Scioto River 59
Scott's Pond 90
Scottville, MI 146
Seahorse Lake 369, 370, 373
Sea Shell City 131
Sebowisha 222
Second Cole Creek 153
Sedge (unspecified) 331
Sedge, Deer's Hair 87
Seneca 25, 290, 319, 323
Seneca Chief 319
Seneca Fire Tower 297
Serviceberry 171, 252, 275
Shadbush see Serviceberry
Shaiena Ozupi Wakpa 344
Shale 116, 167, 290, 376
Shamu 10, 11, 15, 18, 267, 268, 273
Shawondasee 222
Shawnee 47, 67, 128, 182, 211, 214, 290
Shawnee Glen 47
Sheffield, PA 17
Shelby County, OH 184, 186, 191
Sheriff Run 27
Sheyenne Lake 34
Sheyenne National Grassland 6, 345, 346, 347, 348-351
Sheyenne River 34, 344, 345, 356, 357, 359
Sheyenne River Valley Chapter 344
Sheyenne River Valley Scenic Byway 356-359
Sheyenne State Forest 361
Shinleaf 12, 171
Shore-to-Shore Riding Trail 10, 363
Showy Orchis 214
Silver Creek 257
Silver Lady 267, 268, 272
Sincere Sal 131-143
Six-Mile Creek 145
Skipper (unspecified) 165
Skunk (unspecified) 36

399

Skurka, Andy 387
Skylight Mountain 85
Skyline Parkway 275-277
Slader Creek 340
Slant Rock 81, 82
Slate 376
Slattum, Theodore P, Cabin 356-357
Sleeping Bear Dunes 42
Slime Mold (unspecified) 71, 232
Slime, Chocolate Tube 296
Slime, Insect Egg 296
Slime, Scrambled Egg 171
Slugs 27, 287
Smith, Steve 301-306
Snail (unspecified) 8
Snake (unspecified) 223, 307
Snake, Black Rat 310
Snake, Fox 205
Snake, Garter 113, 205, 337
Snake, Hog-nosed 217
Snake, Timber Rattler 322
Snakeroot, Long Fruited 314
Sneaky Valley 261, 264, 266, 385
Snow (storms) 46, 147-150, 257, 297
Snow Flea 374
Snowshoe 249-254, 255-260, 301-306, 337
Snyder, Brook 50-54
Snyder Hill 118
Soan-ge-taha 224
SOLAR 255, 260
Solon Hill 118
Son of the Evening Star 231
Song of Hiawatha, The 224, 231, 337
Soo Line Depot 175, 385-386
Soo Line RR 351
Sound of Music, The 284
South Branch River 21
South Meadow 90
Southern Tier 5, 283, 338
Sparrow (unspecified) 6, 310
Sparrow, English 310
Sparrow, Field 309
Sparrow, White-throated 278, 369
Sparrow, Vesper 384
Spencer, NY 336
Spider (unspecified) 23, 224, 234, 244, 253, 307, 384
Spider, Wolf 314
Spider Lake Road 140
Spiderwort 348
Spirit of the Woods Chapter 178, 192-193, 209, 219, 244, 248, 293
Spleenwort, Mountain 381
Spring Beauty 59, 309
Spring Peepers 113, 161, 369
Spring Valley, OH 66, 67, 70, 127
Spruce (unspecified) 86, 96, 97, 332
Spruce, Black 333, 363
Spurge, Leafy 348

Squaw Root 12, 160, 170
Squirrel (unspecified) 6, 20, 95, 97, 148, 195, 204, 309, 322
Squirrel, Red 87-88, 379
Starcher, Jerry 187-189
St. Bonaventure's 17
St. Ignace 238, 239, 240, 243
St. Joseph River 184, 185
St. Lawrence River 71, 181, 340
St. Louis River 275, 278, 280
St. Marys, OH 182
St. Marys River 146, 185
St. Patrick 354
St. Paul, Minnesota 29, 30, 41
Star Wars 105
Steinman, D.B. 242, 243
Steuben County, NY 343
Stonecrop (unspecified) 158
Straits of Mackinac 238
Stram, Tiffany (see Halfmann)
Strawberry, Barren 342
Strawberry, Wild 76, 331
Subbekashe 224
Sugar Bay 24
Sugarloaf Cove 330
Suggema 223
Sullivan Fire Trail 165
Sullivan's March 336
Summit Steward 86, 87
Sunfish Run 284
Sunflower, Woodland 142, 345
Sunne Demonstration Farm 357
Superior 319
Superior, WI 274
Superior Hiking Trail 5, 267, 271, 324-335
Superior Hiking Trail Association 267, 273, 324-326
Superior National Forest 365
Susquehanna River 340
Swain, NY 342
Swallow (unspecified) 309
Swallowtail, Pipestem 214
Swallowtail, Zebra 161, 214
Swamp Calla 174
Swan 106, 109
Sweetfern 175, 217
Swiss Family Robinson, The 327
Sycamore 47, 205
Szabo, Irene 113, 249-254, 255, 286-287, 289, 315-316, 321-323, 338, 340, 341, 342, 344-345, 362-364, 389
Tabletop Mountain 85
Tabor, Roxanne, Kelly & Kaity 123-125
Tacoma Narrows Bridge 242
Taconite 71
Tadmore, OH 202
Tahawas 72, 84
Talc 71
Talone, Ed 28, 34, 245, 246, 387
Talus 380
Tamarack (Larch) 63, 333
Tamarack Lean-to 343
Tanager, Scarlet 217

Tar Hollow State Forest 214
Taylor Valley 118
Taylorsville Dam 205
Team Penning 352-353
Tecumseh 128
Tecumseh Lake 159, 160
Te-non-an-at-che 318
Temperance River 324, 330
Temperature Extremes 36, 38, 44, 52, 82, 227, 251, 257, 350
Tenskwatawa 128
Tent Caterpillar 308
Thatcher, Thomas 184
These Are the Good Ole Days 248
Thimbleberry 381
Thomas Hardy Power Plant 279
Thorpe, Rose Hartwick 100
Thousand Island Bridge 242
Thrush, Wood 334
Ticks 39, 371
Tigris Expedition, The 388
Times Square 249
Tinker Falls 388
Tioga County, NY 339
Tioughnioga River 118
Tionesta Scenic Area 25-26, 156
Tionesta Watershed 21
Tipp City, OH 187
Tippecanoe 128
Tittabawassee Chapter 365
Titmouse, Tufted 286, 341
Titusville, PA 299
Toad (unspecified) 94, 307
Toadflax 7
Toadshade 307
Toledo, OH 181
Tom Jenkins Dam 158
Tombolo 330
Tompkins County, NY 9, 14, 339
Toothwort, Cut-leaf 59
Toronto, ON 84
Tower Lake 174
Tracy Ridge 18
Trail Construction/Maintenance 56, 88, 215, 219-220, 263, 265, 300, 339, 376
Trap Hills 378
Trapper's Cabin
Traverse City, MI 384
Treaty of Ghent 238
Trebein, OH 204
Treman State Park 8, 13
Triad 299-300
Triangle Park 203, 388
Trillium, Large White 59, 277, 278, 307
Trillium, Red 307
Trimble Wildlife Area 158
Tripp, Jennifer 389
Trout Brook Pond 306
Trout Creek 118
Troy, OH 187
Truss, Howe 313
Truss, Long 313
Truss, Multiple Kingpost 313

400

Truss, Smith 313
Truss, Wernwag 307, 312
Tulip (unspecified) 62
Tuller Hill 118
Tungee, John 40
Turgeon, Bill & Kathy 133
Turkey 24 62, 160, 309, 341
Turkey Tail 232
Turonie, Tana 174, 175, 176
Turtle, Box 205, 217, 314
Turtle, Painted 205
Turtle, Red-eared 205
Turtle, Spiny Softshell 161, 163
Turtle, Spotted 205
Turtle Lake 37
Twayblade, Heartleaved 171
Twenty-Two Creek 363
Two Harbors, MN 267, 281
Two Harbors Lakewalk 268
Two Harbors Lighthouse 268
Tyler, John 128
Tyler's Cascades 168
Tyler's Fork 165, 168
Uller Ski Trail 165
University of Michigan 15, 28, 49, 59, 99, 112, 315
Upper Falls 292
Valley City, ND 30, 344, 347, 356, 358, 359, 361
Vandalia, IL 202
VanDyke, Phil & Nan 42, 44, 45, 144, 196
VanWert County, OH 54, 146
Vehicle Damage 53, 125
Veit, Werner 389
Venegas, Ramona 192, 234
Vervain, Blue 351
Victoria Reservoir 381
Viking Hill 345
Vince Smith Bridge 244
Vinton County, OH 215
Violet (unspecified) 277, 278
Violet, Dog-toothed see Lily, Trout
Violet Branched Coral 170, 232
Virgil Mountain 118
Virgin Forest 25, 299, 388
Virginia Creeper 363
Volcanic Rock 71, 156, 167, 275, 324, 326, 329, 330, 331
Vole (unspecified) 148
Voyageur 366
Wabash Cannonball Railroad 5
Wabash and Erie Feeder Canal 50
Wabash River 185
Wabun 222
Wakerobin 307
Walk West, The 380
Walking Backwards Down the Stairs 244
Wallface 91
War Club Lake 370
War of 1812 319
Warbler (unspecified) 6, 217
Warbler, Black-throated Blue 217
Warbler, Palm 277

Warbler, Yellow 278
Warren, Minnie 144
Warren County, OH 128
Washington, George 183, 299
Washington County, OH 314
Water Shield 174
Water Strider (unspecified) 375
Waterleaf, Appendaged 307
Waverly, NY 13
Way-muk-kwa-na 232, 235
Wayne, Anthony 48
Wayne National Forest 5, 307, 310, 312-314
Weber Lake 164, 165
Welker, Doug 374, 377, 380
Well-Fed Backpacker, The 172
Wendigoes 223
West Round Lake 367
Western Michigan Chapter 152, 177, 293
Western Waterfront Trail 278
Wexford County, MI 261, 266, 295
Wheeler Creek 263
Whip-Poor-Will 162, 163
Whiskey Bridge 322
White, Peregrine (Pilgrim) 28, 336
White, Susannah 336, 339
White Admiral 165
White Cloud, MI 2, 151
White Pine Campsite 335
White Pine Trail 279
White Sky Rock 327
White Woman of the Genesee 290, 291
Whiteface Mountain 85
Whitefish 319
Wichita, KS 167
Wilderness, Boundary Waters Canoe Area 365-373
Wilderness, Porcupine Lake 174
Wilderness, Rainbow Lake 174
Wilderness, Rock River Canyon 258, 260
Willard Munger Trail 278, 279
Willet 278
William A. Irvin 274
Willow, Bearberry 87
Willow, Black 113
Willow, Pussy 13
Willow Bay 18
Wiltsey Glen 118
Winnebago 182
Winter Hikes 50-54, 102-103, 106-108, 109-111, 147-150, 151-153, 249-254, 255-260, 296-300, 301-306
Wisconsin Central RR 305
Wisconsin & Michigan RR 374
Witch Hazel 252
Witches' Butter 8
Wolf (unspecified) 130, 311, 370
Wolf Creek, OH 310, 313
Wolfe, Peter 152, 387
Wood Sorrel 81
Wood Lily 41
Woodchuck 341

Woodchuck Hollow 118
Woodland Culture 360
Woodpecker (unspecified) 204, 223, 334
Woodpecker, Downy 310
Woodpecker, Hairy 310, 379
Woodpecker, Pileated 230, 310, 341
Woodpecker, Red-bellied 310
Woodpecker, Red-headed 310
Woolgrass 379
World War I 129
World War II 33
Worm, Cherry Scallop 25
Worm, Earth 281
Wright Brothers Memorial 203
Wunsch, Ginny 151-153, 246
Wyoming County, NY 323
Yankee Springs Recreation Area 108
Yellow-headed Blackbirds 38
Yellow Patches 170
Yellow Springs, OH 205
Yellow Tuning Fork 232
Yellowstone (engine) 269
Yellowstone National Park 71
Yosemite National Park 71, 360
Young, Jack & Betty 132
Young, Loretta 66-70, 128
Young, Omer (husband) 6, 7, 15, 28, 45, 55, 73, 99, 104-105, 126-129, 144, 146, 188, 193, 200, 238-240, 301, 332, 385, 389
Young, Sam, Joshua, Steve (sons) 6, 10, 15, 17, 28
Zoar, OH 5

Quick Order Form

on the web: www.booksleavingfootprints.com

email orders: info@booksleavingfootprints.com

postal orders: Books Leaving Footprints, 861 W. US 10, Scottville, MI 49454, USA

Please send information on:
☐ Wholesale Quantities ☐ Speaking/ Media presentations

Name_____

Address_____

City_____ State_____ Zip_____

Phone_____ Email_____

North Country Cache: $24.95 per copy

Sales tax: Please add 6% for shipments to Michigan addresses

Shipping to US address: $5 for one book, $2 each for additional copy

Send check or money order with this form

---

for more information about the

North Country National Scenic Trail

contact: North Country Trail Association
          229 E. Main St.
          Lowell, MI 49339
          1-866-hikeNCT
          www.northcountrytrail.org